"For its journey in the perplexing and thrilling territory of the post-Christian twenty-first century, the church in the West and far beyond has no better traveling companion than Lesslie Newbigin. In this book, some of the world's most sensitive and incisive interpreters trace in almost kaleidoscopic fashion the way Newbigin's central concerns and convictions illumine a wide range of missional challenges. Here is a reliable marker signaling how and why Newbigin's influence continues to expand."

—GEORGE R. HUNSBERGER,
Professor of Missiology, Western Theological Seminary

"This book provides a splendid introduction to the work of a Christian giant who identified major issues for the Christian faith in the modern world. . . . The nature and purpose of the church, the relation of Christian faith to other faiths, the Christian encounter with post-Christian Western culture, were all explored by Newbigin with acuity and integrity, and are interpreted here in a sensitive and stimulating way."

—ANDREW F. WALLS,
Professor, Liverpool Hope University and Akrofi-Christaller Institute, Ghana

Theology in Missionary Perspective

Theology in Missionary Perspective

Lesslie Newbigin's Legacy

Edited by

Mark T. B. Laing
and
Paul Weston

☙PICKWICK *Publications* · Eugene, Oregon

THEOLOGY IN MISSIONARY PERSPECTIVE
Lesslie Newbigin's Legacy

Pickwick Publications
An Imprint of Wipf and Stock Publishers
199 W. 8th Ave., Suite 3
Eugene, OR 97401

Unless otherwise stated, biblical quotations are from the *New Revised Standard Version*.

www.wipfandstock.com

ISBN 13: 978-1-61097-574-2

Cataloging-in-Publication data:

Theology in missionary perspective : Lesslie Newbigin's legacy / edited by Mark T. B. Laing and Paul Weston.

xvi + 318 p. ; 23 cm.

ISBN 13: 978-1-61097-574-2

1. Newbigin, Lesslie. 2. Missions—theory. 3. Christianity and culture—Western countries. I. Laing, Mark T. B. II. Weston, Paul, 1957–. III. Title.

BV2063 .T45 2012

Manufactured in the U.S.A.

Dedicated to the memory of
David Kettle (1947–2011)

Contents

Acknowledgments

THE EARLY MOMENTUM FOR this collection of essays arose out of two Day Conferences that were organized in December 2009 in Birmingham and Edinburgh, UK to mark the centenary of Lesslie Newbigin's birth. Each of the days involved seminars and presentations which explored various aspects of Newbigin's legacy, and featured as their centerpiece two lectures by Veli-Matti Kärkkäinen on Newbigin's "Post-Critical Missional Ecclesiology." These lectures are included in the present volume much as they were presented on those days. We are grateful to all who contributed to these occasions, both in presenting papers, leading seminars, and stimulating discussion. A number of leading thinkers from around the world were also invited to contribute their own reflections and reminiscences about Newbigin and his influence. Some of these reflections are gathered in the Appendix to this volume. We record our thanks to the Gospel and Our Culture Network, UK and to the Churches Together in Britain and Ireland who were involved in organizing these centenary events. In addition to the contributions which arose out of the conferences, many of the other chapters in this volume have been commissioned especially for this book, and again we are grateful to all who have contributed.

David Kettle, to whose memory this collection is dedicated, was co-ordinator of the Gospel and Our Culture Network in the UK from 1997–2011. He was one of the main energizing forces in the early planning of the conferences, and it was his idea to produce a book arising out of them. David's death in March 2011, after a long illness, came at a point when the book was already well under way. As a result, we dedicate this collection to the memory of this quiet but energetic disciple, whose own debt to the work of Lesslie Newbigin had been both profound and influential. We trust that it proves to be both a worthy memorial to his tireless efforts to keep Newbigin's vision of faithful cultural engagement and committed gospel witness alive, and also a stimulus to others to take this engagement on into the future.

Acknowledgments

Finally, our thanks to Christian Amondson and the others at Wipf & Stock who have helped to guide this book through the publication process.

Mark T. B. Laing & Paul Weston
Feast of Advent
December, 2011

Abbreviations

BUL	Birmingham University Library
CLS	Christian Literature Society of India
CSI	Church of South India
CWME	Commission on World Mission and Evangelism (WCC)
DWME	Department of World Mission and Evangelism (WCC)
IMC	International Missionary Council
ISPCK	Indian Society for Promoting Christian Knowledge
NIV	*New International Version*
NLS	National Library of Scotland
NRSV	*New Revised Standard Version*
SCM	Student Christian Movement
TEF	Theological Education Fund
URC	United Reform Church
WCC	World Council of Churches
WMC	World Missionary Conference

Contributors

Ian Barns was Senior Lecturer in Ethics and Technology at Murdoch University, Perth, Western Australia until his retirement in 2011. He now lives in Melbourne and is writing a book on "sustainability, the good life and the question of God."

John G. Flett, a native of New Zealand, completed his PhD at Princeton Theological Seminary, USA on the Trinitarian grounding for mission as summarized by the term *"missio Dei."* He is now a Habilitant at the Kirchliche Hochschule Wuppertal/Bethel in Germany and is working on the theme of "apostolicity."

Michael W. Goheen (Ph.D. Utrecht) is Professor of Missional Theology at Newbigin House of Studies, San Francisco and Professor of Missiology at Calvin Theological Seminary, Grand Rapids. He is author or co-author of four books including a volume on Lesslie Newbigin's missionary ecclesiology.

Kenneth D. Gordon is an Honorary Assistant Priest at St Devenick's Scottish Episcopal Church in Aberdeen, Scotland. Ordained in 1960 and retired in 2001, his MTh (2008) dissertation was on the preaching of Lesslie Newbigin. He is currently engaged in doctoral research on Newbigin and Willem A Visser't Hooft.

Eleanor Jackson had the privilege of Lesslie Newbigin's friendship from 1975–1998 and was herself a missionary in India between 1979 and 1986. A retired lecturer in religious studies, she currently represents Radstock on the Bath and North East Somerset Council, UK.

Veli-Matti Kärkkäinen is Professor of Systematic Theology at Fuller Theological Seminary, Pasadena, CA and Docent of Ecumenics at the University of Helsinki. A native of Finland, he has also lived and taught theology in Thailand and participated widely in ecumenical, theological, and interreligious work. He has authored and edited fifteen books and numerous essays.

David J. Kettle was Coordinator of the Gospel and Our Culture Network in the UK until his death in 2011. From 1991–1997 he worked in New Zealand as the Anglican Tertiary Chaplain in Manawatu and as Minister of Milsom Combined Church. His major book *Western Culture in Gospel Context: Towards the Conversion of the West: Theological Bearings for Mission and Spirituality* was published posthumously by Wipf & Stock in 2011.

J. Andrew Kirk has spent much of his life in theological education in South America and the United Kingdom. He retired in 2002 from his teaching position at the University of Birmingham, UK and now teaches and supervises research students part-time at institutions in England, Central Europe and Latin America. His latest book is *Civilisations in Conflict? Islam, The West and Christian Faith* (2011).

Mark T. B. Laing taught missiology at Union Biblical Seminary in Pune, India for several years. His contribution to this collection is adapted from part of his doctoral thesis, a revised form of which is published as *From Crisis to Creation: Lesslie Newbigin and the Reinvention of Christian Mission*. Material is used here with permission from the publishers, Wipf & Stock.

Murray Rae is Professor of Theology in the Department of Theology and Religion at the University of Otago in New Zealand. His research interests include Māori engagements with Christianity, theology and architecture, theological hermeneutics and the work of Søren Kierkegaard. His recent publications include: *God of Salvation*, edited with Ivor Davidson (Ashgate Press, 2011), and *Kierkegaard and Theology* (Continuum, 2010).

Jürgen Schuster was a missionary in Japan from 1983–1998 with a focus on church-planting. He is currently Professor for Intercultural Theology at the Internationale Hochschule (University of Applied Sciences) at Bad Liebenzell in Germany and is the Director of the Research Center for Intercultural and Religious Studies.

Wilbert R. Shenk is Senior Professor of Mission History and Contemporary Culture in the Graduate School of Intercultural Studies at Fuller Graduate School in Pasadena, California, USA. He is a founding member of the American Society of Missiology, and coordinated the Missiology of Western Culture Project (1992–98). He has authored many books and essays on the theme of mission and culture.

Jenny Taylor is Director of Lapido Media, which seeks to advance religious literacy in the media. She holds a doctorate from SOAS, London, on Islam and secularization. She is a media professional, academic and writer, and an expert on the connection between faith and culture, on which she has addressed UK parliamentary and Commonwealth gatherings. With Lamin Sanneh she co-wrote Newbigin's posthumously published book on the relationship between Christianity and Islam in Britain (entitled *Faith and Power*, 1998).

Geoffrey Wainwright is an ordained minister of the Methodist Church of Great Britain. Since 1983 he has served as the Cushman Professor of Systematic Theology at Duke University, North Carolina, USA. From 1976 to 1991 he was a member of the WCC Faith and Order Commission. He is the author of *Lesslie Newbigin: A Theological Life* (Oxford University Press, 2000).

Ng Kam Weng is Research Director of the Kairos Research Centre in Kuala Lumpur, Malaysia. He is a member of the Center for Theological Inquiry, Princeton, USA and fellow of the Centre for the Study of Christianity in Asia at Trinity Theological College, Singapore.

Paul Weston lectures in mission studies and homiletics at Ridley Hall, Cambridge and is an affiliated lecturer in the Cambridge University Divinity Faculty. He has a PhD on Newbigin, has written widely on his work and is the editor of *Lesslie Newbigin, Missionary Theologian: A Reader* (SPCK/Eerdmans, 2006).

Introduction to the Essays

Mark T. B. Laing and Paul Weston

THE ESSAYS IN THIS collection seek to honor the memory of Lesslie Newbigin (1909–1998) who was born just over one hundred years ago, and to assess and engage with the continuing impact of his thought on the vital theological and missionary tasks facing the church in the twenty-first century. Recognition of the importance of his call for a genuinely missionary theology has been growing steadily over the last thirteen years, with the publication of a number of significant books and monographs, starting with the collection of essays which came out of the "After Newbigin" international conference held in Birmingham, UK in November 1998 ten months after his death.[1] A number of themes are emerging from this evaluation, as the contributions in this volume will demonstrate. But underlying them is a sense that the *approach* to theology that Newbigin espoused is one whose importance is being increasingly recognized. With the breakdown of confidence in some of the central philosophical and theological paradigms that have been shaped and sustained by the culture of modernity, Newbigin's approach to the "doing" of theology seems to offer fresh insights and approaches, even providing something of a prophetic model for the global Christian community in new and challenging times.

The essays in this book have been organized in three sections. Section One examines aspects of Newbigin's way of doing theology. Section Two engages with Newbigin on the issues that exercised him in his retirement to the UK when he sought to provide a missiology that would engage with prevailing forms of Western secularism. Finally, Section Three

---

1. Thomas F. Foust et al., eds., *A Scandalous Prophet: The Way of Mission after Newbigin* (Grand Rapids: Eerdmans, 2002).

broadens the vista beyond the West to demonstrate Newbigin's prescience, prophetic critique and enduring relevance to the global church.

SECTION ONE: A WAY OF DOING THEOLOGY

Section One provides an analysis of central aspects of Newbigin's approach to the theological task from a variety of perspectives. It contains new insights from recent scholarly research by established and emerging experts on Newbigin, and by other theologians who have engaged closely with his work. It is also illustrated from new biographical material which reveals him reflecting theologically as a Christian leader engaged in ministry in particular cultural and historical contexts and arguing graciously but firmly with a diversity of theological perspectives.

David Kettle's contribution was originally published in the New Zealand journal *Stimulus* and is reprinted here as a memorial to his tireless efforts to keep Newbigin's agenda in the realm of public discussion amongst students and teachers of theology and mission. David was a co-editor of this volume before his death in March, 2011. In this chapter he reflects on the reception of Newbigin's thinking in the West, arguing that he was often misunderstood precisely because his approach to theology often challenged the operative assumptions upon which the theological enterprise is itself built. In this context, Newbigin's diagnosis of English theology as "an advanced case of syncretism," captive to assumptions deriving from the European Enlightenment, was never likely to be popular. Kettle proceeds to examine four ways in which Newbigin's theology is sometimes passed over or dismissed, and uses these as an invitation to reflect once again on the engagement between the gospel and our contextual and cultural presuppositions. Kettle's argument is that Newbigin's approach is too often heard by reference to these entrenched cultural presuppositions, but that—should we let them—his insights are ones which open up the possibility of a radical re-orientation and renewal.

Jürgen Schuster shows that throughout Newbigin's career his eschatological orientation was of central importance to his theology. Newbigin used it as a "navigational light" with which to approach new missiological issues. In particular this shaped Newbigin's understanding of human history and the role of the church in relationship to the world. Newbigin argued that the story of the gospel was not to be understood as the private preserve of the church, but as the story which explained the history of all humanity. As the gospel is public truth there can be no dichotomy between salvation history and human history. Schuster first outlines key aspects of how Newbigin interprets history in light of his understanding of biblical eschatology. He then shows how Newbigin's biblical eschatology was relevant for his theology of mission and how this same method can help us to address the various missiological questions that we face today.

Mark Laing's chapter examines the influence of Newbigin's missionary experience in India in shaping his ecclesiology. The chapter argues that, in contrast to his experience of the western church, it was his missionary experience which was critical in determining Newbigin's ecclesiology. As a young Church of Scotland missionary in south India Newbigin experienced the dramatic growth of the village churches in rural Tamil Nadu. He was also exposed to the dichotomous relationship that existed between mission and church expressed in the problematic relationship between the Church of Scotland's mission and that of the church in India. Newbigin witnessed in the Indian church a church which was both missionary and profoundly concerned to regain its unity. This was expressed in the negotiations for church union which concluded successfully with the formation of the Church of South India in 1947. Newbigin entered late into these negotiations, but rapidly assumed prominent responsibility, first in India and then internationally. Newbigin's theological reflections on the Indian church enabled him to develop a missionary ecclesiology, which, throughout his wider ecumenical ministry, he then claimed had universal relevance.

Paul Weston contributes a more systematic analysis of Newbigin's missionary ecclesiology. Taking its cue from a quotation from Newbigin's 1953 book *The Household of God*, the chapter argues that the substance and outworking of his understanding of the church is most clearly understood when seen in an eschatological perspective, with questions about its present-day forms and priorities addressed in the light of its heavenly fulfillment. Within this framework Weston develops Newbigin's understanding of the missionary church under the headings of its corporate expression, its calling to be a foretaste of the kingdom, and the missionary priority of its unity. He shows that Newbigin's approach to the theology of the church consistently connects and interweaves these themes as part of a coherent whole, and demonstrates how Newbigin constantly approached structural and strategic questions from a theological rather than a purely pragmatic point of view. As a result, Newbigin's contribution is shown to challenge much contemporary ecumenical discussion in which significant strands of ecclesiology—such as "mission" and "unity"—are treated either as unrelated topics, or else are dislocated from their theological moorings.

Kenneth Gordon's chapter examines the role that preaching played in the life and ministry of Newbigin. He does so by studying the surviving sermons of Newbigin and by interviewing some of those who heard him preach. Gordon first addresses the role the Bible played in Newbigin's life to determine his understanding of the nature and purpose of Scripture. Gordon argues that Newbigin's public ministry flowed from his regular deep private devotion, always informed by intensive and often wide-ranging personal study. Critical to this was a convictional commitment to the authority of the Bible, particularly in light of modern liberal challenges to its truth claims.

Gordon's chapter proceeds to consider how Newbigin used Scripture in his preaching ministry, examining his exegesis, hermeneutics, and preaching style. In particular, Newbigin's commentary on John's Gospel (*The Light has Come*, 1982) is used to analyze and illustrate his approach to hermeneutics. The chapter also explores the range and variety of Newbigin's sermons throughout his long ministry.

Having had the privilege of Lesslie Newbigin's friendship over many years, **Eleanor Jackson** seeks to illustrate, through Newbigin's life and work, his understanding of "truth." Jackson does this in two ways. First, she examines Newbigin's contemplation of the objective question of what "truth" is. For Newbigin this was not an abstract concept, but dynamically expressed and embodied in Jesus Christ. Here Jackson focuses on Newbigin's lifelong reading and study of John's Gospel. Secondly, Jackson focuses on the influence of his personality and conduct to further illustrate his understanding of "truth." Jackson uses Newbigin's original correspondence and interviews with his friends and colleagues to weave a biographical account which interfaces with his published writings. Using the theme of "truth" Jackson highlights the public quest which Newbigin had for truth in his theology, his understanding of mission, and his approach to interfaith dialogue.

SECTION TWO: THEOLOGY IN WESTERN CONTEXT

Newbigin is perhaps best known in the West for calling the churches to resist the marginalization of Christianity by Western culture. In addressing the church's collusion with the dominant cultural assumption that Christian faith is a private matter, Newbigin helps to provide a theology which enables Christians to reclaim a proper role in the public domain as part of their missionary vocation. This section therefore examines aspects of Newbigin's theological and philosophical account of Western culture in the context of the gospel and outlines some of its central implications for mission in the third millennium.

Veli-Matti Kärkkäinen's contribution comprises the two lectures which he delivered at each of the Newbigin Centenary gatherings in Birmingham and Edinburgh, UK in 2009. Taking the overall theme of Newbigin's approach to missional ecclesiology in the post-Christian West, Kärkkäinen explores two aspects of Newbigin's thought. In the first part he develops a "diagnostic assessment" of Newbigin's estimation of "postmodernism," and argues that this needs to be taken in the context of his overall critique of modernity, to which it is related essentially as a development rather than a departure.

In the light of this assessment, Kärkkäinen proceeds in the second part of the chapter to describe the key aspects of Newbigin's "constructive proposal" for the church's mission in the context of postmodernity. Here he articulates and defends five important strands within Newbigin's thought: namely that Christian truth is "fallibilistic" and yet not captive to the nihilism of postmodernity; is "tradition-based" and yet resistant to the charge of subjectivity; is "public" truth, and yet capable of critiquing the "timeless statements" of modernity; is committed to "pluralism" whilst avoiding the pitfalls of agnosticism; and—finally—is committed to persuasion without embracing the "will to power."

Ian Barns' chapter explores the "dichotomous" nature of Christian living in late modern culture. On the one hand Christians participate in the life of prayer and church worship, whilst on the other they find themselves "immersed in the practices, institutions and disciplines" of a wider secular world in which any talk of "God" is largely irrelevant. He does so by examining Newbigin's treatment of this predicament, and Newbigin's call to live out the Lordship of Christ in public life. He explores the pressures on ordinary Christian living within the taken-for-granted framework of the surrounding culture by examining four "enabling conditions" which will help to equip lay Christians to take up the task of "critical frame-reflection and re-visioning." These center around the need for a re-engagement with the structure of the biblical narrative, a call to re-imagine the world in "gospel shape," the recovery of the "prophetic" role of lay Christians in secular callings, and a challenge to take a full and active part in the public and political life of our communities.

Andrew Kirk reflects both theoretically and practically on Newbigin's insistent call to proclaim the gospel as "public truth." Kirk explores the background to Newbigin's understanding of the term and outlines the implications it carries for the good of the life of the public realm. In doing so, he draws out some of Newbigin's characteristic insights—not least his contention that the distinction to be drawn in the public square is not between belief on the one hand and non-belief on the other, but between belief and false belief.

In the second half of the chapter, Kirk provides a valuable case-study (hitherto undocumented) of a corporate attempt to explore the implications of Newbigin's challenge in the city of Birmingham, UK in the 1990s. This combination of commentary and case-study helps to illuminate both the challenges and responsibilities involved in taking seriously the call to proclaim and live out the gospel as "public truth" in the public square.

Murray Rae's contribution discusses Newbigin's description of the identity and missional character of the local church community as the "hermeneutic of the gospel." He helpfully traces the development of this emphasis upon the church as a visible manifestation of the gospel from Newbigin's early writings, and describes the essential character of the congregation through an exploration of the ministries of "word" and "sacrament." He describes the challenges facing churches in a "post-Christendom" context, not least in holding together the "form" and "content" of authentic church life in the contemporary world. The chapter is a powerful challenge to church life, emphasizing that Newbigin consistently called the local congregation to be "an enacted interpretation of and witness to the good news that in Christ God is making all things new." This, Rae argues, is "the most profound challenge that Newbigin leaves the church of the twenty first century."

Jenny Taylor worked with Lesslie Newbigin in his last years, promoting his concept of the gospel as "public truth" to the media world of television and radio producers, and journalists. Her work continues to find its inspiration in Newbigin's writings. Her contribution to this collection is both personal and passionate: part cultural analysis and part autobiography. In doing so it takes a different, but no less valuable, approach to the significance of Newbigin's thought for our contemporary world. It explores the dialectic between his writing and the charity she set up—called Lapido Media—which set out to promote "religious literacy in world affairs" and to challenge the secular media towards a more truthful journalism. She writes of three experiences which illustrate the opportunities that her calling has opened up. It illustrates by example one of the ways in which Newbigin's commitment to the reality of the gospel as "public truth" has been, and continues to be, worked out in the public realm.

SECTION THREE: THEOLOGY IN GLOBAL CONTEXT

Section Three considers the implications of Newbigin's work in a global context, and illustrates the influence of Newbigin's way of doing theology in a variety of international contexts.

Theological education is the theme explored by **Wilbert Shenk** in his historical essay. He details the struggle, over the course of more than two centuries, to develop appropriate theological training for the churches that were established as a result of the modern mission movement. Shenk argues that western theological education, exported by the modern mission movement, has proved to be a serious impediment to training church leaders in other cultures whose task it was to develop contextually appropriate congregations.

The appropriateness of exporting western theological education was not questioned until well into the twentieth century, when Newbigin, with the benefit of extensive cross-cultural experience, was among the early critics of this model. The establishment of the Theological Education Fund by the International Missionary Council paved the way for a conceptual breakthrough, which came when leaders from the global south, such as Shoki Coe, emphasized the importance of both contextuality and contextualization. Through the 1960s and 70s the focus in the global south shifted to developing contextually appropriate theology and theological education, although Shenk reminds us that this still remains a work-in-progress.

Newbigin's missiological approach to those of other faiths is the topic of **Michael Goheen's** chapter. This is a theme which Newbigin grappled with throughout his life and ministry, his writing on religious pluralism reflecting and being enriched by his missionary career in India. Goheen sees parallels between the often misunderstood, or misrepresented, approach of Hendrick Kraemer and that of Newbigin, and he attributes Newbigin with continuing Kraemer's legacy.

The chapter focuses on Newbigin's understanding of a missionary encounter which he believed to be the correct fundamental stance the church was to take toward other religions. Before elaborating on this, Goheen first highlights the danger inherent in starting with the question, "Who can be saved?". Goheen shows how from the outset, this distorts any discussion of world religions and leads to flawed categorizations, such as the triad of exclusivist, inclusivist, and pluralist positions.

As an alternative, Newbigin's starting point is to acknowledge Jesus as the center of world history; that it is Jesus who stands at the center of universal history and thus reveals God's purpose for all humanity. Goheen concludes his chapter by examining the various implications of Newbigin's starting point for the church's missionary encounter with adherents of other religions.

In theology an entrenched dichotomy has been accepted as normative: to understand "mission" and "spirituality" as being separate entities; that the communicating of faith and the cultivation of faith point in different directions. **John Flett** shows how Newbigin challenges such theological assumptions by grounding his theology of mission in the Trinity.

Flett first details the historical development of Newbigin's theology, in which he made the transition from a church-centric to a trinitarian basis for mission. He then argues that regardless of time or context, the confession that "Jesus as Lord" is continually faced with the question, "Who is Jesus?". A full description of who Jesus Christ is directs the church to the name of the Father, Son and the Spirit. This entrance point shows how Newbigin's account of the Trinity is missiologically and christologically determined. Flett then explores the relationship between the Trinity and the church in Newbigin's Trinitarian formulation. For the church, as the community of the Trinity, no space exists between the communication and the cultivation of the faith. The visible continuity of the Christian community is itself basic to missionary movement, and this movement shapes the church in obedience to the Spirit.

Besides his career in theological education, **Geoffrey Wainwright** was involved in the ecumenical movement, serving as a member of the WCC Faith and Order Commission for several years. From his own involvement in the movement, which intersected with Newbigin on numerous occasions, he gives an account on Newbigin's vast contribution to ecumenism. Acknowledging Newbigin's prescience, Wainwright also explores the challenges left by Newbigin's ecumenical legacy and the challenges Newbigin foresaw.

The modern ecumenical movement has been understood as comprising three streams: faith and order; mission and evangelism; and life and work. Wainwright's chapter follows Newbigin's contribution to each stream and explores the contemporary ecumenical challenges that are bequeathed to us from Newbigin's legacy. These range in scope from his contributions to church unity in India and internationally, to his work in developing a missiological approach to western culture. They range from Newbigin's earliest writing to his work done in "retirement." Wainwright concludes by looking forward to the place of the gospel in a global culture, in which Newbigin predicted that the chief competitors to the gospel would be the free market, and Islam.

Ng Kam Weng's chapter provides a valuable case study of Malaysia and Indonesia. Following decolonization, these two countries initially had secular constitutions, but under pressure from Islamic activists, have both become increasingly Islamicized. In this context, Christians—as a minority group—are under increasing pressure to yield the public arena to Islamic sharia law.

In response to such pressures Kam Weng draws upon Newbigin's theology to propose a way in which the church can continue to exist publically, engage socially, and contribute constructively to the task of nation-building. Whilst eschewing a return to Christendom, Newbigin challenged western Christians to recover the historic role the church played in shaping public life in western society. Kam Weng shows how Newbigin's public theology could also be utilized in Islamic contexts, where religious hegemony seeks to stifle the voice of the church. He calls for Christians to move beyond merely moralizing or generalizing to develop the art of "statecraft," in which the church does not just theorize, but offers options which will deal justly with specific situations. This requires the development of contextualized public theology that can assist citizens in the task of strengthening democratic institutions that uphold freedom and justice.

Lesslie Newbigin

His Writings in Context

Paul Weston

During his lifetime, Newbigin was highly regarded both as an ecumenical and missionary statesman, and as a cross-cultural missiologist of the first order. His obituary in *The Times* newspaper in the UK described him as "one of the foremost missionary statesmen of his generation," and "one of the outstanding figures on the world Christian stage in the second half of the century."[1] His reputation for many rests upon his profound missionary engagement with the post-Enlightenment culture of the West, pursued in the 1980s and 90s following his retirement from India in 1974. But his impact as a missionary statesman was already established well before this final phase of his life. In fact, he had successfully managed to integrate a number of varied but significant roles during his unusually busy life. Geoffrey Wainwright's masterly survey amply illustrates this, with its ten chapters organized around the various dimensions of his ministry.[2]

Newbigin was also a prolific writer. In the annotated bibliography at the end of the collection of essays entitled *Scandalous Prophet* (compiled in 1998), there are 387 separate entries under Newbigin's "Published Materials."[3] These span sixty-five years (from 1933 to 1998), and include

---

1. *The Times*, 31st January 1998, 25.

2. Wainwright, *Lesslie Newbigin*. The main chapter headings describe him as: "Confident Believer," "Direct Evangelist," "Ecumenical Advocate," "Pastoral Bishop," "Missionary Strategist," "Religious Interlocutor," "Social Visionary," "Liturgical Preacher," "Scriptural Teacher," and "Christian Apologist" (with an introduction entitled "Man in Christ").

3. Foust, *Scandalous Prophet*, 252–81.

thirty books, thirty-three shorter pamphlets or booklets, 267 articles or book chapters, twenty-one introductory pieces or prefaces to the work of others, two open letters, and thirty-four book reviews.

The disarming presentational "simplicity" of much of this writing—usually lacking the numerous footnotes characteristic of formal academic pieces[4]—might suggest that his writings are somehow lacking in depth and rigor. This would be a serious misjudgment. For many, they offer a depth of insight and engagement with questions of theology, culture, and ecclesiology which is all-too-rare in many an "academic" work. This engagement is the product of deep analytical reflection on the one hand, and an economy of language and penetrating application on the other. But the characteristically simple "form" of his writings also reflects two other aspects of his life and character. First, he was often compelled to write "on the hoof"—in airport lounges, railway stations and during conference breaks—as one whose hectic schedule did not allow for a more leisurely writing program, much as he might have liked one. Secondly, he was an extraordinarily retentive reader, able to recall and quote the ideas and arguments of other writers and thinkers without always needing to remember (and sometimes without knowing) exactly where they had come from. This capacity to recall, analyze, and then articulate the ideas of others—particularly in later life when his eyesight was failing and he used a team of people to read aloud to him—was quite remarkable.[5]

Newbigin's earliest "formal" theological writings are in the form of student essays written whilst a theological student at Westminster College, Cambridge, where he had gone in 1933 to train for ordained ministry. There survive a number of pieces which presage many of his later emphases, and demonstrate his early abilities as both an analytical thinker and a cogent writer.[6] His theological studies were a time of significant spiritual growth too, which "profoundly changed and deepened" his faith. He had arrived in 1933 as a "typical liberal," but experienced a profound "evangelical conversion" through studying Paul's letter to the Romans, and com-

4. John Flett aptly describes this later in this volume as a "seeming phobia of citation." See also Eleanor Jackson's observations.

5. He had developed a voracious appetite for reading from his schooldays where his geography teacher ("Bill" Brown), not only "created a capacity to think, to break out of stereotypes, to explore new ideas and to question old ones," but also taught Newbigin "to get to the heart of the argument of a big book so that we could expound and defend it in debate" (Newbigin, *Unfinished Agenda*, 5).

6. E.g., the thirty-six page essay on "Revelation" (DA29/3/1/2; extracted in Weston, *Lesslie Newbigin*, 18–21).

pleted his studies with a strong evangelical conviction about the finished work of Christ on the cross which was to prove deeply significant for his future ministry and writing.[7]

Newbigin had gone up to Cambridge as an agnostic undergraduate in 1928. He came to faith through the friendship of members of the Student Christian Movement (SCM), and through a "spiritual awakening" during a Quaker summer camp for unemployed miners in South Wales. His subsequent spiritual pilgrimage led him to work for the SCM in Glasgow where he met Helen his future wife, and to theological training back in Cambridge in preparation for mission overseas.

Hereafter, and for most of his working life, Newbigin's beloved "hub" of activities was India, where he and Helen (whom he had married earlier in the year) went to work in 1936 as Church of Scotland missionaries with the Madras Mission. As part of a developing pattern of writing "on the move," his first book *Christian Freedom in the Modern World* (a critique of the work of John Macmurray whose ideas he had debated energetically with fellow-students at Cambridge) was written during the sea voyage and was published by SCM in 1937.

From Madras, the Newbigins were transferred to Kanchipuram (in Tamil Nadu) as district missionaries in 1939, and stayed there until their first home furlough in 1946. Amongst his wide-ranging responsibilities during this time, Newbigin became involved in the discussions about a long-running plan to unite the various denominations in Southern India in an ecumenical "United Church." In 1942 he was appointed to the central committee, and soon became an energetic advocate of the scheme. Five years later—following protracted discussion and debate both in India and in the UK—the "Union of the Church of South India" (CSI) was finally inaugurated at a celebratory service in Madras Cathedral in September 1947.

Inevitably, much of Newbigin's foundational doctrinal thinking about the nature of the church, and the "forms" in which it is structured and organized, was carried out during these early years of missionary service, and this is reflected in his writings of the period. Significant amongst these is his *The Reunion of the Church: A Defence of the South India Scheme*, published in 1948,[8] which articulated the main contours of this ecclesiology, and formed the background to his still-influential treatise on the church

7. Newbigin, *Unfinished Agenda*, 28–29.
8. It was republished in 1960 with revisions.

entitled *The Household of God: Lectures on the Nature of the Church*, which was published in 1953.[9]

Following his year of furlough, Newbigin returned to India in 1947 in time for the formal inauguration of the CSI in September. He had received a cable five months earlier informing him that he was to be the first bishop of Madurai and Ramnad, and was duly consecrated during the inauguration service for the CSI in Madras Cathedral. He was thirty-seven years old. He held this post for the following twelve years, and alongside his many diocesan responsibilities began to be drawn into the work of the newly formed World Council of Churches (WCC). Newbigin attended its first world assembly in Amsterdam in 1948 as a "consultant," and was invited to join the organizing committee of the second assembly which was held in Chicago in 1954. He was later appointed vice-chair of the WCC's "Faith and Order Commission," which set the ecumenical agenda for the third assembly to be held in New Delhi, India, in 1961. He also became involved in the work of the International Missionary Council (IMC), which had been formally constituted in 1921 to promote the understanding and practice of mission and evangelism alongside the wider ecumenical work of the "Life and Work," and "Faith and Order" movements which had emerged from the 1910 Edinburgh conference. He was largely responsible for the agenda of the IMC's 1952 meeting at Willingen, Germany (entitled "The Missionary Obligation of the Church"). Indeed, so significant was his involvement that he was "seconded" from his work as a bishop in the CSI to work with the WCC in Geneva, in order to spearhead the process of integrating the work of the IMC with the wider organization of the WCC. He duly became the first director of the new WCC division of World Mission and Evangelism in 1961, and at the same time became an assistant general secretary of the WCC itself.

Many of his publications during this period reflect this increasing involvement in ecumenical affairs, with important pieces on the relationship between churches and the WCC, other essays written specifically for various international WCC gatherings, and some significant early pieces on the theme of Christian unity—including his books *One Body, One Gospel, One World: The Christian Mission Today* (1958), and *A Faith for this One World?* (1961). It was during this period that Newbigin also began to give serious thought to the development of a genuinely trinitarian approach to

9. Based on the Kerr lectures given in Glasgow the previous year. The contributions of Mark Laing and Paul Weston in this collection both explore Newbigin's ecclesiology, one from Newbigin's early experience as a missionary, the other from a more systematic perspective.

mission.[10] His small but influential booklet, *The Relevance of Trinitarian Doctrine for Today's Mission*, was published in 1963, and its central ideas provided the basis for his later and larger 1978 work on the theology of mission, *The Open Secret: Sketches for a Missionary Theology*, which was based on a course of lectures he gave on the theology of mission at the Selly Oak Colleges, in Birmingham following his return to England in the mid-1970s.[11]

When the five-year appointment in Switzerland came to an end in 1965, Newbigin returned to India on his election as bishop of Madras. He quickly found himself immersed in the wide-ranging challenges facing a city which then numbered around three million people (and was growing at a rate of 100,000 every year). Under his leadership, a number of evangelistic initiatives and community projects were developed in the extensive slum areas that were mushrooming around the city area. He also continued to travel extensively round the world, responding to invitations to lecture and preach, and maintaining an active involvement in the developing work of the WCC. He was a prominent delegate at the fourth assembly of the WCC at Uppsala, Sweden in 1968, took part in the Louvain meeting of the WCC Commission on Faith and Order in 1971, and attended the Commission on World Mission and Evangelism conference at Bangkok, Thailand in 1973 (with its theme of "Salvation Today").

As before, Newbigin's published output during this period continued to reflect his varied ecumenical and mission involvements. But alongside these he was developing other projects too. His 1966 book *Honest Religion for Secular Man*, for example, was the substance of the Firth Lectures given at Nottingham University in 1964, and was a theological response to the secularization debate that was provoking discussion across many disciplines in the early 1960s.[12] It also includes a significant and prescient central chapter in which Newbigin sets out an approach to the theory of knowledge (much influenced by his first reading of Michael Polanyi's *Personal Knowledge* [1958]) which would inform and undergird many of his later discussions on the epistemological crisis facing the West.[13] There were other books too. *Christ our Eternal Contemporary* (1968) was a write-up of a series of lectures given at the Christian Medical College

10. See Flett's chapter "Who is Jesus Christ?" in this volume.

11. It was republished with minor revisions in 1995.

12. The title is itself a partial rebuttal of John Robinson's book *Honest to God* published in 1963 (see the discussion of Robinson's approach in Newbigin, *Honest Religion*, 88–93).

13. Newbigin, *Honest Religion*, 77–99.

at Vellore, whilst the 1969 book *The Finality of Christ* (based on his 1966 Lyman Beecher Lectures at Yale three years earlier) addressed the question of what it meant to claim the uniqueness of Christ in an increasingly pluralized world. And alongside these he also found time to publish a little evangelistic book entitled *Journey into Joy* (1973).

When Newbigin duly "retired" in 1974 at the age of sixty-five, he and Helen fulfilled a long-cherished ambition to travel back overland from Madras to the UK using only local transport. It took them two months, in the company of two suitcases and a rucksack. On arrival back in the UK, he was invited to join the staff of Selly Oak Colleges in Birmingham where for the next five years he taught courses on "The Theology of Mission" and "Ecumenical Studies" to students training for missionary work. He also became a minister in the United Reformed Church (becoming its national Moderator in 1978–79), and in 1981—at the age of seventy-two—took up the pastoral leadership of a small inner-city congregation in Winson Green, Birmingham, which he was to lead for the following seven years.

Newbigin's return to the UK was also the prelude to a period of intense activity, reflection and writing for which he was to become perhaps best known. He had been shocked by the way in which an increasingly secularized culture in the West had made its impact, not just on the church, but more generally on the wider culture. When asked about the contrast between his experience in India and his return to Britain, he often commented on the "disappearance of hope" that he was encountering in the UK.[14] In response to this he began to engage more seriously with the issues facing the church in this increasingly secularized context. In the early 1980s, this led him to put down on paper some of his thoughts arising from the discussions of a working party convened by the British Council of Churches. The resulting pamphlet was published in 1983 under the title *The Other Side of 1984: Questions for the Churches.* Somewhat to his surprise, it seemed to strike a chord, and quickly became a bestseller, becoming the first in a series of publications by Newbigin focusing on the missionary challenges facing the church in the West. What later became known as "The Gospel and Our Culture" program soon gathered momentum and led to two UK regional conferences in 1990 and 1991, and to an international conference of 400 delegates held at Swanwick in Derbyshire, UK in July 1992.

As the debate around these questions developed, so did the output from Newbigin's pen. A further fourteen books and around 160 articles

14. Newbigin, *Other Side of 1984*, 1.

Paul Weston

and smaller pieces followed the publication of *The Other Side of 1984* in 1983. Perhaps most significant amongst these "retirement" books are *Foolishness to the Greeks* (1986), *The Gospel in a Pluralist Society* (1989), *Proper Confidence* (1995), and *Truth and Authority in Modernity* (1996).

Lesslie Newbigin died in 1998 at the age of eighty-eight.

BIBLIOGRAPHY

Foust, Thomas F., et al., editors. *A Scandalous Prophet: The Way of Mission after Newbigin*. Grand Rapids: Eerdmans, 2002.

Newbigin, Lesslie. *Christian Freedom in the Modern World*. London: SCM, 1937.

———. *Christ Our Eternal Contemporary*. Madras: Christian Literature Society of India, 1968.

———. *A Faith for this One World?* London: SCM, 1961.

———. *The Finality of Christ*. London: SCM, 1969.

———. *Foolishness to the Greeks: The Gospel and Western Culture*. London: SPCK, 1986.

———. *The Gospel in a Pluralist Society*. London: SPCK, 1989.

———. *Honest Religion for Secular Man*. London: SCM, 1966.

———. *The Household of God: Lectures on the Nature of the Church*. London: SCM, 1953.

———. *Journey into Joy*. Madras: Christian Literature Society of India, 1972.

———. *One Body, One Gospel, One World: The Christian Mission Today*. London: International Missionary Council, 1958.

———. *The Open Secret: Sketches for a Missionary Theology*. Grand Rapids: Eerdmans, 1978. (Republished with minor revisions by SPCK/Eerdmans, 1995.)

———. *The Other Side of 1984: Questions for the Churches*. Geneva: World Council of Churches, 1983.

———. *Proper Confidence: Faith, Doubt and Certainty in Christian Discipleship*. London: SPCK, 1995.

———. *The Relevance of Trinitarian Doctrine for Today's Mission*. C.W.M.E. Study Pamphlets, No.2. London: Edinburgh House, 1963.

———. *The Reunion of the Church : A Defence of the South India Scheme*. London: SCM, 1948. (2nd ed. London: SCM, 1960.)

———. *Truth and Authority in Modernity*. Valley Forge, PA: Trinity Press International, 1996.

Polanyi, Michael. *Personal Knowledge: Towards a Post-Critical Philosophy*. Chicago: University of Chicago Press, 1958.

Robinson, John A.T. *Honest to God*. London: SCM, 1963.

Wainwright, Geoffrey. *Lesslie Newbigin: A Theological Life*. Oxford: Oxford University Press, 2000.

Weston, Paul, editor. *Lesslie Newbigin, Missionary Theologian: A Reader*. London: SPCK; Grand Rapids: Eerdmans, 2006.

SECTION ONE

A Way of Doing Theology

Unfinished Dialogue?

The Reception of Lesslie Newbigin's Theology[1]

David J. Kettle

LESSLIE NEWBIGIN WAS ONE of the most significant missiologists of the twentieth century, according to Timothy Yates.[2] In Geoffrey Wainwright's assessment, he was comparable with the Fathers of the Church in spiritual stature and scope of ministry.[3] Tom Wright congratulates "any seminary or degree course that offers a special subject on his thought."[4]

Lesslie Newbigin is best known in New Zealand, Britain and North America for his pursuit of authentic missionary engagement with Western culture through a series of books and his "Gospel and Our Culture" initiative.[5] However, in current conversation about such mission he does not widely receive attention. He is remembered with affection by many who knew him, and his message has inspired many in a general way, but his teaching is not often subject to careful reflection. Indeed many have passed over his message or dismissed it. In Britain, at least, he seems to

---

1. This chapter was originally published in *Stimulus: The New Zealand Journal of Christian Thought & Practice* 16, no.2 (May 2008) and is reprinted with permission.

2. Timothy Yates, in a personal communication to the author.

3. Wainwright, *Lesslie Newbigin*, v.

4. Wright, Review of *Lesslie Newbigin*, 3.

5. The most familiar of these are *The Other Side of 1984* (1983) and the larger *The Gospel in a Pluralist Society* (1989); the most cited (in the present author's experience) by readers as personally formative is *Foolishness to the Greeks* (1986). The wider scope of Newbigin's writing is well reflected in Paul Weston, *Lesslie Newbigin: A Reader* (2006).

have been relegated to the margins. The reasons for this raise questions of importance to theology, church life and mission today.

A MARGINAL FIGURE?

Newbigin was in his time Bishop of Madras, General Secretary of the International Missionary Council, a popular lecturer, and the author of a dozen books and hundreds of articles. It may seem odd, therefore, to suggest that he *always has been* a marginal figure. Yet relative to various well established institutions and parties of allegiance with enduring influence, he has always been so.

Firstly, Newbigin was marginal to both "Evangelical" and "Liberal" parties in their mutual opposition (an opposition which he himself attributed to secular ideology). Presenting challenges to each, he has often been treated with suspicion by both. Evangelicals have often been suspicious of him for his close involvement in the ecumenical movement.[6] Because he refused to pronounce on the eternal destiny of particular souls, he has been suspected of universalism. Because he claimed on behalf of the church in each culture (in dialogue with the church in other cultures) responsibility to discern for itself the gospel he has been accused of an "existentialist contextualization" which absolutizes culture and exalts reception at the expense of objective revelation.[7] Liberals, for their part, have been inclined to dismiss his theology for placing the death and resurrection of Jesus Christ at the center of a true understanding of the world in all its aspects (more of this below). More generally, he has been dismissed as simply "conservative" in outlook.

Secondly, Newbigin was marginal to academic theology. He never held an academic post and did not take bearings from current debates in academic theology. He never provided footnotes. To those schooled in post-Enlightenment, encyclopedic traditions of systematic theology, his theological writing could appear "ad hoc," lacking in comprehensiveness or adequate nuance, or obsessive as he pursues relentlessly one or another key act of illumination and conversion. Intellectually he has been seen more often as a missiologist than a theologian.

Thirdly, Newbigin was marginal to denominational church life. He was the enigma of a Presbyterian bishop. His own episcopal status remained unrecognized by the Anglican Church for many years. The Church

6. See, for example Smith, Review of *Lesslie Newbigin*, 91–94.
7. Nicholls, "Gospel and Culture," 49–62.

of South India union scheme, which he hoped might be seen as pioneering the way for global Christian unity, was not thus received.

Newbigin also sought to pioneer the way in other matters only to find his lead rejected. When the classical Christocentric model for mission was increasingly felt to be inadequate in the World Council of Churches, he formulated a Trinitarian missiology which would reflect more faithfully the activity of the Holy Spirit within and beyond a church called to witness to the truth of the gospel and the finality of Christ. By the 1990s, however, this missiology had been displaced by views he had resisted as failing adequately to reflect this calling of the church.[8]

Then in the 1980s and 1990s Newbigin sought to pioneer "authentic missionary engagement" with Western culture through lectures, books, the "Gospel and Our Culture" initiative and a major consultation at Swanwick in 1992. This in turn has been set aside by many who ponder mission in our culture today. In the remainder of this article I shall consider this last dismissal and the perceptions of Newbigin associated with it, and raise the question of further dialogue with his work. In order to do so, it will be necessary to consider what kind of theological enterprise Newbigin undertakes in the first place.

DOING THEOLOGY: THE EXAMPLE OF NEWBIGIN

When Geoffrey Wainwright conceived writing a "theological biography" of Lesslie Newbigin, he was challenged by his publisher's reader to explain how someone who was in the avant-garde of the theological mainstream in the 40s and 50s "has since been marginalised despite the fact that he has remained remarkably up-to-date intellectually." The reader added "This suggests that the theological mainstream itself is now intellectually marginalised in a way that was not true in Newbigin's youth." Wainwright comments: "Insofar as that may be an accurate reading of the situation, I would suggest that a clue resides in the fact that many theologians in the intervening years, in the chase to remain abreast of fashions in the secular academy, have distanced themselves from the body of the faithful, which has thus itself been diminished in its intellectual life."[9]

Lesslie Newbigin's theological reflection always remained, by contrast, rooted in the mission and ministry of the Church. David Ford writes "Newbigin has had an extraordinary gift of discerning at different periods

8. Newbigin, *Relevance*, recalled to this effect in "Ecumenical Amnesia," 2–5.

9. Wainwright, *Lesslie Newbigin*, 393.

in this century what the fundamental issues are."[10] For Wilbert Shenk, Newbigin was "a frontline thinker because of an uncommon ability to sense the emerging issue that must be addressed at that moment . . . what makes Newbigin consistently compelling is his keen sense of context and his ability to identify with his audience."[11]

These comments recall us to the essential contextual orientation of the gospel as accounting for Newbigin's reiteration of key themes and his apparent lack of nuance: he was concerned, in any given context and moment, to discern and say "the one thing necessary"—to grasp the "Word of the Lord."

Newbigin incorporated into the very basics of "doing theology" the essential drama of the gospel's engagement with multi-layered cultural, and other, contexts. As he himself wrote, "There can never be a culture-free gospel. Yet the gospel, which is from the beginning to the end embodied in culturally conditioned forms, calls into question all cultures, including the one in which it was originally embedded."[12] Such contextualisation is no exercise in cultural compliance. Indeed it may be likened rather to the drama of warfare. Newbigin called for:

> a Christian community equipped for vigorous controversy . . .
> (and) the development of a spirituality for combat, training for
> skill and courage in the use of those spiritual weapons which
> alone are appropriate for Christian warfare. The New Testa-
> ment speaks of the Gospel as a gospel of peace, but this does not
> negate what both our Lord and the apostles have to say about
> conflict, about combat, about the endurance of contradiction.
> I have spoken of the need for a lay theology, but it is equally
> important to develop a type of spiritual and intellectual forma-
> tion for priests and pastors and bishops which will enable them
> in turn to equip the members of the body of Christ in each place
> for this spiritual warfare. I do not think that this is now a feature
> of most ministerial formation.[13]

Newbigin's theology must be understood and appraised by reference to the drama of spiritual warfare. What is the nature of this drama?

---

10. Ford "Letter," 4.

11. Shenk, "Lesslie Newbigin's Contribution," 3–6.

12. Newbigin, *Foolishness*, 4.

13. Newbigin, "Can a Modern Society be Christian?" 6.

GOSPEL AND CONTEXT: THE DRAMA OF ENGAGEMENT AND RECEPTION

Jesus of Nazareth disclosed in word and action the approach of God. His message addressed to their depths people's lives and worlds, assumptions and personal attachments, inviting people to yield all wholeheartedly to receive new and eternal life in which God would be sovereign.

This radical conversion cannot be conceived by reference to any supposedly prior conceptual framework. It can be known only in the gift of oneself and one's world to God for transformation. In it the world comes alive with signs at once pointing from this familiar world to the mystery of God and revealing the world *from* (i.e. by reference to bearings offered by) God.

The gospel of God's kingdom is thus "world-shattering": it addresses every familiar world as a paradox soliciting radical attentiveness to something utterly new. Jesus' words and actions mediate such disclosure provoking, in Ian Ramsey's description, a logically odd discernment and total commitment.[14]

It may happen, however, that the announcement of God's kingdom is not thus received, but is heard by reference precisely to the assumptions and attachments which it addresses: these entrench themselves as a basis on which the gospel is now either rejected as alien or "other," or is domesticated. Whereas these assumptions and attachments are brought to light by the gospel in a world seen with new eyes, instead the gospel may be seen (through blindness or evasion) *from* their own unacknowledged frame. This eventuality, inherent in the coming of the kingdom among fallen humanity, is a recurrent theme in Jesus' parables of the kingdom. It presents the drama of the reception of the kingdom in the "krisis" or judgment precipitated by Jesus' life and proclamation.

NEWBIGIN AND THE DRAMA OF HIS RECEPTION

Newbigin understood the gospel as dramatically engaging cultural and other contextual assumptions and attachments in this way—sometimes only to be domesticated. He diagnosed English theology, in particular, as "an advanced case of syncretism," being domesticated to assumptions deriving from the European Enlightenment.

---

14. Ramsey, *Religious Language*, 15.

David J. Kettle

Of course this diagnosis remains merely a claim until, directing attention back to the issues under debate, it provokes a new recognition, in the light of the gospel, of assumptions operative within such theology and perhaps among ourselves.

Newbigin sought to provoke such recognition by presenting a scandalous challenge to such assumptions. Hence the regret he could express when dismissed precisely by reference to these assumptions. For example, he challenged the ruling exclusion of Christian truth from the realm of public debate by raising the question of a "Christian society." When he was then constantly heard, despite his denials, as wanting to restore Christendom, he lamented: "I have now come to the conclusion that this was a mistake and that I must avoid completely the use of this phrase."[15]

In the drama of such encounters, Newbigin and his critics each see the other as bound by assumptions calling for investigation. Each must therefore be willing to explore their own assumptions and trust the other to do the same. At this point, however, an asymmetry becomes apparent between Newbigin and his critics. Whereas Newbigin typically presents with care his own argument and assumptions and those of his critics, often his critics count him as requiring no response. He is simply dismissed without argument. As Tom Wright remarks, "His insights have not been disproved, only ignored."[16] Also, when a critical response is made, his critic seems often not to have listened to him: much criticism relies precisely on assumptions which Newbigin has identified but which remain unacknowledged and undefended by those who hold them.

In the light of these considerations, Newbigin's writings invite further dialogue. Of course, none of the above *proves* that Newbigin's theology presents the vital message of the gospel and that this has been dismissed. It does, however, invite us to entertain this possibility. Let me indicate briefly some areas for further study and reflection.

I shall consider four broad dismissals of Newbigin's theology: (1) his concerns relate to an age now past, (2) his own thinking belongs to a past age, (3) he unreasonably rejects the Enlightenment, and (4) his own theory of knowledge is (ironically) relativistic. In each case I shall raise the question of further dialogue.

15. Newbigin, "Response," 2.
16. Wright, Review of *Lesslie Newbigin*.

WAS HE OCCUPIED WITH "YESTERDAY'S WORLD"?

Firstly, Newbigin's writings have been dismissed as no longer relevant today because they are concerned with an earlier phase of modern culture and not with today's pluralist, postmodern western culture(s): it is claimed he does not "speak to" our situation. This view is associated with two perceptions: (1) that Newbigin's repeated references to "our culture" *in the singular* show him to be occupied with an age now past, and (2) that his focus is upon "modern" rather than "postmodern" culture.

Further dialogue with Newbigin requires us to conceive that he may have discerned and challenged assumptions which in reality still prevail among us today unacknowledged and which give rise precisely to such dismissal of himself.

(1) It can hardly be claimed that Newbigin was unaware of or inattentive towards plurality in Western culture. Already, twelve years before *The Gospel in a Pluralist Society* (1989), he had written such papers as *Christian Witness in a Plural Society* (1977).[17] As early as 1962 he could write of Western society, "What we have now is a world in which wholly different faiths, faiths mutually contradictory at the deepest points of human conviction, compete freely and openly in a plural society."[18]

Newbigin's cross-cultural experience had revealed western society to him as a distinct way of life grounded in its own assumptions. The West does not readily see this, however: rather we take pride precisely in being autonomous individuals open to wherever the exercise of our reason and choice may lead, and pride also in cultural diversity: we see the West as sponsoring freedom and inclusiveness.

(2) Newbigin *did* make many references to the postmodern but he saw it negatively, as reflecting the collapse of modern confidence. The key to understanding postmodernism therefore lay in understanding this confidence and its collapse. Moreover, the modern remained dominant: "Modernism is still the major challenge which the world faces, primarily because it is embodied in the global-financial-industrial system which is now more powerful than even the most powerful nation-states and which is rapidly engulfing traditional societies and their 'autonomous economies' into its mindless operations."[19]

17. Newbigin, *Christian Witness*.

18. Newbigin, "Unfaith," 1.

19. Newbigin, "Modernity in Context," 8.

David J. Kettle

Also, the cultural tendencies which Newbigin highlighted included "postmodern" ones even though he may not have identified them as such. Take, for example, the separation posited in our culture between "facts" and "values," or more precisely between (a) questions of objective truth which invite public examination and debate, and (b) subjective personal "values" which are held or adopted privately. Another example is the *pagan* (as opposed to *secular*) character of western culture: "the elimination of religion from the public square . . . produces a society in which public life is controlled by a set of beliefs which make claims on human allegiance no less comprehensive than those of religion . . . there does not appear to be any logical stopping place on the slope which leads a purely secular society into a pagan society."[20]

Finally, there is a sense in which Newbigin himself precisely *anticipated* the postmodern turn by urging the role of commitment or "faith" in all thinking including that associated with the Enlightenment. Accordingly Paul Weston has described him as a postmodern missiologist before his time.[21]

AN OLD-FASHIONED THINKER?

Newbigin has also been dismissed as no longer relevant because his own writings reflect features of Enlightenment thinking widely held in opprobrium today. Three claims have been made: (1) that he pursues an oppressively "totalising" gospel rather than celebrating human diversity; (2) that he is "elitist" in regarding intellectual ideas as determinative in shaping society; (3) that he attaches too much importance to a right theory of knowledge as constitutive of faith, assuming "that somehow if we can only get straight on our theory of knowledge and the appropriate doctrine that can be derived from it we will be well on our way to renewal."[22]

Here again, further dialogue requires us to allow that Newbigin may have challenged assumptions which are actually still prevalent, unacknowledged, among those who dismiss him in these terms.

(1) Within the Church, Newbigin criticized the imposition by missionaries, albeit often unwittingly, of their own cultural norms upon their hearers. However, he was also wary of a certain "postmodern" celebration of difference which ultimately sponsors indifference both towards

20. Newbigin, "Gospel in Today's Global City," 4.

21. Weston, "Lesslie Newbigin: A Postmodern Missiologist?"

22. Abraham, *Logic*, ch.3.

the other and towards the truth. Christians should not "settle for mutual recognition and co-existence, for a relationship of conviviality but not of total mutual commitment". This, he said, ". . . is the easy way . . . It is cheap, and (one is bound to say) it almost inevitably tends to reduce the value of what it deals with."[23] Mutual learning and correction are vital. Something analogous applies beyond the church, in dialogue with other people including those of other faiths: "There has to be a kenosis, a 'self-emptying'. The Christian does not meet his partner in dialogue as one who possesses the truth and the holiness of God but as one who bears witness to a truth and holiness which are God's judgement on him and who is ready to hear the judgement spoken through the lips and life of his partner of another faith."[24] Such dialogue represents, for Newbigin, a bold investment of God's gift in the world like that acclaimed in Jesus' parable of the talents.

(2) Newbigin understood the authority exercised by intellectuals in the modern period. However, his attention to ideas reflected no mere concern over "common-room skepticism" in academic circles; nor is it robbed of warrant today by a change in status among intellectuals from "legislators" to "interpreters" or by the rise of popular movements and interest groups displacing public debate as the agent of social change. Rather, Newbigin was attentive to the assumptions operative behind social change itself: the assumptions driving consumerism, global capitalism and human rights ideology, mediated socially through "plausibility structures." Indeed he described as a powerful kind of mind-control the contemporary pumping of ideas of "the good life" insistently into every home.

It would be ironic if for our own part we dismissed the power of ideas just when this power is being recognized and employed, e.g. by Islamists who reshape traditional Muslim societies according to their ideology and by al Qaeda leaders who inspire their followers with the philosophy of Sayid Q'tab.

(3) Newbigin did not attribute the modern rejection of the gospel merely to "epistemological" doubt.[25] He did, however, see a distorted theory of knowledge as contributing to the modern dismissal and cultural domestication of the gospel. His attack on the Cartesian "method of doubt" drew upon an older Christian understanding of personal doubt as "something evil, something of which the symbol was the sin of Adam and Eve in doubting the goodness of God's prohibition": the displacement of

---

23. Newbigin, "Ecumenical Amnesia," 4.

24. Newbigin, *Open Secret*, 205.

25. *Pace* Williams, *Revelation*.

David J. Kettle

"basic trust" by suspicion, as we might say. "According to the biblical story
..." Newbigin wrote, "... the primal sin ... was the willingness to entertain
a suspicion that God could not be wholly trusted."[26] In matters of faith,
"epistemological doubt" and "moral rebellion" were interwoven.

AN ENLIGHTENMENT-BASHER?

Newbigin has also been dismissed for being "anti-Enlightenment." He has
been seen as opposing the freedom for critical thought which Enlightenment thinkers claimed and which we support today (with "postmodern"
adjustments, as necessary), and as wanting to restore "Christendom."

Here, further dialogue requires us to conceive that these charges
against Newbigin may arise precisely from our own domestication to Enlightenment assumptions, as he claimed.

Newbigin denied repeatedly that he wanted to restore Constantini-
anism.[27] He also acknowledged great debt to the Enlightenment:

> For Christians it is particularly necessary to acknowledge that
> the Bible and the teaching office of the Church had become
> fetters upon the human spirit; that the removal of barriers to
> freedom of conscience and of intellectual enquiry was achieved
> by the leaders of the Enlightenment against the resistance of the
> churches; that this made possible the ending of much cruelty,
> oppression and ignorance; and that the developments in sci-
> ence and technology which this liberation has made possible
> have brought vast benefit to succeeding generations. It would
> be dishonest to fail to recognise our debt to the Enlightenment.
> Moreover there is much to be said for the view that the unfin-
> ished work of the Enlightenment is still a large part of our con-
> temporary agenda ...[28]

What, then, was Newbigin's criticism of the Enlightenment? He saw
it as imagining that human social flourishing could be pursued without
attention to God's self-revelation in Christ. He saw it as placing trust
fundamentally elsewhere than in God—in reason and sure knowledge
conceived in radical distinction from this revelation. Thus where John
Locke distinguished knowledge from belief, Newbigin maintained that
the former entailed trust just as surely as the latter; similarly when Locke

26. Newbigin, *Other Side*, 19.
27. On this, see Kettle, "Lesslie Newbigin."
28. Newbigin, *Other Side*, 16.

distinguished reason from the reception of revelation. The key question, for Newbigin, was whether people were willing to acknowledge where they put their deepest trust, or where their ultimate commitments lay, and examine these in the light of the gospel.

A RELATIVIST?

Newbigin's insistence that all knowing entails commitment has attracted another and different criticism: that his argument is relativistic. Thus Kevin Gill claims: "Newbigin seeks to avoid charges of relativism by resorting to relativistic arguments that are self-referentially incoherent . . . arguing this way seem to imply that Newbigin is, in fact, a relativist."[29]

Here, further dialogue with Newbigin calls us to allow that this charge reflects an assumption which Newbigin himself challenged—an assumed analogy between such commitment and occupying a discrete vantage point from which objects are viewed. This assumption rules out anything analogous to a "view from nowhere" or a privileged viewpoint.

The analogy between commitment and vantage point reflects Cartesian habits of imagination and underpins, I believe, each of the charges that Newbigin is anti-Enlightenment, and a fideist, and a relativist. It is vital, therefore, that we ponder the sources from which Newbigin drew his understanding of how commitment informs knowing. These are briefly:

(1) *Revelation*: Newbigin saw revelation as fundamentally the self-disclosure of a personal God[30] through particular acts within history and uniquely through Jesus Christ. This revelation cannot be reduced to a set of timeless propositions. In knowledge of God, commitment is about entrusting oneself with loving attention to a God who acts and guides with sovereign freedom. Commitment entails more here than it does in routine knowledge of information.

(2) *Michael Polanyi*: Newbigin found the place of commitment within personal knowledge elucidated well by Michael Polanyi. For Polanyi, in the act of knowing we always rely upon and attend "from" as well as attending "to." Fundamentally this is not a matter of attending from one specifiable thing to another, as from a vantage-point to an object viewed, but rather of attending to the world in *two different ways*.

Unfortunately Polanyi himself has often been misunderstood in this matter and interpreted casually as a relativist or a constructivist superseded

29. Gill, "Critical Review," 8.
30. Newbigin, *Christ*, 14–16.

by Thomas Kuhn. Thus William Abraham has charged Newbigin with "a kind of fideism based on the work of Michael Polanyi."[31] Although Maben Poirier (for example) has refuted this interpretation of Polanyi,[32] fascinating questions remain concerning both Polanyi's theory of knowledge and Newbigin's interpretation of it.

(3) *The cross*: Christian commitment stood for Newbigin in unique relation to other human commitments. His words spoken in 1962 deserve quoting at length:

> What then is that to which I am committed? . . . Here one has to say, perhaps paradoxically, that it is the standpoint which is given at the point of ultimate despair—given by God in Jesus Christ . . . given at the place where the road of commitment ends in a precipice. Every rational commitment to action implies some kind of faith that human life can be shaped to a meaningful and worthy end. And the cross of Christ is the end of that faith. It is the point at which a sentence of death is pronounced on man's quest for the good, the reasonable, the coherent . . . It is, at the same time, the point at which a wholly new possibility is given because Jesus, the crucified, is the risen and ascended Lord—the . . . possibility of living a life of hope in the midst of despair, or victory in the midst of defeat . . . This paradox remains the central core of the Christian faith, not at its beginning only, but through to its end . . . Faith, the commitment from which alone I can speak, is that paradoxical commitment which is given at the point when all other commitment ends in a precipice.[33]

CONCLUSION

Lesslie Newbigin's theology and its marginalization today invite us to reflect on the engagement between the gospel of God's kingdom and contextual presuppositions including those of modern Western culture. This engagement provokes a drama in which either the gospel breaks open these commitments and re-orients its hearers radically towards God, or else the gospel is heard by reference to these entrenched presuppositions and dismissed or domesticated by them.

31. Abraham, *Logic*, ch.3.

32. Poirier, "Comment."

33. Newbigin, "Unfaith," 2–3.

The drama of this engagement cannot be grasped by modern or post-modern thinking insofar as this understands knowledge and presupposition by reference, unacknowledged, to Cartesian habits of imagination. Newbigin's theology, however, breaks with Cartesian assumptions by seeking to understand knowledge and presupposition by reference to commitment in the context of the personal self-disclosure of God, of Polanyi's theory of knowledge, and of the cross. In this matter of vital relevance for authentic missionary engagement with our culture today, the theology of Lesslie Newbigin invites further dialogue.

BIBLIOGRAPHY

Abraham, William J. *The Logic of Renewal*. Grand Rapids: Eerdmans, 2003.

Ford, David. "Letter." *The Gospel and Our Culture Newsletter* 5 (1990) 4.

Gill, Kevin. "A Critical Review of *The Gospel in a Pluralist Society*." *Ratio* (Spring 1993) 1–8.

Kettle, David. "Cartesian Habits and the 'Radical Line' of Inquiry." *Tradition & Discovery* 27/1 (2000/1) 22–32.

———. "Lesslie Newbigin, Christendom and the Public Truth of the Gospel." *Anvil* 18/2 (2001) 107–15.

Newbigin, Lesslie. "Can a Modern Society Be Christian?" In *Christian Witness in Society: A Tribute to M.M. Thomas*, edited by K. C. Abraham, 95–108. Bangalore: Board of Theological Education—Senate of Serampore College, 1998.

———. *Christ Our Eternal Contemporary*. Madras: Christian Literature Society of India, 1968.

———. *Christian Witness in a Plural Society*. London: British Council of Churches, 1977.

———. "Ecumenical Amnesia." *International Bulletin of Missionary Research* 18 (1994) 2–5.

———. *Foolishness to the Greeks: The Gospel and Western Culture*. London: SPCK, 1986.

———. *The Gospel in a Pluralist Society*. London: SPCK, 1989.

———. *The Gospel in Today's Global City*. Selly Oak Colleges Occasional Papers, 16. Birmingham, UK: Selly Oak Colleges, 1996.

———. "Modernity in Context." In *Modern, Postmodern and Christian*, co-authored with John Reid and David Pullinger, 1–12. Carberry: Handsel, 1996.

———. "On the Gospel as Public Truth: Response to the Colloquium." (Leeds, UK, 1996). Unpublished manuscript in *Lesslie Newbigin Papers, Library Special Collections, The University of Birmingham, U.K.*

———. *The Open Secret*. Grand Rapids: Eerdmans, 1978.

———. *The Other Side of 1984: Questions for the Churches*. Geneva: World Council of Churches, 1983.

———. *The Relevance of Trinitarian Doctrine for Today's Mission*, C.W.M.E. Study Pamphlets, 2. London: Edinburgh House, 1963.

————. "Unfaith and Other Faiths" (1962). Unpublished manuscript in *World Council of Churches, Ecumenical Centre Library, Geneva, Switzerland.*

Nicholls, Bruce. "Towards a Theology of Gospel and Culture." In *Down to Earth: Studies in Christianity and Culture*, edited by John Stott et al., 49–62. Grand Rapids: Eerdmans, 1980.

Poirier, Maben W. "A Comment on Polanyi and Kuhn." *The Thomist* 53 (1989) 259–79.

Ramsey, Ian T. *Religious Language*. London: SCM, 1957.

Shenk, Wilbert R. "Lesslie Newbigin's Contribution to the Theology of Mission." *TransMission* (Special Issue: "Tribute to Lesslie Newbigin") (1998) 3–6.

Smith, David. Review of *Lesslie Newbigin: A Theological Life*, by Geoffrey Wainwright. *Themelios* 28/1 (2003) 91–94.

Wainwright, Geoffrey. *Lesslie Newbigin: A Theological Life*. Oxford: Oxford University Press, 2000.

Weston, Paul D.A. "Lesslie Newbigin: A Postmodern Missiologist?" *Mission Studies* 21 (2004) 229–48.

————. editor. *Lesslie Newbigin, Missionary Theologian: A Reader*. London/Grand Rapids: SPCK/Eerdmans, 2006.

Williams, Stephen N. *Revelation and Reconciliation: A Window on Modernity*. Cambridge: Cambridge University Press, 1995.

Wright, N.T. Review of *Lesslie Newbigin: A Theological Life*, by Geoffrey Wainwright. *Gospel and Our Culture Network Newsletter* 32 (Autumn 2001) 3.

The Clue to History

Jürgen Schuster

"The question is whether the faith that finds its focus in Jesus is the faith with which we seek to understand the whole of history, or whether we limit this faith to a private world of religion and hand over the public history of the world to other principles of explanation."[1]

AMONG WESTERN MISSIOLOGISTS NEWBIGIN is probably best known for creating an awareness for the fact that the split between the public and private sphere of life is in conflict with the character and aspiration of the gospel. Newbigin has insisted on questioning this dichotomy. History is much more than a mere backdrop for individual encounters between God and human beings. History itself is the arena of the particular acts of a particular God, who purposefully acts for the sake of his creation in order to bring about salvation and shalom. As Bishop N.T. Wright states: "The whole point of Christianity is that it offers a story which is the story of the whole world. It is public truth."[2]

This interconnection between salvation and history occupied Newbigin since his student days and the beginning of his ministry.[3] One of the earliest documents of Newbigin's public ministry in India was published only after his death in the year 2003.[4] In a series of lectures he gave at Union Theological College, in 1941, on the subject of "The Kingdom of God and the Idea of Progress," Newbigin outlined his understanding of

1. Newbigin, *Foolishness to the Greeks*, 61.
2. Wright, *New Testament and the People of God*, 41–42.
3. Newbigin, *Unfinished Agenda*, 31.
4. Newbigin, "Kingdom of God," 1–55.

biblical eschatology and its relevance for the engagement with the secular idea of progress and human history. Geoffrey Wainwright, in the introduction to his book on Newbigin, shares: "Lesslie himself pressed on me the significance of these Bangalore lectures as his first full treatment of themes that would continue to occupy him throughout his life."[5] The "fully real character of biblical eschatology" which Newbigin reflected upon and defended at the beginning of his public ministry turned out to be one of the marks of his theology and shaped his understanding of human history and the role of the church in relationship to the world. This article attempts first, to outline some key points of Newbigin's understanding of history in light of his understanding of biblical eschatology, and second, to sketch out the relevance of biblical eschatology for his theology of mission.

HISTORY AND ESCHATOLOGY

> The Bible is unique among the sacred scriptures of the religions in that it offers an interpretation of history as a whole, human history and cosmic history, and not just of the life of man apart from this history. Its centre of attention is not, if one may put it so, the possibility of man's escaping out of this world into another; it is the promise of God coming to this world to redeem it and to complete what he has begun.[6]

History is God's story with his creation and humankind. In contrast to Hindu beliefs with which Newbigin engaged in India, the gospel presents history as reality (as opposed to illusion—*maya*) in which God is actively involved. In contrast to a post-Christendom western worldview which relegates any reference to God to the sphere of private values, Newbigin insisted that history is the sphere in which God deliberately acts and reveals himself. We will focus on four key aspects of Newbigin's understanding of history.

The Rediscovery of Purpose

> It is impossible to write history without some vision of its meaning from which judgments of significance can be made . . . History . . . is not the story of the development of forces immanent

5. Wainwright, *Signs amid the Rubble*, viii.
6. Newbigin, "Bible Study," 8.

within history; it is a matter of the promise of God. History has
a goal only in the sense that God has promised it.[7]

History can only be told if there is a story, a meta-narrative which determines the significance of certain events and the irrelevance of others.
There may be different interpretations regarding the significance of events,
depending on the story line in the interpreter's mind. However, the study
of history can never yield results if it is seen simply as the lining up of an
endless number of events and historical facts. Scientific research in the
Western world has taught us to focus on the cause and effect relationship
in order to understand. If our universe were a closed system, developing
on its own, focusing on cause and effect would be our primary means
to give meaning to the vast data of human experience. If, on the other
hand, we understand God as a personal and acting God, involved in his
creation, purpose becomes a major factor for understanding what is going
on. God's actions and words must necessarily be particular events, rooted
in specific times and places in history. But the purpose of a single action
may extend way beyond the specific individual person and the particular
story involved. To understand meaning in history we have to consider the
purposeful acts of the living God, who is pursuing his purpose with his
creation in and through particular historic events. God reveals himself to
us not just as one player among many others, intervening in history every
now and then. He appears as the main actor in the story. And we as human
beings are responsive and responsible actors.[8]

Given that purpose plays a major role in determining meaning, a
particular purpose may not always be apparent while the actors are still
in the middle of the story. It may become obvious only at the end. In the
meantime the only option is to listen to the person acting, explaining the
purpose of his or her particular acts.

"Suppose that going along a street, we observe men at work with piles
of bricks and bags of cement, and we guess that a building is being erected.
What is it to be? An office? A house? A chapel? There are only two ways
to discover the answer: we can wait around until the work is complete and
inspection enables us to discover what it is. If we cannot wait until then,
we must ask the architect, and we will have to take his word for it."[9]

7. Newbigin, *Gospel in a Pluralist Society*, 72, 103.

8. Newbigin, *Proper Confidence*, 52–53.

9. Newbigin, *Proper Confidence*, 57. See also "Purpose is a personal word. It im-
plies a mind which has a purpose real in the mind though not yet realized in the
world of objects; it can be known only by listening to the person whose purpose it is"

Understanding history as *story* in which God is acting intentionally corresponds to understanding the Holy Scriptures as the revelation of God's purpose, witnessing to God's actions in history and conveying God's own elucidation of what his purpose is in acting the way he does.

Secularized and Privatized forms of Eschatological Hope

> The horizon of all our action in the world, therefore, is not an earthly utopia but the heavenly city which is God's new creation . . . The Bible closes with a vision of the holy city coming down from heaven to earth. It is the vision of a consummation which embraces both the public and the private life of men and women. There is no dichotomy between these two. Those who die before that day are laid to rest in a "dormitory" around the church where the living continue to worship. When the Day comes, all together will share the same end—judgment and, for the blessed, the heavenly city.[10]

Modernity with its strong focus on human agency and humankind's mastery of nature led to a secularized version of Christian eschatology. The otherworldly focus of the Christian hope was translated into an earthly expectation which was to be realized by human agency. Christian eschatology gave way to the idea of progress. This idea took shape in two different forms. Both Marxism and capitalism were built on secularized understandings of history. Marxism obviously failed to reach the utopia of a just society. This failure is deeply related to its romantic and idealistic view of human nature. Humans are seen as basically good and merely hampered in their development by suppressing social structures. This naïve view of the human being goes hand in hand with the denial of God as creator and savior. Capitalism on the other hand has continued to gain tremendous momentum, despite recent financial crises. It is still seen by many as the unrivalled solution to our current worldwide economic problems, suggesting that the possibilities for the increase of material goods and prosperity are without limitation and form the basis for the pursuit of individual happiness. Newbigin calls for a critical engagement with the theory of a market economy which builds on the principle of self regulation according to the market's inherent rules and demands. Economic systems are not intrinsically good or neutral

(Newbigin, "Can the West be Converted?", 6).

10. Newbigin, *Other Side of 1984*, 34–35.

systems which could be left to their own devices. They too have to be brought under the lordship of Christ.[11]

While the idea of progress is still prevalent in the global economic market, the relegation of faith into the sphere of private values rather than public facts, as well as the dualism of spirit and matter based on Greek philosophy, have led to a change of focus in Christian eschatology. The Christian understanding of purpose and hope has focused almost exclusively on a merely private future, on personal salvation. "My living relationship with God now," and "my future with him in heaven," have become the locus of attention. "This naturally diminishes the sense of responsibility for public affairs."[12]

Newbigin deliberately challenged the dichotomy of private versus communitarian hope. Both of these aspects are fragmentary and need correction. A strict focus on communitarian hope—as in the Marxist utopia of a just society—marginalizes human beings as individuals. They may serve to advance the cause, even though they may never participate in the desired goal. The human being "becomes instrumental to history, for the individual does not live to participate in the realisation of history's meaning."[13] The fixation on individual hope, on the other hand, diminishes the meaning of history as such. All that counts is the eternal destiny of the individual human soul.

True Christian eschatology holds together personal and corporate hope in the expectation of the final resurrection, based on the historical fact that Christ has been raised from the dead and has thus overcome transience and futility. The hope of a future resurrection and participation in the new creation builds on this historical event.[14] The fact that there is no dichotomy between personal and corporate hope means that Christian eschatology embraces both the public and the private life of men and women. This is the necessary framework for Christian engagement in holistic mission. Newbigin emphasized that: "[Christ] is coming to meet us, and whatever we do—whether it is our most private prayers or our most public political action—is simply offered to him for whatever place it may have in his blessed kingdom. Here is the clue to meaningful action in

---

11. See Newbigin, "End of History," 2.
12. Newbigin, *Gospel in a Pluralist Society*, 113; also 67–68.
13. Newbigin, "Bible Study," 8.
14. 1 Cor 15:13–20

a meaningful history: it is the translation into action of the prayer: 'Your kingdom come, your will be done, as in heaven so on earth.'"[15]

Christian involvement in the matters of this world occurs in light of the future advent of Christ; it is an enacted prayer for the coming, visible manifestation of Christ's rule.

The Relationship between the Universal and the Particular

> The Christian tradition affirms that God has made his mind and purpose known to some (not to all) people through events in history—not all events but some, the memory of which is treasured in the Christian tradition . . . The biblical record as we have it comes from a community which (with wide diversities of interpretation at many points) understood history in terms of a purpose of God to bring salvation to the world through a particular people among all the peoples of the world.[16]

One of the major challenges for a theology of religions today is the question of the relationship between the particularity of the Christ event and the universality of God's saving will. The pluralistic view relegates the NT insistence on the centrality of Christ to the area of love-language,[17] opening the door for other religious experiences to be seen as equally valid and commensurable experiences with salvific character. This corresponds to the postmodern rejection of a universal meta-narrative and its insistence on individual stories, unconnected and detached from each other.

The gospel however, presents a universal story of one God and one humankind in which all the individual stories not only find their specific niche but also their true meaning as part of the whole. The universal character of the cosmic story and the particular character of each individual life story are intrinsically intertwined. This is also true of the particularity of the Christ event und the universality of the saving will of God. Newbigin addresses this last question in light of the biblical pattern of election. The few are elected for the sake of the many. The purpose of God electing a few out of the many is not to focus on their salvation and leave others outside of his salvation story. Genesis 12:1–3 states clearly that Abraham—and, in continuation of the story, Israel and the church—is called for the sake

---

15. Newbigin, *Gospel in a Pluralist Society*, 102.

16. Ibid., 72, 76.

17. See Hick and Meltzer, *Three Faiths—One God*, 197–210.

of the nations, in order that "all the families of the earth" will be blessed through him. It corresponds to the nature of salvation as it is presented in the biblical story that God's salvific intention for humankind must find its expression in a community which is shaped by his truth and love. Election is thus understood not as a privilege for the few but as a responsibility of the few for the sake of the many.[18] Hunsberger specifies Newbigin's view of election as follows:

> One is chosen by God to bear the blessing to another. The particularity of the choice reflects both the personal character of God (which implies the freedom to act and to choose the time and place of such action) and the social character of human life. It is congruent with the nature of salvation (it reconciles as it is received at the hand of an "other") and the scope of it (it is intended for all). Far from creating or intensifying the "problem" of particularity, election for witness is the pattern which makes the inevitable particularity of a personal God's historical actions universal. The particular choice is designed to bear the blessing to all.[19]

Newbigin was convinced of the universal significance of the particular Christ event and never wavered in his insistence on the centrality of the person of Christ.[20]

> [W]e are making the tremendously bold claim that God really has a purpose for the world and for all men . . . [W]e ask them to read the Bible. There they will find a sort of outline of world history, beginning with the creation and ending with the glory of God's perfect kingdom; but the central thread of the history is the story of God's people. And the centre point of the story is the birth, life, death, resurrection and ascension of Jesus and the coming of His Spirit to His disciples. It is from that centre point that we understand the whole Bible, both the Old Testament and the New. Everything in the Bible points towards Him, and then points outward from Him to the end of the world and the ends of the earth.[21]

---

18. See Newbigin, *Gospel in a Pluralist Society*, 85–86.
19. Hunsberger, *Bearing the Witness of the Spirit*, 235.
20. See Anastasios (Yannoulatos), "Tribute to Bishop Lesslie Newbigin," 95–96.
21. Newbigin, "Why Study the Old Testament?", 75–76.

Jürgen Schuster

Newbigin can thus call Christ the "clue to history."[22] Christ is the centre of world history, its turning point, because in him the reign of God has been established and revealed on earth, even though it is at the same time still hidden from the eyes of the world. It is in Christ that the universal saving will of God finds its particular expression, and salvation is brought by the one for the many. The community of the elect is bearing witness in this world to this particular act of salvation with its universal focus by living as a sign, an instrument, and a foretaste of God's reign in the present.

Revelation and Eschatological Verification: Participation and Witness

> Normally you cannot be sure what is the point of the story until you have reached the end. There can always be surprises at the end, and in the best stories there are. How then can we, who are still in the middle of the cosmic story, know what the point of the story is, or whether it has any point at all? Only if the author of the story has let us into the secret while we are still in the middle. There can be no other possibility. And here of course, when we speak of "the author letting us into the secret," we are talking the language of revelation.[23]

The fact that we are still in the middle of an ongoing story and that its outcome is still ahead of us entails the necessity that we can only respond in belief or in unbelief to the claims the author of the story makes about its interpretation; "There can be no indubitable proofs."[24] Here the eschatological orientation of history based on the will of a personal God presents itself as the key for Newbigin's epistemology. We are part of an ongoing story. Therefore we don't have access to an outside view. We are given God's word regarding the outcome of the story. But there is no way to verify it objectively. We need to commit ourselves in faith to a specific view of the world. We all have to follow Augustine's creed, "credo ut intelligam," "I believe (i.e. I commit myself to a specific worldview) in order that I may know." For the final verification of the Christian truth claim Newbigin can only point to the end of history.[25]

22. See Newbigin, "Life and Mission of the Church," 61; Newbigin, *Finality of Christ*, 65, 69; Newbigin, *Gospel in a Pluralist Society*, 103.

23. Newbigin, *Gospel in a Pluralist Society*, 91.

24. Ibid., 55.

25. See ibid., 65.

For the time being there remains only the "test of adequacy."[26] The goal of Christian witness and apologetics is to demonstrate—not only in words—that the gospel "does provide the best foundation for a way of grasping and dealing with the mystery of our existence in this universe."[27] This demonstration is not based on a universally accessible set of meta-criteria by which to judge the different plausibility structures, and it will not lead to indubitable certainty. It is, however, an invitation by the witness (*martyr*), who has staked his life on a specific truth claim,[28] to people of other persuasions to engage in an exploration of the adequacy of the Christian plausibility structure, and to commit themselves to this particular view of the world.

Based on this outline of Newbigin's understanding of history in light of the biblical eschatology we will now consider some implications for his theology of mission.

THEOLOGY OF MISSION AND ESCHATOLOGY

The eschatological framework of Newbigin's theology is characterized by two poles, the inauguration of Christ as Lord at his first coming in the past, and the visible manifestation of his reign at his second coming in the future. The implications of this eschatological framework for Newbigin's theology of mission can be seen in at least five areas.[29]

Holistic Mission

The missiological controversy of the 1960s and 1970s on the relationship between witness in word or/and deed, which led to a split between the evangelical and the ecumenical mission movement, may seem to be a matter of the past when we consider the widespread use of terms like "holistic mission." However, the theological basis for holistic mission is still somewhat ambiguous. It is worth considering the implications of Newbigin's eschatological framework for this question.

The incident which caused the apostles and the church to be sent into the world was the inauguration of Christ's Lordship, his accession to the

26. Newbigin, "Truth and Authority," 81.

27. Newbigin, *Proper Confidence*, 94.

28. Vanhoozer, "Trials of Truth," 120–56.

29. For a detailed discussion of these issues, see Schuster, *Christian Mission in Eschatological Perspective*.

throne at the right hand of the Father (Rev 5). The public proclamation of Christ's kingship—the advent of the reign of God in the person of Jesus Christ—has thus become the church's mission. This proclamation is to be done by both word and deed. Both are meant to be signs of God's kingdom, pointing to the final consummation of God's reign at Christ's return.[30] Understanding holistic mission in this eschatological framework helps the church to be both hopeful and realistic in its engagement with the challenges the world faces today. The church is not called to bring about the kingdom of God through its activities. This would be a grossly distorted assessment of its own capabilities. However, the church is also not allowed to leave the social and political issues aside in its participation in God's mission. The New Testament does not permit this kind of privatization of hope and salvation. The deeds of the church are significant because of their sign-character, pointing to Christ, the Lord. The verbal proclamation of the church is significant because it explains what the church is doing in the world and proclaims the name of the one who is Lord of all.

Among evangelicals the Greek dualism of spirit versus matter has sometimes led to a dissolution of the eschatological tension of the "already now" and the "not yet" of God's reign. De-facto it has been dissolved into a temporal sequence of Christ taking care of the spiritual matters at his first coming ("dying for our sins"), and the relegation of the solution to social, political, and material matters to his second coming. This is of course a distortion of the biblical mission mandate. On the other hand, seminal voices in the ecumenical mission movement tended towards a world-immanent understanding of salvation ("shalom as humanization of the world"), overestimating the church's capabilities, and neglecting the eschatological future. The hermeneutical key for a balanced understanding of holistic mission is the recovery of the eschatological vision of God's story and the fact that the lordship of Christ can only be understood in light of the eschatological tension which the New Testament presents. As Newbigin says, the church must have a point of reference outside of this world in order to be significant for the world.[31]

30. In a personal letter to Albrecht Hauser (at that time a member of the ecclesiastical council in Stuttgart and in charge of matters regarding world mission) Newbigin wrote, "I am very interested in your comments on Manila. How sad that we seem to be unnecessarily polarized. I have just come from a missionary conference where the dominant note was 'We must keep our mouth shut and listen to the poor'—the polar opposite of Manila. How I long for a great body of people who can say 'Yes, we must listen but we must also speak of what God has done in Jesus Christ.'" Newbigin to Hauser, 19/12/1989.

31. Newbigin, "Church, World, Kingdom," 106–7.

The Gospel as Public Truth

In presenting the gospel to the world the church in the West today faces a double challenge. On the one hand, religion is generally understood as a private matter with limited or no influence on public life. It is presumed that a secular worldview provides a "neutral" foundation on which each individual can build his or her own religious convictions regarding his or her private life, aiming for private salvation and happiness. Christianity has to take its stand among other religions in this pluralistic marketplace. The church is easily misled into presenting the gospel as just such a way to private salvation. This in fact changes the character of the gospel in a fundamental way by giving up the meta-narrative which encompasses the whole human story from creation to new creation.

On the other hand, meta-narratives are very much a matter of modern or pre-modern worldviews and immediately encounter suspicion and resistance in a pluralistic, post-modern world. Islam runs into this problem when it tries to understand and present itself in the West as providing both religious and social order. Post-modernity with its emphasis on diverse, unrelated individual life stories rejects any claim of a universal meta-narrative, even though it actually continues to draw heavily on the modern materialistic paradigm with its emphasis on progress and prosperity.

In this kind of a context the church is challenged to present the gospel as relevant to the individual life stories without conceding to the rejection of an overarching meta-narrative. The gospel must not be presented nor perceived as simply enrichment for individual spiritual experience or an importunate will to power and control. It needs to be understood as the framework in which each individual life story can find ultimate meaning as part of God's story, and especially in relation to the person of Christ, who is the centre of history.

Here eschatology plays an important role. Christ has established his reign on earth, but it is not yet manifest to all. The presentation of the gospel meta-narrative can and must therefore be presented as an invitation to believe, not as a constraint to be subjugated to. Charles Taber has drawn attention to the fact that the authenticity of the gospel meta-narrative can only be perceived when it is presented as neither totalitarian nor homogenizing. He points to the events of Christ's crucifixion (God suffers rejection rather than imposing his way on human beings), and of the plural character of unity at Pentecost (unity in diversity): "I suggest, in fact, that the gospel of the kingdom of God is the only valid universal meta-narrative, the only one which is not ruthlessly homogenizing and totalitarian, because it is the only one based on self-sacrificing love instead of worldly power, the only one offered by a king on a cross, the only one offered by a conquering lion who turns out to be a slaughtered lamb (Rev 5:1–10). This is the guarantee that it is not totalitarian. Pentecost, if correctly understood, is the guarantee that it is not homogenizing."[32]

This calls for a solid reflection on the interpretation of the gospel and its character, as well as the methods of presentation of the gospel to the world. The church must resist the pressure to reduce the gospel to the area of private religion. And it must be prepared to present the adequacy of the gospel meta-narrative for both individuals and humankind, not only verbally, but also in the life of the community of believers.

The Church as Hermeneutic of the Gospel

If the gospel must not be reduced to the area of private religion, the church must not be reduced to a religious club of like-minded people who support each other in their pursuit of religious interests. The church takes its bearings for its being in the world from the fact that Christ is inaugurated as Lord of all. Newbigin coined the famous triad: The church is "sign, instrument, and foretaste" of God's reign. It is a sign to the world, demonstrating what it is like to live under the salvific lordship of Christ, exemplifying what it means to find meaning for one's individual life story in the framework of the gospel meta-narrative. It is an instrument of God's reign, proclaiming in word and deed the lordship of Christ and bringing about real change in this world. The contributions to current social issues may be numerically insignificant. However, they are significant because of their sign-character, pointing to Christ as Lord. Finally, the church is a foretaste of God's reign in this world. As a community of believers it continues to strive to bring all aspects of life under the lordship of Christ, beginning in its own community, exemplifying a biblical perspective of human existence in a local community, contributing a biblical view of humanity to the public discourse, and unmasking and challenging ungodly powers. As such the church is a hermeneutic of the gospel to the world. It is the provisional incorporation of humankind into Christ which will find its consummation in the eschatological establishment of the new humankind in the new creation.

32. Taber, "Gospel as Authentic Meta-Narrative", 189.

The eschatological tension between the inauguration of Christ's reign in the past and the manifestation of his reign in the future characterizes the life of the church. As the first-fruits of renewed humankind the church must never be church-centered and complacent as it participates in God's mission. Together with its Lord it is looking forward to the manifestation of Christ's reign. In the meantime it is called to be a hermeneutic of the gospel, inviting people to a new worldview and an allegiance to Christ as Lord.

The Gospel among the Religions

The claim that the gospel is public truth and must not be squeezed into the private mold, has characterized Newbigin's engagement with the plurality of religions and his critique of a pluralistic paradigm. While the church must take its stand on the religious marketplace together with other religious communities, it must take into consideration the unique character of the gospel in its conversation with people of other faiths and in its presentation of the good news. The gospel is neither a way to private salvation, nor is it the announcement or enforcement of a theocratic kingdom.[33] Communicating with people of other faiths is essential in the church's encounter with others, but this dialogue—Newbigin didn't really like the word—must not become a substitute for witness. The telling of the story of Jesus is rather the "essential contribution of the Christian to the dialogue."[34] The church contributes the biblical story not out of a conviction of superiority, neither the superiority of itself as a community nor of its own religious practice and teaching. Instead it does so because it is entrusted with the gospel story. At the centre of the story is the fact that God meets us not at the top of the staircases of our religious efforts, but rather at the foot of the cross, where we can only meet him with empty hands (see Matt 5:3), leaving our own religious achievements behind.[35]

The encounter in dialogue and witness inevitably raises the question as to which tradition we trust and to which tradition we commit ourselves. Increasingly theologians with a pluralist conviction have drawn upon Eastern religious traditions with their embrace of diversity, and these philosophical and religious constructs have gained popularity in both East and West. However, popularity and general acceptance do not necessarily

33. Newbigin, *Finality of Christ*, 48–49.
34. Newbigin, *Gospel in a Pluralist Society*, 182.
35. See Newbigin, *Open Secret*, 181; see also Phil 3:5–9.

make these constructs true. We all have to concede that no-one can claim complete knowledge of God's point of view. Everybody has to participate in the interreligious dialogue with his own particular view of the truth and her own commitment to a specific tradition.[36] Verification or falsification of truth claims is, in the end, an eschatological matter;[37] which brings us to our final section.

Eschatology and Hermeneutics

Confidence and certainty in the endeavor of knowing are for Newbigin intrinsically bound to the faithfulness and fidelity of God. They do not rest in human decisions or in human reason, but in a "personal commitment to a personal Lord" who will lead us "into a fuller understanding of the truth."[38] All attempts to gain a Cartesian certainty, which is ultimately based on the knowing subject, are bound to fail.[39] Following Polanyi Newbigin holds that there is no possibility of knowing anything apart from initially believing something. Critical doubt is only the second step in the process of knowing. It requires the initial acceptance of something as true. Thus, knowing is never something merely objective. It requires a commitment on the part of the knowing subject. This epistemological approach seamlessly integrates with the biblical claim that God has revealed himself in human history in deed and accompanying word. In fact it allows for making this revelation the point of departure for the exercise of knowing. The commitment to this tradition includes the recognition that the truth claim of the gospel can only be verified by God himself when he brings the story to its end. In the meantime the credibility of the gospel can only be witnessed to, and advocated provisionally.

Newbigin thus argued for—what Hiebert calls—a critical realist epistemology[40] which affirms the subjective nature of knowledge and yet—in contrast to an instrumentalist paradigm—regains the reference to an external reality which is distinct from the knowing subject. This epistemological approach calls for a hermeneutical community, in which the epistemological foundations can be expressed and debated, and in which the results of the ongoing process of knowing can be shared and discussed.

36. Newbigin, *Open Secret,* 166–68.

37. See Foust, "Lesslie Newbigin's Epistemology," 162.

38. Newbigin, *Proper Confidence,* 66.

39. Newbigin, *Truth and Authority in Modernity,* 68.

40. Hiebert, *Missiological Implications,* 68ff.

It remains the task of the church today to participate in the public discourse, to clarify and explain its epistemological foundations, and to witness to the story which was entrusted to it in a manner which invites people to discover the true meaning of their own life story in the context of the meta-narrative of God's story with humankind. Newbigin has pointed us in a direction where we can genuinely be committed to the claim of God's revelation and honestly participate in the public and religious discourse of our times.

CONCLUSION

It should be clear by now that the eschatological orientation of Newbigin's theology is not a peripheral matter. Newbigin throughout his ministry used this framework as a navigational light to get his theological bearings when addressing new missiological issues. Thus, the eschatological orientation becomes something of a central thread throughout his writings. This paper is presented in the hope that the recognition of the story-character of the gospel may lead us also to understand the missional challenges of our time as part of the ongoing story, and may help us to address missiological questions in light of the eschatological outcome of that story.

BIBLIOGRAPHY

Anastasios (Yannoulatos). "In Tribute to Bishop Lesslie Newbigin." *International Review of Mission* 79 (1990) 86–101.

Foust, Thomas F. "Lesslie Newbigin's Epistemology: A Dual Discourse?" In *A Scandalous Prophet. The Way of Mission after Newbigin*, edited by Thomas F. Foust et al., 153–62. Grand Rapids: Eerdmans, 2002.

Hick, John, and Edmund S. Meltzer, editors. *Three Faiths—One God. A Jewish, Christian, Muslim Encounter*. London: Macmillan, 1989.

Hiebert, Paul G. *The Missiological Implications of Epistemological Shifts. Affirming Truth in a Modern/Postmodern World*. Harrisburg: Trinity Press International, 1999.

Hunsberger, George R. *Bearing the Witness of the Spirit. Lesslie Newbigin's Theology of Cultural Plurality*. Grand Rapids: Eerdmans, 1998.

Newbigin, Lesslie. "Bible Study on Romans 8." Unpublished Paper, 1976. Online: http://www.newbigin.net/assets/pdf/76bsr8.pdf.

———. "Can the West Be Converted?" *International Bulletin of Missionary Research* 11 (1987) 2–7.

———. "Church, World, Kingdom." Henry Martyn Lecture, Cambridge University, 1986. In *Signs Amid the Rubble. The Purposes of God in Human History*, edited by Geoffrey Wainwright, 95–109. Grand Rapids: Eerdmans, 2003.

———. "The End of History." *The Gospel and Our Culture Newsletter (U.K.)* 13 (1992) 1–2.

———. *The Finality of Christ.* London/Richmond, VA: SCM/John Knox, 1969.

———. *Foolishness to the Greeks: The Gospel and Western Culture.* London: SPCK, 1986.

———. *The Gospel in a Pluralist Society.* Geneva: WCC, 1989.

———. "The Kingdom of God and the Idea of Progress." Bangalore Lectures, 1941. In *Signs Amid the Rubble. The Purposes of God in Human History,* edited by Geoffrey Wainwright, 1–55. Grand Rapids: Eerdmans, 2003.

———. "The Life and Mission of the Church." In *We Were Brought Together,* edited by David M. Taylor, 59–69. Sydney: Australian Council for the WCC, 1960.

———. *The Open Secret: An Introduction to the Theology of Mission.* Rev ed. Grand Rapids: Eerdmans, 1995.

———. *The Other Side of 1984. Questions for the Churches.* Geneva: WCC, 1983.

———. *Proper Confidence: Faith, Doubt, and Certainty in Christian Discipleship.* Grand Rapids: Eerdmans, 1995.

———. "Truth and Authority in Modernity." In *Faith and Modernity,* edited by Philip Sampson et al., 60–88. Oxford: Regnum, 1994.

———. *Unfinished Agenda: An Autobiography.* Grand Rapids: Eerdmans, 1985.

———. "Why Study the Old Testament?" *National Christian Council Review* 74 (1954) 71–76.

Schuster, Jürgen. *Christian Mission in Eschatological Perspective: Lesslie Newbigin's Contribution.* Nürnberg: VTR, 2009.

Taber, Charles R. "The Gospel as Authentic Meta-Narrative." In *A Scandalous Prophet. The Way of Mission after Newbigin,* edited by Thomas F. Foust et al., 182–94. Grand Rapids: Eerdmans, 2002.

Vanhoozer, Kevin J. "The Trials of Truth. Mission, Martyrdom and the Epistemology of the Cross." In *To Stake a Claim: Mission and the Western Crisis of Knowledge,* edited by J. Andrew Kirk and Kevin J. Vanhoozer, 120–56. Maryknoll, NY: Orbis, 1999.

Wainwright, Geoffrey. *Signs Amid the Rubble: The Purposes of God in Human History.* Grand Rapids: Eerdmans, 2003.

Wright, N. T. *The New Testament and the People of God.* London: SPCK, 1992.

The Indian Church and the Formation of Lesslie Newbigin's Ecclesiology

Mark T. B. Laing

THIS CHAPTER SEEKS TO examine how Newbigin's ecclesiology was shaped through his missionary experience in India. It argues that his missionary experience, including his role in the formation of the Church of South India (CSI), were critical in determining Newbigin's ecclesiology. A colleague, who worked under Newbigin in the International Missionary Council (IMC), recalled how Newbigin would repeatedly refer to his Indian experiences, "to an extent that I would judge them to be fundamental for his orientation."[1]

As a young Church of Scotland (CofS) missionary in south India Newbigin experienced the dramatic growth of the village churches in rural Tamil Nadu. And, as a missionary, he was exposed to the dichotomous relationship that existed between mission and church expressed in the problematic relationship between the Church of Scotland's mission and that of the Indian church. Newbigin saw in the Indian church a church which was both missionary and profoundly concerned to regain its unity.

This was expressed in the negotiations for church union which concluded successfully with the formation of the Church of South India in 1947. Newbigin entered late into the negotiation process but rapidly assumed prominent responsibility, first in India and then internationally. Newbigin's theological reflections and apologetic for the south Indian union scheme enabled him to develop an ecclesiology in which the eschatological dimension was prominent. This gave credence to his claim that his experience of the Indian church was of relevance beyond the confines of south Asia.

1. Paul Löffler, email to Laing, 28/9/2007.

NEWBIGIN AND THE INDIAN CHURCH

As a young missionary Newbigin experienced the dramatic growth of village churches in rural Tamil Nadu. These experiences provided him with a definitive model of the church—orientated towards the world and missionary in its essential nature.[2] Through these churches Newbigin believed he was witnessing a recovery in the relationship between mission and church. This contrasted with the dichotomous and problematic relationship between the Indian church and Foreign Mission of the Church of Scotland (FM) which Newbigin faced as a missionary. These formative years in India imbued Newbigin with a vision of the church which he carried with him for the rest of his life. In contrast, he rarely spoke of the western church except to reprimand it for abandoning its missionary nature and being woefully fragmented.

Newbigin, with his wife Helen, were missionaries with the Church of Scotland, serving in the Madras district of south India from 1936.[3] For the majority of that time Newbigin served as the "district missionary" in Kanchipuram, Madras District until furlough in 1946. During this period there was considerable correspondence between Newbigin and the Rev Alexander S Kydd. Kydd served as the general secretary of the Foreign Mission Committee of the Church of Scotland (FMC) from 1931 until forced to retire due to illness in 1945.[4] This archival material—which to date has not been utilized—provides an early insight into Newbigin's developing vision of the church, formed as India prepared for independence.

By way of background it is important to remember that this period was a difficult one for the international mission of the CofS. There was retrenchment, reduction in missionary numbers, problems in recruiting missionaries and accumulative financial deficits. These deficits, because of their persistent nature, even caused the FMC to consider the total abandonment of one of its fields, or alternatively reduction to their work across the board. Kydd lamented: "I do not want to be too gloomy, but I feel very doubtful about the financial position getting markedly better in the

2. Newbigin would repeatedly return to this defining model of the church. E.g., Newbigin, *Mission in Christ's Way*, 23.

3. For Newbigin's personal account see: Newbigin, *Unfinished Agenda*, chs. 5–8.

4. The 1945 FMC report records the committee's regret over Kydd's illness and an appreciation of his service. He was succeeded by the Rev JWC Dougall, "Report of the Foreign Mission Committee for 1945," in *Reports to the General Assembly of the Church of Scotland*, 292–95. Kydd's obituary appeared in *The Scotsman*, 19/7/1950, page 3, digital archive, http://edu.archive.scotsman.com/article.cfm?id=TSC/1950/07/19/A r00307.

near future and by "near" I mean within ten years… The truth about the situation into which the country and Empire has moved is only gradually dawning upon us."[5]

Living Epistles

Although he had just arrived in India, due to a serious leg injury Newbigin was invalided home in late 1937, and from June of 1938, *inter alia*, was working as the Candidates Secretary for the FMC in Edinburgh during his recuperation. During this time he edited *Living Epistles*.[6] This report, based on the annual reports of several hundred missionaries, was published for the General Assembly and available for sale in the churches; its target audience being the grassroots supporters of the FM in the local congregations.

Although *Living Epistles* was written for a popular audience, the booklet demonstrated Newbigin's prescience in his assessment of the future relationship between missions and the indigenous churches. Newbigin's foreword in *Living Epistles* focused on the profound growth of the "indigenous church" rather than the FM—it is noteworthy that Newbigin used this term and refrained from using the accepted term "younger church." Newbigin, influenced by his reading of Hendrick Kraemer,[7] already understood the form of mission in which "The Church thought of the world in regional terms, and of missionary work as a kind of 'colonizing' activity" as being anachronistic, the thinking of a previous generation.[8] The redundancy of such a model was exposed in the decline of Christianity in the west: "the moral and spiritual unity of the West has been so shattered by the manifest departure of the majority of its inhabitants from any faith in God as He is revealed in Jesus Christ."[9] Already by 1939 Newbigin (in contrast to Kydd) had moved from understanding mission directionally, in terms of giving and receiving. After the IMC Tambaram conference of 1938 it "became abundantly manifest that the problems facing the Church

5. Kydd to Newbigin 3/2/1940, NLS: Acc7548/A23. For Kydd's annual report see the respective: "Report of the Foreign Mission Committee." In *Reports to the General Assembly of the Church of Scotland*, 1936–1946.

6. Newbigin, *Living Epistles*. Although the report was compiled and edited by Newbigin it was published as an official document from the FMC.

7. Kraemer, *Christian Message*.

8. Newbigin, *Living Epistles*, 3.

9. Ibid.

all over the world are identical. In every land, 'Christian' and non-Christian alike, the Church is in a minority."[10] Newbigin understood that, in the early twentieth century, a fundamental shift had taken place away from the association of land with Christian faith. The church wherever it was located, was in a missionary situation.

Newbigin thus spoke of a new "sense of community" with the indigenous church, aware of "this new perception of the old truth that we without them, and they without us, shall not be made perfect."[11] At the commencement of his missionary career Newbigin had moved beyond the prevalent paternalistic language of the "younger church" which was dependent upon the "older church," to return to the more fundamental Pauline image of mutuality, and co-dependency.

Newbigin's Church-centric Approach

But how was that new relationship with the indigenous church to be worked out in practice? Back in India Newbigin was struck by the rapid church growth occurring in rural villages, which was seemingly independent of the FM. He notes for example the birth and development of a church in a remote "outcaste" village called Thirupanamur in which, "from the first the initiative was taken by the villagers, not by us."[12] This repeated pattern of the "spontaneous" expansion of village churches profoundly influenced Newbigin: "In my mind at least there were visions of a new missionary movement reaching out from that village to the untouched areas round about it, based not on a new effort from the headquarters, but on the new-found faith and conviction of the village people themselves."[13] From these experiences Newbigin understood that his role as a missionary was to *respond* to the village initiative. His rationale being that the work of the gospel was being prosecuted by divine agency rather than through any human agency, centered in the local or international headquarters of the FM.[14]

10. Ibid., 4.

11. Ibid., 6.

12. Newbigin to Kydd, 28/1/1940, NLS: Acc7548/B130.

13. Newbigin to Kydd, 28/1/1940. A more generalized account of the growth of such churches, stripped of geographic references, can be found in Newbigin's influential work *South India Diary*. This portrait of the non-western church opened a new world for many in the West.

14. At this early stage in his career Newbigin did not attribute his indebtedness to Roland Allen. Later he acknowledged that he was attempting to apply Allen's ideas.

Concerning Newbigin's own methodology in village evangelism, with hindsight he recognized similarities and his indebtedness to Karl Barth. Rather than seek some rational common ground between himself as a westerner and Hindus in the villages by an appeal to an apologetic which sought stability external to the gospel, Newbigin instead was unapologetic about speaking from within the framework of the gospel, narrating the story of which he believed he was a part.[15]

Having recognized that the centers for church growth lay in the villages Newbigin endeavored to facilitate that growth. Rather than extracting key Christian converts from their context to train them in mission compounds, Newbigin did the reverse. During the quieter (but hotter) part of the agricultural year, rather than retreat to the cooler climes of Kodaikanal in the Nilgiri Mountains—the missionary norm—Newbigin initiated village camps. "The whole thing aims at creating the conditions in which the village churches can be as far as possible self-supporting, by laying the maximum possible responsibility on the shoulders of the ordinary, barely literate, but often shrewd and sensible, subaiyan [village elder]. It means a conception of the Church which is extremely primitive as far as all the outward things go — but which at least is soundly based on the real condition of the people."[16]

For Newbigin, on the basis of his theological convictions, historical entities needed to be realigned. To this end he advocated a more general change in mission policy with new initiatives: "[in] training in worship for the Christian groups; training lay leadership by means of hot-weather retreat courses; [and] strengthening the evangelistic staff."[17] Fundamental to facilitating this change in emphasis was Newbigin's realization of the essential role of both missionary and national women.[18]

These early missionary experiences were to be determinative for Newbigin. At both a practical and theological level he continued to maintain his church-centric focus. Early in the correspondence with Kydd it becomes evident that Newbigin was aware that the Indian church was growing in spite of, rather than because of, the efforts of the CofS. This led to protracted discussion with Kydd and more widely within IMC circles

---

15. Weston, interview, 11/9/2008.
16. Newbigin to Kydd 3/5/1940, NLS: Acc7548/B130.
17. Newbigin to Kydd 27/12/1939, NLS: Acc7548/ B130.
18. Newbigin to Kydd 27/12/1939.

on the nature and priorities which should determine the inevitable devolution to the "younger church."[19]

For the FMC, maintenance of prestigious institutions was a central priority. In contrast to prevalent missionary attitudes which saw the urban institutional work of the mission as being central, Newbigin took a different tack. He argued that the role of the district missionary should be abolished in non-pioneering situations as the perpetuation of this model was detrimental to the development of an indigenous church. Newbigin recognized that what was considered peripheral and insignificant—the village work—should be given central priority to facilitate "building up the church in the only place where it is growing."[20]

Newbigin reasoned that rather than the FM facilitating the growth of the church, its policy of city based institutions was profoundly detrimental to the village church. Through education and the promise of better job prospects the best and brightest from the village were lured into mission institutions. This was doubly detrimental, in that it drained leadership from the true centers of church growth and, having done so, then stunted their development by placing them in unhealthy city churches, where energy was dissipated in internal strife rather than harnessed for evangelism.[21] Paramount for Newbigin was the need to facilitate the growth of the village churches because: "[I]t does seem that the village Church is the place where a truly indigenous Christianity can come into being—not the indigenousness of Western enthusiasts for indigenousness, but the real indigenousness of Indian Christians slowly developing their own modes of expression."[22]

Newbigin recognized the problematic relationship between mission and church which the mission policy of the FMC, in its relationship with the Indian church, had established: "The Mission [Council] employs catechists and evangelists and runs big schools, hospitals etc. The [Indian] Church is poor and pays small salaries. The Mission is rich and pays big ones. The missionaries are the most powerful people in the Christian community. They accept the authority of the Mission over themselves, but not the authority of the Church. The Mission controls the livelihood of most

19. This correspondence is located in NLS: Acc7548/A24–27; B130.

20. Newbigin to Kydd 27/12/1939, NLS: Acc7548/B130.

21. Newbigin to Kydd 26/7/1941, NLS: Acc7548/B130.

22. Newbigin to Kydd 26/7/1941.

of the leading members of the Church, but has no official relationship to the courts of the Church."[23]

Newbigin argued that the historical reality of the missionary movement, in this case the FM, had produced and then perpetuated this dichotomy between mission and church. Newbigin understood this to be the outworking of a defective ecclesiology: "The fundamental reason is that it is based on a false doctrine of the Church. The idea of a permanent dichotomy of Church and Mission as two separate organizations is totally foreign to the NT and destructive of any growth in Churchmanship."[24] This dichotomy was alien to Newbigin's reading of the NT which held the church as central: "The life of the Church is radically corrupted if it is separated from the missionary task, and evangelistic effort is corrupted if it does not spring from the Church and lead back into the Church."[25] Determinative for Newbigin was his theological understanding that: "The Church exists by mission and mission is a function of the Church. A permanent organizational dichotomy of Church and Mission is [therefore] intolerable."[26]

Here Newbigin, from his first-hand experience is focusing on the dichotomy that mission organizations have created on the "mission fields." The outcome of a dichotomous relationship between foreign missions and the Indian church occurred regardless of the actual organization of the mission organization.

In the case of the CofS the mission remained wholly accountable to the church, this being expressed in the FMC's total subservience to the General Assembly. This contrasted with English or American voluntary societies which operated largely independently from the "home church." Regardless of a mission's relationship to its "home church" Newbigin was critical of all agencies in perpetuating a dichotomy *on the field* between their mission work and the indigenous church.

Newbigin identified several consequences from the separation of mission from the church. First, it encouraged the "Development of a type of self-sufficient, introverted congregation, lacking all sense of the Church catholic, priding itself chiefly on its ability to pay its pastor, and

---

23. Newbigin, "Relation of Older and Younger Churches in India: Uncensored Remarks," 1947, NLS: Acc7548/B43, 1.

24. Newbigin, "Uncensored Remarks," 1.

25. Ibid.

26. Ibid., 3.

disclaiming responsibility for missionary work around it."[27] Newbigin was critical of the prevalent assumption in mission theory that the objective of a mission organization was to establish churches according to the three-selfs principle:[28] "Our thought of the Church was wrong because we began from the principle of self-support and produced an emaciated affair with many of the full functions of a Church reserved for the Mission, instead of starting with the biblical and apostolic ideal of one catholic Church in which we and they are one."[29] The church, the world over, is one, and together shares a common orientation of facing outwards towards the world. Newbigin argued that the Pauline model was for churches to cooperate in partnership rather than aim at disparate and isolating self-sufficiency.

The second consequence Newbigin identified was the failure to develop an adequate ministry. The mission policy of the CofS was actually undermining the ministry of the indigenous church. The "organizational dichotomy" between church and mission was expressed by the office of the district missionary who operated independently of the Indian church. The result of this was that key positions sought after by the best educated and most able Indian Christians were not as pastors but as administrators and mission-employed managers. Newbigin asserted that, "This is understandable, for we missionaries have been predominantly not pastors and evangelists, but administrators, and the typical position of a missionary is not in a pulpit but behind a big desk."[30] Newbigin maintained that a minister's central focus should be to do pastoral work and evangelism rather than become a kind of "office-wallah that most district missionaries become"; and that the "district missionary [wa]s an anachronism who ought to be abolished."[31] The bureaucratization that missions brought had a disastrous impact on the pastorate: "Consequently all the Pastors have this ambition, to get out of the Pastorate—which is very much a slave's

---

27. Ibid., 1.

28. History attributes Henry Venn and Rufus Anderson with independently formulating that newly established churches should become self-supporting, self-governing, and self-propagating. WR Shenk, "Rufus Anderson and Henry Venn: A Special Relationship?" Missionary commitment to this *principle* continued into the Edwardian period. B Stanley, "The Remedy Lies with Themselves: Edinburgh 1910 on the Self-Supporting Indigenous Church," in *Yale-Edinburgh Group on the History of the Missionary Movement and Non-Western Christianity*, 1.

29. Newbigin, "Uncensored Remarks," 2.

30. Newbigin to Kydd 13/6/1943, NLS: Acc7548/B130.

31. Newbigin to Kydd 11/6/1942, NLS: Acc7548/B130.

job—into the position of the Circle Chairman [of the mission]."[32] Newbigin was concerned to recover the importance and biblical understanding of the scope of the ordained ministry which he proposed would enable these organizational problems to be overcome.

Third, Newbigin was critical of the "'Overseas Presbyteries' of the CofS [operating] alongside the courts of the Indian Church."[33] CofS missionaries understood themselves to be under the authority of the CofS through the Overseas Presbytery of the CofS, rather than being accountable to the Indian church. This parallel, independent existence undermined the authority of the Indian church. Newbigin had personally witnessed this authority being disregarded by a CofS missionary colleague who stated that he was only under the jurisdiction of the CofS—an incident which profoundly affected his attitude to the authority of the Indian church.[34]

At a time when mission agencies were devolving responsibility and authority to the Indian church Newbigin argued that all foreign personnel should also be under the full authority of the indigenous church. Acting upon this conviction, in an unprecedented and pioneering move, Newbigin—along with fellow clergy Ellis O Shaw and Robert P Mackenzie—applied for full membership of the Indian church and relinquished any anomalous claims to simultaneously be accountable to a "higher jurisdiction"—the Overseas Presbytery of the CofS. In the dichotomy that existed between the mission and the church, Newbigin as a *missionary*, was aligning himself with the indigenous church rather than with his mission organization. As this was unprecedented, the actual process of this change of allegiance was a rather protracted affair passing through several CofS committees and being discussed at the General Assembly before CofS approval was finally given.[35] Newbigin's initiative demonstrated that missionaries were prepared to recognize the authority of the Indian church, that the proper place of mission (and missionaries) was in *subservience* to the national church. For the Indian church it demonstrated a new era in missionary deployment which coincided with Indian independence from colonial rule.

32. Newbigin to Kydd 13/6/1943, NLS: Acc7548/B130.

33. Newbigin, "Uncensored Remarks," 1.

34. Newbigin, *Unfinished Agenda*, 72.

35. A Special Committee was established to confer with the General Administration Committee, the Inter-Church Relations Committee, and the FMC, with a view to the matter being brought before the General Assembly for decision. Minute 7279, 21/3/1944, NLS: Dep298/Box191.

The fourth consequence of the dichotomy, according to Newbigin, was the current stalemate in the process of devolution. Newbigin argued that although the FM, in principle, proposed to be church-centric, in reality it: "shrank from handing over a fine well-run institution to a body so weak and unimpressive as this 'Indian Church'. We thought in terms of 'Us' and 'Them', and 'they' were clearly inadequate for the job."[36] Newbigin posited that the source of this dichotomous thinking again stemmed from a defective ecclesiology.

This early correspondence shows that Newbigin at the start of his missionary career was articulating a missionary ecclesiology in which the church was central to his thinking. His missionary experience, in which he wrestled with the historical legacy of the dichotomy between mission and church, served to reinforce and clarify these presuppositions as he sought an organizational expression of his theological convictions. The seemingly insignificant and unimportant village churches gave Newbigin an enduring vision of the church—a non-western missionary church which he contrasted with the stagnant, introverted western church. In his emphasis on decentralized control, and the vitality of the village church one is reminded of the recurring refrain Newbigin imbued from earlier Student Christian Mission influences: "that the health of the body depends upon the health of the smallest units."[37]

THE FORMATION OF THE CHURCH OF SOUTH INDIA

A further factor shaping Newbigin's ecclesiology was his involvement in the Church of South India (CSI) negotiations. The formation of the CSI in 1947 was looked upon with great interest around the world, particularly as it pioneered the reunion of episcopal with non-episcopal churches. It not only affected India but reverberated globally, and especially it challenged old assumptions within the western church. At the formation of the CSI there was the bright hope that the scheme would prove to be a catalyst for other reunion schemes: "I vividly remember how firmly we believed in those exciting days that our union in India would open the way for similar unions all over the world."[38]

Newbigin, in his young maturity, hit the crest, coming late to the CSI negotiations. Newbigin's ecclesiology was very much shaped by the

36. Newbigin, "Uncensored Remarks," 2.
37. Newbigin, *Unfinished Agenda*, 105.
38. Newbigin, "Basis and the Forms of Unity," 1.

CSI, an Asian church which has no equivalent in western experience. The CSI was forward looking, always in the process of formation. Newbigin himself is a product of these developments, his experience, and ideas of the church being formed by his experiences in south India.

Newbigin's model of the church, formed in the non-western world, clashed with those holding to the historical church, his greatest difficulty being with Anglo-Catholic ecclesiology. His experience (and defense) of the Indian church prepared him for the ecumenical agenda on a world scale. The Indian church, which was missionary and profoundly committed to unity, provided Newbigin with a starting point on these key themes on which he later built his theology during his involvement in the ecumenical movement.

His experience of the formation of the CSI and his subsequent reflections on that led him to believe that in south India, beyond the abnormal, distorted ecclesiology of Christendom, he was partaking in a recovery of true biblical ecclesiology. He could discern two key aspects in this recovery. First, that the church was missionary, orientated towards the world, rather than towards itself. The second aspect recovered was that churches orientated towards the world also recovered a profound concern to overcome their divisions and become organically united—one visible body in each location.

Newbigin's Involvement in the South India Scheme

Newbigin entered into the South India Scheme for Church Union (SIS) late in its history and at a time when the process was languishing. Although a relatively young and inexperienced missionary he was quickly entrusted with considerable responsibility. In 1942 Newbigin was invited to succeed Rev Dr J. H. Maclean[39] as convener of the Union Committee of the Madras Church Council, Maclean nominating Newbigin as his successor.[40] A year later Newbigin was elected convener of the Union Committee for the whole of the South India United Church (SIUC) at a time of weariness and general despondency about the scheme.[41]

As chairman of the SIUC committee on union Newbigin was aware that for the scheme to succeed, he must fight for it on three fronts: first,

39. Maclean was a CofS missionary and Newbigin's predecessor as district missionary at Kanchipuram.

40. Maclean to Newbigin, 15/10/1942, BUL: DA29/2/4/16.

41. Newbigin, *Unfinished Agenda*, 74.

in India, the arguments for union needed to be disseminated to the level of the grassroots of the church, shifting the centre of gravity away from missionary domination; second, the importing of western ecclesiastical debate into India needed to be curtailed; and third, internationally, the "propaganda" of Anglo-Catholic opposition to the scheme needed to be countered.

To enable the scheme to succeed Newbigin appealed to the Church of Scotland and the American Board of Commissioners for Foreign Missions for funds to allow the reports of the proposed union to be translated into Tamil and Telugu in preparation for the SIUC assembly in 1944. To support his case he cited the result from the Madras Church Council: "We badly lack machinery for adequate discussion of the Scheme in the vernaculars. The Scheme itself has never ever been translated. The discussion has therefore been dominated by missionaries. At last year's Madras Church Council I created a record by giving the entire report in Tamil and having the debate on it in Tamil. We got, as you know, a thumping majority for union, and several Indians told me it was the first time they had ever understood what the issues were. I know that this is symptomatic of a much wider situation."[42]

Newbigin's chairmanship was decisive in enabling the debate to move beyond the confines of English to reach ordinary south Indian Christians. Early calls for union had been Indian initiatives.[43] But subsequent missionary involvement had entangled the debate in problems inherent within western ecclesiology; in particular the relation between episcopally and non-episcopally ordered churches, and how they could be united to the satisfaction of the parent churches. The CSI was the pioneer in bringing together episcopal and non-episcopal churches, overcoming the biggest division that had beset the Protestant church.

One of the tactics of attack against the union scheme, employed by the Anglo-Catholics, was to ridicule it as being theologically insufficient: "A certain amount of somewhat lofty scorn seems to be being sprinkled on the Scheme of Union by those in the West who regard it as theologically inadequate."[44] Whilst in India Newbigin called for international support to combat Anglo-Catholic attacks on the union scheme.[45] Later he was to en-

---

42. Newbigin to Kydd, 13/9/1943, NLS: Acc7548/B130.

43. For a history see: B Sundkler, *Church of South India.*

44. Newbigin to "Dear Friends" [circular letter], October 1944, NLS: Acc7548/C1.

45. For details see: Laing, "Advocates and Opponents of Church Union in South India."

ter the fray, becoming the main international advocate of the scheme, representing the scheme at various Anglican conferences and consultations.[46] Newbigin's role effectively became that of international ambassador for the SIS.

The Reunion of the Church

In response to Anglo-Catholic opposition Newbigin developed his theological defense of the SIS, in *The Reunion of the Church*,[47] in which he mainly dealt with the struggle to reconcile Catholic and Protestant ecclesiologies.

Newbigin observed the impetus for mission and unity that emerged, unexpectedly, from the missionary practice of comity.[48] The emergence of those concerns in the South Indian church led Newbigin to believe that he was partaking in a recovery of ecclesiology. If the events in south India were truly a "recovery of the heart of the gospel" as Newbigin understood them to be, then they had implications beyond the remit of south India, they were of import for the global church. The recovery of these twin concerns enabled Newbigin to critique the abnormal ecclesiology of Christendom which had grown complacent about both mission and unity.

For Newbigin church unity had to be organic: "As the Body of Christ, the church is an organism 'joined and knit together by every joint with which it is supplied when each part is working properly' (Eph. 4:16). Its unity is therefore properly described as organic."[49] This was a conviction that he held throughout his life: "for so long as I have breath, I must continue to confess my belief that God intends his Church to be — in the words of the Lambeth Appeal — 'an outward, visible and united society.'"[50]

Unity was never to be understood as a goal in and of itself, but was for the purpose of mission. Newbigin's "primary concern in developing, articulating, and defending this view of unity was that the church might

46. Described in Newbigin, *Unfinished Agenda*, Ch 11.

47. Newbigin, *Reunion*.

48. Arrangements of "comity" between different mission organizations divided mission fields into defined geographic areas with the agreement between these organizations not to then interfere in one another's affairs. The following are the main references in Newbigin's writing on comity: Newbigin, *Reunion*, 1–25, Newbigin, "Unity and Mission"; Newbigin, "Missions in an Ecumenical Perspective," Newbigin, "Cooperation and Unity."

49. Newbigin, "Union, Organic," 1028.

50. Newbigin, *Unfinished Agenda*, 253.

remain true to its missionary nature."[51] The form of organic unity embodied in the CSI was, for Newbigin, the best recovery of unity that had yet been devised; other alternative forms of union such as the Ceylon scheme and the north India scheme proffered more problematic solutions, particularly to the question of how to unite episcopal with non-episcopal churches.[52] Newbigin's advocacy of the SIS scheme led him into prolonged debate with the Anglican Church on the best solution to disunity. His dual concern for unity *and* mission undergirded and was foundational to his detailed defense of the SIS.

For the "younger churches" not to respond to the theological impetus for unity that comes from the practice of comity, but rather ape western denominationalism would "be the public denial of the Gospel which we preach, the good news of Him who, being lifted up, will draw all men to Himself."[53] "It is not possible to account for the contentment with the divisions of the Church except upon the basis of a loss of the conviction that the Church exists to bring all men to Christ. There is the closest possible connection between the acceptance of the missionary obligation and the acceptance of the obligation of unity. That which makes the Church one is what makes it a mission to the world."[54]

Newbigin argued that a static definition of the church which only states what the church *is* without also proposing what the church is *becoming* sustains this impasse between God's will for episcopacy and the reality of non-episcopal church traditions. A central method in Newbigin's argument for reconciliation is to apply Paul's theology of justification by faith collectively to the church. "Only in terms of the mystery of justification by faith, of the God who calleth things that are not as though they were, is the dilemma to be resolved. The central purpose of this book [*Reunion of the Church*] was to place the discussion of the question of Church union in that perspective."[55]

In the age of the *eschaton*, the Spirit enables the church to witness, to the ends of the earth, and until the end of time. The perspective of the

51. Goheen, "*As the Father*," 201.

52. The Church of North India, and the Church of Pakistan were inaugurated in 1970, negotiations to unite the Ceylon Church collapsed.

53. Newbigin, *Reunion*, 21.

54. Ibid., 11.

55. Newbigin, *Reunion*, xvi, xxvii, xxxiv. This critical point was missed by all reviewers of the 1948 edition, except for one, who complained that it did not belong to a book on the church. Newbigin thus felt justified in publishing a second edition, hoping that, this time, his central thesis would be understood.

eschaton enables the church to live with the inherent tension of being holy and sinful; and of defining itself in terms of what it is, and *also* in terms of what it is becoming. "This acceptance of a real end means that the dimension of time is a reality within the life of the Church."[56] This theology of time was reflected in the constitution of the CSI which explicitly confessed that the church is not what it ought to be—it is in process.[57] The CSI constitution acknowledged the theological principle that the church was provisional, a temporary construct.[58] The church, caught up in the dynamic work of the Spirit, accepted that it was incomplete and open to change: "If the Church is the sign and fruit and instrument of Christ's purpose to draw all men to Himself; . . . and if the ultimate purpose is the union in one fellowship of all who accept Christ as Lord; then movement belongs to the very nature of the Church. It is, in its very nature, a pilgrim people."[59]

The Household of God

Encouraged by others, Newbigin sought to release the theology implicit in his defense from the particularity of the south Indian situation, and develop it to give support for the ecumenical movement, which, he perceived, was progressing without an adequate ecclesiological foundation.[60] The invitation to deliver the Kerr Lectures at Trinity College in Glasgow gave Newbigin the impetus to further develop his argument. He sought to "wrestle with the issues raised" on the doctrine of the church at the first assembly of the World Council of Churches (WCC), reflecting on what answers the formation of the CSI might contribute.[61] The lecture series subsequently was published as *The Household of God.*[62]

Central to Newbigin's thesis (and the book) was the question "By what is the Church constituted?" Although "We are all agreed that the Church is constituted by God's atoning acts in Christ Jesus" the question the church faced throughout history was "how are we of the subsequent generations made participants in that atonement? *What is the manner of*

56. Newbigin, *Household of God*, 133.

57. Ibid., 25.

58. This was manifest in "The Pledge" and "The Thirty-Year Period" as means to gradually unite the ministry. Newbigin, *Reunion*, 107, 114–19.

59. Newbigin, *Reunion*, xxx.

60. Newbigin, *Unfinished Agenda*, 136–137.

61. Newbigin to Dr Millar Patrick, 9/8/1950, BUL: DA29/1/6/113.

62. Newbigin, *Household of God*.

our engrafting into Christ?[63] Newbigin moved beyond the polarity of the Protestant-Catholic ecclesiologies to offer three answers: first "that we are incorporated in Christ by hearing and believing the Gospel," this was the Protestant answer; the second was the Catholic answer that "we are incorporated by sacramental participation in the life of the historically continuous Church"; the third, what Newbigin hesitatingly called the Pentecostal answer, was that "we are incorporated by receiving and abiding in the Holy Spirit."[64] Each of these answers, which Newbigin explored in subsequent chapters, had dominated traditions of the church's self-understanding and definition, possessing an aspect of the church's essence, but each in and of itself was incomplete. And in relation to other traditions it was problematic if one tradition maintained an exclusive definition of the church, which thus negated dissenting ecclesiologies, as "none of us can be said to possess the *esse* of the Church."[65] This created an impasse in reunion movements as each tradition was unable to give up an aspect of what it considered was the *esse* of the church. Each tradition was rooted in the gospel, and "the denial of any of them leads to the disfigurement of the Church and the distortion of its message."[66] Whilst each tradition sought to remain true to its self-understanding of the essence of the church, yet there was the acknowledgement that, "We are drawn to one another by a real working of the Holy Spirit which we dare not resist."[67]

As "The Church is not merely a historical reality but also an eschatological one" it can be rightly understood only in an eschatological perspective:[68] "The meaning of this 'overlap of the ages' in which we live, the time between the coming of Christ and His coming again, is that it is the time given for the witness of the apostolic Church to the ends of the earth. The end of all things, which has been revealed in Christ, is . . . held back until witness has been borne to the whole world . . . The implication of a true eschatological perspective will be missionary obedience . . ."[69]

As before, Newbigin maintained that two implications emerge from the *eschaton*, that the church is concurrently called to organic unity and to mission, the relationship between them emanating from the heart of the

---

63. Ibid., 30 (original emphasis).
64. Ibid.
65. Ibid., 134.
66. Ibid., 111.
67. Ibid.
68. Ibid., 135.
69. Ibid.

gospel, and animated by the gift of the Holy Spirit. It is by the Holy Spirit that the church is incorporated into Christ; "that we are made participants in the victory yet to be revealed"; and we are empowered for mission.[70]

Missionary obedience of the church orientated the church outwards towards the world, "Evangelistic work places the Church in a situation in which the stark contrast between Christ and no-Christ is constantly being faced. In such a situation other matters necessarily fall into second place."[71] This had been Newbigin's shared experience as the CSI was formed. The mission experience of the church had forced critical examination of the disunity of the church and inspired efforts to recover unity. This recovery in the key themes of mission and unity, which the western church had neglected, "must be prosecuted together and in indissoluble relation one with the other."[72]

Newbigin explored those implications from his reading of John 17:21. Unity is missional, "in order that the world may believe": "The Church's unity is the sign and the instrument of the salvation which Christ has wrought and whose final fruition is the summing-up of all things in Christ."[73] The organic unity of the church demonstrated the efficacy of Christ's salvation to make us one. And conversely, the disunity of the church was a contradiction of the gospel, undermining the credibility of Christ's prayer and his ability to reconcile all things in himself.

A crucial question was *how*; in progress from disunity to union, how were the disunited churches to be brought together? Newbigin, as one of the fourteen original bishops in the CSI, urged others contemplating union to look to the SIS, as a model for full organic union of the visible church, the first of its kind which had actually come to fruition. Newbigin's insistence on the SIS path towards unity, as opposed to other schemes which were more palatable to Anglicans, led him into prolonged theological debate which impacted the heart of the ecumenical movement and the outcome of other union schemes.[74]

70. Ibid., 142.
71. Ibid., 151.
72. Ibid., 144, 152.
73. Ibid., 149.
74. For details of this debate, see M. T. B. Laing, " International Impact of the Formation of the Church of South India: Bishop Newbigin Versus the Anglican Fathers." "The Faith and Order 'survey of church union negotiations 1959–1961' reported on the progress of some fifty sets of conversations and plans toward unity that were being conducted or drawn up at national and regional levels on every continent." Wainwright, *Newbigin*, 113. Of all those schemes only those in the Indian subcontinent

Later Newbigin reflected on how the Lambeth Conferences of 1948 and 1958 had been *kairos* moments in the history of the church, which provided rare opportunities for dramatic progress. Rather than the opportunity being embraced, it had been squandered. Newbigin expected that if Lambeth had responded positively to the CSI, "I am sure that the whole worldwide movement for unity among the Churches would have gone forward . . . [Instead] [t]hat opportunity was lost, and is not likely to come again."[75]

Newbigin was a task theologian; his theological reflection emerged, not *in abstracto*, but out of the particular struggles the church faced and the organizational solutions he proposed to those problems. Newbigin's theology of time links the history of reunion with the theology which informed it and the reflection it produced. The church in eschatological perspective is not a static entity, but is in process and must, at certain junctures, make decisions which will have profound repercussions. Newbigin was well aware that the process of union created a tension between the theological formulation upon which union was based and the time lag of the organizational expression of that union. Thus, in the case of the CSI, ecclesiological expression was founded upon provisional theological formulations. The new united church needed to be defined in terms of what it was becoming rather than in static formulations. Newbigin insisted that "God demands decisions in time."[76] In 1947 a vote had to be taken for the CSI to become a reality. To demand at that time yet another delay to allow for a reformulation of the basis of union would be a *de facto* rejection of the scheme.[77]

From these experiences Newbigin understood the church's concern with mission and unity to be a recovery of the "heart of the gospel." In his work with the ecumenical movement he sought the proper embodiment of the relationship between mission and unity which was coupled with a sense of urgency, that "God demands decisions in time."

---

succeeded in uniting with episcopal churches.

75. Newbigin, *Unfinished Agenda*, 114.

76. Newbigin cited in Hollis to Newbigin, 2/11/1958, BUL: DA29/2/8/17.

77. Newbigin to Archbishop Fisher, 15/4/1961, BUL: DA29/2/8/52. Newbigin, "Anglicans, Methodists and Intercommunion," 282.

CONCLUSION

This chapter has argued that Newbigin's India experience was determinative in shaping his thinking on the church. This then equipped him for further, international leadership in the ecumenical movement. As a young CofS missionary in Tamil Nadu Newbigin was introduced to the "intolerable dichotomy" between mission and church. He experienced this in the problematic relation between the CofS mission and the Indian church, the quest for devolution bringing this into sharp focus.

His early missionary correspondence reveals his church-centricism in which he argued for the realignment of the mission to effectively serve the rural and rudimentary village churches. The vision of these churches expanding "spontaneously" provided Newbigin with a model of the church to which he would often return. Through Kraemer Newbigin recognized that a new epoch had dawned in the relationship between mission organizations and indigenous churches. Newbigin's correspondence with Kydd reveals his prescience—in contrast to Kydd's intransigence—which was demonstrated in his own personal commitment to be accountable to the Indian church.

Facing the practical issues of how the Indian church should relate to the CofS mission led Newbigin to a more fundamental theological assessment of the importance of the church in general. With hindsight he realized that his theological position on the church had been profoundly changed as a consequence of his missionary experience. He wrote, when drafting his 1956 book *Sin and Salvation*: "I found as I wrote that book that my thinking had changed in a significant way. Twenty years earlier [at Cambridge] in writing on this theme I had referred to the Church only in a very marginal way at the end of the essay . . . Now I found that I had to begin with the Church—the point at which the unbeliever first comes into contact with the redemptive work of Christ."[78] The reason for this profound shift in thinking Newbigin attributed to his missionary experience: "I did not make that switch easily but I found that the experience of missionary work compelled me to make it. I saw that the kind of Protestantism in which I had been nourished belonged to a 'Christendom' context. In a missionary situation the Church had to have a different logical place."[79]

Newbigin's late entry into the practical negotiations of the SIS gave him a wealth of experience in committees and then of defending the

---

78. Newbigin, *Unfinished Agenda*, 146.
79. Ibid.

scheme against critics. But more importantly the formation of the CSI gave Newbigin the task of formulating a theological defense. Newbigin argued that the CSI, rather than being an Indian oddity, was a demonstration of a recovered ecclesiology. The church's dual call to mission and unity was inextricably linked and emanated from the heart of the gospel. In India the impetus for these factors had emerged as a consequence of comity agreements. Newbigin argued that the church's call to mission and unity must also be understood in eschatological perspective. An eschatological perspective had to take a theology of time seriously. The church was defined not just in static terms of its essence, but also in terms of what it was *becoming*. The prospect of the *eschaton* universalized the need for these concerns to be recovered, particularly by the western church. The success of the CSI was a universal sign to the churches that reunion was possible.

Newbigin, in his transition from the arena of the CSI to the larger ecumenical movement, carried these concerns. As the CSI was a sign to the churches that reunion was possible, he later argued that integration of the IMC with the WCC was, in an analogous way, as a sign to the world. For Newbigin the basis of world unity was reconciliation in Christ mediated through the church, the new community, which, in reunion, demonstrated Christ's efficacy to make us one and, in mission, declared this to the world.

BIBLIOGRAPHY

Archives

Foreign Mission Records of the Church of Scotland, (Acc 7548). The National Library of Scotland, George IV Bridge, Edinburgh, EH1 1EW, Scotland, UK. Catalogued at: http://www.nls.uk./catalogues/online/mss/index.html.

The Papers of Lesslie Newbigin (DA29). Special Collections, Main Library, University of Birmingham, Edgbaston, Birmingham B15 2TT, UK Catalogued at: http://www.special-coll.bham.ac.uk/index.shtml.

Books and Articles

Goheen, Michael W. *"As the Father Has Sent Me, I Am Sending You": J.E. Lesslie Newbigin's Missionary Ecclesiology*. Zoetermeer: Boekencentrum, 2000.

Kraemer, Hendrik. *The Christian Message in a Non-Christian World*. London: Edinburgh House, 1938.

Laing, Mark T. B. "The Advocates and Opponents of Church Union in South India: Perceptions and Portrayals of 'the Other.'" In *Yale-Edinburgh Group on the*

History of the Missionary Movement and Non-Western Christianity. New College, University of Edinburgh, 2008.

———. "The International Impact of the Formation of the Church of South India: Bishop Newbigin Versus the Anglican Fathers." *IBMR* 33, no. 1 (2009) 18–24.

Newbigin, Lesslie. "Anglicans, Methodists and Intercommunion: A Moment for Decision." *Churchman* 82, no. 4 (1968) 281–85.

———. "The Basis and the Forms of Unity." *Mid-Stream: The Ecumenical Movement Today* 23 (1984) 1–12.

———. "Cooperation and Unity." *IRM* 59, no. 233 (1970) 67–74.

———. *The Household of God: Lectures on the Nature of the Church*. London: SCM, 1953.

———. *Living Epistles: Impressions of the Foreign Mission Work of the Church of Scotland in 1938*. Edinburgh: Church of Scotland Foreign Missions Committee, 1939.

———. *Mission in Christ's Way: Bible Studies*. Geneva: WCC Publications, 1987.

———. "Missions in an Ecumenical Perspective", 1962. WCC, Ecumenical Centre Library: Geneva.

———. *The Reunion of the Church: A Defence of the South India Scheme*. London: SCM, 1948, reprinted 1960.

———. *Sin and Salvation*. London: SCM, 1956.

———. *A South India Diary*. London: SCM, 1951.

———. *Unfinished Agenda: An Autobiography*. Grand Rapids: Eerdmans, 1985.

———. "Union, Organic." In *Dictionary of the Ecumenical Movement*, ed. Nicholas Lossky, José Míguez Bonino and et al., 1028–1030. Geneva: WCC Publications, 1991.

———. "Unity and Mission." *Covenant Quarterly*, no. 19 (1961) 3–6.

Reports to the General Assembly of the Church of Scotland. Edinburgh: W. Blackwood, 1936–1946.

Shenk, Wilbert R. "Rufus Anderson and Henry Venn: A Special Relationship?" *IBMR* 5, no. 4 (1981) 168–72.

Stanley, Brian. "The Remedy Lies with Themselves: Edinburgh 1910 on the Self-Supporting Indigenous Church." In *Yale-Edinburgh Group on the History of the Missionary Movement and Non-Western Christianity*, 1–13. Edinburgh, July 2004.

Sundkler, Bengt. *Church of South India: The Movement Towards Union, 1900–1947*. London: Lutterworth, 1954.

Wainwright, Geoffrey. *Lesslie Newbigin: A Theological Life*. Oxford: OUP, 2000.

Ecclesiology in Eschatological Perspective

Newbigin's Understanding of the Missionary Church[1]

Paul Weston

INTRODUCTION

QUESTIONS ABOUT THE MEANING of the word "church" have gained a fresh relevance in our day. Whether these relate to debates about "emerging" congregations, to the identity of "fresh expressions" of church, or to the question of how the quest for unity is related to mission, ecclesiology is very much on the agenda. These discussions have been given impetus by the decline of congregations in the West on the one hand, and by the missionary impulse on the other to plant congregations where no church exists. In choosing Newbigin's understanding of the missionary church as the theme for this chapter, my aim is to complement Mark Laing's more biographical contribution in the previous chapter. Here I will take a more systematic approach, and show that many of the questions facing the contemporary church—particularly in the West—had already been high on Newbigin's agenda for some years, and were being addressed by him with that same missionary incentive that is rightly being urged upon us today. By doing so, I hope to show that though Newbigin's theological method is always culturally attuned, it is never at the expense of theological coherence. Indeed I will argue that it is this coherence that most challenges our discussions of ecclesiology today.

---

1. This chapter is a revised version of a paper delivered at the 2011 Meissen Theological Conference and is published here with permission.

We begin with a quotation from Newbigin's classic 1953 book *The Household of God.* As Laing has shown, this book expresses the essential characteristics of Newbigin's approach to the understanding of the church which he had already thought about and labored over for many years as a young missionary in India, and which had been formative in the discussions leading up to the inauguration of the Church of South India (CSI) in 1947.[2] It comes at point where, having surveyed the three "streams" of church tradition ("Protestant," "Catholic," and "Pentecostal"), Newbigin draws together the implications of what he has been saying. He writes:

> a salvation whose very essence is that it is corporate and cosmic, the restoration of the broken harmony between all men and between man and God and man and nature, must be communicated . . . by the actual development of a community which embodies—if only in foretaste—the restored harmony of which it speaks. A gospel of reconciliation can only be communicated by a reconciled fellowship.[3]

This quotation is deeply characteristic of the flow of Newbigin's thought, and my aim in what follows is in part to offer an exposition of it, developing Newbigin's understanding of the missionary church under the headings of its corporate perspective, its function as a foretaste of the kingdom, and its ecumenical obligation. I will distinguish these themes in order to analyze them, but it is important to remember that they are always connected in Newbigin's thinking, both theologically and structurally. We begin, however, by looking at the framework which holds them together, namely eschatology.

ECCLESIOLOGY IN ESCHATOLOGICAL PERSPECTIVE

The key to understanding Newbigin's theology of the church is that he sees its earthly nature and purpose as only properly understood when "read back" from its eschatological reality.[4] It is in this sense what we might describe Newbigin's understanding of the church as a "retrospective" ecclesiology, with questions about its present-day forms and priorities

2. See Laing's chapter in the present volume.

3. Newbigin, *Household of God,* 141.

4. See the discussions on this theme in Goheen's detailed doctoral study of Newbigin's ecclesiology (Goheen, *"As the Father,"* e.g., 136–52). He rightly states here that "Newbigin's eschatology forms the firm basis for his missionary ecclesiology" (142). See also Goheen, "Missional Calling," 41–43.

addressed in the light of its heavenly fulfillment. As he puts it: "The salvation of which the Gospel speaks and which is determinative of the nature and function of the Church is—as the very word itself should teach us—a making whole, a healing. It is the summing-up of all things in Christ."[5] The church on earth is therefore to be "proleptic" in its forms and functions, precisely because its vital characteristics are eschatologically and salvifically determined. As he puts it: "The Church is the pilgrim people of God. It is on the move—hastening to the ends of the earth to beseech all men to be reconciled to God, and hastening to the end of time to meet its Lord who will gather all into one. Therefore the nature of the Church is never to be finally defined in static terms, but only in terms of that to which it is going. It cannot be understood rightly except in a perspective which is at once missionary and eschatological . . ."[6]

With this eschatological hermeneutic as the key to understanding the different aspects of Newbigin's ecclesiology, we will now examine its outworking under the three themes referred to earlier.

THE MISSIONARY CHURCH IN CORPORATE PERSPECTIVE

In our opening quotation from *Household of God*, Newbigin describes the gospel as a "gospel of reconciliation"—involving the bringing together of the different elements of an estranged creation: reconciliation with the Creator, reconciliation with other human beings, and reconciliation with the created order itself. As a community reconciled by the good news of this gospel, Newbigin continually insists that the church must itself become a reconciling community, bearing in turn—as it has done down the Ages, the very message of reconciliation that brought it into being. As a result of this fundamental connection between the church's "nature" and "function," the idea of mission in Newbigin's thinking is never "attached" to a theology of the church as if it were one amongst many activities of similar importance. Rather, it is absolutely integral to its nature and being. Missiology and ecclesiology are already theologically fused in Newbigin's thought as two sides of the same coin.

To put this another way, Newbigin argues that if the church is the corporate expression of salvation, it is also the mediator of that salvation. Here we come across the inter-personal and corporate "logic" of salvation,

5. Ibid., 140.
6. Ibid., 25.

so characteristic of Newbigin's thinking. We encounter the truth about God, he argues, not by coming to accept impersonal propositions or generalized ideas about the "meaning" of faith, but through the mediation of God's people—the faith-communities brought into being by the revelation of the gospel itself. And this meeting with God through the "body" of his church is itself a reflection of the way in which all true knowledge is mediated: as revelatory mediation between personal beings. Newbigin was to become well-known for his discussions of epistemology in his later writings, but the conviction that "the meaning of the world is personal," and that all true knowledge is therefore personally mediated forms the bedrock of his theological method.[7]

This general truth is formalized in Newbigin's ecclesial thinking by his understanding of the doctrine of "election." Newbigin was well aware of the distortions and arguments sparked historically by the idea of "election." But he is much more interested in the biblical purposes of election than he is in its relationship to the doctrines of assurance or perseverance. For him, a biblical understanding is summed up by the fact that "One race is chosen in order that through it God's salvation may be mediated to others, and . . . may thus become the nucleus of a new redeemed humanity."[8] In saying this he was aware that it sharpened a further, and different, kind of problem: the potential "scandal of particularity" in the minds of those who cannot accept the idea that the final truth about the universe should be "carried" by a *particular* group of people. However, he insists that it is precisely this strange doctrine which ultimately resolves the awkward tension between the "universal," "cosmic" nature of the gospel on the one hand, and the "particularity" of the communities that bear its message on the other. He addresses this point in a paper prepared for an ecumenical study under the auspices of the World Council of Churches (WCC) in 1948, arguing that: "To demand that the doctrine of God's universal love be dissociated from the history of a particular people is to expect it to conform to the pattern of general propositions or laws which are typical of human reasoning. To demand that the knowledge of God's universal love

7. See, for example, the extract from his 1936 student essay "Revelation" in Weston, *Lesslie Newbigin*, 18–21. The original is in the Birmingham University Archives (DA 29/3/1/2). For a development of these themes in the 1960s (following his reading of Michael Polanyi's *Personal Knowledge*, published in 1958), see Newbigin, *Honest Religion*, 77–99. For later discussions, cf.—amongst many examples—*Gospel in a Pluralist Society*, 27–38.

8. Newbigin, *Household of God*, 100.

be available to all men equally is to expect that I should know it without the actual experience of meeting my neighbour."[9]

So then, Newbigin developed from the outset a strong sense of the ontology of the church as a divinely-ordained missionary *community*, bearing in its own life and relationships the very message of the salvation through which it was brought into being. As a result, it would have been inconceivable to Newbigin to construe an ecclesiology which was not at one and the same time communitarian in character and missionary in expression, since "wherever the missionary character of the doctrine of election is forgotten . . . God's people have betrayed their trust."[10]

Newbigin was to return repeatedly to the theme of the church as a missionary community, but it is worth touching on a late "variation" of it at this point. I refer to his description of the local congregation as the "hermeneutic of the gospel" which was to become a central feature of his later thinking in the context of the missionary challenge of Western culture in the 1980s and 90s. In some ways this development appears newly formulated, but in the light of the foregoing discussion, it can be seen to be right in line with Newbigin's earliest ecclesiological thinking. He first used the phrase "hermeneutic of the gospel" in his 1980 booklet *Your Kingdom Come* to emphasize the embodying of the gospel by the "Church as a whole" in its witness to the Kingdom.[11] The actual phrase is not used again until the late 1980s where it re-emerges as a key expression in Newbigin's articulation of the missiological significance of the local church congregation in the context of the post-Enlightenment culture in the West. In his 1987 article, "Evangelism in the City," for example, he addresses the profound missionary need of the hour by posing the question: "How can this strange story of God made flesh, of a crucified Saviour, of resurrection and new creation become credible for those whose entire mental training has conditioned them to believe that the real world is the world which can be satisfactorily explained and managed without the hypothesis of God? . . . I know of only one clue to the answering of that question, only one real hermeneutic of the gospel: a congregation which believes it."[12]

In important respects, this conception finds its roots in Newbigin's understanding of the "corporality" of the gospel: that salvation is

9. Newbigin, "Duty and Authority," 29.

10. Newbigin, *Household of God,* 101.

11. Newbigin, *Your Kingdom Come,* 38, in the context of Newbigin's arguments about holding together the ideas of "church" and "kingdom" which had been separated (to the detriment of both) by contrasting approaches to mission in the 20th century.

12. Newbigin, "Evangelism," 4.

mediated through the body of Christ to those around it, and—in the particular sense of the phrase "hermeneutic of the gospel"—that it is "interpreted" or "made understandable" by means of the life of the body of Christ. If there is a fresh development here from his earlier thought, it is the idea that whereas before, mission was conceived in largely "centrifugal" terms—of the church going *towards* those outside and bearing the gospel witness in deed and word, here there is a greater "centripetal" stress on the incarnational attraction of the local congregation as it "indwells" and "embodies" Christ.

Two years later in *The Gospel in a Pluralist Society* Newbigin devoted a whole chapter to this missionary conception of the local congregation,[13] arguing that a critical problem in the West was that the Church had surrendered itself to the dominant assumptions of the culture of the Enlightenment. In his view, this "domestication of the gospel"[14] to the "reigning plausibility structure" of a secular culture must be faced honestly, and then set aside by a fundamental re-orientation of cultural assumptions within the Church. Only so will it be in a position to demonstrate once more in its life and worship the *alternative* "plausibility structure" of the gospel. Indeed, Newbigin's late thinking insists that it is only in this renewal of corporate congregational life that the secularized society of the West can be reached. He sums up the challenge by saying that Western culture's "reigning plausibility structure can only be effectively challenged by people who are fully integrated inhabitants of another."[15] By embodying the life of the risen Jesus *within* the varied life-settings of Western contemporary culture, Newbigin calls the church once more to demonstrate the quality of life and liberty revealed in the gospel.

So, to conclude this section, we have seen that from the start of Newbigin's thinking about ecclesiology there is a fusion of "being" and "function": the church is not called into mission as something somehow separate from its essential being and nature. In a vital way the "medium" of the church *is* the message of the gospel. Or as he put it in the 1948 paper referred to earlier: "The preaching of the Gospel is indissolubly linked with the existence of a people called and set apart by God to be its bearers."[16]

13. Newbigin, *Gospel in a Pluralist Society*, 222–33.

14. Ibid., 10–11.

15. Ibid., 228. The term "plausibility structure" comes from Peter Berger (see e.g., his *Social Reality*, 45–46).

16. Newbigin, "Duty and Authority," 29.

THE MISSIONARY CHURCH AS FORETASTE
OF THE KINGDOM

We move now to a connected theme in Newbigin's understanding of the church expressed in the quotation from *Household of God* with which this chapter began. There he spoke of the church as the "community which embodies—if only in foretaste—the restored harmony of which it speaks."[17] It is immediately apparent from this that the idea of the church as the "foretaste" or "sign" of the kingdom is characteristically (and logically) anchored in an eschatological framework. But what is of special interest in this regard is that Newbigin often uses the phrase to clarify particular sets of relationships; especially the church's role in God's sovereign work in relation to the "kingdom" on the one hand and to the "world" on the other.

Developing this theme, it is significant to bear in mind Newbigin's reaction to the various world missionary conferences of the first half of the twentieth century, for it was in this context—and in response to the discussions that they stimulated—that his thinking evolved and clarified. The confident missionary energy that had inspired the 1910 Edinburgh World Missionary Conference, with its expectation of the imminent coming of the Kingdom of God, was soon to be severely tested in the trenches of the First World War, where any optimism about the Kingdom's arrival was met with the grim realities of human barbarity and suffering. The missionary conferences that followed Edinburgh were far less hopeful about the task facing a now-chastened church. At the International Missionary Council (IMC) meeting at Jerusalem in 1928, for example, there was much talk of the "secular," and of the attempt to understand what God was doing in the world outside the church. As Newbigin was later to comment: "Its closing words were of 'hope and expectation of His glorious Kingdom,' though perhaps the whole context leads one to infer that for many of the delegates this kingdom was conceived rather in terms of 'a Christ-like world' than in terms of 'a new heaven and a new earth.'"[18]

By contrast the theme of the 1938 IMC meeting at Tambaram was entitled "The World Mission of the Church." Its tone was set in the opening address, in which John Mott declared that "it is the Church which is to be at the centre of our thinking and resolving these creative days—the Divine Society founded by Christ and His apostles to accomplish His will in the world." The church was back on the agenda once more, and Newbigin saw

17. Newbigin, *Household of God,* 141.
18. Newbigin, *Relevance,* 23.

this as the beginning of an "exceedingly necessary and fruitful period" in which mission-thinking became "church-centric"—as he later described it.[19] But he was not uncritical of some of its emphases, as we will see.

The counter reaction to Tambaram's emphasis on the church became sharpened as a result of the IMC meeting at Willingen in 1952. Here, the conference tried to wrestle with the question of how God's work in and through the church could be related to his activity *outside* the church in "secular" history. In particular Johannes Hoekendijk had argued that the mission of God (the *Missio Dei*) was the primary reality in mission, and that this movement of God was not limited to the church, but included various kinds of secular movements, in both personal, public, and political life.[20]

Although no convergence of opinion came out of Willingen on this issue, the emphasis on the realm of the "secular" dominated missionary thinking throughout the 1950s and 60s, with the church somewhat sidelined. Indeed, one of the stream papers at the Strasbourg conference of 1960 argued that the Tambaram conviction that God blesses the world *through the church* had to be abandoned, and replaced by the view that God addresses the church *through the world*. This conception of the secular as the primary context of God's redemptive work heralded the publication of books by a number of leading thinkers, including Harvey Cox and Paul van Buren.[21]

Newbigin's reaction to these developments was nuanced. He was positive about some of the fruits of the so-called "church-centric" era, not least the formal integration of the WCC with the IMC in 1961 which helped to cement the connection between "church" and "mission" for which Newbigin had always argued.[22] At the same time, he was wary of the attempt to limit God's activity to the work of the church. "The Church is indeed the agent of God's mission and a clue to his dealing with mankind," he wrote in 1963, "but this does not mean that the work of God in the world is to be simply identified with the progress of the Church in mission and unity." Nor did it mean that the events of secular history were "mere background for the story of the Church, or merely scenery for

19. Ibid., 23.

20. His (unadopted) report was co-written with Paul Lehmann, and is reproduced in Goodall, *Missions Under the Cross*, 238–45.

21. Cox, *Secular City* (1965), and van Buren, *Secular Meaning* (1968).

22. Newbigin became the first director of the new WCC division of "World Mission and Evangelism."

the drama of salvation."[23] Moreover, he often felt that discussions about God's redemptive activity outside the church were marred by two kinds of theological separation: firstly between the kingdom of God and the person of Jesus, and secondly between the kingdom of God and the church.[24] Newbigin continued to insist theologically on the need to maintain these connections, and it was partly in response to the debates raised by the WCC missionary conferences that Newbigin developed his committed trinitarian approach to mission in the late 1950s and early 1960s,[25] which was to be given its fullest treatment in his 1978 book *The Open Secret*.[26]

Here, he develops and interweaves trinitarian themes: the Father's kingship over all creation (and the church's call to bear witness to this kingdom); the continuing "presence" of the kingdom in the church of Jesus Christ; and what he calls the "prevenience" of the kingdom in the mysterious work of the Spirit.[27] In agreement with aspects of the "church-centric" emphasis at Tambaram he argues that the kingdom is genuinely present in the church as the body of Christ—as it had been embodied historically in the person of Jesus. Yet at the same time he insists that the kingdom is not the "property of the church," nor can it be "domesticated" by the church.[28] There is always an intrinsic "otherness" about the kingdom which points to the fact that it is yet to be fully realized. As a result, whilst embodying something of the reality and power of the kingdom in its ongoing life, the church must also continue to point *away* from itself to that fuller realization. Equally, in developing the discussion of the ministry of the Spirit, Newbigin clearly aims to expand the narrower "church-centric" approach to mission (thereby countering the idea for example that mission is to be understood merely as the church's "self-propagation" through the "putting forth of the power that inheres in its life"[29]). On the contrary, he insists, the Spirit is sovereign in mission (it is *he* rather than the church who is the "agent" of mission), and that the church will often find itself straining to keep pace with what the Spirit is doing.

23. Newbigin, *Relevance*, 24.

24. See his discussion in *Your Kingdom Come*, 11–12.

25. See, e.g., Newbigin, "Mission"; *Relevance*.

26. Republished in 1995 with minor revisions.

27. For discussion of Newbigin's trinitarian theology, see the contribution of John Flett in this volume.

28. Newbigin, *Open Secret*, 62.

29. Ibid. Cf. Newbigin's criticism of certain strands of church-growth thinking in making the church the "goal" of mission rather than a "sign" of the kingdom (e.g., "On being the Church," 35–36; *Gospel in a Pluralist Society*, 184ff.).

But at the same time, Newbigin is always careful to link the work of the Spirit to the community of faith. By doing so he clearly has an eye on addressing some of the developments in "secular" mission characterized by Willingen in 1952 and its aftermath. So the Spirit "rules, guides, and goes before the church"; or "is himself the witness, who changes both the world and the church," and is the one "who always goes before the church in its missionary journey."[30]

How then is the missionary church related to "kingdom" and "world"? Newbigin's trinitarian approach enabled him to clarify these relationships in the context of the ongoing WCC discussions, whilst at the same time continue to underscore their eschatological framework. His characteristic answer was therefore that the church relates to the world as its setting, and to the kingdom as a sign. As he puts it in *The Open Secret*: "The church lives in the midst of history as a sign, instrument, and foretaste of the reign of God."[31]

THE MISSIONARY CHURCH AND ITS ECUMENICAL OBLIGATION

Returning a final time to our opening quotation from *The Household of God*, Newbigin writes that the consummation of God's salvation purposes will be a "restored harmony." The church is called to become a living demonstration of the gospel which it proclaims, because "a gospel of reconciliation can only be communicated by a reconciled fellowship."[32] "If this be true," he asserts a few pages later "then it is high time that its implications for the ecumenical discussion of the nature of the Church were realistically faced."[33]

The ecumenical outworking of the "logic" of salvation was a hallmark of Newbigin's ecclesiological passion to which he was committed throughout his adult life.[34] In his autobiography he wrote that as an undergraduate at Cambridge in the late 1920s, it was his membership of the Student Christian Movement under the influence of speakers like Joe Oldham and John Mott that taught him "to see unity and mission as two sides of a

30. Newbigin, *Open Secret*, 62–63.

31. Ibid., 124.

32. Newbigin, *Household of God*, 141.

33. Ibid., 143.

34. See the discussion in Goheen, *"As the Father,"* 200–227.

single commitment."[35] In his own ministry, the pinnacle of his ecumenical achievements was undoubtedly the formal inauguration of the Church of South India in 1947, which remained a source of great joy and exhilaration to him. He served as one of its founding bishops—first in Madurai,[36] and later in Madras.[37] Indeed, so committed was he to its vision of ecumenism that he saw its establishment as somehow pioneering a way forward for the worldwide church. This was never to be, and Newbigin was to experience desperate personal disappointments in his struggles to defend the validity of the CSI against its detractors—not least at successive Lambeth Conferences. Nonetheless, in the years that followed the foundation of the CSI, Newbigin's passion for unity remained undaunted, and during the 1950s in particular he was deeply and energetically involved in the discussions over the nature of unity within the WCC, which was to become a key theme of its Third Assembly at New Delhi in 1961.

Unity and Theology

The debates around the question of church unity had been gathering momentum for some years, and Newbigin's thinking can be seen in his Thomas Memorial Lecture (entitled "The Quest for Unity through Religion"[38]) which was delivered at the University of Chicago in 1954 (shortly before the Second Assembly of the WCC in Evanston that year). Here, Newbigin develops the argument that church unity derives from the once-for-all historical demonstration of the love of God in the atoning cross of Christ, which brings into being a reconciled community. In developing this thought, Newbigin contrasts the Christian community of faith with the enlightenment quest enshrined in the philosophy of the Hindu *Vedanta*. This resulted in a very different kind of social outworking, characterized by more individualized forms (for example the solitary dedication of the *sannyasi*), and therefore by a mutual tolerance of others on the journey rather than by a commitment to community. In contrast with this *Vedantic* quest, Newbigin argues that Christian "enlightenment" centers around an historic act of divine love which draws men and women together in mutual forgiveness and harmony. As he puts it: "Tolerance requires no visible community to express it, but love does. The deeper and stronger

35. Newbigin, *Unfinished Agenda*, 239.

36. 1947–1957.

37. 1965–1974.

38. Newbigin, "Quest for Unity."

the love, the more binding will be the mutual obligations to which it will lead. Therefore, it belongs to the very essence of the atonement wrought by Christ, that it leads to the creation of a visible community binding men together in all nations and all generations."[39]

Once again Newbigin connects soteriology and ecclesiology, writing that "The church is organic to the gospel."[40] But the corollary of this is equally important for him, which is to fuse the theological grounding of the church in the gospel with a corresponding imperative in mission. For the atoning work of Christ immediately places believers in a new set of relationships, not only with fellow Christians but with every human being, for the "atoning act is directed to the whole human race, and not to anything less."[41] As a result, "Those who have been, by the power of the Holy Spirit, brought within the circle of that reconciling power and reborn into the new system of relationships which it creates are by that very fact committed to participation in that reconciling ministry."[42] Indeed, "by their membership in the church [believers] are committed to a mission to the world. They cannot abandon the latter without forfeiting the former."[43]

So if Christ is the center around which humankind is to be unified, then the cause of Christian mission is seriously hampered, even "flagrantly contradicted" "by the disunity of Christendom itself."[44] "The disunity of the church" he writes, "is a public denial of the sufficiency of the atonement. It is quite unthinkable that the church should be able effectively to preach that atonement and to become, in fact, the nucleus of the reconciled humanity, while that denial stands."[45]

In the light of these convictions it is not surprising that Newbigin wrote with regard to the inauguration of the CSI in 1947 that he was "so utterly sure that what we are doing is not patching things together, but being led by the Holy Spirit back to the fullness and simplicity of gospel truth."[46] For him, the gospel was the only hope around which the unity of humankind could be envisaged, and a unified church its only demonstration this side of heaven.

---

39. Ibid., 26.
40. Ibid., 28.
41. Ibid.
42. "Quest for Unity," 28.
43. Ibid.
44. Ibid., 29.
45. Ibid.
46. Newbigin, *Unfinished Agenda*, 91.

These early ecumenical convictions re-appear at several points in his later work. What is consistent about them is the belief that the unity of the church is a matter of theological principle rather than pragmatic expediency. Writing in 1993, for example, he argues that "The Church cannot abandon this struggle [for unity] for the sake of a comfortable tolerance, without betraying its calling."[47] Accordingly, Newbigin warns that disunity in the Church is damaging to Christian witness precisely because it is a denial of the gospel. As he puts it in a 1992 sermon: "We cannot, with any hope of being believed, preach to men the word of our Lord that he, when he is lifted up from the earth, will draw all men to himself, if we continue stubbornly to say that even his love is not enough to draw us close to one another and enable us to live together as brethren in one family."[48]

The force of this apologetic is hard to resist, even if there are understandable questions about its application to the realities of church life. For example: are denominational boundaries legitimized by a real difference of opinion over what is considered to be of "primary" and what of "secondary" importance?; or, what is the appropriate "form" of local or global unity?; and again, to what extent is the commitment to a "united local church"—a phrase much-used by Newbigin—always best for missionary advance?

Unity and Structure

Newbigin was conscious of the significance of such questions, and wrestled with them throughout his ministry. In the 1954 lecture in Chicago, for example, he addresses the question of boundaries. "How" he asks "are we to understand the bond which binds together churches in the World Council which are deeply divided from one another on matters of truth?"[49] The answer he gives here and elsewhere is that we must always return to the "starting point" of the finished work of Christ on the cross. When we encounter those who acknowledge the fact of this finality but who differ in their interpretation of it, the believer is nonetheless "placed in an existential relation" which cannot be denied—even though there may be "acute disagreement" in points of application.[50] "The bond that unites us, therefore, is not a mere feeling, not a mere agreement in thought, not a

47. Newbigin, "Pluralism," 6.
48. Newbigin, "Riverside Sermon," 4.
49. Newbigin, "Quest for Unity," 26.
50. Ibid.

merely natural sympathy, it is an actual knitting-together of two persons, which can be described either by saying that the Holy Spirit unites us or by saying that the death of Christ for us both places us in a relation to each other wherein we can but acknowledge each other as brothers." [51]

In terms of formal and organizational unity, Newbigin is more circumspect in this early lecture, but makes two points. First, he urges that Christians should strive to demonstrate their unity "visibly" within their localities, and that this requires a continual process of "death and rebirth, to the place where forgiveness and reconciliation are alone to be had." For, as long as "separated churches cling to their own individuality and seek to evade that dying, they cannot be reborn into the one fellowship which mankind will recognize as the nucleus of its remaking into one".[52] Second, he argues that each local community should maintain a clear relationship to the worldwide community of faith: meaning, for example, that forms of ministry employed in local contexts should be universally recognized. But he concludes that "within these wide limits there are vast areas where we must simply say that we have yet to learn what is required of a fellowship which is truly to embody Christ's atonement in and for the world."[53]

Newbigin continued to reflect on the challenge of "visible unity" throughout his later ministry,[54] and was much involved in the discussions leading to the statement on unity (known as "All in Each Place") which came out of the 1961 WCC Assembly at New Delhi, and in which he had a significant drafting role.[55] In general, during the 60s and 70s—amidst a plethora of issues impinging upon its discussions—two broad approaches to the question of unity were emerging within WCC circles. One sought local organic forms of union in which churches surrendered their separate identities in order to form new local bodies; the other operated at a more global level and took the form of bilateral dialogues between the different world confessions. These two strands were acknowledged at the Nairobi conference in 1975 which spoke of the global Church being "a conciliar fellowship of local churches which are themselves truly united."[56] This significant statement sought to hold together both the global confes-

51. Ibid., 26–27.

52. Ibid., 31.

53. Ibid., 31–32.

54. See Wainwright, *Lesslie Newbigin*, 88–134.

55. The statement is reproduced in Visser 't Hooft, *New Delhi Report*, 116–35; for discussion, see Wainwright, *Lesslie Newbigin*, 113–15.

56. Paton, *Breaking Barriers*, 60.

sional elements of unity alongside their more local organic expressions. Newbigin favored this "conciliar" approach, believing that when local churches were truly united in vision and purpose, the broader context of unity was best served by a "conciliarity" which affirmed local varieties of church expression. This was not a "substitute" for unity in each locality, but rather the most helpful context in which local moves toward unity could be "progressively learned and experienced."[57]

But the Nairobi statement also raised the question: what is *meant* by "a local church truly united"? Newbigin sought to address this in the 1977 article just quoted which was published in the *Ecumenical Review*.[58] In it he repeated his view that the local church is to be Christologically defined as being Christ *for* that local "place," but he is now more expansive in his description of how the concept of "place" is to be interpreted. It is not simply "the latitude and longitude of the spot where this church happens to be" but rather the "place in the fabric of human society" in which it is set.[59] In this sense, the "relation of the Church to the place is a dynamic one and not a static one" because people live in a "variety of secular realities, each of which has to be taken seriously." These comprise the geographical location, but also include places of work, of kinship and shared language, of political or ideological commitment and so forth.[60] What then determines the validity of different expressions of the church in these many interlocking "places"? Newbigin responds by acknowledging that whilst "diversity is part of God's gracious purpose for the human family," "separation and mutual rejection is not," and that the local expression of the church calls for a unity which "neither negates diversity nor permits diversity to be the basis for mutual rejection."[61]

On the other hand, in order to take its role seriously as the "first-fruits" of the kingdom in the web of secular "places" in which it is set, the church must make every effort to reach those elements of the community which are "alien to the present membership of the local church."[62] Newbigin argues therefore, that there must be new "forms" of church—"outside the walls" of the existing church, each with its own proper character, and distinct from the community from which it came. "Separation there must

57. Newbigin, "What Is 'A Local Church Truly United'?" 127.
58. Ibid.
59. Ibid., 118.
60. Ibid.
61. Ibid., 122.
62. Ibid., 123.

be—for the sake of mission" he argues, but equally "separation cannot be the last word," for the gospel is about God's purpose to "unite *all* things in Christ."[63] His conclusion is that:

> The existence of separate congregations in the same geographical area on the basis of language and culture may have to be accepted as a necessary, but provisional, measure for the sake of the fulfilment of Christ's mission. Necessary because there must be the possibility to bring to full ripeness the special gifts and insights that God has given to peoples of different language and culture and this cannot happen if some have no place except on the margin of a community of another language or culture. Provisional because the Gospel is good news of God's purpose to bring all these gifts to their perfection in his new creation where—all together—they will shine in their true glory.[64]

We note once again that Newbigin finds the fundamental clues to the questions of church form and function by reference to eschatological realities. "Unity must be defined in terms of movement, not *stasis*," he argues. The key question is not "Is this body of Christians truly united within itself?" but "Is this body of Christians functioning as a true sign, foretaste and instrument of God's purpose in Christ to draw *all in that place* into unity in Christ?"[65] As a result, Newbigin is sympathetic to those "provisional" forms of church "beyond the walls" which exist for the sake of mission, and are future-orientated towards the ultimate goal of unity which lies at the heart of the gospel. But he is correspondingly critical of those forms of denominationalism which: "look to the past, which are determined not by the future hope that all shall be one, but by the past quarrels through which the Church has been divided, which takes out of the past not the one name of Jesus but other names by which the identity of a congregation is to be defined. This is not part of missionary obedience."[66] Newbigin concludes the article characteristically by tracing the connections between salvation, ecclesiology and unity, saying that, "Only if the Church at every level is moving towards the unity to which God calls all human kind is it true to its nature."[67]

---

63. Ibid., 123–24.
64. Ibid., 124.
65. Ibid., 125 (emphasis original).
66. Ibid., 127.
67. Ibid., 128.

CONCLUSION

Newbigin's understanding of the "missionary church" was passionate and committed. It was both lived "in" and lived "out." We have shown that it was also theologically driven and doctrinally integrated, and that the reason for this is that it is essentially an ecclesiology "in reverse", its central contours read back from a unified eschatological perspective. Its radically *theological* nature is one of the reasons why Newbigin's work in this area demands continued attention. Moreover, the coherence of his approach holds together important elements in the theology of the church that are too easily disconnected—not least in contemporary debates. In this context it is perhaps his insistence on the missional dimensions of unity that has yet to be taken seriously enough. For Newbigin, unity was never a narrowly ecclesiastical affair, but is always theologically anchored to the meaning of the gospel itself, and to its missionary outworking: *that the world may know.*

In light of this, Newbigin's vision of the missionary church remains ever-contemporary, both as an invitation to re-imagine as well as a challenge to engage. Perhaps this is particularly so in the light of the waning of the influence of the WCC and its ecumenical emphases on the one hand, and yet an increasing awareness on the other that the unity of the church is once more a vital concern for mission. So let the last words be his: "Can there be in each place such a shared common life in Christ as can be a credible sign of the unity of all mankind? God knows. But to give up the quest of such unity is to settle for something less than the Gospel."[68]

BIBLIOGRAPHY

Berger, Peter L. *The Social Reality of Religion.* London: Faber & Faber, 1969. (Originally published in the US as *The Sacred Canopy* (1967).

Cox, Harvey. *The Secular City: Secularization and Urbanization in Theological Perspective.* London: SCM, 1965.

Goheen, Michael W. "The Missional Calling of Believers in the World: Lesslie Newbigin's Contribution." In *A Scandalous Prophet: The Way of Mission after Newbigin,* edited by Thomas F. Foust, et al., 37-54. Grand Rapids: Eerdmans, 1998.

———. *"As the Father Has Sent Me, I Am Sending You": J. E. Lesslie Newbigin's Missionary Ecclesiology.* Zoetermeer: Boekencentrum, 2000.

Goodall, Norman, editor. *Missions Under the Cross: Addresses delivered at the Enlarged Meeting of the IMC at Willingen, in Germany, 1952.* London: Edinburgh House, 1953.

68. Newbigin, "All in One Place," 306.

Newbigin, Lesslie. "All in One Place or All of One Sort? On Unity and Diversity in the Church." In *Creation, Christ and Culture: Studies in Honour of T.F. Torrance*, edited by Richard W.A. McKinney, 288–306. Edinburgh: T. & T. Clark, 1976.

———. "The Duty and Authority of the Church to Preach the Gospel." In *The Church's Witness to God's Design: An Ecumenical Study Prepared under the Auspices of the World Council of Churches*, 19–35. London: SCM, 1948.

———. "Evangelism in the City." *Reformed Review* 41 (1987) 3–8.

———. *The Gospel in a Pluralist Society*. London: SPCK, 1989.

———. *Honest Religion for Secular Man*. London: SCM, 1966.

———. *The Household of God: Lectures on the Nature of the Church*. London: SCM, 1953.

———. "The Mission of the Triune God." Unpublished manuscript, Geneva: WCC, Ecumenical Centre Library, 1962.

———. "On Being the Church for the World." In *The Parish Church?: Explorations in the Relationship of the Church and the World*, edited by Giles Ecclestone, 25–42. Oxford: Mowbray, 1988.

———. *The Open Secret: Sketches for a Missionary Theology*. Grand Rapids: Eerdmans, 1978.

———. "Pluralism in the Church." *ReNews (Presbyterians For Renewal)* 4, no. 2 (1993) 1, 6–7.

———. "The Quest for Unity through Religion." *Journal of Religion* 35 (1955) 17–33.

———. *The Relevance of Trinitarian Doctrine for Today's Mission*, CWME Study Pamphlets, No.2. London: Edinburgh House, 1963.

———. "A Riverside Sermon" (1992). In *A Word in Season: Perspectives on Christian World Missions*, edited by E. Jackson, 1–6. Grand Rapids: Eerdmans; Edinburgh: Saint Andrew, 1994.

———. *Unfinished Agenda: An Updated Autobiography*. 2nd ed. Edinburgh: Saint Andrew, 1993.

———. "What Is 'A Local Church Truly United'?" *Ecumenical Review* 29 (1977) 115–28.

———. *Your Kingdom Come: Reflections on the Theme of the Melbourne Conference on World Mission and Evangelism 1980*. Leeds: John Paul the Preacher's Press, 1980.

Paton, David M., editor. *Breaking Barriers*, WCC Fifth Assembly (Nairobi). London: SPCK, 1975.

Polanyi, Michael. *Personal Knowledge: Towards a Post-Critical Philosophy*. Chicago: University of Chicago Press, 1958.

van Buren, Paul. *The Secular Meaning of the Gospel*. Harmondsworth: Pelican, 1968.

Weston, Paul, editor. *Lesslie Newbigin, Missionary Theologian: A Reader*. Grand Rapids: Eerdmans; London: SPCK, 2006.

Newbigin as Preacher and Exegete

Kenneth D. Gordon

UNDERSTANDING SCRIPTURE: NATURE AND PURPOSE

NEWBIGIN'S WRITINGS DISPLAY HIS clear conviction of the importance of Scripture and his desire to promote a proper understanding of its function in the life of the church.[1] He was however no fundamentalist, having begun "as a typical liberal."[2] His move rightwards appears to have stayed with him and he remained intentionally biblical in his thought and preaching.[3]

There can be no doubting the centrality of the Bible in Newbigin's personal life. During his final years he wrote, "I more and more find the precious part of each day to be the thirty or forty minutes I spend each morning before breakfast with the Bible." [4] This was in fact his lifelong practice, together with personal praise and prayer,[5] from which all else

1. This conviction was displayed in other contexts than his writings. For example, Dr Hans-Ruedi Weber—one time Director of Biblical Studies at the WCC—was made graphically aware of Newbigin's concern for exegetical exactitude as a young man who had been, as Newbigin put it, "carried away by rhetoric and had made Paul say things which were not in the text." "Lesslie," he said, "took me aside and severely criticized something I had said during . . . the bible studies on Galatians." (Quoted from a letter to Newbigin's biographer—see Wainwright, *Theological Life*, 17 and the book's corresponding note 26.)

2. Newbigin, *Unfinished Agenda*, 29.

3. The Rev Murdoch MacKenzie spoke of this at the Service of Thanksgiving for the Life of Lesslie Newbigin, in Southwark Cathedral on 28 March 1998, saying, "He lived and moved, and had his being soaked in the words of Scripture."

4. Newbigin, *Word in Season*, 204.

5. Newbigin preached a sermon on "Individual Prayer" at Holy Trinity Brompton,

in his work and writing flowed. It is therefore hardly surprising that he regarded "the crisis of faith in the modern West" as "bound up with the question of biblical authority."[6] In this he was probably even more prescient than he knew, in light of the confusion and turmoil evident in the churches today, which, it could be claimed, is associated with the same fundamental question.[7] Thus Newbigin continues to speak with typical relevance and perceptiveness.

The matter of biblical authority is allied with the concept of revelation. The possibility and necessity of divine revelation brings with it questions about the manner and means of God's self-disclosure, and Newbigin settled some of these questions in his own mind very early on.[8] He acknowledges the place of Scripture in the total concept of Christian revelation when he appeals to "the teaching of the New Testament about revelation" as part of the "down-reach of God's saving grace."[9] Precisely how at that time he understood the nature of biblical authority and its place in the process of revelation is unclear, but we can be pretty sure that even then he would have regarded ultimate authority as residing in a Person, not in a text. The question for us now, however, as for him then, is still, what is the nature of biblical authority? For the mature Newbigin, this was answered carefully and sensitively.[10] Care was necessary in order to avoid both fundamentalist and liberal extremes, and sensitivity to demonstrate an awareness of the genuine difficulties that arise for the contemporary interpreter in a postmodern world.[11]

London. In this, he spoke of the method and style of his own personal practice of daily prayer (HTB Catalogue No. 411). The exact date of this sermon is not known, but it was probably in 1994/5.

6. Wainwright, *Theological Life*, 299.

7. For example, the Anglican Communion's ongoing internal problems arising from issues of sexuality, in which scriptural authority is evidently a critical consideration.

8. See his student essay on "Revelation," in Newbigin archives, Birmingham University Library, Special Collections section, UK, (DA29/3/1/2). (An extract from this essay is reproduced in Weston, *Lesslie Newbigin*, 18–21.)

9. Weston, *Lesslie Newbigin*, 19.

10. Thus, e.g., in Newbigin, *Foolishness to the Greeks*, in his chapter on "The Word in the World" he calls western culture "to a new plausibility structure in which the most real of all realities is the living God whose character is 'rendered' for us in the pages of Scripture," 64. "Rendered" is, it may be surmised, intended to gloss over some detailed implications and to emphasize the "story" of the Bible.

11. Cf., Stott, *Living Church*, 104–7, where the same point is made by another well-known preacher of a slightly different stripe.

Newbigin directly addressed the liberal/fundamentalist controversy in *Proper Confidence,*[12] and devoted an entire chapter to Holy Scripture. While he was fully open to the fruits of critical biblical study, he was also aware that the historical-critical method had perhaps over-reached itself, held inherent contradictions, and could no longer claim ultimate superiority in the academy or in the church.[13] His strictures were even more severe in regard to any fundamentalist doctrine of biblical inerrancy, which he regarded as "a direct denial of the way in which God has chosen to make himself known to us …"[14] In typically incisive words, Newbigin rightly asserts that "the important thing is not how we formulate a doctrine of biblical authority but how we allow the Bible to function in our daily lives."[15] For him, this meant letting the Bible's world and story shape and determine ours.

In *Truth and Authority in Modernity,*[16] Newbigin again has a section specifically on "Scripture." This is set, however, in the context of a chapter entitled "The Mediation of Divine Authority," in which tradition, reason, and experience are also part of the mediatory process. Thus we can see that, although Scripture is the foundation block on which his hermeneutical work is constructed, his method is properly holistic, and the Bible cannot be used as a set of propositions or statements of bare truth in themselves. He was evidently attracted by George Lindbeck's "cultural-linguistic model,"[17] which he considered applicable to the understanding of Scripture and with which he paraphrases the Bible as "a narrative that structures human experience and understanding."[18] Thus, he concludes, "The Bible, I suggest, functions properly in the life of the church when it functions in the way Lindbeck's language suggests. It functions as the true story of which our story is a part, and therefore we do not so much look *at* it as *through* it in order to understand and deal with the real world."[19]

12. Newbigin, *Proper Confidence.*

13. Thus, he writes, "The practice of the historical-critical method, in spite of the useful results it has produced in our understanding of the ways in which the biblical material was formed, is nevertheless full of self-contradictions" (Ibid., 84).

14. Ibid., 89.

15. Ibid., 91.

16. This was a revision and expansion of previously published essays, including a working paper on "Authority" for The Gospel and Our Culture's discussion group, meeting at St. Andrew's Hall, Selly Oak, Birmingham (U.K.) on 4 September 1989.

17. This is set out in Lindbeck, *Nature of Doctrine.*

18. Newbigin, *Truth and Authority,* 38.

19. Ibid., 42.

One might therefore conclude that, as with the Eucharist so with Scripture, it is a case of discerning and receiving "the things of God for the people of God." [20]

USING SCRIPTURE: EXEGESIS

It is not surprising to find Newbigin, in the preface to his commentary on John's Gospel,[21] approaching his expository task from an ecclesiastical perspective, and basing his *apologia* for the manner and style adopted in the commentary on his ordination vows[22] as a bishop in the Church of South India.[23] He had first been ordained as a Church of Scotland presbyter in 1936, and he would then also have made comparable vows.[24] Newbigin (unlike some modern ordinands) took these vows, we can reasonably infer, very seriously and without any "mental reservation." To "cross his fingers" intellectually would have been contrary to the very essence of the man.

Any interpreter of the Fourth Gospel must see John 20:31 as a key verse and Newbigin is no exception. The Gospel writer, whose work is often described as "the theological gospel," was undoubtedly a pastoral theologian—and that is what Newbigin clearly is in this commentary, a pastor to his flock. His purpose too is to bring others to faith in Jesus as Messiah and Son of God, and his book comes from long years of pastoral reflection and activity.

20. This analogy is applied and explored in Wright, "Bible as Sacrament."

21. Newbigin, *Light Has Come.*

22. It may be noted that, although "consecration" is the commonly used term, "ordination" is liturgically correct, being applicable to all three orders of ministry.

23. These include an affirmation of acceptance of "the Holy Scriptures as containing all things necessary for salvation, and as the supreme and decisive standard of faith," and a promise to be diligent in the study of the Holy Scriptures, praying for a true understanding of them, that you may be able to feed your people with the bread of life, to lead them in accordance with God's will, and to withstand and convince false teachers" (ibid., vii).

24. Question 2 in the Church of Scotland Ordinal and Service Book of 1931 reads as follows, "Do you believe the Word of God, which is contained in the Scriptures of the Old and New Testaments, to be the supreme rule of faith and life?" (*Church of Scotland Ordinal*, 21).

Kenneth D. Gordon

USING SCRIPTURE: HERMENEUTICAL STYLE

An example from *The Light has Come* may serve to illustrate Newbigin's hermeneutical style. His commentary on John 21:1–25 provides illuminating insights.[25] If chapter 21 of John is a later addition, Newbigin sees it as nevertheless coming from the same hand as the writer of the preceding twenty chapters. He reaches this conclusion on the basis of literary style, textual integrity, theological content and interpretation, and by a link to chapter 20 in the words of 21:14.[26]

In his discussion of how this final chapter came to be added, Newbigin presents his arguments as "a *reasonable* way of interpreting the evidence."[27] With problematical issues in hermeneutics, this is often the best (or only available) method of finding a solution. Newbigin assesses the evidence on its merits and applies common sense (reason?) in interpreting known pre-suppositions provided by other branches of the study of the gospels—referring, for instance, to "the great reservoir of memory treasured in the early Church and presumably existing in many varied units of both oral and written tradition."[28]

Each of the four gospel writers had a discrete purpose in writing, and a specific target audience in mind. The different communities of which they were part, Newbigin surmises, no doubt each had their specific store of memories. For this final chapter, John perhaps drew on memories from a community that treasured the Galilee resurrection appearances, which John had not previously mentioned (as opposed to those in Jerusalem). And, of course, John's selection was made for a decidedly theological purpose (cf. 20:31). The theological meaning of the Lord's commission to his disciples (John 20:19–23) is in fact brought out even more clearly, Newbigin says,[29] in chapter 21, and the special roles of Peter and John are also explained.

Commenting on the apparent discontinuity between the two closing chapters of John, Newbigin compares this with a similar "break" at

25. Wainwright chooses the Johannine Prologue in his section on "The Reading of the Text" (*Theological Life*, 308–12). Newbigin entitles this "Overture," although he does not carry the operatic theme through the rest of his exposition.

26. "This was now the third time that Jesus was revealed . . . after he was raised from the dead."

27. Newbigin, *Light Has Come*, 274 (my italics).

28. Ibid.

29. Cf. "As chapters 20 and 21 now stand there is a continuity of theological theme . . . envisaged more explicitly in chapter 21 than in chapter 20" (ibid., 275).

the end of chapter 14, and concludes, "we may believe that the author of the Gospel in its final form has—in arranging the units of tradition that came to his hand—given a higher priority to continuity of theological development than to preserving the order of events as they happened. We conclude . . . that chapter 21 records meetings which took place before the meetings of 20:19–29."[30]

Thus, Newbigin has evidently studied the works of critical scholars and made appropriate hermeneutical use of their evidence and opinions, but with judicious application of his own intellectual insight and judgment (human reason) and his devotional experience of scriptural meditation (the work of the Holy Spirit).

His commentary on verses 1–14 of chapter 21 shows a clear application of the principle of interpreting Scripture with Scripture. This is a feature of Newbigin's hermeneutics which may be observed also in regard to his preaching.[31] Here, he sees the two resurrection appearances as "the conflation of two distinct memories" recounted in Luke's Gospel (5:1–11; 24:30–43). As with Luke's language about the breaking of bread at Emmaus, so here with John, Newbigin interprets the words "*Jesus came and took the bread and gave it to them, and so with the fish*" eucharistically, as "sharing in the meal is the unveiling of the presence." The catch of fish is interpreted as "an acted parable" in fulfillment of the promise of Jesus, "*I will make you become fishers of men.*" Similarly (with verses 15–19) the commission given to Peter is "another parable" with the image of shepherd replacing that of fisherman. This style of interpretation is clearly both stimulating and suggestive for homiletical and devotional purposes.

These words from the commentary, "to 'follow Jesus' is what it means to be a disciple," are typical Newbigin words, expressed in the very same terms in both his writing and his preaching. In his hands, they convey the essence of the matter unequivocally. Following Jesus means here for Peter "the way of the cross," but the beloved disciple "bears witness in a different way." Commenting on verses 20–25, Newbigin is clear that John's "witness is embodied in the book which lies before us." Newbigin links this with the First Letter of John (possibly implying Johannine authorship of that book too). Quoting its opening verse,[32] he comments, "The witness of the

---

30. Ibid.

31. E.g., in his sermon delivered at the Uniting Service of Congregational and Evangelical & Reformed Churches, Cleveland, Ohio, USA on 26 June 1957. See "Minutes of the Uniting General Synod of the United Church of Christ," Appendix 13.

32. "*That . . . which we have seen with our eyes, which we have looked upon, and touched with our hands . . .*" (1 John 1:1).

beloved disciple comes not as a disembodied word, but as the witness of a community which has found and still finds in that word the power of everlasting life."[33] For Newbigin, "the witness of a community" is in reality "the hermeneutic of the Gospel," as he succinctly expressed it many times. It is always the church that matters, and that needs to be addressed with the call to *"follow me."*

It is clear that Newbigin's hermeneutical style is very well suited to the task of preaching, which was always his primary work.

PREACHING SCRIPTURE: RANGE AND VARIETY

The dedicated Newbigin website contains a large amount of material for study and research purposes.[34] But only four sermon scripts are available on the site. With one exception, these are sermons preached on special occasions, such as anniversaries or celebrations, and appear to have been chosen for their theological or missiological, rather than homiletical, significance. Not many other examples of Newbigin's preaching are extant in a form readily transferable to a website. The bulk of his homiletical material is contained in the Newbigin archives.[35] Approximately one hundred scripts are held there,[36] along with much other material pertaining to various aspects of Newbigin's life and work.

In light of the range and style of Lesslie Newbigin's work and thought, the question might legitimately be asked, "When is a sermon not a sermon?" This is both legitimate and necessary, since many of the lectures, talks, broadcasts, and writings that he has bequeathed to us bear distinct sermonic characteristics.[37] And, it might be contended that at least some of his sermons could be classified as talks or lectures, albeit given in a context of worship. Ruth Conway has stated this succinctly, "it was often difficult to distinguish between his lectures and his preaching,"[38] and her

33. Newbigin, *Light Has Come*, 281.

34. Http://www.newbigin.net. In version 2009/05, there are 279 documents, mostly by Newbigin, but many by others writing about him.

35. See note 8 above for location of archives.

36. This is supplemented by talks, broadcasts, and written pieces with some homiletical connection or relevance.

37. Newbigin was not the only one of whom this could be true. His contemporary and friend, the Sri Lankan evangelist and theologian D. T. Niles' Warrack Lectures (1957–58) were apparently described thus by one knowledgeable hearer, "These were not lectures, but sermons" (Visser 't Hooft, "Foreword," 9).

38. In a conversation in Oxford, 3 December 2003.

husband concurred with this opinion.[39] What both were expressing (and others besides have spoken similarly[40]) seems to indicate that Newbigin was no ivory-tower theologian but one who really believed what he said and said what he truly believed. His theological thinking was always done spiritually and from deep personal conviction, while his preaching was both spiritually and theologically informed.

The sermon scripts in the archives cover a period from 1955 to 1991, together with about a dozen that bear no date but give no indication of being from an earlier period. Most, by far, are from the 1970s and 1980s. Some decades are extremely thinly represented.[41] There appears to be virtually no surviving homiletical material from before the 1950s. Dates shown on the scripts indicate that many were used on numerous occasions, and they were evidently often delivered in widely varying contexts and locations, and sometimes adapted for situations quite different from the original.

During his final retirement in London, Newbigin had significant involvement in the life of Holy Trinity Church, Brompton.[42] Sermons and talks delivered there are usually recorded on tape and the church's holding includes five sermons preached by Newbigin as guest preacher during regular Sunday morning worship. Two have no date given, one is from 1995, and two are from 1996. In addition a further twenty-six recordings are of Bible studies, talks and lectures given in the church's Bible school program (School of Theology) or at "Away Days" for members of the congregation. These all date from 1994–1997.[43] A further two tapes, of talks given during a Mission led by Newbigin at Emmanuel URC Church, Cambridge, England are now in the possession of the present writer, as are a series of

39. Martin Conway, one-time President of Selly Oak Colleges, Birmingham, UK, is the author of the entry on Newbigin in the *Oxford Dictionary of National Biography*.

40. One such is Eleanor Jackson, Newbigin's (forthcoming) biographer, who has made a similar observation—"I was reading these 'talks' to students in Kerala last night. I think it is very hard to decide what is a sermon and what is a talk because they read more like extended sermons" (email to author 21 March 2006).

41. This is particularly so for the 1950s.

42. His links with HTB, a Church of England parish church in London and the home of the Alpha Course, is well-known. His friend and colleague, Dan Beeby, reckoned that Newbigin was willing to become involved partly in order to inject some good strong theology into the charismatic ethos of the church, so that it would be kept "on the right lines" (interview with author, 5 December 2003).

43. Two collections of the School of Theology talks were published in 2003 as Newbigin, *Discovering Truth*, and *Living Hope*. A combined volume (*Faith in a Changing World*, edited and introduced by Paul Weston) was published in 2012 (see bibliography).

talks given at a (URC) Group for Evangelism and Renewal Conference (GEAR)[44] which took place in Swanwick, Derbyshire, in 1986. Five further tapes of sermons, or full services including sermon, are in the William Smith Morton Library of Union Theological Seminary & Presbyterian School of Christian Education, Richmond, Virginia, USA.[45] These are from such diverse occasions as a CBS "Church of the Air" broadcast and a service at Seabury-Western Theological Seminary, Evanston, Illinois.[46] A script of a sermon delivered at the formation of the United Church of Christ, in USA, is also extant.[47]

Looking at the entire range of extant sermons, covering a period of about forty years, one might expect that large tracts of Bible territory would be traversed in the texts and themes dealt with. This is indeed the case, and there is an unsurprising weighting in favor of the New Testament as against the Old Testament.[48] However, over half of the books of the Old Testament and just a third of the New Testament books do not feature in the overall tally of sermon texts at all. Of the New Testament books that are used for sermon texts, the Fourth Gospel far outstrips any

44. Of which Malcolm Hanson has written as follows: "As founding chairman of GEAR I always maintained as a principle that no one could join GEAR. It was simply an informal group of people seeking to stimulate evangelism and renewal within the URC and to serve the whole church, and that to have our own membership would be (a) divisive—our commitment was to Christ, the church and the URC in particular—and (b) it might exclude from our activities and influence some who would not want to identify too closely with us. Despite this, some people, including . . . Lesslie, would sometimes say they did belong to GEAR, which was a great encouragement to us, even if not strictly accurate. However, at a later point, and against my better judgment (!), the committee decided to invite people to join GEAR so that they might show their commitment through membership. I have always refused to take that step, and one of the last conversations I had with Lesslie was a few months before his death, when he asked me whether he should become a member. I outlined my own position which he graciously accepted as his own and so did not join, though also continuing to support and value GEAR" (email to author, 18 December 2005).

45. The writer is indebted to the Director of the Instructional Resource Centre, at UTS (Ann Knox), and the Executor of Bishop Newbigin's Literary Estate (his daughter, Mrs Margaret Beetham), for the provision of and permission for copies of these tapes. The tapes of sermons are part of a total holding of nineteen Newbigin cassettes.

46. Two of the sermons in the William Smith Morton Library holding may be the oldest surviving sermons in existence, dating from 1954, and delivered in the Chapel of UTS, Richmond, Virginia, USA.

47. See footnote 31, above.

48. No use appears to be made of the Apocrypha, although lectionaries (which Newbigin liked to follow) usually include certain parts of the Apocrypha.

other book.[49] This is not surprising when we remember that Newbigin devoted many years to the study of John's Gospel and that his only published commentary, "developed over a period of thirty years," was on this book.[50] Chapters 10, 12, 14, and 17 of John are the most frequently used sources of sermon texts, excepting the multiple uses of many sermons.

PREACHING SCRIPTURE: FIRST LOVE

In *Unfinished Agenda*, Newbigin's first reference to preaching is to "open-air preaching" in the course of a Cambridge Evangelistic Campaign to the city of Preston (probably in 1929/30), in which he participated as a student. He says of that experience, "it was an enormously fruitful, if sometimes frightening exercise."[51] His thoughts of possible ordination began not long after this particular preaching experience.[52] References to "preach(ing)," and "sermon(s)" abound throughout the book, mostly to his own preaching, but also to that of others whom he mentions. It is an indication of the importance he attached to preaching that in a book of 260 pages, such references occur on fifty pages.[53] He cannot, it seems, give an account of his life without referring to preaching almost constantly.[54] It was not just that he preached a lot, but that preaching clearly mattered greatly to him. This was evident from the beginning of his ministry as a young missionary in India, where his "street preaching" was a staple diet of the daily menu of work. In the nature of things, preaching of this kind would have been quite informal, normally spontaneous and certainly not rehearsed or over-prepared. Newbigin loved it, and developed great proficiency at it—in due course, in the Tamil language.[55] Looking at sermons

---

49. Almost a third of the overall total is on Johannine texts.

50. Newbigin, *Light Has Come*, x.

51. Newbigin, *Unfinished Agenda*, 12.

52. At an SCM Conference at Swanwick in 1929/30 (his second year at Cambridge University): "While I was praying . . . I suddenly knew that I must offer for ordination" (ibid.,15).

53. Ibid.

54. The longest part of the book without such reference is just twenty-five pages long: this is exceptional. More commonly, these references occur at intervals of four or five pages.

55. Murdoch MacKenzie, who served as a missionary during Newbigin's episcopate in Madras, testifies that, "with people in villages, Lesslie felt very much at home and his sermons whilst biblical were couched in the everyday experiences of village people and laced with humour at which Lesslie was a master in the Tamil language"

which have no specific biblical text as a basis or starting point, but are simply on a theme, it is clear that the central Christian events (the cross and the resurrection) predominated, and that practical Christian living mattered greatly too.[56]

The period when Newbigin had the longest continuous and sustained preaching ministry in one pulpit was the eight and a half years he spent as minister at Winson Green URC Church in Birmingham, England, after his years in India.[57] It is therefore deeply regrettable that it is now no longer possible to add significantly to (or to gainsay) the laudatory verdict of his Indian colleague at Winson Green, the Rev Hakkim Singh Rahi, from the Church of North India. Newbigin, he says, "was gifted to put his ideas across in the layman's tongue . . . he preached profound messages from the Word of God . . . he never read his messages . . . he always looked into the eyes of the people while preaching, which secured full attention from his audience . . . the people were greatly blessed."[58]

Such a testimony to the appropriateness of Newbigin's preaching is indicative of his gift for "reading" an audience well,[59] and this gift clearly stood him in good stead throughout his life—in many widely divergent settings as well as in many different pulpits.[60]

Based on the evidence of extant sermons, in both textual and tape recorded format, it would be true to say that they are intellectually well thought-out and usually require careful attention on the part of hearers. Many are quite challenging in the sense that the thought-forms used and the rigorously rational development of arguments forces hearers to concentrate closely throughout. This impression is given added weight by the

---

(email to author, 22 April 2006).

56. There are sermons, for example, on "Christian Aid" and "Money Matters." Much of the correspondence in the archives bears even clearer and fuller witness to his social and political concerns.

57. Described by Newbigin as "much harder than anything I met in India" (*Unfinished Agenda*, 235).

58. Quoted in Wainwright, *Theological Life*, 279.

59. Dan Beeby has also testified to this: "he knew and read an audience well" (interview with author, 5 December 2003).

60. This, however, was not invariably the case. A one-time Oxford University college chaplain recalls an occasion in 1987 when "the sermon was much too long, a closely developed argument which had all the Senior Fellows agitated not about the theme but about their dinner!" (email from the then chaplain to author, 16 March 2005). But, cf. Dan Beeby's opinion, "he never preached for too long and was never boring." Interview as in previous note.

fact that scripts are full texts and not simply outline notes.[61] The frequent editing of these texts, with stylistic and verbal alterations or improvements, indicates a concern for good presentation and striving for accuracy and impact.

Did Newbigin display characteristics in his preaching which might indicate a breadth of style and type? Most sermons display to a greater or lesser extent the features of his preaching which could be said to be characteristic—such that a blind hearer might readily recognize them as authentically Newbigin's sermons. The one clear exception to this is the sermon preached in the chapel of Rugby School,[62] characterized by the staccato style of short sentences, and the use of graphic imagery designed to appeal to a discrete audience and context. This alone is sufficient to indicate that Newbigin's preaching was not altogether stereotyped.

All preachers develop homiletically in a number of ways. Practice and experience normally ensure that early weaknesses are gradually overcome. Maturing knowledge of Scripture, of people and of life increasingly enhances preaching content and skills. Some preachers seek consciously to widen their style and type of preaching, recognizing the need to adapt to changing times. Most, however, recognize that their gifts do not lie in every possible preaching method and settle for their "natural" way. No less than any other part of a service of worship, however, preaching does have to move on in order to maintain relevance and facilitate effective communication. This affects all aspects of what might be called the "superstructure" of preaching. The ship's hull, however, is already solidly built and long since launched in the form of the divinely given revelation in Christ and the scriptures.

Comparison of the "feel" of Newbigin's extant sermons in different periods suggests to the present writer that he remained constantly faithful to the biblical basis of preaching, and also maintained his "superstructure" in good and useful condition. If we did not know the date of a given sermon, it would not necessarily be easy (or even possible) to place it in the correct period simply from reading or hearing it. Things about his preaching that did change were mainly superficial and occasional. He does not appear to have altered his basic design strategy,[63] or to have deviated from

61. Wainwright states that "the briefest hand-written sermon outlines" do exist (Wainwright, *Theological Life,* 279). However, no catalogue references are given and the present writer has found difficulty in locating any in the archives.

62. See Archives, DA29/4/2/12.

63. Even his use of three points, although less obviously made, could still be a feature of some late sermons.

his primarily intellectual style. Many of his illustrations from early periods re-appeared in later periods too.

Was Newbigin a leading preacher, an outstanding preacher, or a giant among preachers? Unquestionably he was a leading preacher (that would be hard to deny), and—on the basis of this study—he would seem to have been outstanding in many respects (perhaps specifically of his type and in his milieu), but probably not as great a giant in his preaching as in his other activities.

However, in an address at Newbigin's funeral service, at Dulwich Grove URC Church, London, on 7 February 1998, Dan Beeby truthfully described him as "a world-famous preacher," averred that he would always prefer to preach than to occupy a bureaucrat's desk, and added—most tellingly of the man—"when he dropped a name, it was always the name of Jesus."[64]

BIBLIOGRAPHY

Archives

The Papers of Lesslie Newbigin (DA29). Special Collections, Main Library, University of Birmingham, Edgbaston, Birmingham B15 2TT, UK. Catalogued at: http://www.special-coll.bham.ac.uk/index.shtml.

Books and Articles

The Church of Scotland Ordinal and Service Book for use in Courts of the Church Prepared by the General Assembly's Committee on Public Worship and Aids to Devotion. Edinburgh and Glasgow: The Church of Scotland Committee on Publications, 1931.

Conway, Martin., "Lesslie Newbigin." In *Oxford Dictionary of National Biography*, edited by Henry Matthew & Brian Harrison, 40:577–9. Oxford: OUP, 2004.

Lindbeck, George A. *The Nature of Doctrine: Religion and Theology in a Postliberal Age*. Louisville: Westminster John Knox, 1984.

Newbigin, Lesslie. *Discovering Truth in a Changing World*, London: Alpha International, Holy Trinity Brompton, 2003.

———. *Faith in a Changing World*, edited and introduced by Paul Weston. London: St Paul's Theological Centre, 2012.

———. *Foolishness to the Greeks*. London: SPCK, 1986.

———. *The Light Has Come: An Exposition of the Fourth Gospel*. Grand Rapids: Eerdmans, 1982.

64. The writer is indebted to the late Rev Dr Arthur MacArthur for a copy of the address.

————. *Living Hope in a Changing World* London: Alpha International, Holy Trinity Brompton, 2003.

————. *Proper Confidence: Faith, Doubt, and Certainty in Christian Discipleship.* Grand Rapids: Eerdmans, 1995.

————. *Truth and Authority in Modernity.* Valley Forge, VA: Trinity Press International, 1996.

————. *Unfinished Agenda, An Updated Autobiography.* Edinburgh: Saint Andrew, 1985, Updated 1993.

————. *A Word in Season.* Edinburgh: Saint Andrew, 1994.

Stott, John R.W. *The Living Church: Convictions of a Lifelong Pastor.* Nottingham: Inter-Varsity, 2007.

Visser 't Hooft, Willem A. "Foreword." In *The Preacher's Calling to be Servant,* by D.T. Niles. London: Lutterworth, 1959.

Wainwright, Geoffrey. *Lesslie Newbigin: A Theological Life.* Oxford: OUP, 2000.

Weston, Paul, editor. *Lesslie Newbigin: Missionary Theologian—A Reader.* London: SPCK, 2006.

Wright, Stephen. "The Bible as Sacrament." *Anvil* 19/2 (2002) 81–87.

"And the Truth Shall Set You Free"

Lesslie Newbigin's Understanding of "Truth" as Illustrated by His Life and Work

Eleanor Jackson

INTRODUCTION

T HE QUESTION OF NEWBIGIN's understanding of "truth" can be considered in two ways. First, there is his contemplation of the objective question of what "truth" is. Newbigin did not consider it a topic for abstract philosophical debate, nor as a lofty principle in Christian ethics to which one might aspire as an unattainable standard in human life, nor as an impersonal transcendent force as Gandhi did.[1] Rather, it was the dynamic personal force embodied in Jesus Christ as found in the Fourth Gospel. His concept of truth is the key to his theology of mission, to his approach to dialogue with other faiths, and to his critique of post-modern society. Secondly, subjectively, there is the influence on his personality and conduct. I shall never forget seeing a long shadow cross his face as though he was in acute physical pain when he realized someone had lied to him, and his letters display his anguish as Bishop in Madurai-Ramnad when he had to deal with a corrupt bursar of a Christian college who was massaging the accounts to the benefit of her caste folk.[2] Nevertheless Newbigin himself was adept at "spin," for example, concealing in his autobiography

---

1. Significantly, Gandhi's autobiography (1927) was entitled *An Autobiography or the Story of My Experiments With Truth*.

2. On caste conflicts in the church generally: see Birmingham University Library (BUL), DA29/1/2/68.

the true facts about the way he was badly swindled by the sculptor of the statues of Christian Tamil scholars displayed on the marina in Madras.[3]

Given his parents' Presbyterian integrity and his childhood upbringing, the impact of his Quaker schooling and his encounter with the Moral Re-armament (or Oxford Movement), it is important to understand the roots of this ambiguity and examine the interaction between his personal convictions and his intellectual reasoning on the subject. The sources for this chapter will be limited to his private letters, especially those to his younger sister Frances, interviews with his friends and colleagues and his writings—particularly his study of the Fourth Gospel, *The Light has Come*. This is because it was so important to him that faith, ethics, and theology be biblically grounded and all things cohere in Christ.

NEWBIGIN'S UNDERSTANDING OF TRUTH AND ITS ROLE IN HIS THEOLOGY OF MISSION

In my forthcoming biography of Lesslie Newbigin, *Walking in the Light*, I argue that Newbigin's approach has much in common with the liberation theology he criticized so much.[4] It was profoundly contextual, developed in response to a particular need and engaged with the situation which produced that need, whether pastoral or apologetic. Theological reflection followed his experiences, although that does not mean that he did not also act out of given principles derived from Christian revelation.[5] Consequently, he accepted "truth" as a working concept, and did not defend his definition of it until the 1980s when the different strands of his thought become woven together. For example:

> We need cross-cultural missions to bear witness to that which
> is beyond every national and local culture, the story which is
> the real story of the human race in God's purpose. We bear
> witness to it because we believe that it is not just a symbolic
> way of expressing our values but the truth about human nature

3. Newbigin, *Unfinished Agenda*, 206–7; interviews with Bishop Sundar Clarke 14/9/01 and Revd Dr Noel Jason 22/3/06; letters to Frances Newbigin dated 4/11/73 on costs reaching Rs 45,000/- (DA29/1/10/29 and 13/3/74 on police intervention, DA29/1/10/16).

4. Due to be completed in 2012.

5. This can be demonstrated by comparing the lectures he gave to students at the Christian Medical College, Vellore, S India in 1971, published as *Journey into Joy*, and lectures given at Holy Trinity Church, Brompton in 1994–5 (Newbigin, *Discovering the Truth*).

and destiny . . . we proclaim it as public truth in the sense that it is the truth by which all other claims to truth will finally be judged . . . We are witnesses—witnesses not of our religious experiences but of Jesus, his incarnation, ministry, death and resurrection. We cannot keep silent about this, because it is the truth that concerns every human being. It is the truth about the human story. And so it must be told to every human being. That obligation remains until the end of time.[6]

This 1987 quotation demonstrates very precisely not only how the concept of truth provides the missionary imperative for Newbigin, but also how it is personalized by him as the life, death, and resurrection of Jesus, and drives everything else. When he was a young SCM graduate staff member Newbigin began, it seems, by internalizing what Archbishop William Temple wrote in the "Statement" adopted by the International Missionary Council Meeting in Jerusalem in 1928: "Our Message is Jesus Christ. Either it is true for all, or it is not true at all."[7] He made this the cornerstone of his appeal and his missiology in later years. In one of the closing speeches at the SCM's 1933 Edinburgh Quadrennial conference, for example, as one of the newest volunteers for lifelong missionary service, he declared: "But this, too, must be said, that what matters is the truth or otherwise of that revelation, and that if it is true, it is true for all men and cannot be kept for one nation or one community."[8] His speech is remarkable for anticipating other key themes of his, for example: the "privatization of Christian faith" and "western individualism" (here denounced in terms of a warning to students against "smacking their lips at the private enjoyment of an intellectual satisfaction"). He also rejects what is now called "religious pluralism" just as firmly as he was to do in the 1980s and 1990s, not because the world religions are false or lacking in common values but because what matters is the truth behind religious practice, and for him that can only be Christ. Faith is a matter of life and death, of confronting the reality of the universe, rather than intellectual persuasion or the pursuit of an interesting hobby. Hence the equation of truth with Christ which underlies his thought.

6. "Mission in the World Today" an address given to New College Missionary Society, New College, Edinburgh, 12th November 1987, in Newbigin, *Word in Season*, 130–31.

7. See Paton, *Christian Message*, 483. Temple reconciled conflicting theologies among IMC members with the statement (Iremonger, *William Temple*, 396).

8. Newbigin, "Student Volunteer," 102.

Newbigin elaborates this point in a discussion paper he wrote in 1961[9] and which evolved into the work he published as *The Relevance of Trinitarian Doctrine for Today's Mission.* The desire to help those in need should not be confused with the requirement to go and make disciples of all nations: "The issue, in fact, is one of truth. Are the churches acting as though they were persuaded that Jesus Christ is the final and determinative truth for every man and for all mankind, so that for every human being and for every nation the most important question of all is: 'What is your relation to Jesus Christ?'" There could hardly be a clearer statement of the centrality of Christ to Newbigin's theology of mission as he goes on to suggest that a failure of belief is as much responsible for the decline in commitment as the changing global situation.[10] The truth, however, is not a matter of private conviction for one's "private life," but is the means of relating Christ's sovereignty to secular world history.[11]

In *The Open Secret* Newbigin reverts to the theme that there is no human salvation except in relatedness.[12] Salvation is the consequence of shared activity, not individual enlightenment as in Hindu Vedanta.[13] So it is not a question of communicating with each individual soul but of a collective effort because of mutual responsibilities. If this is so, then "salvation must be an action that binds us together and restores for us the true mutual relation to each other and the true shared relation to the world of nature."[14] The Gospel will not be revealed in a blinding flash of light coming to each individual Christian but through individual Christians talking to and helping their neighbors. They will not do this of their own volition but because they are sent with the blessing (Rom 10:14). Here his concept of truth has been recast in terms of the integrity of human relationships.

---

9. Newbigin, "First Tentative Draft." It was a sequel to his 1958 study, *One Body, One Gospel, One World* and translated into several languages. Geoffrey Wainwright in *Lesslie Newbigin: A Theological Life* developed the methodology of analysing Newbigin's thought by taking "early," "middle," and "late" period writings on each topic he studies, which I am adopting here.

10. "First Tentative Draft", 10.

11. Orchard, *Witness in Six Continents,* 174.

12. Newbigin, *Open Secret,* 70. He sees John 17:20–23 as a paradigm of this.

13. The Vedantic schools of philosophy, which are based on the later sacred scriptures, presuppose an experience of enlightenment similar to the better known experience of the Buddha. Flood, *Introduction to Hinduism,* 229, 238f.; Brockington, *Sacred Thread,* 29–50.

14. Newbigin, *Open Secret,* 70.

The Truth in Christ and Inter-religious Dialogue

It is due to the value he sets on this integrity, that he arrived at his final position on inter-faith dialogue, which is very different from the "exclusivist" position which is usually attributed to him.[15] In this he was influenced not only by his experience as a young missionary of studying the Hindu scriptures and the Fourth Gospel with the members of the Ramakrishna Mission ashram in Kanchipuram but by his friendship over four decades with Chaturvedi Badrinath ICS, a senior Indian civil servant.[16] Badrinath is the proof of his assertion that, "It is possible to have a firm belief in the uniqueness and finality of Jesus and *on the basis of that belief* to have respectful and loving relationships with people of other faiths."[17] Admittedly, his purposes are evangelical and pastoral in every inter-faith encounter, but that is no different from the position of a sincere Muslim or any dialogue partner whose faith permits conversion.[18] Newbigin's approach is personal, though he may conceive of another faith as a social and intellectual system as well. He believed that dialogue was about co-operation at a personal level, as when he worked with Muslims on the City of Birmingham Education Department's SACRE committee to revise the authority's RE syllabus.[19] The benefits of this approach in terms of inter-personal and

15. Race, *Christians and Religious Pluralism*, 7 and D'Costa, *Theology and Pluralism*, 10. Owen C. Thomas was probably the first to attempt this kind of classification in *Attitudes towards Other Religions*. A radical critique of it is provided in Perry, *Radical Difference*.

16. Badrinath was Deputy Governor of Madras, and they got to know each other when both were official guests sat, garlanded, on platforms at interminable functions. "Badri," as he always called him, was deeply read in Sanskrit scriptures and had his own idiosyncratic interpretation as a result of having gained a very deep and critical understanding of western philosophical traditions. After Newbigin left India and Badrinath was demoted for failing to show Mrs Gandhi sufficient deference, he wrote a massive tome which he dedicated to Lesslie in gratitude for their friendship. See his *Dharma, India and World Order* with a foreword by Newbigin; also the extract reproduced in *Finding Jesus in Dharma* in which Newbigin's influence is praised .

17. He goes on to say how honoured he is that his friend has dedicated "a big book" to him, and that he is to write the foreword (Letter, DA29/2/3/27).

18. Newbigin insists, though, that he argued his case on the basis of the Bible, not the principles of the western Enlightenment. He points out that Hindus are just as intolerant, in a different way, in that "It is the essence of the Hindu attitude that it claims to know the truth of which all existing religions are but distortions and retractions" ("Quest for Unity," 19).

19. Newbigin, *Unfinished Agenda*, 231. He had much sympathy for Muslim parents who objected to Birmingham's secular approach ("Muslims, Christians and Public Doctrine," 1).

inter-societal relationships in a modern multi-faith society should be obvious but it only works when those involved are open to change, and are prepared to take the risk that they may be wrong, which Newbigin himself admits. Indeed in 1975 he declared, "One has not really heard the message of one of the great religions that have moved millions of people for centuries if one has not been really moved by it, if one has not felt in one's own soul the power of it." [20]

Nevertheless, he did not like the concept of "dialogue" in twentieth century Britain. Newbigin's concept of dialogue itself was constricted by his concept of truth, and by a negative assessment of Greek philosophy, as this passage demonstrates:

> The concept of dialogue . . . is rooted in the Greek elements of our culture. Here ultimate truth is sought in the realm of ideas, of eternal truths transcending the accidental happenings of history. Dialogue in this sense seeks an ultimate agreement about what must be true for all people through probing, testing, enlarging, and correcting the insights of the participants in an exchange of wisdom. But in the Biblical parts of our cultural inheritance, ultimate truth is found not in time-transcending ideas (Plato) or forms (Aristotle) but in particular events in recorded history. Dialogue cannot discover these events. They have to be reported. Someone who knows the facts has to report them to those who do not. This is the starting point of a dialogue, not its product.[21]

These "particular events"—as he saw them—were God's intervention in history, real events in people's lives, which caused them to engage in salvation. Newbigin came to the conclusion that, "The sphere of religion is a battlefield for the demonic [because] . . . religion is the sphere in which a person surrenders himself to something greater than himself." This includes Christianity.[22] He justifies this position from his exegesis of the Fourth Gospel, but of course one can hear the voice of his friend Hendrik Kraemer in the background.[23] Newbigin did not see himself as a superior

20. Newbigin, "Basis," 267–68. Sentence repeated in *Open Secret*, 184.

21. Newbigin, *Gospel in Today's Global City*, 6. This was why he appreciated Justin Martyr's work, *Dialogue with Trypho the Jew*.

22. Newbigin, "Basis," 253. The idea is expanded in *Open Secret*, chapter 8 but by the 1990s he had decided religion was *a* sphere, not *the* sphere because such an encounter could take place outside.

23. ". . . where we are told that Jesus is the light that shines on every human being, and that this light shines in the darkness, it is made clear in the story that it is religion

sort of human being because of his knowledge of the truth in Christ, but rather as a sinner saved by grace, whose sins included his share of the collective responsibility for a racist approach to those of other faiths.[24] Rather, he took the story of Cornelius and Peter as a paradigm for dialogue in that Cornelius was led by a vision to seek Peter out, and was converted, but Peter had to change his understanding of the truth in Christ radically and accept gentiles into the church (Acts 10).

So when he became minister of the URC Church in Winson Green, Birmingham, he rejected suggestions that he should confine inner city evangelism to "Anglo-Saxons" and engage people of other faiths in "dialogue." He asserts:

> The sharing of the good news takes place in the context of a shared human life, and that means in part the context of shared conversation. In such conversation we talk about real things, and we try both to communicate what we know and to learn what we do not know. The sharing of the good news about the kingdom is part of that conversation and cannot happen without it. But why do we have to substitute the high-sounding word "dialogue" at this point? Is it because we fail in the simple business of ordinary human conversation? I confess that in the Winson Green neighborhood we have not established any "dialogue" between representatives of the different faiths, but we do have quite a lot of conversation. It is the kind of conversation that is not an alternative to but the occasion for sharing our hope. And it leads some people to ask the sort of questions that lead further.[25]

---

which is the area of darkness and that it is the common people, unversed in religion, who respond to the light." (Statement prepared for the URC General Assembly in 1988 entitled *A Theological Perspective on Inter-Faith Dialogue*). Hendrik Kraemer (1888–1965) was the controversial author of *The Christian Message in a non-Christian World*. He derived from Karl Barth the idea that religion is a sinful barrier constructed by humans as a shield between them and God.

24. When the church adopted a position of superiority, it was false to its "title deeds" (Newbigin: "Religion for the Marketplace," 145–6). See letter dated 21/4/92 to "Tom" (DA29/2/3/27).

25. Newbigin, "Evangelism in the City." Reproduced in Newbigin, *Word in Season*, 46–47.

A Theological Approach to Truth

We turn now to consider the concept of truth in Newbigin's more theological later writings. This is because in earlier works he does not consider the question in any degree of depth, and it would seem that it was only when confronted with the collapse of confidence in overseas missions among Western church congregations on the one hand, and assailed by the claims of post-modernism on the other that he rectified this. He was much troubled by the currents stirred up by the publication of J.A.T Robinson's *Honest to God* in 1963, which popularized theological discussion of the question of the existence of God, and he responded with two popular paperbacks of his own: *Honest Religion for Secular Man* (1966) and *Christ our Eternal Contemporary* (1968). But these are basically "in-house" attempts to restate Christian faith in modern, reasonable terms, as William Temple had done for Newbigin's generation of students.

Rather, in the 1950s and 1960s he was concerned with integrating his theology of mission with his understanding of the Trinity, which is how— almost by accident— he produced ground-breaking ideas on the work of the Spirit, thereby anticipating the arrival of the Pentecostal churches in the ecumenical movement. Only when he published his Selly Oak Colleges lectures, as *The Open Secret* in 1978, just when the "The Myth of God Incarnate" debates were at their height, does he change his agenda.[26] Nevertheless, this sequence re-enforced his concern with *who* the Truth is, rather than *what* it is. He had by then digested the work that was the biggest single influence on him, namely *Personal Knowledge*, published in 1958 by the scientist turned philosopher, Michael Polanyi. Its principal appeal would seem to be that Polanyi, like Newbigin himself, was concerned that "truth" must be fact based on verification as far as is humanly possible, just as scientific theories must be, but nevertheless that the knower is psychologically involved with what is known, and that therefore the "objectivity" of the scientist is a myth.[27] Newbigin also accepted that the philosophy underlying modern western science was culturally conditioned, just as theology is. The post-modern assertion that all truths are relative

26. Newbigin, *Open Secret*. The "Myth of God Incarnate" debate was triggered by the publication of the same name (SCM 1977) in which John Hick, Michael Goulder and others debated the incarnation. (Cf. Newbigin's later contribution to the debate: "Centrality of Christ for History.")

27. He could never accept the Hindu viewpoint that it did not ultimately matter whether Krishna was Arjuna's charioteer in a specific historical battle, as his teaching in the *Bhagavadgita* is eternally true.

and dependent on a person's subjective evaluation in order to be perceived as true is itself the product of a "subjective" value judgment. In his search for an effective epistemology, Newbigin writes, "What is at stake is the meaning of 'knowing.' It is a question of the way in which humans are enabled to come to a true understanding of and a practical relation to the realities within which life is set."[28] He wants to see the church and other parties engage in a dialogue as to what this might be.

In connection with this, Newbigin constantly wrestled with the question, "By what authority?" not only to validate his own vocation but also to vindicate the church's witness to Christ. If truth is a matter of individual subjective perception, and not even a matter for community consensus, then the search for the meaning of life is futile because the answer cannot be verified. But if truth can be realized through the Christian scriptures, and interpreted through received doctrine, then the situation is altogether different.[29] Newbigin is scathing about the reductionism of "historical-textual criticism," though it has its place as a tool to understand the communities which produced the scriptures. For him the truth emerges through "faith seeking understanding," as Augustine and then Anselm had envisaged it. As a result, Newbigin calls for a "genuinely missionary encounter between a scriptural faith and modern culture."[30]

If truth can only be defined by personal experience and one's own interpretation of it, then it is impossible to establish what is objectively true, or to evaluate one form of truth as being better or worse than another. It becomes a matter of private conviction, not public witness and contrary to what was required of Jesus' disciples in apostolic times. The message as well as the messengers are then marginalized and have no impact on standards in public life or the transformation of society. Newbigin finds it perverse that modern society finds doubt a more credible option than faith, and clearly thinks that church and state in western Europe have "lost the plot" by downgrading their Christian heritage in the name of reason and religious tolerance. Not that he finds so-called "fundamentalism" any more meritorious than the liberals who are at least trying to engage with contemporary ideas even if the sacrifice of core principles is too much. Although not overtly "Barthian" in his position, and given to quoting Dietrich Bonhoeffer rather than Barth, there is a "given" element to his

28. Newbigin, *Other Side of 1984*, 30.

29. The issue of the authority of biblical revelation is most thoroughly discussed in Newbigin, *Gospel in a Pluralist Society*, e.g., 39–51; also *Proper Confidence*, e.g., 79–92.

30. That is, an attempt to interpret what God has done in history in the challenges of modern society (Newbigin, *Other Side of 1984*, 49).

thought, in the form of his acceptance of revelation through Scripture and his insistence that truth, to be the truth, must be universal and lead to further insights, not to a dogmatic dead end.

As is well-known, Newbigin traces the problem to John Locke and René Descartes, though he can appreciate what they were trying to do in the context of the seventeenth century scientific revolution when the post-Reformation wars of religion left educated people disillusioned with the established churches. He sees parallels between the intellectual confidence of the 18th century and the present day.[31] He speculates on what would have happened if Descartes had proved his existence to himself not with "I think, therefore I am," but "I love, therefore I am." At root the problem is that since the fracturing of Christendom (to which, he insists, he has no desire to return), there has been a dichotomy between the so-called fact based, material world, and anything relating to the spiritual dimension.[32] For Newbigin truth must be all-embracing, just as Christ relates to all things, or it is an illusion, and he attempts to map out how this might be understood: "The truth is not imposed upon us, for indeed truth has not done its work unless and until we have learned to honor and love it from our hearts as truth. But we do not reach truth unless we allow ourselves to be exposed to and drawn by a truth which is beyond our present understanding." This is what Jesus is teaching his disciples (John 15:15) and is the essence not only of scriptural authority but our approach to life.[33]

Influences and Experiences Which Shaped His Understanding of Truth

To understand how Newbigin arrived at these positions, it is necessary to examine the experiences which made him who he was.

It is clear from his autobiography, *Unfinished Agenda*, that Newbigin was profoundly influenced by his parents, especially his father, who was a deacon at Jesmond Presbyterian Church, Newcastle from 1910–1940, and by his education at the Quaker public school, Leighton Park School, Reading. The importance of this should not be under-estimated even though he only devoted ten pages in his autobiography to his childhood, education, family background, and life in general before his conversion.[34] He was,

31. Newbigin, *Truth to Tell*, 21.
32. Ibid., 42f.; *Proper Confidence*, 35f.
33. Newbigin, *Proper Confidence*, 90.
34. Newbigin, *Unfinished Agenda*, 1–10. Perhaps this is because compared with his

he says, almost always very happy. He had the gift of making friends easily, which assuaged the desperate homesickness he felt in his first year at Leighton Park, aged thirteen, and where—being small for his age, he was bullied. He was hopeless at team sports in an era when athletic prowess counted more than academic success, but socially it was different. About a third of the boys came from the great Quaker business dynasties and were expected to go into their fathers' companies, as he was. His father also tried to manage his business by Christian principles, and "his word was his bond."[35] There is an exchange of letters between his father and the headmaster as evidence of the one time he got into real trouble, for smoking. He was made to promise not to smoke again while he was still growing, and as far as I can tell, he never did smoke again.[36] Quaker education eschewed the rote learning so common in the 1920s in favor of encouraging the pupils to explore subjects and think for themselves. Newbigin flourished under the influence of "Bill" Brown, the outstanding geography teacher, and an atheist.[37]

The Quaker tradition of worship did not appeal to him, especially on Sundays after a wet and cold march in a crocodile formation to the Meeting House in Reading, but he did imbibe Quaker values of integrity, self-discipline, and social service because the school scout troop was a joint venture with boys coming from the poorest local families, and summer camps were also held for them. The forces of evil were seen by Newbigin and his father to be cut-throat capitalism, exploitation of the workers and militarism but the faith he had that these sins could be overcome was that of humanist belief in progress and moral integrity. He was also a pacifist, his father having deliberately sent him to a school which, unusually in the 1920s, did not have an "Officer Training Corps."[38]

Newbigin's conversion, the turning point in his life, could be portrayed as a quest for truth, or at least for a rational answer to the meaning

---

life after his conversion those years seemed dull and insignificant.

35. See e.g., ibid., 7. In 1932 as Inter-Collegiate SCM Secretary he got his father to address students in Edinburgh on the subject of business ethics.

36. Letters in Leighton Park School archive, kindly shown to the author by the archivist, Tim Newell Price. It was typical of the school that when Duncan Wood got into serious trouble, he was made a prefect to deter him from offending again (Interview, 13/10/ 2005).

37. There was a great mutual affection and respect between them, as is evidenced from occasional letters inviting Newbigin to preach when he was on furlough and so on (e.g., DA29/1/2/247).

38. Newbigin, *Unfinished Agenda*, 6–7.

of life. There is an element of this in the emphasis he places on books which made him re-think his position as he left school.[39] Significantly, when he arrived at Queens' College, Cambridge, he was befriended by members of the Student Christian Movement (an inter-denominational and very open fellowship), and warmed to their rather untidy questioning faith, rather than to the Cambridge Inter-Collegiate Christian Union's evangelical fervor.[40] The fun-loving but prayerful Christians he met convinced him to keep on seeking, and he began studying the Bible and praying himself. What finally brought him to Christ after nearly two years of SCM friendship, attending choral Evensong in Queens' College chapel, and helping at the boys' club run by the Cambridge Society of Friends, was not a stereotypical sudden conviction of sin, a loathing for a "decadent" and "frivolous" life, bereavement, or heartbreak in a romantic relationship. It was a crushing sense of his own personal inadequacy and the lack of answers for a whole generation of working men now enduring crippling poverty as a result of the Depression.

Newbigin and another "old Leightonian," Jim Cottle, had volunteered to spend the summer vacation helping at a Men's Recreation Club, in Trealaw, South Wales. For the final week of their stay it was decided to take about sixty men camping by the sea at Llantwit Major. One night things got out of hand because the men managed to bring enough alcohol back to the camp for a number to get roaring drunk. Fights broke out. The students had absolutely no idea how to cope with the situation. Eventually the noise subsided and Newbigin slunk to his tent, overwhelmed with a sense of his own inadequacy. What happened next he describes as follows:

> As I lay awake a vision came to my mind, perhaps arising from something I had read a few weeks before by William Temple. It was a vision of the cross, but it was the cross spanning the space between heaven and earth, between ideals and present realities, and with arms that embraced the whole world. I saw it as something which reached down to the most hopeless and sordid of human misery and yet promised life and victory. I was sure that night, in a way I had never been before, that this was the clue that I must follow if I were to make any kind of sense

39. One was William James' essay, *The Will to Believe* and the other was an exposition of Christian faith by the popular Presbyterian preacher, Herbert Gray (Newbigin, *Unfinished Agenda*, 6).

40. The Student Christian Movement was formed in 1903 from the earlier British Colleges Christian Union, itself formed to support the Student Volunteer Movement Union. See Jackson, *Red Tape and the Gospel*, 31–36.

of the world. From that moment I would always know how to take bearings when I was lost. I would know where to begin again when I had come to the end of all my own resources of understanding or courage.[41]

The Cross became his touchstone, a certainty which would always be there in his thoughts and prayers, and thus the symbol of truth in practical terms, by which he would be led into all truth. Although Newbigin was now convinced that in it there was life and hope, he does not seem to have been overwhelmed by a sense of the love of Christ for him personally—as many converts do—but to have grown into such a relationship of love. It is probably not a co-incidence that William Temple, whom he would get to know because he was involved in the SCM until his tragically premature death in 1944, now influenced him so much. Temple never suffered a moment's doubt in God his whole life, even though when as a young philosophy don, he had problems with the doctrine of the Virgin Birth.[42] Rather, he just grew in grace in a Johannine conversion, and but for this passage in his autobiography, it is tempting to see the same in Newbigin because it cannot be said that conversion immediately produced in him a radical change of lifestyle or character. However, if his was not a classic evangelical conversion, there are classic elements: the so-called "push factor"—his sensitivity to the misery of unemployment, a crisis—the camp fights—and a "pull factor"—the fellowship of the SCM and the examples of Christian lives among his new friends.[43] Yet the sense of inadequacy still haunted him, for his autobiography opens with the lines:

It is not finished, Lord.
There is not one thing done;
There is no battle of my life
That I have really won.[44]

It is significant that Newbigin's path to faith came through an ethical issue, the challenge of unemployment, and the misery that economic depression had created in the traditional Welsh mining communities. In 1969 he was to define conversion as follows: "Conversion to Christ, properly understood, is such a turning round that, in the fellowship of those

41. Newbigin, *Unfinished Agenda*, 11–12.

42. This comment was made to me by David Paton, because his father was often compared with his friend William Temple.

43. Wingate, *Church and Conversion*, 245–7, 258.

44. The opening lines of "It Is Not Finished" by G. A. Studdert Kennedy.

similarly committed, one is enabled to act in history in a way that bears witness to and carries forward God's real purpose for the creation."[45]

Though conversion does lead to "the deepest kind of personal cleansing, forgiveness, reconciliation and renewal," and involves "the replacement of alienation by a loving personal relationship, constantly renewed, between the self and the source of its being,"[46] for Newbigin it is not a question of "being saved" (or not), but of whether one becomes committed to doing the will of God in the world. It is a process which does not take part in isolation, but in relation to the work of the church in the world. It gives one a foretaste of the Kingdom of God. The young Newbigin's belief in the gradual transformation of society by all working together for good became over time transformed into a conviction that conversion had an eschatological dimension and that it was not an individualistic affair, but participation in God's purpose in the church and the world. So redemption is not a question of individual pre-destined human souls being selected for salvation, but the corporate redemption of humankind through Christ, as outlined in Romans chapter 8.

This understanding of the process of salvation was re-iterated in a series of Bible Studies he conducted on Paul's Letter to the Galatians in 1969. Discussing Paul's experience on the road to Damascus (Gal 1:13–17) he declares that:

> of course it was a conversion, but we misunderstand conversion if we think of it as "being saved." Paul never speaks of what happened to him that day as his "being saved." Paul is sure that he will be saved on the last day, but his conversion was not a matter of his own salvation, it was his commissioning for service. And that is the truth of all real conversion. Conversion is for action. It is being turned around from trying to find our own salvation to serving God's saving purpose for the world.[47]

The challenge of Moral Rearmament and "absolute truth"

At a time when America and Europe were convulsed by the economic collapse known as "the Great Depression," debate on international affairs centered on military re-armament as a means of resisting fascism and

45. Newbigin, *Finality of Christ,* 110–11.

46. Ibid., 111–12.

47. Newbigin, *Set Free to be a Servant,* 14.

communism. As Germany was believed to be re-arming in defiance of international treaties, reviving the specter of another terrifying world war, the Moral Rearmament movement, under its charismatic leader Frank Buchman, erupted and targeted British universities. Originally called "The First Century Christian Fellowship," and then "The Oxford Group Movement," it harnessed the idealism of young people in particular with demands for total commitment to a simple evangelical faith and lifestyle supported by membership of local non-denominational prayer groups.[48] Society could be changed and the church revived through the personal transformation of individuals inspired by absolute principles of love and truth. Friendships must be true, and those one disliked "forgiven." Taking Jesus' commands literally in this way was symptomatic of the Group approach, and is reflected in the way Lesslie took in a down-and-out tramp, shared his lodgings with him and helped him until his death many years later.[49] Mary MacDonald Smith, Helen and Lesslie Newbigin's life long friend, is convinced both were members and much influenced. However, Newbigin himself writes: "I think most of us in the SCM were both disturbed and attracted by 'the Groups,' as they were called, and I had many occasions then and in later years to be grateful for their witness. But I could not accept their view of Christian faith and life as adequate and I never committed myself to them."[50]

With his many interests—mountaineering, music, local history, helping at boys' camps, debating society and the SCM—Newbigin never lacked for friends at university, but the Oxford Groups' warmth and focus on personal spiritual development and improving one's personal relationships would have appealed. The hot-headed student who got involved, with the Cambridge SCM, in a peace demonstration during the Remembrance Day commemoration at the Cenotaph in Cambridge in 1933 also shared their pacifist viewpoint at that time. Newbigin, however, became increasingly dubious about the integrity of the pacifist position as the Spanish Civil War broke out, and his school friend Julian Bell (of the Bloomsbury set) died for his principles there. As war itself approached,

48. See Jarlert, *Oxford Group,* 65 for a discussion of the "utopianism" of the movement which countered that of national socialism and communism. Newbigin accepted an invitation to one of the "house parties" hosted to win those they believed would be influential in society.

49. Newbigin, *Unfinished Agenda* 21

50. Ibid., 13. Contrast Letter to Frances 17/5/42 (DA29/1/2/173) and 13/8/48 (DA29/1/6/61). My uncle, Revd Thomas Harwood, met Lesslie in a Group and is convinced of his membership.

the SCM came increasingly under the influence of Reinhold Niebuhr and Karl Barth, who mediated to students the theological stiffening of purpose they needed while criticizing "The Groups."[51] The question is whether Newbigin distanced himself from the movement because it did not engage his reason as a scientist who must always start with the facts, or whether he felt— as others have done—that there was a fundamental intellectual dishonesty about their position, especially their pacifism.

THE CONVERGENCE OF NEWBIGIN'S LIFE AND THOUGHT

In conclusion, it is to his exposition of John's Gospel (*The Light has Come*) that one must turn to understand the source of Newbigin's beliefs, and their inner coherence. Written shortly after he retired from lecturing at the Selly Oak Colleges, and published in 1982, it is typical of many of his books, being the product of decades of reflection and preaching. Kenneth Gordon points out, in his recent study of Newbigin's sermons, that from the evidence of the extant material, the text he preached on most often was John 14:6, "I am the Way, the Truth and the Life: no-one comes to the Father except by me." He uses the analogy of fell-walking, his favorite "hobby," and the importance of following the path. According to Kenneth Gordon's summary,

> There are often signposts (clues) along the way which are in-tended to keep the walker in the right path to his destination. Newbigin, of course, observes that Jesus is not, in this context, a mere signpost or clue, but is in reality the track along which we are to walk. Thus although we may intellectually interpret life through the cross and resurrection, we are called to live our life in Jesus . . . with the cross and resurrection applied in baptism at the outset and in the eucharist throughout life. In practice this means that we too follow the pattern of our Lord's suffering and resurrection as we live out our eternal life in him.[52]

In *The Light Has Come* Newbigin explains that he sees his task as explaining the word contained in the Gospel in such a way that it provides

---

51. Busch, *Karl Barth*, 276. In 1936 Barth wrote, ". . . if the church does not resist this movement, in the end it will be completely ruined by it."

52. Gordon, "Preaching of Lesslie Newbigin," 38. Sermon archived at DA 29/4/1/8 and used at least twelve times.

a critique of his culture.[53] He is doing this by reading it as a witness to the truth, enabled to do so by the promise of the Spirit that the disciples would be witnesses.[54] Jesus is himself the gospel which is preached and "it is in his name 'that there is life' (John 20:31)."[55] He emphasizes how the Gospel writer wishes to demonstrate what is true and how Jesus is "full of grace and truth." Considering John 5:30–40, he asks how anyone can recognize divine revelation when his or her culturally conditioned intelligence is so limited: "The ultimate answer to the problem can only be given in terms of a trinitarian doctrine of God—of the Father who is the source of all being and of all truth, of the Son by whose perfect obedience the being and truth are present in a human life as part of public history, and of the Spirit of the Father and the Son by whose sovereign and gracious action my reason and conscience are enabled to acknowledge the Son and through him to join in glorifying the Father." [56]

One can also argue that it is through this insight that one can reconcile both the public quest which Newbigin had for truth in his theology, his understanding of mission, and his approach to inter-faith dialogue. He believes that there is liberation through the personal knowledge of Jesus, who is truth and alone can deliver those who are bound by sin. Therefore he could overcome his personal weaknesses and achieve Christ-like integrity.[57] One of the most vivid stories about Newbigin the young missionary came from a Tamil villager who witnessed him losing his temper with a builder who wanted a bribe to complete the work.[58] For Newbigin believed truth should be lived. His life was a continual dialogue with Scripture. He was keenly aware of his flaws, but believed that through life in the community of Christ he could find forgiveness. With regard to Christ's postresurrection disciples he says, "They will also be a learning community, not pretending to possess all the truth, but having the promise that, as they bear witness among all the nations, the Spirit will lead them into all the truth . . . This community is therefore no triumphant company of the

53. Newbigin, *Light Has Come*, ix.

54. John 14:25.

55. Newbigin, *Light Has Come*, 3.

56. Ibid., 69.

57. Ibid., 109.

58. Interviews conducted in Kanchipuram by Revd P. J. Chellappa in August 1996 for the Newbigin biography.

saved surrounded by the multitude of the lost. It is the sign and first fruit of God's purpose to save all." [59]

This seems a good place to end an appreciation not just of what Newbigin did, but who he was to us a hundred years after his birth.

BIBLIOGRAPHY

Archives

The Papers of Lesslie Newbigin (DA29). Special Collections, Main Library, University of Birmingham, Edgbaston, Birmingham B15 2TT, UK. Catalogued at: http://www.special-coll.bham.ac.uk/index.shtml.

Books and Articles

Badrinath, C. *Dharma, India and World Order*. Edinburgh: Saint Andrew, 1993.

———. *Finding Jesus in Dharma: Christianity in India*. Delhi: ISPCK, 2004.

Brockington, J. L. *The Sacred Thread: Hinduism in its Continuity and Diversity*. Edinburgh: Edinburgh University Press, 1996.

Busch, Eberhard. *Karl Barth: His Life from Letters and Autobiographical Texts*. Translated by John Bowden. London: SCM, 1976.

D'Costa, Gavin. *Theology and Religious Pluralism: The Challenge of Other Religions*. Oxford: Blackwell, 1986.

Flood, Gavin. *An Introduction to Hinduism*. Cambridge: Cambridge University Press, 1996.

Gandhi, Mahatma K. *An Autobiography or the Story of My Experiments with Truth*. New Delhi: Penguin, 1927.

Gordon, Kenneth D. "A Critical Examination of the Preaching of Lesslie Newbigin and its Implications for Preachers Today." MTh diss., University of Wales, 2008.

Hick, John, editor. *The Myth of God Incarnate*. London: SCM, 1977.

Iremonger, Frederic A. *William Temple, Archbishop of Canterbury: His Life and Letters*. London: Oxford University Press, 1949.

Jackson, Eleanor M. *Red Tape and the Gospel: A Study of the Significance of the Ecumenical Missionary Struggle of William Paton (1886–1943)*. Birmingham: Phlogiston, 1980.

Jarlert, Anders. *The Oxford Group, Group Revivalism, and the Churches in Northern Europe, 1930–1945: with special reference to Scandinavia and Germany*. Lund: Lund University Press/Chartwell-Bratt, 1995.

Kraemer, Hendrik. *The Christian Message in a Non-Christian World*. London: Edinburgh House, 1938.

Newbigin, Lesslie. "The Basis, Purpose and Manner of Inter Faith Dialogue." *Scottish Journal of Theology* 30 (1977) 253–70.

59. Newbigin, "Christian Faith and the World Religions," 332.

Eleanor Jackson

―――. "The Centrality of Jesus for History." In *Incarnation and Myth: The Debate Continued*, edited by Michael Goulder, 197–210. London: SCM, 1979.

―――. "The Christian Faith and the World Religions." In *Keeping the Faith: Essays to Mark the Centenary of Lux Mundi*, edited by Geoffrey Wainwright, 310–340. London: SPCK, 1988.

―――. *Discovering Truth in a Changing World*. London: Alpha International, 2003.

―――. "Evangelism in the City," *Reformed Review* 41 (Autumn 1987) 3–8.

―――. *The Finality of Christ*. London: SCM, 1969.

―――. "First Tentative Draft of a Paper to Follow the IMC Paper 'One Body, One Gospel, One World.'" Unpublished manuscript, 1961. WCC Archives: Geneva.

―――. *The Gospel in a Pluralist Society*. London: SPCK, 1989.

―――. *The Gospel in Today's Global City*. Selly Oak Colleges Occasional Paper no 16. Birmingham: Selly Oak Colleges, 1997.

―――. *Journey into Joy*. Madras: CLS, 1972.

―――. *The Light has Come: An Exposition of the Fourth Gospel*. Edinburgh: Handsel, 1982.

―――. "Muslims, Christians and Public Doctrine." *The Gospel and Our Culture Newsletter* 6 (1990) 1–2.

―――. *One Body, One Gospel, One World: The Christian Mission Today*. London: International Missionary Council, 1959.

―――. *The Open Secret: An Introduction to the Theology of Mission*. Rev ed. London: SPCK, 1995.

―――. *The Other Side of 1984: Questions for the Churches*. Geneva: WCC, 1983.

―――. *Proper Confidence: Faith, Doubt and Certainty in Christian Discipleship*. London: SPCK; Grand Rapids: Eerdmans, 1995.

―――. "The Quest for Unity through Religion." *Journal of Religion* 35 (January 1955), 17–33.

―――. *The Relevance of Trinitarian Doctrine for Today's Mission*. CWME Study Pamphlets, No.2. London: Edinburgh House, 1963. (Republished as *Trinitarian Doctrine for Today's Mission*, with an introduction by Eleanor Jackson. Carlisle: Paternoster, 1998.)

―――. "Religion for the Marketplace." In *Christian Uniqueness Reconsidered: The Myth of a Pluralistic Theology of Religions*, edited by Gavin D'Costa, 135–48. Maryknoll, NY: Orbis, 1990.

―――. *Set Free to be a Servant: Studies in Paul's Letter to the Galatians*. Madras: CLS, 1969.

―――. "The Student Volunteer Missionary Union." In *The Christian Faith Today*, 94–104. London: SCM, 1933.

―――. *Truth to Tell: The Gospel as Public Truth*. Geneva: WCC, 1991.

―――. *Unfinished Agenda: An Updated Autobiography*. Edinburgh: Saint Andrew, 1993.

―――. *A Word in Season: Perspectives on Christian World Mission*. Grand Rapids: Eerdmans, 1994.

Orchard, Ronald K., editor. *Witness in Six Continents: records of the meeting of the Commission on World Mission and Evangelism of the World Council of Churches held in Mexico City, December 8th to 19th, 1963*. London: Edinburgh House, 1964.

Paton, William, editor. *The Christian Life and Message in Relation to Non-Christian Systems.* Report of the Jerusalem Meeting of the IMC. London: Oxford University Press, 1928.

Perry, Tim S. *Radical Difference: A Defence of Hendrik Kraemer's Theology of Religions.* Editions SR vol.27. Ontario: Wilfred Laurier University Press, 2001.

Polanyi, Michael. *Personal Knowledge: Towards a Post-Critical Philosophy.* Chicago: University of Chicago Press, 1958.

Race, Alan. *Christians and Religious Pluralism: Patterns in the Christian Theology of Religions.* London: SCM, 1993.

Thomas, Owen C. *Attitudes Toward Other Religions: Some Christian Interpretations.* London: SCM, 1969.

Wainwright, Geoffrey. *Lesslie Newbigin: A Theological Life.* Oxford: OUP, 2000.

Wingate, Andrew. *The Church and Conversion: a study of recent conversions to and from Christianity in the Tamil area of South India.* Delhi: ISPCK, 1997.

SECTION TWO

Theology in Western Context

The Church in the Post-Christian Society Between Modernity and Late Modernity

Lesslie Newbigin's Post-Critical Missional Ecclesiology[1]

Veli-Matti Kärkkäinen

INTRODUCTION: SETTING NEWBIGIN IN THE CONTEXT OF POSTMODERNISM

SIMILARLY TO THE BISHOP of Hippo whom he greatly admired, the Bishop of South India felt like he was living in between the times, in a transitional era. Whereas for St. Augustine the transition had to do with the falling apart of the worldwide political empire of Rome, for Newbigin the transformation had to do with the dismantling of the foundations of the worldwide intellectual empire, the Enlightenment. Newbigin often expressed this dynamic and anguish in the words of the Chinese Christian thinker Carver Yu, who claimed that the contemporary culture of the West lives in the dynamic of "technological optimism and literary pessimism."[2] Again, similarly to the early fifth-century critic of Ancient Rome, the late twentieth-century critic of the Modern West, did not live long enough to

---

1. This chapter was originally delivered as two lectures at the Newbigin Centenary gatherings in Birmingham and Edinburgh, UK in 2009 and subsequently published in Kirk, *Mission and Postmodernities*. It is reprinted here with minor revisions by permission of Regnum Books and the editors of the volume.

2. Newbigin, *Gospel in a Pluralist Society*, 232; Newbigin, *Truth to Tell*, 19, 24.

Veli-Matti Kärkkäinen

see what the new empire was that replaced the old one and what the implications of that shift were for the life and mission of *City of God* on earth.

It has been noted recently that it was only during the last decade of his productive life that Newbigin intentionally and explicitly started addressing the challenge of postmodernism. Paul Weston, in his important essay on Newbigin's relation to postmodernism, mentions that all references to that concept occur after 1991 when he was already eighty-two years old.[3] Had he lived longer, Newbigin's engagement with postmodernism would have loomed large in the horizon of his cultural critique. At the same time—and this is the key to my own investigation—as Weston rightly notes, "Newbigin can be shown to have developed a missiological approach that effectively anticipates many of the questions raised by contemporary postmodern perspectives."[4] I attempt to show in this essay that the English bishop's engagement of postmodernism goes way beyond the year 1991. Indeed, I set forth an argument according to which Newbigin's cultural critique of Modernity offers a fruitful and a fresh way of considering the church's relation to the postmodern condition. However, what is ironic about this contribution is that the bishop himself neither attempted a response to postmodernism nor was by and large conscious of it.

Rather than considering Newbigin a "crypto-Postmodernist," I argue that a careful analysis of his writings over a longer period of time reveals that while he saw in some features of postmodernism orientations that helped clarify the critique of Modernity, by and large he was extremely critical of key features of what he thought makes postmodernism. At no point did Newbigin consider the program of postmodernism as a whole an ally to his own pursuit of "the gospel as public truth." I fear that one of the titles the bishop would absolutely eschew having attached to his legacy is "postmodern." The reason for this assessment is simply the fact that, in the bishop's understanding, postmodernism represented to him everything destructive, almost as much as his arch enemy, Modernity.

My approach in this investigation is based on the methodological conviction—or at least, a hypothesis—according to which Newbigin's thinking reveals a remarkable integrity and consistency throughout the period of his mature life, beginning from the late seventies or early eighties, when he began focusing on the critique of the church's mistaken "contextualization" strategy into the Western (European-American) culture. This is not to say that his thinking was systematic or always even tightly

3. Weston, "Postmodern Missiologist?" 229.
4. Ibid., 230.

126

ordered. It was not, he was no scholar but rather a preacher and independent thinker—and he himself was often the first one to acknowledge it.[5] It is simply to say that upon his return from India, in a relatively short period of time the key theses of a missionally driven post-critical thinking emerged. Therefore, methodologically, the best way to determine his relation and contribution to postmodernism is to look broadly at the writings of the whole of his mature career. Indeed, my reading of his writings has assured me, against my own initial suspicions, that his critique—as well as the occasional affirmation—of postmodernism is to a large extent unspoken and tacit in the texture of the cultural critique whose main target was Modernity.[6] Consequently, I fear, those who critique Newbigin for the lack of a nuanced understanding of postmodernism[7] not only miss the point but expect of him something he never set out to do.

One of the reasons why I think along those lines is that, as I will have an opportunity to explain in the following, for Newbigin postmodernism was parasitic on Modernity. Postmodernism in his judgment had no independent existence, it was rather an offshoot from Modernity. He didn't see postmodernism as a "savior" to the church, but rather another challenger along with Modernity—even when occasionally he affirmed some elements of this new epistemological approach.

5. As a preacher rather than an academic scholar, Newbigin often used ideas and movements as heuristic "talking points" and examples rather than as showcases of detailed academic analysis. His writing style was occasional rather than systematic. To take up obvious examples: his tracing of the pre-history and development of Modernity from antiquity (in terms of the two narratives of Christian faith and Hellenistic philosophy) or his treatment and contrasting of Augustine and Aquinas, in its details hardly stands the scrutiny of rigorous academic investigation. Similarly, his preference for "good guys" in history such as Athanasius and Augustine and disdain for "bad guys" such as Aquinas and Descartes reflect much more their role in the unfolding intentionally biased reading of history than anything else. While for the purposes of academic scholarship the acknowledgment of those kinds of biases should not go unnoticed, in my opinion, they should not blur the significance of Newbigin's critique and constructive proposal. In many ways, it can be said that his innovative and bold proposal can stand on its own feet even if it can be shown—unfortunately—that not all the historical and philosophical judgments do.

6. One of the many contributions of Weston's "Postmodern Missiologist?" essay is that it outlines the key aspects of Newbigin's indebtedness to Michael Polanyi, the philosopher of science from whom the bishop borrowed well-known ideas such as "universal intention," testimonies "from within the tradition," and so forth. These are concepts that helped the mature Newbigin to construct his cultural critique and point the way towards his view of "the gospel as public truth."

7. Graham and Walton, "Walk on the Wild Side," 5–7.

My discussion is composed of two main parts. In part one, I will attempt a diagnostic assessment of Newbigin's view of postmodernism. Rather than trying to judge whether Newbigin's vision of postmodernism was correct or even balanced, my task is simply to analyze the bishop's view. Part two then attempts to determine what would be the key aspects of Newbigin's constructive proposal with regard to the church's mission under the postmodern condition. Not surprisingly, in light of my methodological remarks above, I contend that Newbigin's response to postmodernism is not radically different from his response to Modernism. To both Modernists and postmodernists, he offered as an alternative the view of the gospel as public truth.

I repeat myself: My aim is neither to try to make the bishop postmodern nor even try to align his thinking with postmodern orientations. Rather, my ultimate goal is to use his cultural critique of Modernity as a way to help the church in the beginning of the third millennium to reappraise her mission and existence in the world.

Needless to say that all of the essay is necessarily reconstructive from the author's point of view, particularly in view of my stated purpose above: rather than searching for the term *postmodern* in his writings or even trying to determine veiled references to postmodernism, I reconstruct the bishop's viewpoint on the basis of his overall missional thinking and epistemology.[8]

PART 1: NEWBIGIN'S VIEW OF POSTMODERNITY

Rather than first attempting a generic description of postmodernism—if there is such a generic concept about an intellectual movement which intentionally opposes any generalizations—my approach is "from below." What I mean is this: I will do my best to discern from Newbigin's own writings the way he discerned the effects and implications of the transition underway in the cultures of the West as the Enlightenment was slowly giving way to a new way of thinking and being. The term "transition" in the subheading below is intentional and important: it seems to me that the

8. In my investigation of many aspects of Newbigin's thinking I am indebted to the published doctoral dissertation submitted to the Faculty of Theology at the University of Helsinki by Jukka Keskitalo (see bibliography). This careful study is the most comprehensive theological analysis of Newbigin's thinking. Unfortunately, it is written in Finnish and has only a brief English summary. Therefore, I do not give references to it unless there is a direct citation or otherwise important reason in terms of academic integrity.

best way—and to a large extent, the only way—to determine what New-bigin opined about postmodernism appears in the contexts in which he is discussing the move away, the transition, from Modernity to postmodern-ism. Thus, seeking for and counting terms such as "postmodernism" is to miss the point. Without often naming what this "post-" or "late-" was, he focused his reflections on the implications of the transition away from Modernism to the church's mission.

The Epistemological Challenge of the Transition from Modernity to Late Modernity.

I will divide Newbigin's diagnosis of postmodernism into two interrelated themes: epistemology and lifestyle. The first one gets the lion's share in this discussion, and is further divided into two segments. While epistemology and lifestyle are interrelated, they can also be distinguished for the sake of clarity of analysis.

The key to properly understanding Newbigin's diagnosis of postmod-ernism is to acknowledge its parasitic nature. As mentioned above, for Newbigin postmodernism had no independent existence; rather it was an extension of and offshoot from Modernity. This may also help to explain the lack of sustained analysis of postmodernity.[9] It only came to the fore as the bishop was reflecting on the transition away from Modernity. This state of affairs is reflected in his choice of terminology. A number of terms appear in his writings such as "postmodern culture" or "postmodernity,"[10] "the postmodern development of modernism,"[11] as well as "postmod-ern reaction."[12] I believe the term "*late* modern" might best characterize Newbigin's view which builds on the idea of continuity.[13] In the follow-ing, while I continue using the term "postmodern(ism)" as the general nomenclature, I will at times use the term "late modern" to highlight New-bigin's take on the topic. In keeping with his idea of the parasitic nature of postmodernism, one of the key observations of the bishop was that the advent of postmodernism, if such has already happened, does not mean

9. Keskitalo, *Kristillinen usko*, 214 notes that Colin Gunton's view of postmoder-nity is similarly parasitic.

10. Among others, Newbigin, *Proper Confidence*, 27, 51; Newbigin, *Truth and Authority*, 82.

11. Among others, Newbigin, *Proper Confidence*, 83.

12. Among others, Newbigin, *Truth and Authority*, 7.

13. So also Keskitalo, *Kristillinen usko*, 214.

a complete shift in terms of replacement of the old for new but rather a co-habitation of a sort. This co-habitation includes both intellectual and lifestyle issues, as the discussion will show.

There are a number of internal dynamics, even contradistinctions in postmodernism in Newbigin's analysis. On the one hand, there are many who have grown very suspicious of the project of the Enlightenment with its search for Cartesian indubitable certainty. On the other hand, this is only one side of contemporary Western intellectual culture. Among the ordinary folks—and in many ways among the educated as well—there is still a firm trust in the facts of science and Modernity. This confidence in the project of Modernity is greatly aided by the economic and scientific-technological globalization process.[14]

Over against this continuing confidence in the Enlightenment, there is a definite shift that, for the bishop, signals the transition away from Modernity: for "an increasing number of people . . . there is no longer any confidence in the alleged 'eternal truths of reason' of . . . Lessing."[15] The following "working definition" of postmodernism by Newbigin is as illustrative of his perception of that movement as any: "Its main feature is the abandonment of any claim to know the truth in an absolute sense. Ultimate reality is not single but diverse and chaotic. Truth-claims are really concealed claims to power, and this applies as much to the claims of science as to those of religion. The father of this whole movement is the German philosopher F. W. Nietzsche. Nietzsche was the one who foresaw, in the closing years of the 19th century, that the methods of the Enlightenment must in the end lead to total scepticism and nihilism."[16]

At the heart of Newbigin's analysis of postmodernity is thus the loss of confidence in any kind of universal truth of reason after the Enlightenment,[17] a feature he also calls "the sickness of our culture."[18] In Newbigin's mind, the "foundationalism" of the Enlightenment with its belief in grandiose truths has been replaced in postmodern culture with the idea of "regimes of truth," which stand next to each other in a pluralist society:

14. Newbigin, "Modernity in Context," 8.

15. Newbigin, *Truth and Authority*, 77.

16. Newbigin, "Religious Pluralism: A Missiological Approach," 231.

17. See again, e.g., Newbigin, *Truth and Authority*, 77 cited above.

18. Newbigin, "Religious Pluralism and the Uniqueness of Jesus Christ," 50. Newbigin refers several times to the well-known ideas of the Jewish-American philosopher Alan Bloom, who in his influential work *The Closing of the American Mind* (New York: Simon & Schuster, 1987) sees a total relativism as the dominant feature of Western culture; see e.g., Newbigin, *Word in Season*, 105–6.

> In the last decades of the this century, the intellectual leadership of Europe has begun to turn its back on modernity. We are in the age of postmodernity. The mark of this is a suspicion of all claims to universal truth. Such claims have to be deconstructed. The "metanarratives" told by societies to validate their claim to global power are to be rejected. There are no privileged cultures and no privileged histories. All human cultures are equally entitled to respect. There are only different "regimes of truth" (Michael Foucault) which succeed one another . . . There are no overarching criteria by which these regimes can be judged.[19]

In order to properly understand the parasitic nature of postmodernity, one needs to acknowledge the bridge from Descartes via Friedrich Nietzsche—the "spiritual father" of all postmodernists—to contemporary elimination of the original Enlightenment dream of the certainty of knowledge.[20] Ironically the method of doubt—which was made the main way of achieving indubitable certainty—was changed in the hands of Nietzsche into the main weapon against Modernity which in turn paved the way for the total loss of confidence manifested in postmodernity. "The Cartesian invitation to make doubt the primary tool in the search for knowledge was bound to lead to the triumph of skepticism and eventually of nihilism, as Nietzsche foresaw."[21] Nietzsche replaced rational argument as the means of arbitrating between competing truth claims with "will to power."[22] Terms such as "true" and "untrue" have simply lost their meaning,[23] what remains is simply different "narratives," themselves historically conditioned.[24] Even science—believed by the Enlightenment pioneers to be the source of indisputable truths—becomes yet another expression of the will to power.[25]

Not surprisingly, Newbigin did not tire himself with highlighting this built-in irony of the line of development from the dream of indubitable certainty coupled with the method of doubt from Descartes to Nietzsche's rejection and replacement of all such "uncritical" attitudes for historization of all knowledge which finally led to the total loss of confidence of postmodernity. "It is deeply ironic that this method has led us directly into

19. Newbigin, *Proper Confidence*, 27.

20. See, e.g., ibid., 26–27.

21. Newbigin, *Truth and Authority*, 8.

22. Ibid.

23. Newbigin, *Proper Confidence*, 26.

24. Ibid., 73–74.

25. Ibid., 27.

the program of skepticism of the postmodern world."[26] Ultimately, the fact that postmodern culture doesn't allow us to know which God really is the "true" God is for Newbigin a sign of a "dying culture."[27]

A Pluralist Society

A virtual synonym for Newbigin for postmodern culture is "pluralist culture." While pluralism as such is nothing new to Christian faith, which was born in a religiously pluralistic environment, what is new is the form of contemporary pluralism: "The kind of western thought which has described itself as 'modern' is rapidly sinking into a kind of pluralism which is indistinguishable from nihilism—a pluralism which denies the possibility of making any universally justifiable truth-claims on any matter, whether religious or otherwise."[28]

An important aid to Newbigin in his analysis of the nature and effects of the late Modern pluralism is offered by Peter Berger's *Heretical Imperative*,[29] with which he interacted extensively in several writings.[30] Berger's well-known thesis is that whereas in pre-Modern societies heretical views were discouraged at the expense of communal and cultural uniformity, in contemporary[31] Western culture there is no "plausibility structure," acceptance of which is taken for granted without argument, and dissent from which is considered heresy. "Plausibility structure" simply means both ideas and practices in a given culture which help determine whether a belief is plausible or not. To doubt these given beliefs and believe differently makes a heresy. Understandably, the number of those in pre-Modern society who wanted to be labeled heretics was small, whereas in the contemporary culture formulating one's own views—apart from given plausibility structures or even in defiance of them—has become an imperative. Consequently, all are heretics! The corollary thesis of Berger is that in this situation Christian affirmations can be negotiated in three

26. Ibid., 27; see also 36, 105; and Newbigin, *Truth and Authority*, 9.

27. Newbigin, "Religious Pluralism and the Uniqueness of Jesus," 52.

28. Newbigin, "Religious Pluralism: A Missiological Approach," 227–28.

29. Berger, *Heretical Imperative*.

30. Newbigin, "Can the West be Converted?" 2–7; Newbigin, *Gospel in a Pluralist Society*, 39–40, 53.

31. Berger uses the term "modern" when speaking of contemporary Western culture. I have changed it to "contemporary" to avoid confusion: obviously, what Berger is describing is the culture of postmodernity which encourages each individual to have his or her own beliefs.

different ways: either in terms of choosing one's belief from a pool of many views, or making a distinction between beliefs that are still viable and ones that are not in light of current knowledge, or finally, building one's beliefs on a universal religious experience (as in Schleiermacher's vision) which precedes any rational affirmation.[32] Berger himself opts for the last one.

While Newbigin appreciates Berger's analysis and affirms its basic idea concerning the radically widening array of choices in late Modern culture,[33] he also critiques it for lack of nuance. First, Newbigin complains that the pluralism of Berger's scheme is selective and it does not include all areas of culture: "The principle of pluralism is not universally accepted in our culture. It is one of the key features of our culture . . . that we make a sharp distinction between . . . 'values' and . . . 'facts.' In the former world we are pluralists; values are a matter of personal choice. In the latter we are not; facts are facts, whether you like them or not. . . About 'beliefs' we agree to differ. Pluralism reigns. About what are called 'facts' everyone is expected to agree."[34]

This takes us to another main dilemma of late Modern culture in the West, which—ironically—is also the malaise of the whole culture of the Enlightenment, as repeatedly lamented by Newbigin.[35] This irony couldn't be more pointed, and I think highlighting its significance takes us to the heart of the highly dynamic and tension-filled nature of postmodernism in the bishop's thinking. Briefly put: the fatal distinction between values and facts—as Newbigin believes—is not only the undergirding weakness of the culture of Modernity; this very same obscurity characterizes also late Modern culture. Consequently, the culture of Modernity would not be cured by the transition to postmodernism (any more than postmodern culture with the shift to Modernity). Both are plagued by the distinction which makes any talk about the gospel as public truth meaningless!

The second complaint against Berger's analysis of contemporary culture is Newbigin's incisive observation that while "the traditional plausibility structures are dissolved by contact with this modern world-view, and while . . . the prevalence and power of this world-view gives no ground for believing it to be true, he [Berger] does not seem to al-low for the fact that it is itself a plausibility structure and functions as

---

32. Berger has named these three options deductive (Karl Barth as an example), reductive (Bultmann's demythologization program as a paradigm), and inductive (Schleiermacher, as mentioned, as the showcase).

33. See, e.g., Newbigin, *Foolishness to the Greeks*, 13.

34. Newbigin, *Gospel in a Pluralist Society*, 14–15.

35. E.g., ch. 2, "Roots of Pluralism," in Newbigin, *Gospel in a Pluralist Society*.

such."[36] In other words, the pluralist postmodern culture has not done away with plausibility structures but instead has replaced the traditional for another one, namely, the presupposition that individual choices only apply to certain aspects of reality: values but not to facts. This is a selective heretical imperative. The person who sets himself or herself against this plausibility structure—in other words, attempts to be a heretic in relation to established "facts"—is called just that, the *heretic*. Here Newbigin sides with Alasdair MacIntyre, who argued that "'Facts' is in modern culture a folk-concept with an aristocratic ancestry," "aristocratic" referring to the Enlightenment philosopher Bacon's admonition to seek for "facts" instead of "speculations."[37] In one word, for Newbigin Modernity and postmodernism do not represent two different species but rather both represent the Enlightenment project.[38]

The Effects on Lifestyle of the Transition to Late Modernity

So far we have been looking at Newbigin's analysis of the intellectual climate in the culture which is transitioning from Modernity to Late Modernity. With regard to lifestyle and cultural ethos, the transition to late Modernity is causing "nihilism and hopelessness."[39] Along with the loss of confidence in truth, postmodern society has also lost the hope and optimism of progress, so typical of Modernity.[40] This loss of confidence not only in reason but also in the future can be discerned both in the lives of individuals and the society as a whole: "In the closing decades of this century it is difficult to find Europeans who have any belief in a significant future which is worth working for and investing in. A society which believes in a worthwhile future saves in the present so as to invest in the future. Contemporary Western society spends in the present and piles up debts for the future, ravages the environment, and leaves its grandchildren to cope with the results as best they can."[41]

36. Newbigin, *Foolishness to the Greeks*, 13–14.

37. MacIntyre, *After Virtue*, 79. For references to this phrase, see Newbigin, *Foolishness to the Greeks*, 76–77; also *Proper Confidence*, 55.

38. Keskitalo, *Kristillinen usko*, 230.

39. Newbigin, *Proper Confidence*, 47 (again, in reference to Yu's phrase, cited above).

40. Newbigin, *Other Side of 1984*, 1–2, 6; Newbigin, *Gospel in a Pluralist Society*, 112; Newbigin, *Proper Confidence*, 46–47.

41. Newbigin, *Gospel in a Pluralist Society*, 90–91.

Newbigin painfully found that out as he was returning to his homeland after a considerable period of missionary work in Asia. When asked what might have been the greatest difficulty in his homecoming, his response was the "disappearance of hope"[42] and the increase of "pessimism."[43] All this in turn has led particularly the young generation to the culture of "instant gratification." Whereas in the past people invested in the future, contemporary people in the West just live for today and do not see it meaningful to think of the future.[44]

While this kind of perception can be—and has been—critiqued[45] as a function of reverse culture shock, there is no denying the fact that these negative effects of postmodernity play a significant role in Newbigin's cultural analysis. The main point I want to make here is that in Newbigin's cultural analysis there is a direct link between the transition away from Modernity with its loss of confidence in reason and the lifestyle of people living under those transitional forces. The implications for the church's mission are of course obvious: Should the church attempt a proper response, which would entail both epistemological and lifestyle-driving reorientation of thinking and practices?

PART 2: MISSIONAL RESPONSE TO THE CULTURE IN TRANSITION BETWEEN MODERNITY AND LATE MODERNITY

Having looked at Newbigin's diagnosis of postmodernism, through the lens of the effects of the transition away from Modernity, the second part of this essay attempts to discern the main responses of the bishop. To repeat myself: rather than focusing on themes related to postmodernism, I will continue gleaning widely from Newbigin's writings in order to show that his response to late Modernity can only be reconstructed from his response to Modernity.

In order to bring to light the dynamic nature of Newbigin's thinking, I wish to reconstruct his response to late Modernity along the lines of several polarities. Clearly, the bishop envisioned the mission of the church in this transitional period being faced with a number of dynamic tensions.

42. Newbigin, *Other Side of* 1984, 1.

43. Newbigin, "Secular Myth," 13.

44. Newbigin, *Gospel in a Pluralist Society*, 90–91; see also 111–12.

45. Ustorf, *Christianized Africa*, 108–10; for Newbigin's response, see "Secular Myth," 6, 13.

While the notion of a safe middle-ground hardly does justice to his radical program, in many ways I hear him calling the church to locate herself at the midpoint of various polarities, such as the following ones:

- Calling the church to be "relevant" while declining from explaining the gospel in terms of late Modernism

- Adopting a fallibilistic epistemology while resisting the nihilism of postmodernism

- Standing on a particular tradition while rejecting subjectivism

- Holding on to the gospel as public truth while critiquing the "timeless statements" of Modernity

- Affirming "Committed Pluralism" while condemning "Agnostic Pluralism"

- Trusting the power of persuasion while abandoning any notion of the will to power

Calling the Church to Be "Relevant" while Declining from Explaining the Gospel in Terms of Late Modernism

For the church to fulfill her mission in any culture, Newbigin argues, she has to be relevant on the one hand, and to confront the culture, on the other hand.[46] One of the recurring complaints of the bishop against the church of Modern Western culture is her unapologetic and uncritical desire to be only relevant. This is the crux of the mistaken contextualization strategy of the church vis-à-vis Modernity: the church has completely accommodated herself to the culture of Modernity. At the heart of this mistaken strategy is the apologetic defense of the rationality of Christianity to the Enlightenment mind. The only way this strategy of "tactical retreat" may wish to defend the "reasonable" nature of Christian faith is to stick with the standards of rationality of Modernity.[47] But those standards are of course not in keeping with the "Christian worldview." Among other deviations from the Christian view, those standards operate with the fatal split between values and facts, as explained above.

The reason the church of Modernity attempts to accommodate herself to the strictures of the Enlightenment is the need to be "relevant." The church that is being pushed into the margins of the society, to cater

46. See, e.g., Newbigin, *Other Side of 1984*, 55.
47. Newbigin, *Gospel in a Pluralist Society*, 3; *Proper Confidence*, 93.

"values" while science, politics, and the rest of the public arena takes care of facts, feels she needs to be acknowledged. Consequently, the church purports to influence choices in the private area alone and shies away from any attempt to present the gospel as any kind of "universal truth."[48] In Modern theology this move away from the idea of the gospel as public truth to catering of personal values was aided and guided by Liberal Theology, under the tutelage of Friedrich Schleiermacher and others which finally led to the "anthropologization" of theology.[49] When the statements of theology are noncognitive descriptions of religious "feelings" rather than "personal knowledge" with "universal intention"—to use Newbigin's key phrases borrowed from Polanyi—an attitude of "timidity" follows.[50]

Now, someone may ask why am I rehearsing this familiar Newbigin critique, the target of which is Modernity rather than postmodernism, the topic under discussion. The reason is what I argued above, namely, that because in Newbigin's diagnosis postmodernism is but an offshoot from Modernity, the church's response to postmodernism can only be reconstructed from the initial reaction to Modernity.

Similarly to the culture of Modernity, I argue on behalf of Newbigin, the culture of postmodernity is willing to tolerate the church as long as she "behaves" according to the rules. As shown above, with all their differences, both cultures operate with the same distinction between values and facts. The difference is this: while the culture of Modernity really believed that there are facts—and thus indubitable certainty—to be distinguished from personal, noncognitive values, postmodernism regards both "facts" and "values" as personal opinions.

The end result with regard to the church's mission, however, is the same: In this transitional period of time the church is tolerated only if she suffices to be "relevant" under the rules now of late Modernity with its idea of "regimes of truths," none of which is better or worse off and none of which has any right whatsoever to consider other "truths" as less valuable or less "true." For the church now to succumb to the temptation of being silent about the gospel as public truth would in Newbigin's opinion just repeat the same old mistake of the church of Modernity.

As an alternative—again following Newbigin's program for the church that wants to recover from the Babylonian Captivity of Modernity—there has to be a new initiative to question the basic beliefs of postmodern

48. Newbigin, *Foolishness to the Greeks*, 19; *Gospel in a Pluralist Society*, 2.

49. Newbigin, *Foolishness to the Greeks*, 40–41, 45.

50. Newbigin, *Truth and Authority*, 81.

culture.[51] This means a shift from explaining the gospel in terms of the postmodern worldview with its denial of any kind of "universal truth" to explaining the postmodern worldview in terms of the gospel.[52] This bold initiative means nothing less than confronting the "revolution of expectations" in the postmodern world.[53] Similarly to the call to the church facing the forces of Modernity, the bishop would call the church of this transitional period to the "conversion of the mind," not only of the "soul." The reason is simply that there is a radical discontinuity between the gospel and the beliefs of both Modernity and late Modernity.[54]

Interestingly enough, Newbigin compares his own view of the Bible and revelation to that of the Liberation theologies. The basic purpose of Liberationists is not to explain the text but rather to understand the world in light of the Bible. Liberationists resist the idea of the Bible student being a neutral, noncommitted outsider.[55] Newbigin's theological hero St. Augustine is also commended in this regard. Augustine was the first "postcritical" theologian and philosopher who subjected the prevailing culture, Greek rationalism which was falling apart, to biblical critique. Rather than living in nostalgia, the Christian church should learn from Augustine a bold and unabashed approach to culture by taking the biblical message as an alternative worldview.[56]

Only this kind of bold initiative would help the church balance the dual need to be relevant and to be faithful. How that may happen is the focus of the continuing discussion here.

Adopting a Fallibilistic Epistemology while Resisting the Nihilism of Postmodernism

A tempting way for the church to question late Modernity's lack of confidence in knowledge would be simply to adopt an opposite standpoint of affirming the Modernist program of indubitable certainty. This is not the way the bishop wants the church to perceive her role in this transitional

---

51. Cf. Newbigin, *Other Side of 1984*, 55 (which of course speaks of an initiative in relation to the culture of Modernity).

52 Cf. Newbigin, *Foolishness to the Greeks*, 22; Newbigin, *Gospel in a Pluralist Society*, 222 (which, again, speaks of the Church in relation to Modernity).

53. Cf. Newbigin, *Other Side of 1984*, 55.

54. Cf. Newbigin, *Gospel in a Pluralist Society*, 9–10.

55. Newbigin, *Gospel in a Pluralist Society*, 97–99; *Word in Season*, 111.

56. Newbigin, *Other Side of 1984*, 24.

period. Rather, in a surprising move he seems to be echoing some of the key concerns of postmodern epistemology by affirming a fallibilistic epistemology. Indeed, says the bishop: "We have to abandon the idea that there is available to us or any other human beings the sort of certitude that Descartes wanted to provide and that the scientific part of our culture has sometimes claimed to offer."[57] Here there is a link with postmodern orientations, and the bishop is happy to acknowledge it:

> We accept the post-modernist position that all human reasoning is socially, culturally, historically embodied. We have left behind the illusion that there is available some kind of neutral stand-point from which one can judge the different stories and decide which is true. The "Age of Reason" supposed that there is available to human beings a kind of indubitable knowledge, capable of being grasped by all human beings which was more reliable than any alleged revelation, and which could therefore provide the criteria by which any alleged divine revelation could be assessed. This immensely powerful hang-over from the "modernist" position still haunts many discussions of religious pluralism. . . But in a post-modernist context all this is swept away.[58]

Part of the situatedness of knowledge is to acknowledge—in the British bishop's case—its Euro-centric nature: "My proposal will, I know, be criticised as Euro-centric, but this must be rejected. We cannot disown our responsibility as Europeans within the whole evangelical fellowship. It is simply a fact that it is ideas and practices developed in Europe over the past three centuries which now dominate the world, for good and for ill."[59] That said, the bishop of course also calls himself and other Europeans to take another look at how that legacy has been passed on with regard to other cultures; the acknowledgment of the situatedness of knowledge and preaching the gospel does not save Europeans from helping their "brothers and sisters in the 'Third World' [in] the task of recovering the gospel in its integrity from its false entanglement with European culture, and so seek together to find the true path of inculturation."[60]

Because of the socially and locationally conditioned nature of human knowledge, Newbigin condemns any form of Fundamentalism, a

57. Newbigin, *Truth to Tell*, 35.
58. Newbigin, "Religious Pluralism: A Missiological Approach," 233.
59. Newbigin, "Gospel and Culture," 8.
60. Ibid.

mistaken approach to revelation and the Bible in its search for an indubitable certainty by appealing to "evidence" to prove the Bible.[61]

If the Scylla of Modernity is the illusion of indubitable certainty, the Charybdis of postmodernism is the lack of confidence in anything certain. As implied above, the way from the search of indubitable certainty to virtual epistemological nihilism goes via the way of doubt. The built-in self-contradiction of the Cartesian program is the necessity of doubt as the way to certainty. This "hermeneutics of suspicion," when taken to its logical end, of course leads to the doubting of everything, in other words, the dismantling of all certainty. At the end of this road, as explained above, there is the Nietzschean nihilism. This would close all doors to affirming the gospel as public truth.

Differently from both Modernity and postmodernism, the bishop—in keeping with Augustine's dictum *credo ut intelligam*—considers belief as the beginning of knowledge. Both Descartes and Nietzsche would disagree. Belief as the beginning of knowledge does not mean leaving behind critique and doubt. Rather, it means that doubt and critique are put in perspective.[62] Even doubt entails some assumptions, the doubter begins with something else, a "tradition," an idea Newbigin borrows from Alasdair MacIntyre.[63] "But the questioning, if it is to be rational, has to rely on other fundamental assumptions which can in turn be questioned."[64] Briefly put: certainty unrelated to faith is simply an impossible and unwarranted goal.[65] Newbigin makes the delightful remark that both faith and doubt can be either honest or blind; it is not always the case that faith is blind while doubt is honest. One can also envision honest faith and blind doubt.[66]

---

61. Newbigin finds many faults in the Fundamentalistic Bible interpretation: (1) "It is difficult to maintain without a kind of split personality if one is going to live an active life in the modern world." (2) "Those who hold this position are themselves part of the modern world; consequently, when they say that the Bible is factually accurate, they are working with a whole context of meaning, within a concept of factuality that is foreign to the Bible." (3) In the final analysis, to "prove" the Bible, Fundamentalists must appeal to experience, the experience of the Church concerning the Bible; if so, then Fundamentalists have succumbed to the same trap as Liberalism, their arch-enemy. Newbigin, *Foolishness to the Greeks*, 46; see also *Gospel in a Pluralist Society*, 42–43, 49; *Proper Confidence*, 85–86.

62. Newbigin, *Gospel in a Pluralist Society*, 19.

63. Ibid., 82.

64. Newbigin, *Proper Confidence*, 50.

65. Newbigin, *Gospel in a Pluralist Society*, 28; see also 4–5.

66. Newbigin, *Proper Confidence*, 24; *Truth and Authority*, 7.

While the Christian tradition represents confidence and "fullness of truth" promised by Jesus, the Christian concept of truth is not an "illusion" that "imagine[s] that there can be available to us a kind of certainty that does not involve . . . personal commitment," for the simple reason that the "supreme reality is a personal God." Thus, those who "claim infallible certainty about God in their own right on the strength of their rational powers are mistaken." Bishop Newbigin reminds us that in interpersonal relationships we would never claim that![67]

As an alternative and cure for both the Modernist illusion of indubitable certainty and the postmodern lapse into nihilism, the bishop presents his own view of human knowledge as "personal knowledge." It is borrowed from Polanyi, who negotiated between Cartesian certainty and pure subjectivism. "Personal knowledge" "is neither subjective nor objective. In so far as the personal submits to requirements acknowledged by itself as independent of itself, it is not subjective; but in so far as it is an action guided by individual passion, it is not objective either. It transcends the disjunction between subjective and objective."[68]

Polanyi's concept of personal knowledge serves the bishop well in that it fits in with his view of reality as personal, as mentioned above. The "object" of Christian knowledge is not a "thing" but rather "who," a person, the incarnated Lord.[69] Being "personal" means that this kind of knowledge entails a risk, it is "risky business."[70] It is "subjective in that it is I who know, or seek to know, and that the enterprise of knowing is one which requires my personal commitment. . . And it is subjective in that, in the end, I have to take personal responsibility for my beliefs."[71] Yet, this kind of knowledge is not subjectivistic because, again borrowing from Polanyi, it has a "universal intention." It is meant to be shared, critiqued, tested, and perhaps even corrected. It engages and does not remain only my own insight. It is not only "true for me."[72] Thus, to repeat what was mentioned above: doubt and critique should not be abandoned, rather they should be put in a perspective by seeing them as secondary to faith.[73] Only this

67. Newbigin, *Proper Confidence*, 67.

68. Polanyi, *Personal Knowledge*, 300; see, e.g., Newbigin, *Gospel in a Pluralist Society*, 51–52, 54–55.

69. Newbigin, *Proper Confidence*, 67.

70. Newbigin, *Gospel in a Pluralist Society*, 35.

71. Ibid., 23.

72. Ibid., 33.

73. Newbigin, *Proper Confidence*, 48, 105; *Other Side of 1984*, 20; *Gospel in a Pluralist Society*, 20.

kind of epistemology might offer for church that lives under the under the forces of Modernity and postmodernism an opportunity to attain *Proper Confidence.*

Standing on a Particular Tradition while Rejecting Subjectivism

While half of contemporary Western culture still lives under the illusion of the possibility of indubitable certainty, the other half, the late Modern one, "has lapsed into subjectivism" which is the "tragic legacy of Descartes' proposal" and even more ironically, the half into which theology usually falls.[74] Modernity, on the one hand, denies the whole concept of tradition in its alleged "neutral" standpoint. The Cartesian method mistakenly believes itself to be tradition-free. Postmodernism enthusiastically affirms traditions, "regimes of truth," happily existing side-by-side. No one tradition is better or worse, and no one tradition has the right to impose its own rationality upon the others.[75] The implications for the church's mission are obvious. For the Modern hearer of the gospel, any appeal to a particular tradition is an anathema and a step away from the alleged neutral, tradition-free search for certainty. For the postmodern hearer, the gospel is *a* good-news but not *the* good news.

The way out of this dilemma for the bishop is to take a lesson from both Polanyi and the ethicist-philosopher Alasdair MacIntyre[76] and speak robustly of the need to stand on a particular tradition. The necessity of acknowledging the tradition-laden nature of all human knowledge is based on the shared postmodern conviction, nurtured by contemporary sociology of knowledge, according to which all knowledge is socially and thus "contextually" shaped. "There is no rationality except a socially embodied rationality."[77] Any knowledge is rooted in and emerges out of a particular context, location, situation. The bishop boldly accepts that all truth is socially and historically embodied and thus aligns himself with a leading postmodern idea. Another ally here is, as mentioned, Alasdair MacIntyre: "As Alasdair MacIntyre so brilliantly documents in his book *Whose Justice,*

74. Newbigin, *Gospel in a Pluralist Society*, 35.

75. See Newbigin, *Word in Season*, 187.

76. Newbigin also refers at times to the well-known philosopher of science Thomas Kuhn (*The Structure of Scientific Revolutions* [Chicago: University of Chicago Press, 1970]), who spoke of dramatic turning points in the development of science when new paradigms emerge and transform not only the methods and results but also the whole way of thinking scientifically; see, e.g., Newbigin, *Word in Season*, 91–92.

77. Newbigin, *Gospel in a Pluralist Society*, 87.

What Rationality? the idea that there can be a kind of reason that is supra-cultural and that would enable us to view all the culturally conditioned traditions of rationality from a standpoint above them all is one of the illusions of our contemporary culture. All rationality is socially embodied, developed in human tradition and using some human language. The fact that biblical thought shares this with all other forms of human thought in no way disqualifies it from providing the needed center."[78]

The "situational" nature of human knowledge means that knowing can only happen from within tradition: This state of affairs, however, does not mean that therefore no one can claim to speak truth. Indeed, to "pretend to *possess* the truth in its fullness is arrogance," whereas, the "claim to have been given the decisive clue for the human search after truth is not arrogant; it is the exercise of our responsibility as part of the human family."[79] This seeking after the truth happens first and foremost in the Christian community. Whereas Modernity focuses on the individual person's knowledge, Christian rationality—in this regard, aligning with the ethos of postmodernism—believes in a communally received knowledge, even when the act of knowing is personal, as explained above. "It would contradict the whole message of the Bible itself if one were to speak of the book apart from the church, the community shaped by the story that the book tells."[80]

For Newbigin, the church is a truth-seeking community that seeks to understand reality from its own vantage point. Again learning from Polanyi, Newbigin claims that there is a certain kind of correspondence between the Christian and scientific community as both build on "tradition" and "authority." Even new investigations happen on the basis of and in critical dialogue with accumulated tradition, represented by scholars who are regarded as authoritative. For the Christian church this tradition is the narrative, the story of the gospel confessed by all Christians:

> The Christian community, the universal Church, embracing more and more fully all the cultural traditions of humankind, is called to be that community in which a tradition of rational discourse is developed which leads to a true understanding of reality; because it takes as its starting point and as its permanent criterion of truth the self-revelation of God in Jesus Christ. It is

78. Newbigin, "Religious Pluralism and the Uniqueness of Jesus Christ," 50; so also p. 52; the reference is to MacIntyre, *Whose Justice, What Rationality?*

79. Newbigin, "Religious Pluralism and the Uniqueness of Jesus Christ," 54.

80. Newbigin, *Proper Confidence*, 53.

necessarily a particular community, among all the human communities. . . But it has a universal mission, for it is the community chosen and sent by God for this purpose. This particularity,
however scandalous it may seem to a certain kind of cosmopolitan mind, is inescapable.[81]

There is always the danger of domestication of the tradition or, as
in postmodernism, its reduction into *a* story among other equal stories—that, in Newbigin's mind, would lead to pluralism and denial of the
particularity of the gospel. The gospel can be protected from this kind of
domestication, he believes. "The truth is that the gospel escapes domestication, retains its proper strangeness, its power to question us, only when
we are faithful to its universal, supranational, supracultural nature."[82] By
making universal truth claims, Christian faith coexists with other traditions and their claims to truth.[83] Out of the framework of the gospel narrative, Christian tradition, the church seeks to understand reality—rather
than vice versa.[84]

As mentioned before, rather than explaining the gospel through the
lens of postmodern culture—or Modern culture for that matter—this
missional ecclesiology seeks to explain the world through the lens of the
gospel. Here there is of course a link with the thinking of George Lindbeck and Postliberal thought. Dissatisfied with both the Fundamentalistic
"Propositional Model" of revelation and the Liberal "Experiential Model,"
Lindbeck suggests an alternative that he calls the "Cultural Linguistic
Model." That model sees Christian claims and doctrines as "rules" that
govern our way of speaking not only of faith but also of the world. While
sympathetic to Postliberalism's insight,[85] Newbigin's thinking also differs
from Lindbeck's in that Newbigin still considers Christian doctrines,
based as they are on the dynamic narrative of the Bible, as historically
factual and thus in some sense "propositional." For Newbigin, the crux of
the matter is to raise the question "Which is the *real* story?"[86]

The insistence on the factual, not only "linguistic" basis of Christian
narrative is essential to Newbigin as he willingly admits the "confessional"

81. Newbigin, *Gospel in a Pluralist Society*, 87–88.
82. Newbigin, "Enduring Validity," 50.
83. Newbigin, *Gospel in a Pluralist Society*, 64; *Truth and Authority*, 52.
84. Newbigin, *Gospel in a Pluralist Society*, 53.
85. See, e.g., ibid., 24–25; *A Word in Season*, 83–84.
86. Newbigin, *Word in Season*, 85 (emphasis mine).

nature of his starting point. This confessional standpoint, however, in his opinion is no affirmation of the fideism or subjectivism of postmodernism:

> I am, of course, aware that this position will be challenged. It will be seen as arbitrary and irrational. It may be dismissed as "fideism", or as a blind "leap of faith". But these charges have to be thrown back at those who make them. Every claim to show grounds for believing the gospel which lie outside the gospel itself can be shown to rest ultimately on faith-commitments which can be questioned. There is, indeed, a very proper exercise of reason in showing the coherence which is found in the whole of human experience when it is illuminated by the gospel, but this is to be distinguished from the supposition that there are grounds for ultimate confidence more reliable than those furnished in God's revelation of himself in Jesus Christ, grounds on which, therefore, one may affirm the reliability of Christian belief. The final authority for the Christian faith is the self-revelation of God in Jesus Christ.[87]

This clinging to the historical event of Jesus Christ takes us to the heart of his desire to defend the gospel as public truth.

Holding On to the Gospel as Public Truth while Critiquing the "Timeless Statements" of Modernity

The church and her mission in this transitional period finds herself faced with a twofold challenge: on the one hand, there is the Modernist search for indubitable certainty, and on the other hand, the nihilism of postmodernism. At least this is the way the bishop paints the picture.

In order to continue reconstructing the proper response to such a transitional era, a brief summary of our findings so far is in order. First, while the church seeks to be relevant, it has to resist the temptation to accommodate herself to the strictures of the existing culture. Second, this can be done best on the basis of committed, personal knowledge which avoids the trap of the nihilism of postmodernism and the illusion of Modernity. It is a knowledge with the aim to be shared with the rest of creation. Third, this kind of committed, "proper confidence" can only be had from within a particular tradition. This tradition-driven knowledge is an alternative to the alleged neutral standpoint of Modernity and the subjectivistic, noncommitted "regimes of truth"–driven view of postmodernism.

87. Newbigin, "Religious Pluralism: A Missiological Approach," 236.

Christian tradition avoids the dangers of domestication because it is a tradition shared and tested by an international community and it is based on a universally oriented "true" story of the gospel. Now, this all leads to the affirmation of the gospel as public truth while resisting any notion of the timeless truths of Modernity.

Where Modernity fails is that it does not acknowledge the social nature of its knowledge. Where postmodernism fails is in its one-sided focus on the socially embodied nature of human knowledge to the point where there is no overarching Story, framework, criterion. All stories just exist side by side and everyone is free to choose.

The affirmation of the gospel as public truth is based on the "foundation" of the unique authority of Christian tradition based on God's self-revelation. That self-revelation happens in secular history[88] to which Christ is the clue.[89] The peculiar nature of the Christian story with regard to its truth claims is the "Total Fact of Christ."[90] The *factum*-nature (from Latin [*factum est*]: "it's done") of Christian claims to truth in Christ has to do with history.[91] While the Christ-event is part of salvific history, it is also an event in universal history. Therefore, the subjectivistic interpretation of Existentialism according to which the events of salvation history such as the resurrection only "happened to me" is a totally mistaken view. The Christian gospel is story, narrative, but is more than that: "Christian doctrine is a form of rational discourse."[92] Happening in secular history, its claims are subject to historical scrutiny. The historicity of the Christian story, then, is the reason why "its starting point [is] is not any alleged self-evident truth. Its starting point is events in which God made himself known to men and women in particular circumstances. . ." In a sense, the argument is of course thus circular: the church interprets God's actions in history as God's actions, yet regards them as happening in history. But,

88. Ch. 8 in Newbigin, *Gospel in a Pluralist Society* is titled "The Bible as Universal History." This view of course resonates with Wolfhart Pannenberg's view of revelation as history. For some reason, Newbigin does not engage this Lutheran theologian's ideas even though many of them, including the historicity of the resurrection or the importance of eschatology, are obvious common points.

89. Ch. 9 in Newbigin, *Gospel in a Pluralist Society* is titled "Christ, the Clue to History."

90. Ibid., 5.

91. Newbigin, *Open Secret*, 50–52.

92. Newbigin, *Truth and Authority*, 52.

says the bishop, the same principle applies to science, too, which is in this sense circular in its reasoning.[93]

If the historical nature of the Christian tradition is the safeguard against the charge of the Modernist self-evidence of truth, the historical and thus factual nature also marks it off from the postmodern view with no interest in the historical basis. Christian rationality necessarily has to raise the question of its "objective" basis:

> The central question is not "How shall I be saved?" but "How shall I glorify God by understanding, loving, and doing God's will—here and now in this earthly life?" To answer that question I must insistently ask: "How and where is God's purpose for the whole of creation and the human family made visible and credible?" That is the question about the truth—objective truth—which is true whether or not it coincides with my "values." And I know of no place in the public history of the world where the dark mystery of human life is illuminated, and the dark power of all that denies human well-being is met and measured and mastered, except in those events that have their focus in what happened "under Pontius Pilate."[94]

In other words, with all his insistence on the socially embodied nature of human knowledge and its tradition-driven nature, the bishop is not willing to succumb to the postmodern temptation of leaving behind the "facts." True, against the Modernists, Newbigin claims the risky, "personal" nature of human knowledge; but at the same time, against postmodernists, he sets forth the argument for the historical and factual nature of key Christian claims. This is no easy middle way but rather a radical middle!

Affirming "Committed Pluralism" while Condemning "Agnostic Pluralism"

In light of the fact that for Newbigin "pluralism" is a virtual synonym for late Modernity—as observed above—it is surprising that he is not willing to abandon the concept altogether. Rather, to paraphrase MacIntyre, he is raising the all-important question: Whose pluralism? Which pluralism? The bishop is against that kind of pluralistic ethos of contemporary Western society in which no truth can be considered truth, an ideology of parallel and equal "regimes of truth" without any criteria or parameters.

93. Newbigin, *Gospel in a Pluralist Society*, 63.

94. Newbigin, "Religious Pluralism and the Uniqueness of Jesus Christ," 54.

In his opinion, this kind of pluralism is based on the fatal distinction between facts and values. Whereas in the area of values no criteria exist, in the domain of facts, mutually assumed criteria can still be applied quite similarly to the ethos of Modernity. In other words: while, say, a scientist as a private person may have no right to argue for the supremacy of his personal values, as a *scientist*, however, she is supposed to stick with the rules of the game. In medicine, physics, and chemistry there is no "Wild West" of pluralism, some claims and results are considered to be true, while others false. "No society is totally pluralist."[95] As mentioned above, this "heretical imperative" is highly selective.

A significant contribution to the discussion comes from the bishop's distinction between two kinds of pluralism, one desired, the other one to be rejected, namely, "agnostic pluralism" and "committed pluralism." He defines agnostic—sometimes also called anarchic—pluralism in this way: "[I]t is assumed that ultimate truth is unknowable and that there are therefore no criteria by which different beliefs and different patterns of behavior may be judged. In this situation one belief is as good as another and one lifestyle is as good as another. No judgments are to be made, for there are no given criteria, no truth by which error could be recognized. There is to be no discrimination between better and worse."[96]

In other words, this is the pluralism stemming from the failure of the Modernist program in delivering its main product, indubitable certainty. The latter type of pluralism, committed pluralism, is an alternative to the former. The best way to illustrate its nature is again to refer to the way the scientific community functions. That community is "pluralist in the sense that is it not controlled or directed from one center. Scientists are free to pursue their own investigations and to develop their own lines of research." This type of pluralism is committed to the search of the truth following mutually established guidelines and operating "from within the tradition." It takes into consideration the authority of tradition while maintaining the freedom to pursue new ways of understanding the reality and truth.[97] In order for the church to come to such a place, she has to appreciate her tradition in a way similar to the scientific community.[98]

95. Newbigin, *Word in Season*, 158.
96. Ibid., 168.
97. Ibid., 168–69.
98. Ibid., 170.

In a pluralist society of late Modernity, says the bishop, "There are only stories, and the Christian story is one among them."[99] The attitude of committed pluralism drives the church to dialogue with other traditions and modes of rationalities. If the church believes it is a witness to—if not the possessor of—the gospel as public truth, the "Logic of Mission"[100] pushes the church out of her comfort zone to share the gospel. While the gospel truth does not arise out of the dialogue, it calls for a dialogue with a specific goal in mind, namely to present the gospel faithfully and authentically:

> [T]he message of Christianity is essentially a story, report of things which have happened. At its heart is the statement that "the word was made flesh." This is a statement of a fact of history which the original evangelists are careful to locate exactly within the continuum of recorded human history. A fact of history does not arise out dialogue; it has to be unilaterally reported by those who, as witnesses, can truly report of things which have happened. Of course there will then be dialogue about the way in which what has happened is to be understood, how it is to be related to other things which we know, or think that we know. The story itself does not arise out of dialogue; it simply has to be told.[101]

This Christian view of dialogue thus differs radically from the understanding of dialogue under the influence of agnostic pluralism. For that mind-set, "Dialogue is seen not as a means of coming nearer to the truth but as a way of life in which different truth-claims no longer conflict with one another but seek friendly co-existence." That kind of model of dialogue bluntly rejects any kind of "instrumental" view of dialogue as a means to try to persuade. It only speaks of "the dialogue of cultures and of dialogue as a celebration of the rich variety of human life. Religious communities are not regarded as bearers of truth-claims. There is no talk about evangelization and conversion."[102]

Since for the Christian church dialogue is not an alternative to evangelization, one has to think carefully of how the attempt to persuade with the power of the gospel may best happen in late Modernity.

---

99. Newbigin, "Religious Pluralism: A Missiological Approach," 233.

100. Newbigin, *Gospel in a Pluralist Society*, ch. 10 is titled "The Logic of Mission."

101. Newbigin, "Religious Pluralism: A Missiological Approach," 233.

102. Ibid., 240.

Trusting the Power of Persuasion while Abandoning
Any Notion of the Will to Power

In late Modernity, any hint of the old Christendom way of resorting to political power as a means of furthering a religious cause is a red flag. Bishop Newbigin was the first one to condemn any such attempt on the church's part: "I have argued that a claim that the Christian faith must be affirmed as a public truth does not mean a demand for a return to 'Christendom' or to some kind of theocracy. It does not mean that the coercive power of the state and its institutions should be at the service of the Church."[103]

The suspicion of the "will to power" in late Modernity, however, is deeper and more subtle than the fear of the church's political power. The postmodern suspicion has to do with the church's desire to confront epistemology that has lost all criteria in negotiating between true and false. Therefore, postmodernists argue, "There is to be no discrimination between better and worse. All beliefs and all lifestyles are to be equally respected. To make judgments is, on this view, *an exercise of power* and is therefore oppressive and demeaning to human dignity. The 'normal' replaces the 'normative.'"[104] It is here where the church, rather than succumbing to the mindset of agnostic pluralism, should confront the people of late Modernity with the offer of the gospel as public truth. While there is no way for the church faithful to her mission to avoid this confrontation, the church should also do everything in her power to cast off any sign of the will to power.

In Newbigin's vision, the church is a Pilgrim People, on the way, and thus does not claim the fullness of truth on this side of the eschaton, it only testifies to it and seeks to understand it more appropriately.[105] Even the Christian witness waits for the final eschatological verification of the truth of the gospel.[106] Such a witness does not resort to any earthly power, rather he or she only trusts the power of the persuasion of the truth.

---

103. Newbigin, *Word in Season*, 170. Newbigin notes in another context how ironic it is that the introduction by the West of ideas, science, technology, and such products of "development" were for the most part not considered as the "will to power" in the Third World. Rather, they were "welcomed and embraced." (Ibid., 122–23.)

104. Ibid., 168 (emphasis mine).

105. Newbigin at times calls the witnesses "seekers of the truth" and commends the apophatic tradition of Christian theology for its acknowledgment that "no human image or concept can grasp the reality of God" (Newbigin, *Gospel in a Pluralist Society*, 12).

106. Ibid., 53–54.

Consequently, time after time, the bishop recommends to the church an attitude of humility and respect for others. While witnesses, Christians are also "learners."[107] The church does not possess the truth but rather testifies to it, carries it on as a truth-seeking community and tradition.[108]

The refusal of the "will to power" goes even deeper than that of the cultivation of a humble and respectful attitude towards others. It grows from the center of the gospel truth as it is based on the cross of the Savior:

> What is unique in the Christian story is that the cross and resurrection of Jesus are at its heart. Taken together (as they must always be) they are the public affirmation of the fact that God rules, but that his rule is (in this age) hidden; that the ultimate union of truth with power lies beyond history, but can yet be declared and portrayed within history. The fact that the crucifixion of the Incarnate Lord stands at the centre of the Christian story ought to have made it forever impossible that the Christian story should have been made into a validation of imperial power. Any exposition of a missionary approach to religious pluralism must include the penitent acknowledgement that the Church has been guilty of contradicting its own gospel by using it as an instrument of imperial power.[109]

In other words, any attempt to usurp power means nothing less than a perversion of the message of the gospel.

IN LIEU OF CONCLUSION: SEED-THOUGHTS FOR FURTHER REFLECTION

It seems to me it is in keeping with Lesslie Newbigin's evolving and dynamic way of thinking that no "closing chapter" be offered to the reflections on the mission and life of the church in the transitional era between Modernity and postmodernism. More helpful, I think, is to reflect on some tasks and questions for the future and map out some remaining areas of interest.

Let me first return to my methodological musings in the beginning of the essay. Again, in this context I am not concerned about methodology primarily for the sake of academic competence; rather, my interest in it has everything to do with the material presentation of Newbigin's missional

107. Ibid., 34–35.

108. Ibid., 12.

109. Newbigin, "Religious Pluralism: A Missiological Approach," 234.

ecclesiology and epistemology. I argued that rather than tabulating references to postmodernism in the bishop's writings, nor even looking primarily at those passages which may have a more or less direct reference to postmodernism, a more helpful way of proceeding would be to take lessons from his response to Modernity, particularly with regard to the transitional period when the church lives under two modes of rationalities. This kind of methodology seemed to be viable in light of Newbigin's conviction that postmodernism is parasitic on Modernity. If my methodology is appropriate and does justice to Newbigin's own approach, then it means that his writings on missional ecclesiology and cultural critique continue to have their relevance even if the shift to postmodernism will intensify in the future.[110]

If my hunch is correct then a main task for the church of the West at this period of time would be to pay attention to the nature of the transition. I do not believe that we live in a culture in which Modernity has given way to postmodernism. Rather, I regard Newbigin's insight that what makes the end of the twentieth and the beginning of the twenty-first century unique culturally is the process of transition. Modernity is alive and well not only in the West but also in the Global South. At the same time, as a result of the massive critique of and disappointment with it, there is an intensifying desire to cast off the reins of Modernity. However, that distancing from the Enlightenment heritage does not mean leaving behind its influence; rather, it is a continual reassessment of Modernity as we continue living under its massive influence. To repeat myself: it is the transition that makes our time unique. To that dynamic Bishop Newbigin's thinking speaks loud and clear.

I have mentioned in my discussion several movements of thought and thinkers to which Newbigin either gives a direct reference such as Lindbeck and Postliberalism or Reformed Epistemology or, say, Stanley Hauerwas with which he clearly has some affinity. It would be a worthwhile exercise to reflect on similarities and differences between the Reformed Epistemology of Alvin Plantinga and others who maintain that Christian faith should unabashedly adopt God as the "foundation" rather than trying to look somewhere else.[111] Similarly the Hauerwasian connec-

---

110. My own growing conviction is that, similarly to Modernity, postmodernism has such built-in contradistinctions in its texture that it may not survive for a long time. Its contribution in my opinion has been mainly deconstructive: it has helped the culture of the West to wake up from the Modernist slumber. What becomes "post" this, I am not yet sure about.

111. Keskitalo (*Kristillinen usko*, 167–72) offers an insightful excursus on the topic; unfortunately, it is not accessible for English readers.

tion with its idea of the church as a unique "colony" and thus unique way of understanding reality would make a helpful contribution to our thinking of missional ecclesiology. When it comes to Postliberalism, it seems to me that Newbigin's sympathies—even with some critical notes—might have been a bit misplaced. I personally do not think that Postliberalism is a viable alternative as it advocates a "sectarian" rather than public understanding of truth, by speaking of truth only in terms of inner-Christian convictions and personalized ways of viewing the world.

I am not mentioning these tasks for further study primarily to advance academic inquiry but rather in my desire to better understand the scope and location of Newbigin's missional ecclesiology in the larger matrix of contemporary thinking. Is it the case that Newbigin's missional ecclesiology and epistemology represents a movement *sui generis* or is it rather that—like any creative and constructive thinker—he has listened carefully to a number of contemporary voices and echoes their motifs in a fresh way?

BIBLIOGRAPHY

Berger, Peter L. *The Heretical Imperative: Contemporary Possibilities of Religious Affirmation*. London: Collins, 1980.

Graham, Elaine, and Heather Walton. "A Walk on the Wild Side: A Critique of *the Gospel and Our Culture*." *Modern Churchman* 33 (1991) 1–7.

Keskitalo, Jukka. *Kristillinen usko ja moderni kulttuuri: Lesslie Newbigin käsitys kirkon missiosta modernissa länsimaisessa kulttuurissa* ["The Christian Faith and Modern Culture: Lesslie Newbigin's View of the Church's Mission in Modern Western Culture"], Suomalaisen Teologisen Kirjallisuusseuran Julkaisuja 218. Helsinki: Suomalainen Teologinen Kirjallisuusseura, 1999.

Kirk, J. Andrew, et al., editors. *Mission and Postmodernities*, Edinburgh 2010 Studies. London, UK: Regnum, 2011.

MacIntyre, Alasdair. *After Virtue: A Study in Moral Theory*. London: Duckworth, 1981.

———. *Whose Justice? Which Rationality?* London: Duckworth, 1988.

Newbigin, Lesslie. "Can the West Be Converted?" *International Bulletin of Missionary Research* 11, no. January (1987) 2–7.

———. "The Enduring Validity of Cross–Cultural Mission." *International Bulletin of Missionary Research* 12 (1988) 50–53.

———. *Foolishness to the Greeks: The Gospel and Western Culture*. London: SPCK, 1986.

———. "Gospel and Culture." Address given to a conference organized by Danish Missions Council and the Danish Churches Ecumenical Council in Denmark (3 November 1995). Online: http://www.newbigin.net/assets/pdf/95gc.pdf.

———. *The Gospel in a Pluralist Society*. London: SPCK, 1989.

———. "Modernity in Context." In *Modern, Postmodern and Christian*, co-authored with John Reid and David Pullinger, 1–12. Carberry: Handsel, 1996.

Veli-Matti Kärkkäinen

——— . *The Open Secret: An Introduction to the Theology of Mission.* 2nd ed. London: SPCK, 1995 (originally published 1978).

——— . *The Other Side of 1984: Questions for the Churches.* Geneva: World Council of Churches, 1983.

——— . *Proper Confidence: Faith, Doubt and Certainty in Christian Discipleship.* London: SPCK, 1995.

——— . "Religious Pluralism: A Missiological Approach." *Studia Missionalia* 42 (1993) 227–44.

——— . "Religious Pluralism and the Uniqueness of Jesus Christ." *International Bulletin of Missionary Research* 13 (1989) 50–54.

——— . "The Secular Myth." In *Faith and Power: Christianity and Islam in "Secular" Britain*, edited by Lesslie Newbigin, Lamin Sanneh and Jenny Taylor, 1–24. London: SPCK, 1998.

——— . *Truth and Authority in Modernity.* Valley Forge, PA: Gracewing/Trinity Press International, 1996.

——— . *Truth to Tell: The Gospel as Public Truth.* London: SPCK, 1991.

——— . *A Word in Season: Perspectives on Christian World Missions.* Edited by Eleanor Jackson. Grand Rapids: Eerdmans, 1994.

Polanyi, Michael. *Personal Knowledge: Towards a Post-Critical Philosophy.* Chicago: University of Chicago Press, 1958.

Ustorf, Werner. *Christianized Africa—De-Christianized Europe? Missionary Inquiries into the Polycentric Epoch of Christian History.* Ammersbek bei Hamburg: Verlag an der Lottbeck, 1992.

Weston, Paul D. A. "Lesslie Newbigin: A Postmodern Missiologist?" *Mission Studies* 21, no. 2 (2004) 229–48.

Re-imagining the Gospel as Public Truth

Ian Barns

INTRODUCTION: A CHALLENGE OF FRAMEWORKS

I WAS AN ELEVEN year old boy when I became a Christian. At the time I
was living with my parents in a little town on the south coast of Western
Australia. I had become curious about Christianity and went along one
Sunday evening to the local Baptist church where, in response to an evangelistic challenge, I made a commitment to follow Jesus. It was for me
a surprisingly transformative and life-changing moment. Over fifty years
later, I continue to live within and "towards" that commitment and experience. However, like most Christians, I suppose, mine has been a journey marked as much by spiritual struggle as anything like a "victorious
Christian life." A particular point of perplexity has been the experience
of living a dichotomous existence: one part actively Christian, participating in the life of prayer, Bible study, Christian community and theological
learning; but the other part immersed in the practices, institutions and
disciplines of a wider secular world in which talk of "God" was completely
irrelevant.

Lesslie Newbigin has been important to me as one who has both explored this predicament of a privatized Christian form of life with insight
and urgency and has also offered a way of living out the vision of the Lordship of Christ with greater public integrity and wholeness. There is a passage in his little book, *Foolishness to the Greeks* which is never far from my
mind and which captures the urgent need to contest the way our culture
pressures us to restrict faith in Jesus to the "religious" part of our lives:

A private truth for a limited circle of believers is no truth at all. Even the most devout faith will sooner or later falter and fail unless those who hold it are willing to bring it into public debate and to test it against experience in every area of life. If the Christian faith about the source and goal of human life is to be denied access to the human realm, where decisions are made on the great issues of the common life, then it cannot in the long run survive even as an option for a minority."[1]

Yet how do we live out a gospel that claims to be "public truth" in our late modern western culture: a culture that has become increasingly influential—both intensively through the milieu of electronic media and the incredible density of knowledge, ideas and information, and extensively through the processes of economic and cultural globalization? In this chapter I want to explore that question by considering the "gospel as public truth" agenda that Newbigin outlined in several of his books and how it needs to be applied by "ordinary" Christians in the contexts of everyday life.

In my experience, most Christians adopt a basically utilitarian approach to the secular world in our various forms of employment, business and finance, home-building, study, entertainment, leisure and so on. To be sure, we recognize that these are significant locations for Christian discipleship, but we usually consider the spiritual challenges that arise as basically subjective and inter-personal and not to do with the larger structures and systems themselves. Indeed, despite ongoing secularization we still generally feel at home in the spaces, practices and institutions of a liberal-democratic-capitalist society and economy, comforted by a sense of the continuing influence or legacy of Judeo-Christian values.

For Newbigin this was a deeply mistaken approach. Rather than "our culture" being a neutral space, he argued that it was shaped by a now well-entrenched "fiduciary framework" that at a fundamental level undercuts or displaces a Christian apprehension of the world. The awkward term "fiduciary framework" is one that Newbigin drew from Michael Polanyi's writings on the personal nature of scientific knowledge: that our lives are embedded within a taken-for-granted and collective way of experiencing the world, that includes assumptions about the nature of reality, the purpose of human life and the ordering of human society, as well as ethical and aesthetic meanings and values. We don't necessarily "believe" in the framework of our culture: rather it is a way of being in the world that is

1. Newbigin, *Foolishness to the Greeks*, 117.

"sedimented" in our everyday practices and norms of social behavior. It is coded into our laws, institutions, artifacts, styles of clothing, forms of greeting, architecture, buildings and streets. It shapes our thinking, feeling and imagination at a most basic level.

Newbigin's challenge for us is to become aware of—and to actively contest—the dominant fiduciary framework of our time, which expresses an enlightenment humanist vision of knowledge, reality and human existence. He reminds us that whilst we may feel quite at home within this framework, since it continues to draw on many of the moral and social values of the antecedent Christendom framework (the Judeo-Christian tradition), we should recognize that at a fundamental epistemological level it is deeply antithetical to a Christian vision of reality. For Newbigin a key aspect of this framework is an assumed division between factual knowledge about the world, which is to be obtained through the objective methods of science, and "values," which—whilst important for human politics and social relations—are ultimately matters of preference and tradition. This division is reflected in the authority and prestige accorded to scientists and technically-trained experts, in the construction of school curricula, and in a liberal pluralism that generally celebrates diversity with respect to moral and religious beliefs.

Whilst it is convenient for Christians to accept a position of being one—albeit still politically privileged—religious tradition amongst an increasing religious plurality, the acceptance of the dominant epistemology of our culture implicitly denies the objective truthfulness of the gospel's message about God in Christ. In response to this, said Newbigin, our task is not only to bring to bear the message of the gospel to the issues of the day, but to do so in a way that is critically "frame-reflective," contesting the reigning fiduciary framework and embodying the alternative framework entailed by the gospel of Christ.

SOME POST-NEWBIGIN INITIATIVES

In the decades since Newbigin's writing gave rise to the "gospel and our culture" movement, his call for a more "frame-reflective" approach to public life has been taken up by a wide range of theologians and other scholars. In North America, an influential reformed tradition has fostered a fairly widespread interest in the question of "worldviews": of the need to challenge a secular and enlightenment worldview and to articulate an alternative Christian worldview. A rather different approach has been that of so-called "post-liberal" school of theology and biblical studies, originating with Hans Frei and George Lindbeck at Yale and becoming widely influential through the writings of Stanley Hauerwas and his former students such as Gregory Jones, Stephen Long and William Cavanaugh. In Europe, Pope Benedict has forcefully argued against the cultural and political dominance of "secular humanism" and for the defence of the moral objectivism of the Christian faith. In Britain the "radical orthodoxy" movement associated with John Milbank, Catherine Pickstock and Graham Ward and others is developing an approach that contests the assumed separation of religion and public life, exposing the deeply "religious" character of the supposedly secular spheres of economics, politics, sexuality and art, and is seeking to reframe them in Christian trinitarian and sacramental terms. More recently, Charles Taylor in his massive book, *A Secular Age*,[2] has developed an analysis of the profound shifts in the cultural framework of the West that parallels that of Newbigin, albeit in a more nuanced way.

Despite these encouraging developments, Newbigin's challenge remains a daunting one. The kind of frame-reflective public engagement he called for has not been taken up in any significant way by most church traditions, mainstream or otherwise. Although there have been various initiatives in "public theology," by and large the usual approach has been to contribute a "biblical perspective" (often together with other "faith traditions") within a taken-for-granted enlightenment framework. At the level of ordinary, church-going Christians there are diverse and encouraging efforts to connect faith and life in areas such as medical ethics and science and religion. However, any talk about "fiduciary frameworks" or "cultural imaginaries" seems highly abstract and academic, remote from the pragmatic concerns of negotiating or debating the issues of everyday life. Yet as Newbigin and others remind us, the question of a world-shaping cultural framework is far from being merely academic. In fact it confronts us most directly in the most immediate experiences of everyday life: in our means of subsistence (how we get our money, food, water, electricity), in the newspapers we read, the electronic media we participate in, the movies we watch, the books we read, and so on.

It is encouraging that within the wider culture there is a growing and interest in the way collective life is "framed." For example, in 2004 the US political scientist George Lakoff published a widely read book on the importance of "framing" in political campaigning, entitled *Don't Think of an*

---

2. Published in 2007.

Elephant.[3] More recently in Britain, a study by Tom Crompton (for WWF on consumer attitudes),[4] focused on the way issues are framed in the mass media and television. More generally in a media saturated-environment, there is at least some awareness of the ways in which particular issues—and the world in general—are not simply *given*, but constructed within a particular discursive frame. Most of us have learnt to recognize "spin," whether in advertising or politics. Moreover, despite the recent prominence of a more aggressive atheism, there is a growing "post-secular" questioning of the adequacy of modernity's secularist frame.

Still, it's a lot to ask of congregations made up of people with a wide diversity of spiritual orientations, educational backgrounds and cultural awareness to reflect on the fundamental framework of our culture and to become aware of how it shapes the way we think and live. Yet this is a challenge that comes not just from academic theologians, but from Scripture itself. St Paul urges his readers, for example, to "offer your bodies as a living sacrifice, holy and pleasing to God—this is your true and proper worship. Do not conform to the pattern of this world, but be transformed by the renewing of your mind" (Rom 12:1–2 NIV).

THE CHALLENGE FOR ORDINARY CHRISTIANS

What then is required for ordinary Christians immersed in the cultural density of our late modern culture to engage in the kind of constructive frame-reflective public theology that Newbigin was calling for? It's not an easy task and one that requires more serious attention at all levels of church life. It's not something for which most congregations, trained to participate passively in in-house church activities, are at all well-equipped. It requires an ability to "read" or to discern in our everyday culture the influence of background frameworks. It requires the fostering of various skills and virtues, not least a capacity to engage in respectful dialogical listening and learning, even with those with whom we disagree. To develop such skills will require in many congregational contexts a significant shift from a pre-occupation with "in-house" maintenance to equipping people for creative discipleship within the wider culture.

Following Newbigin I suggest that there are several important "enabling conditions" for the equipping of lay Christians to take up the task of critical frame-reflection and re-visioning. These are:

3. Lakoff, *Don't Think of an Elephant.*
4. Crompton, *Common Cause.*

- a deep immersion in the larger kingdom story of the Bible;

- experience in creatively re-telling the story of the world (and its extraordinary history and diversity) in a way that counters the presently dominant humanist meta-narrative;

- a congregational commitment to work out our collective and individual vocation as God's renewed "image-bearers" within the various spheres of life, including work;

- an understanding and defence of the key leavening role that the church plays in maintaining the proper "Christian secularity" of the modern state.

1. GETTING THE GOSPEL'S STORY RIGHT

At the heart of any faithful Christian response to our culture is our understanding of the gospel itself. Newbigin recognized that our capacity to defend the gospel as public truth was severely undermined by the truncated version that dominated much of Christian thinking and practice. He urged us to re-discover the "big picture" gospel that the Bible was actually all about. As he put it with characteristic clarity and simplicity: "In distinction from a great deal of Christian writing which takes the individual person as its starting point for the understanding of salvation and then extrapolates from that to the wider issues of social, political, and economic life, I am suggesting that, with the Bible as our guide, we should proceed in the opposite direction, that we begin with the Bible as the unique interpretation of human and cosmic history and move from that starting point to an understanding of what the Bible shows us of the meaning of personal life."[5]

It is still the case that in much of mainstream Christianity the prevailing understanding of the gospel continues to be individualistic and anthropocentric. Personal experience and discipleship, communal worship and evangelism are generally framed within a message of God's action to save each individual from the consequences of their sin. As one popular song puts it, "Jesus died, just for me." This message touches our hearts and lifts our spirits, especially when expressed communally in "Jesus and me" love songs. But it is also a message that does little to encourage or help us to think about the wider culture in which we live in discerning, Christian terms.

5. Newbigin, *Gospel in a Pluralist Society*, 128.

Sadly, when Christians whose thinking has been shaped by a truncated individualistic gospel do engage with political issues, they often do so either in progressive enlightenment terms, merely adding a religious gloss to various secular causes, or in reactionary fundamentalist terms hostile to secular disciplines and suspicious of government action. The growth of the Christian right in the United States—pre-occupied with the issues of abortion, gay marriage and economic freedom—is a tragic parody of what a faithful witness to the gospel of public truth might look like in an American context. The damage that right wing Christianity does to the communication of the gospel in our world is massive and reinforces the urgent need to get the Bible's big story right.

There is still the immense challenge of re-shaping the minds—and lives—of ordinary church-going Christians in terms of a kingdom/new creation paradigm. Tom Wright's image of regarding Christian life as becoming part of a five-act play in which we are called to improvise sections of the play on the basis of a deep knowledge of the overall script has been helpful in thinking about how we might best connect a knowledge of Scripture to the circumstances of everyday life.[6] Robert Webber's argument for re-shaping liturgical worship in terms of the Bible's big story[7] and John Wright's *Telling God's Story,* which argues for the faithful preaching of Scripture's larger narrative,[8] identify some of the critical tasks in fostering a kingdom imagination and praxis amongst ordinary Christians.

2. RE-IMAGINING A GOSPEL-SHAPED WORLD

A society's cultural framework is expressed and communicated most powerfully in the mythic stories it tells: of its origins, its struggles of identity, of its axial events, of its heroes and exemplars, and of its place within the wider scope of history. Even our ostensibly disenchanted, technologically sophisticated culture is shaped and sustained by its mythic stories: in our case a story of humanity's coming of age through the advance of reason and the displacement of the gods of religion and superstition. To be sure our nineteenth century forebears' sunny confidence that through reason humanity would progressively create a more enlightened and humane world has been chastened by the horrors of the twentieth century. Yet it seems premature for postmodernists to assert that modernity's mythic

6. Wright, *New Testament and the People of God,* 140–41.

7. Webber, *Ancient-Future,* passim.

8. Wright, *Telling God's Story.*

progress story has lost all credibility. Our culture's collective imagination is still soaked in dreams of secular human flourishing and the mastery of nature. Notwithstanding the enduring problems of poverty, inequality, disease and civil conflicts, most moderns still have faith in progress. It's a faith validated in several ways: by continuing improvements in living standards made possible by more and more powerful technologies—in energy, food production, medicine, transportation, communication and social administration; by an ever-deepening scientific knowledge of the human condition; and, less clearly, by progressive improvements in personal rights and freedoms.

Even so the progress story is now being challenged as never before by the deepening crises of modernity in our time: ecological, political, social, psychological and moral. Most deeply the myth of secular human flourishing is undermined by the implicit nihilism of the modernity's scientistic view of reality and of human origins. Paradoxically, one of the greatest achievements of enlightenment humanism—the enormous advances in our understanding of the physical world, from the big bang to the human brain—brings into question the sense of ontological uniqueness that has been central to the humanist project. As physicist Steven Weinberg put it, "The more the universe seems comprehensible, the more it also seems pointless."[9] For many people the "malaises of modernity" have led to a greater open-ness to seeing the world differently. As social theorist Jonathan Rutherford put it: "We are living through an age of transition. The new co-exists with the old. We can identify political, economic and cultural elements of this change, but we do not yet have a way of describing the kind of society we are living in. The great explanatory frameworks of political economy and sociology inherited from the industrial modernity of the nineteenth century leave too much unsaid. Theories of the moment tend to skip from one modern phenomenon to another. They are like stones skimming across the surface of water. We lack a story of these times."[10]

Countering modernity's grand story with the alternative story of God's kingdom was for Newbigin a crucial aspect of communicating the gospel as public truth:

> The way we understand human life depends on what conception we have of the human story. What is the real story of which my

9. Weinberg, *First Three Minutes*, 154. Cf. the discussion in his *Dreams of a Final Theory*, 255.

10. Rutherford, "Culture of Capitalism," 8.

life story is a part? That is the question which determines what we believe to be success and what failure. In our contemporary culture, as exemplified in the curriculum of teaching in the public schools, two quite different stories are told. One is the story of evolution, of the development of species through the survival of the strong, and the story of the rise of civilization, and its success in giving humankind mastery of nature. The other story is the one embodied in the Bible, the story of creation and fall, of God's election of a people to be the bearers of his purpose for humankind, and of the coming of the one in whom that purpose is to be fulfilled. These are two different and incompatible stories.[11]

Is it possible that the Bible's story—the story of creation, human rebellion against God and the subsequent descent into violence, God's election of Israel, the saga of Israel's life in the land and exile, the coming of Jesus, his life, death and resurrection, the outpouring of the Spirit and the preaching of the gospel to all peoples, and the expectation of a time when God judges all things and establishes the kingdom in a perfected creation—might once again shape the imagination and hopes of a whole society as it did in the era of Christendom? At one level it seems highly unlikely. For many people, modernity has opened up a story of human life on this earth and in the cosmos that seems vastly more authoritative and powerful than the Christian story centred on an obscure people and its messiah. And yet as the statement by Jonathan Rutherford indicates, people are looking for a story that provides a better spiritual framework for our lives. So could the Bible's story meet the need of our times?

Opposition or Dialectic?

Newbigin assumes a radical opposition between the "enlightenment progress/mastery of nature" story and the Bible's story, and that the Christian task is one of simply narrating the world differently. However, I believe that a more dialectical approach is needed: one that recognizes the deep connection as well as difference between these two stories. In my view a more constructive Christian approach recognizes the continuing Christian "core" of modernity's story—for example, with respect to a vision of the dignity of the human person, regardless of race, status, gender etc.; the conviction that cosmic and human history has a purpose and a direction;

11. Newbigin, *Gospel in a Pluralist Society*, 15–16.

and that humanity has a special place as the lords of creation. Our critical task is to make explicit the ways in which modernity's story represents an heretical—and ultimately monstrous—perversion of Christianity, since the displacement of God unfolds not in a just and peaceable world but in the violent assertion of Promethean will and desire. Constructively, we also need to recognize that the enlightenment pursuit of these Christian goods is an indictment on the failure of Christians—both past and present—to do so. Any re-narration of the world in biblical terms needs to incorporate the positive achievements of an enlightenment culture—for example, with respect to its deepened scientific understanding of the natural world and the many ways in which the condition of human life has been vastly improved through economic development and technological innovation.

Creative Re-narration

I can only touch on what such a creative re-narration might involve. Against the cosmic story of a universe shaped by the blind forces of chance and necessity, the gospel story tells of God's act of creation in which the created order is able over time to bring forth the incredible diversity of life, including human creatures able to participate in the personal and relational love of the creator. Against the image of Promethean man whose assertive will and technological daring has inspired much of modernity's march of progress, the gospel story centres on the figure of Jesus as the one who faithfully reflects and embodies the self-giving love of the Creator God. Against the notion that moral and material progress can be achieved through autonomous human endeavor, the gospel story tells of the need for the redemption of humans from the malign fruits of our rebellion and sin.

The question of how we narrate or re-narrate the world is not something to be left to cultural theorists and the like. All of us are continuously engaged in storytelling, either as the tellers or the hearers. The primary mythic stories of our culture pervade the more specific stories we tell of our communities, our nations, our heroes and ourselves. The characters and plots of novels, films and TV dramas resonate with the myths of human self-discovery and freedom, of progress and prevailing against all odds. Even the dramas of political life and of the business world are suffused with myth. So being able to discern and respond to the narrative forms of our cultural life is thus an important skill for us to develop as

Christians, as is the capacity to re-narrate the extraordinary story of scientific and technological discovery, medical advances and the processes of globalization in terms of the gospel story.

3. RE-IMAGING THE PROPHETIC ROLE OF LAY CHRISTIANS WITHIN A SECULAR PUBLIC REALM

For Newbigin the everyday endeavors of lay Christians were as important if not more so than the pronouncements of ecclesiastical spokesmen in demonstrating the public truth of the gospel in contemporary society:

> The missionary encounter with our culture for which I am pleading will require the energetic fostering of a declericalized, lay theology . . . We need a multitude of places where this kind of lay theology can be nourished. We need much better provision to ensure that when church leaders make pronouncements on ethical, political, and economic questions, their words are informed by a theology that has been wrought out of the coal face, at the place where faith wrestles at personal cost with the hard issues of public life. And we need to create, above all, possibilities in every congregation for lay people to share with one another the actual experience of their weekday work and to seek illumination from the gospel for their daily secular duty. Only thus shall we begin to bring together what our culture has divided—the private and public. Only thus will the church fulfill its proper missionary role. For while there are occasions when it is proper for the church, through its synods and hierarchies, to make pronouncements on public issues, it is much more important that all its lay members be prepared and equipped to think out the relationship of their faith to their secular work. Here is where the real missionary encounter takes place.[12]

In terms of what is surely needed for Christian laypeople to be appropriately resourced as agents of the gospel as public truth, much more needs to be done, both practically and theologically. Within many churches, there is still a culture that privileges church-oriented ministries over secular occupations as the primary domain of Christian vocation. Moreover, even where there is pastoral support for church members within their "secular" occupations, this is typically framed in terms of personal discipleship or taking up opportunities for personal evangelism.

12. Newbigin, *Foolishness to the Greeks*, 143.

There is an urgent need for congregations to address the key question: does the substantive professional work of architects, builders, investors, farmers etc. have a kingdom significance beyond their recognized utilitarian value? Do we say simply that the "kingdom value" of the many and varied secular occupations that Christians may choose to practice lies in the service they offer to other people: that they can become vehicles of God's love and compassion?

In his books, *The Challenge of Jesus* and *Surprised by Hope*, Tom Wright argues along these lines. He suggests that we ought to see the diverse professional activities in which Christians are engaged as "building blocks" for God's kingdom. It is wrong for us to think that we are "building the kingdom." Rather, it is God who can and will make use of the "work" in which we are engaged (gold, silver and precious stones vs. wood, hay and stubble):

> Every act of love, gratitude, and kindness; every work of art
> or music inspired by the love of God and delight in the beauty
> of his creation; every minute spent teaching a severely handi-
> capped child to read or to walk; every act of care and nurture,
> of comfort and support, for one's fellow human beings and for
> that matter one's fellow nonhuman creatures; and of course ev-
> ery prayer, all Spirit-led teaching, every deed that spreads the
> gospel, builds up the church, embraces and embodies holiness
> rather than corruption, and makes the name of Jesus honoured
> in the world—all of this will find its way, through the resur-
> recting power of God, into the new creation that God will one
> day make.[13]

However, Wright's perspective of human vocation needs to be spelt out more fully by saying not just that the faithful and loving service of Christians will be redeemed in the new heavens and the new earth, but that the task of "world building" is integral to our human calling to be God's image bearers within the creation. Rikk Watts speaks of this in terms of the vocation of "building a city." Watts sees that the extraordinary development of civilization—of crafting a human-shaped world—arises out of our proper calling as God's agents within the creation.[14] To be sure, this calling has been pursued not faithfully, but in idolatrous rebellion, giving rise not to the beautiful city that God intends, but the monstrous city of which "Babylon" is the archetype. Yet as Jacques Ellul argued in

13. Wright, *Surprised by Hope*, 219.

14. Watts, *Making Sense of Genesis 1*, 8f.

The Meaning of the City, God does not abandon humanity or its proud creation, but bears its sin and opens the way for its ultimate redemption.[15]

What Kind of City?

This dynamic of creational calling, rebellious world-building and cruciform redemption provides the theological framework for the understanding of Christian participation in the many and diverse activities that build, maintain and extend the human city. Thus a further key question arises: what kind of city are we participating in building? Of course this question relates not just to the urban centers that have been and have become ever more so extraordinarily central to the human enterprise, but to the emergent global civilization that reflects both the glory and tragedy of humanity.

Such questions are certainly on the agenda, at least in secular form, in much public policy debate. We recognize that the human city is where the fate of humanity is being worked out. Will the city be shaped by the relentless drive for corporate profit and be marked by high levels of inequality, a weakened civic culture and a degraded physical environment? Or is a more just, peaceable and sustainable city possible?

It is easy for progressive Christians to identify with the vision of a just, peaceable and sustainable city. Clearly such a vision resonates with the gospel, and with the OT prophets' denunciation of oppression and violence, of the failure to care for the poor, the widow and the orphans in the land. Yet a gospel vision is also very different. It is about the creation of a city centered on the worship of the servant king, and one in which human creative world building has a sacramental character, reflecting the self-giving life of the triune God. How can this counter vision be made visible in the cultural spaces, places and flows of contemporary cities?

4. WHAT DOES "PUBLIC TRUTH" MEAN IN POLITICS? DEFENDING THE CHRISTIAN SECULARITY OF LIBERAL POLITICAL INSTITUTIONS

A particularly important—and challenging—arena in which we are called to communicate the gospel as public truth is that of politics: public policy, legislation, public administration, public opinion, election campaigns and

15. Ellul, *Meaning of the City*, 180.

so on. Until fairly recently, it seemed that the political domain was becoming irreversibly more secular or at least "de-Christianized." From being close to the centres of institutional and discursive power, churches have been reduced to being one set of pressure groups ("faith groups") among many in a pluralistic, secular public domain. In government, academia, business, the media and advertising it is now the discourses of economics, of market processes, of scientific expertise and psychology that frame much of public knowledge and opinion.

By and large over the past half-century most Christians have adapted happily enough to these shifts, finding some comfort in the belief that, even if God had been relegated to the private sphere, nonetheless public life was still shaped by a strong heritage of Judeo-Christian values. Yet in recent years, as public attitudes have become more pluralistic and post-Christian, fundamentalist Christians have become more politically active. In the United States in particular right wing Christians have pursued an openly "Christian" political agenda, seeking to change laws and public policy in relation to abortion, gay rights and so forth, and beyond that to bring into question the very legitimacy of secular government itself. The most extreme expression of the Christian right movement is the so-called "'dominion theology," associated with people like Rousas Rushdoony and Gary North, whose explicit aim is to (re-)establish the United States as a theocracy under "God's law."

The rather surprising (at least in the eyes of secular liberals) re-assertion of religious ideology (not only Christian but Islamic as well) has triggered a widespread debate amongst liberal political theorists about the legitimate place of religion in the public sphere. Some have argued that religious beliefs and language should be kept firmly within the private domain, whilst others have conceded that it is only fair that religious believers—like all other citizens—should be free to articulate their religiously-based reasons in public debate, but with the proviso that the principle of religious neutrality should be strictly maintained within the formal domain of the state (i.e. in the machinery of government legislation, regulation and administration).

The legitimacy of the liberal democratic state has also been challenged by the processes of globalization, especially where these have been framed within a corporatist free market ideology. As governments have become increasingly subordinate to the imperatives of global capital, their legitimacy as embodiments of democratic processes has been seriously undermined. Thus whilst the radical right wants to minimize the state in order to enhance individual freedom, many on the left have become disillusioned with the state and look to alternative forms of political association that might better reflect collective social purposes.

The Role of the Modern Nation-State.

Thus the question of "religion in the public sphere" is entwined with the question of the proper role of the state itself. Both of these questions should be of vital interest to Christians seeking to articulate the gospel as public truth. How are we to understand the nature and purpose of the modern nation state theologically?

Newbigin argued for the Christian defence of a secular state and secular public sphere: a position he described in terms of "committed pluralism." He opposed both the project of restoring Christendom and also any Christian withdrawal from participation in political processes:

> The Enlightenment's vision of the heavenly city has failed. We are in a new situation, and we cannot turn back the clock. It is certain that we cannot go back to the *corpus Christianum*. It is also certain—and this needs to be said sharply in view of the prevalence among Christians of a kind of anarchistic romanticism—that we cannot go back to a pre-Constantinian innocence. We cannot use the example of the early church to encourage us in a Manichaean attempt to treat all power as evil and to wash our hands of responsibility for the realities of political power. We cannot go back on history. But perhaps we can learn from history. Perhaps we can learn how to embody in the life of the church a witness to the kingship of Christ over all life—its politics and economics no less than its personal and domestic morals—yet without falling into the Constantinian trap. That is the new, unprecedented, and immensely challenging task given to our generation. The resolute undertaking of it is fundamental to any genuinely missionary encounter of the gospel with our culture.[16]

A defense of the Christian secularity of the state is a particularly urgent aspect of any "gospel as public truth" agenda. One is that we should not be complacent, taking for granted the freedoms and benefits of a state constrained by the rule of law and systems of democratic accountability. Our freedoms and the limitations of the powerful are precarious outcomes

---

16. Newbigin, *Foolishness to the Greeks*, 102.

of the struggle to acknowledge the sovereign lordship of Christ. A second is that we should not imagine that the political expression of the lordship of Christ is a theocracy, involving rule by a Christian elite and the enforcement of "Christian" laws. The history of Christendom makes clear that in our present age, the eschatological reign of Christ is expressed not through the enforcement of Christian power, but rather through creating and maintaining public spaces of free association and expression, and the fostering of public discussion of the goods of human life.

CONCLUSION

As late modern Christians we do inhabit two worlds. We are unavoidably part of the wider world with its Promethean energies, driving our economic life, our politics and our culture in unknown and probably precarious directions. Yet we are also, by faith, members of that "civic assembly of the eschatological city" centred on the risen Christ, who is our sovereign Lord, and who through the work of his Spirit and his people will bring God's creation to its intended perfection. These are not separate and autonomous worlds, but exist in a dialectic that is deeply oppositional yet in which the fruits of God's kingdom are being and will be realized.

Once again, Newbigin expresses this vision of an alternative gospel-based form of citizenship in a wonderfully challenging way:

> Christian discipleship . . . is neither the way of purely interior spiritual pilgrimage, nor is it the way of realpolitik for the creation of a new social order. It goes the way that Jesus went, right into the heart of the world's business and politics, with a claim which is both uncompromising and vulnerable. It looks for a world of justice and peace, not as the product of its own action, but as the gift of God who raises the dead and "calls into existence the things that do not exist" (Rom 4:17). It looks for the holy city not as the product of its policies but as the gift of God. Yet it knows that to seek to escape from politics into private spirituality would be to turn one's back on the true city. It looks for the city "whose builder and maker is God," but it knows that the road to the city goes down out of sight, the way Jesus went, into that dark valley where both our selves and all our works must disappear and be buried under the rubble of history . . . Such discipleship will be concerned equally in the private and the public spheres to make visible that understanding and ordering of life which takes as its "fiduciary framework"

the revelation of himself which God has given in Jesus. It will provide occasions for the creation of visible signs of the invisible kingship of God.[17]

BIBLIOGRAPHY

Crompton, Tom. *Common Cause: The Case for Working with Our Cultural Values.* WWF Report (September, 2010). Online: http://assets.wwf.org.uk/downloads/common_cause_report.pdf.

Ellul, Jacques. *The Meaning of the City.* Translated by Dennis Pardee. Grand Rapids: Eerdmans, 1970.

Lakoff, George. *Don't Think of an Elephant: Know Your Values and Frame the Debate.* White River Junction, VT: Chelsea Green, 2004.

Newbigin, Lesslie. *Foolishness to the Greeks: The Gospel and Western Culture.* London: SPCK, 1986.

———. *The Gospel in a Pluralist Society.* London: SPCK, 1989.

———. *The Other Side of 1984: Questions for the Churches.* Geneva: World Council of Churches, 1983.

Rutherford, Jonathan. "The Culture of Capitalism." *Soundings* 38 (Spring 2008) 8–18.

Taylor, Charles. *A Secular Age.* Cambridge, MA: Belknap, 2007.

Watts, Rikk. "Making Sense of Genesis 1," *Stimulus* 12/4 (November 2004) 2–12.

Webber, Robert E. *Ancient-Future Evangelism: Making Your Church a Faith-Forming Community.* Grand Rapids: Baker, 2003.

Weinberg, Steven. *Dreams of a Final Theory: The Search for the Fundamental Laws of Nature.* London: Vintage, 1993.

———. *First Three Minutes: A Modern View of the Origin of the Universe.* London: Fontana, 1983.

Wright, John. *Telling God's Story: Narrative Preaching for Christian Formation.* Downers Grove, IL: IVP Academic, 2009.

Wright, N. T., *The Challenge of Jesus.* London: SPCK, 2000.

———. *Christian Origins and the Question of God. Vol. 1: The New Testament and the People of God.* London: SPCK, 1992.

———. *Surprised by Hope.* London: SPCK, 2007.

17. Newbigin, *Other Side of 1984,* 37.

Newbigin at the Areopagus

Arguing for Truth in the Market Place

J. Andrew Kirk

THE VISION

THE INTENTION OF THIS article is to reflect on Lesslie Newbigin's concern that the Christian Gospel should be presented to the world as public truth. I will divide it into two main parts. The first section will explore briefly how Newbigin understood the concept of the Gospel[1] as public truth. The second section will review a discussion process that took place in the 1990s in Birmingham under the title, "The Gospel as Public Truth . . . in Birmingham." I hope that together they will illuminate the theme of the proclamation of the Gospel in the public square. This aspect of Newbigin's thinking is informed by other aspects of his analysis of contemporary culture, such as the notion of "plausibility structures," the public-private and fact-value splits and the assertion of human autonomy.

Newbigin understood the three terms in the following ways. "The Gospel" is the message about Jesus Christ as revealed by the Holy Spirit to the apostolic church and recorded in Scripture. It is good news in two essential dimensions. Firstly, it tells the story of what God in Christ has

---

1. The capital letter is used to indicate that, from a Christian perspective, there is ultimately only one good news story for the whole world. The events of Jesus of Nazareth's life, teaching, sacrificial death and resurrection to new life as presented and interpreted by his first disciples alone speak of a genuine and enduring hope for a transformed human existence in all its dimensions. There are, of course, many other pieces of good news; the Jesus narrative, however, is the benchmark by which all the other claims are to be measured.

done to restore creation to the wholeness that God has always intended. Secondly, the act of restoration is a free gift from God to his creatures. God has stepped into the world to bring about a transformation that human beings can never achieve for themselves. His activity is sheer unmerited grace. "Public" refers to whatever affairs are conducted in the domain of the whole human community, and which are open to all. In this sense the Gospel is public good news, for it speaks of actions performed openly on the stage of universal history, which are intended for the whole of humanity (1 John 2:2). The message of Jesus Christ is the exact opposite of esoteric doctrines or mystery cults of any kind. Newbigin loved to quote Paul's affirmation, when on trial before Festus and King Agrippa, that "this was not done in a corner" (Acts 26:26). "Truth" is the whole of reality as disclosed generally in creation and particularly by God's personal communication to humanity through his chosen servants.

Debate in the Civic Arena

Today in Western societies the public sphere (or market place) is "naked" in the sense that Western culture, having abandoned Christian public doctrine about the purpose and destiny of human life, is left only with speculation and an arbitrary choice about what it means to be human. Contemporary culture is characterized by the "nightmare of subjectivism and relativism . . . the captivity of the self turned in on itself."[2] In the long process of secularization in the West, there is a common perception that Nature[3] has taken the place of God as the complete source of knowledge. However, nature is impersonal and indifferent to the plight of humanity.

Moreover, in spite of a current insistence on the value of pluralism,[4] truth-claims are inevitable.[5] However, without the assurance of revealed

2. Newbigin, *Truth to Tell*, 13.

3. The capital letter is used here to point out that nature is often used as a kind of personalised substitute for the divine being. It is as if the words of the Psalmist, "My help comes from the Lord, who made heaven and earth" (Ps 121:2) have become "My help comes from . . . heaven and earth." There is currently a vociferous body of opinion that claims that a complete understanding of the origin and development of life can be fully achieved by investigating the material world.

4. Pluralism is understood as the view that "affirms a rough parity among them (religions) concerning truth and salvation. Pluralism . . . celebrates diversity of religious experience and expression as good and healthy. It maintains that no one tradition can be normative for all, and is sceptical of claims that any particular religious tradition has special access to truth about God." Satyavrata, "Religious Pluralism," 334.

5. It is plain that the statement about pluralism is itself a claim to be affirming the truth in the realm of religious validity.

truth, they easily become the will-to-power. This becomes manifest, for example, in the current imposition of "correct beliefs and practices" through legislation.[6] Without a knowledge of the truth about human life given by its Creator, all social programs and policies will tend to be arbitrary and authoritarian. Newbigin recognized this some time ago and, therefore, asserted that the price of maintaining a genuinely free society against the capricious imposition of constraints on the free expression of beliefs is constant vigilance: "There must be men and women in whom the authentic prophetic spirit is at work, who can speak in the name of the living God, who are ready to be witnesses, if necessary with their blood, to the reality of his rule. If there are not such, secular society is an easy prey for totalitarian ideologies. The house out of which the old gods have been expelled lies open to new demons."[7]

The notion of a secular society as the impartial arbiter of conflicting religious truth-claims is a myth. A religion-free society (as hoped for by the "new atheists") is unattainable, because human beings are inherently worshipping beings. Therefore, the God-shaped void at the heart of the secularist project will be filled, not with reasonable, detached, non-partisan and unprejudiced ideas and programs, but with other deities, which are basically pagan. Newbigin maintained characteristically that the distinction that has to be drawn, even in the most secular society, is not between religious belief and non-belief (agnosticism), but between belief and false belief. Thus, for example, secular humanism, in its exposition of the experience of human life, appeals (by faith) to the entirely unscientific notion of materialism, as a sufficient explanation for the whole of existence.

The Christian Message in the Civic Arena

The Christian church is called at this specific time to come in from the cold to claim its place as a chosen witness to the truth about the whole of reality as seen in the light of Jesus Christ. It should not allow itself to be marginalized, because of guilt about its Christendom past, as just one voluntary society amongst many, all of them purveyors of partial-truths:

6. I refer to laws that prohibit citizens from discriminatory practices, even on the grounds of well-formed (and, until recently) universally acknowledged moral principles. These laws are based on one particular interpretation of the meaning of equality; see, Jonathan Chaplin, "Equality: of people or reasons?" in Chaplin, *Talking God*, 29–37.

7. Newbigin, *Honest Religion*, 76.

"We are called, I think, to bring our faith into the public arena, to publish it, to put it at risk in the encounter with other faiths and ideologies in open debate and argument."[8] This, says Newbigin, is a fundamental part of its mission calling.

The Christian community, therefore, has a responsibility (beginning with itself) to expose false gods and call people to convert from them. The Barmen Declaration of the German Confessing Church provides an analogy: "The affirmations . . . would have made no impact without the anathemas. The Declaration names and rejects a false ideology . . . It affirms the truth of the gospel and, in its light, condemns the reigning falsehood. I think that perhaps that is the first thing to say about the duty of the Church in relation to political issues. The Church has to unmask ideologies."[9]

The Christian faith is a total alternative to secular faith. It offers, not just a different perspective on reality, but a different location for human accountability. Ultimately, all human beings and the societies they have created will be held answerable to the God of creation and history. In the public arena, accountability to the people (to the *demos*[10]), to the consensus of the majority, is not sufficient. The Gospel contains the ultimate truth about human life in society. There is no secular-sacred divide. This is why one can legitimately liken Newbigin's call to the Christian community to understand and proclaim the Gospel as truth in the public realm to Paul's encounter with the intellectual and political leaders of Athens in the market-place[11] and at the Areopagus. There, Paul preached the public doctrine of "Jesus and the resurrection" (Acts 17:18): "It was the message of the resurrection, rather than the 'creation theology' of the main part of Paul's address, which many of the hearers rejected. So, Paul did not compromise or temporize his message to fit the world-view of the Athenian 'opinion-formers.' He preached a scandalous and costly message which called the Athenians to renounce their mistaken religious views, in order to be able to enjoy fellowship with the true God (compare 1 Thess 1:9)."[12]

In other words, Paul was implying that the Athenians would only understand and practice authentic political life, about which they had such a

---

8. Newbigin, *Truth to Tell*, 59–60.

9. Ibid., 74.

10. Variously translated "people," "populace," "assembly," "crowd."

11. The New Revised Standard Version suggests, as an alternative translation for the Greek word *agora*, "civic centre."

12. Kirk, *Loosing the Chains*, 149; see the whole section, "Paul in Athens," 147–53.

self-consciously vaunted view, when they came to accept the truth of the message about Jesus, which he was announcing to them.

Economic Needs and Human Rights

Two of the most important issues in the public square are market economics and human rights. Newbigin insisted that, in the realm of economic life, in a society that has no accepted public doctrine about the purpose for which all things and persons exist, there is no basis for adjudicating between needs and wants. Therefore, as present circumstances bear witness, the dispute between wants and needs is irresolvable. This is at the heart of the crisis of global Capitalism and one of the main causes of its failure to address adequately the endemic nature of debilitating poverty. He also pointed out that, in the realm of rights, they are devoid of meaning unless there are parties that acknowledge a responsibility to meet the claims. Since there is no public doctrine about human responsibility, contrary claims to rights are likely to pull societies apart. Consequently, rival claims to rights, as is often the case in contemporary secular societies, have become a conflict of interests.

An Open Civic Space?

It should be emphasized that Newbigin's call to see the Gospel as public truth is not a veiled call to return to a lost Constantinian era. He has been much misunderstood at this point. His criticism of the Enlightenment project of modernity is not a veiled wish to return to a pre-modern society (as if such a desire were possible in any case). Christians, he believed, may advocate a "principled pluralism," i.e. one that promotes an open society in which vigorous debate between disparate views is encouraged. A plurality of divergent views should not be equated with a laissez-faire attitude that springs from a basic indifference to truth, but to a civilized way of handling what Polly Toynbee, referring to politics, calls "the clash of moral universes," "fundamentally different world views do(ing) battle."[13]

Since Newbigin was writing and speaking, public life has continued to shift. David Kettle sums up well the transposition that is now going on:

> As far as I can see, Newbigin was more concerned at the unsustainable, indiscriminately liberal face of secular society than

13. Quoted in Chaplin, *Talking God*, 49.

with its hidden tendency towards illiberalism which we see today. Thus when he argued against the secularist state's claim to stand for freedom in opposition to the sacral or Constantinian disposition of religions, he did so by pointing out that no state can allow freedom for *everything*, and so the Christian insistence upon certain *foundations upholding* freedom is by no means outrageous. Newbigin did not, on preliminary enquiry, adopt the argument that the secularist state has a false conception of freedom causing it precisely to *subvert* freedom when it thinks it is *defending* it by legislating against Christianity as (supposedly) freedom-denying. That is to say, he was more concerned, in the late 20th-century culture of his time, with state *disregard for* Christian truth than for state *interference with* those living by Christian truth. Again, he was more concerned to argue that Christians who seek power in the public domain should (unlike in a theocracy) allow space for others to dissent, than to argue that those in the public domain should allow space for Christians to dissent.[14]

However, it is the latter that should now also be of grave disquiet to the Christian community. Responding to this new situation would be one way of continuing Newbigin's concern that the Gospel be proclaimed as public truth. Today, Christians are called to make out a powerful case for society to hear without prejudice, among others, the voice of the Christian community. It is symptomatic of the extent of secularization that such a claim to be heard has to be made at all. Although, as I have argued elsewhere,[15] religious and secular beliefs are species of the same genus, the latter have become the default position for deciding what are and are not acceptable doctrines and practices in our current situation.

THE GOSPEL AS PUBLIC TRUTH . . . IN BIRMINGHAM

In order to see how the notion of the Gospel as public truth might become a mission priority for the Christian community, it may be helpful to tell something of the story of a study process that took place in Birmingham during the 1990s. As far as I am aware, this story has never been explicitly

---

14. In a private communication to me, dated 27 October 2009 (the emphasis is original).

15. See the chapter, "Mission as Dialogue: The Case of Secular Faith" in Kirk, *Mission under Scrutiny*.

J. Andrew Kirk

documented.[16] It illustrates, however, something of the thinking that has gone on among a group of Christians influenced by the challenge that Newbigin has set out and motivated to engage with its implications. Newbigin personally (at that time a resident of Birmingham) encouraged the group to see Birmingham as the place where a "pilot project" might happen, seeing how the Gospel could be declared public truth in a specific social context.[17]

The Background

The decade leading up to the second millennium was designated by a number of Churches as a decade of evangelism. There was a move among some churches in Birmingham to look at evangelism, not only as a way of communicating the gospel of Jesus Christ to individuals (essential though that focal point remains), but also as a way of addressing a whole city. A small, ad hoc working group was set up under the auspices of the Birmingham Council of Christian Churches (BC3) to consider the question of evangelism in respect of the whole city. After a couple of years, it became clear that BC3 did not think its work was a priority on its agenda, or perhaps did not believe that it had the resources to carry through the project. The Board of Mission of the Diocese of Birmingham agreed to take over responsibility for furthering the discussion. As a beginning, it set up a theological working group to look at "the meaning and feasibility of addressing the Gospel to the whole city of Birmingham, following an initiative of the Decade of Evangelism Steering Group."[18]

16. I base my version of the story on the official aide-memoirs taken of the various meetings and a number of study papers that were produced for the group and the wider public. I have these collected as a file. I am aware that Keith Sinclair (then rector of the Parish of Aston) also kept a file of all the documents. It is probable that another one exists in the Birmingham Diocesan office. I have checked out this account with Martin Conway (then President of the Selly Oak Colleges), who was also part of the group. He confirms that, according to his memory, this is a more or less reliable account of what transpired.

17. The study process was not formally linked to the Gospel and our Culture Project. However, it was inspired by the questions that Newbigin was raising about mission to culture. It also related to an earlier report concerning "Faith in the City of Birmingham," to which Newbigin was a contributor.

18. *Terms of Reference* (1994). It is interesting to note that, in the context of this study, the group was given the title of "the Gospel as Public Truth theological steering group."

Although the actual priorities to be considered were to be decided by the group itself, some questions were formulated at the beginning that were intended to indicate the kind of direction in which it would go. Thus, does it make sense to evangelize a city like Birmingham? If so, by what means may this be achieved? What is the relationship between communicating the Gospel to the city and to individuals? What powers and forces shape the life of a city? What do they exist for? What impact do they make on the lives of city dwellers? What bearing does the life, death, resurrection and ascension of Jesus Christ have on these powers?

The original ad hoc working group had been thinking (creatively) along fairly traditional lines about organizing significant events that would take up the challenge of the Decade of Evangelism for the whole city. Thus, for example, a series of sermons on topical issues from a Christian perspective in the cathedral, a public lecture(s) or public debates at the International Conference Centre or on central TV, public discussions on moral issues facing the city and the nation, an inquiry center under the auspices of the churches, and practical training in personal evangelism were all mooted. The vision was fairly ample. Nevertheless, the theological reflection group decided that none of these were really adequate to the task and, therefore, it would try to think through anew the issues that arise when communication of the Gospel as public truth becomes the central focus. The challenge it set itself was to move from thinking immediately about evangelistic *events* to an evangelistic *mind-set* that would first ponder the public nature of the good news of Jesus.

A New Direction

Two members of the group wrote a preparatory paper. It was designed to make proposals for a study process on engaging theologically and practically with the Gospel as public truth . . . in Birmingham. There were two clear antecedent events that inspired this new direction. The first was a paper contributed by a group, under Lesslie Newbigin as the chair person, to a book published in 1988 with the title *Faith in the City of Birmingham*. The chapter was called "Christian Perspectives on the City." The second was a major conference held at Swanwick in July 1992 under the auspices of The Gospel and our Culture Network. The title of the conference was "The Gospel as Public Truth," and its main concern was to relate the Gospel to the public domain by not allowing it to be "privatized," i.e. to become merely an interesting option for individuals rather than good news with crucial implications for the public square.

The initial paper set out the preliminary task of the reflection group as that of gaining a historical perspective on the Gospel as an instrument in the shaping of Birmingham as a city, considering recent and current initiatives (especially the "City Pride" process) which gave significant statements of the place of the city within contemporary culture and listening to what God is saying through the voice of many different people in the city at present. The paper continued by considering the theme of the evangelization of a city. It mentioned that an initial and partial bibliographical search had failed to produce "a single example of Christians having thought of evangelization and the corporate reality of the city as belonging together." "There may be a recognition (in the literature surveyed) that communication requires a thorough understanding of how the urban context shapes the lifestyles and values of the city-dweller, leading to a careful appraisal of what methods might be appropriate for ensuring that people hear the message in the city. However, the emphasis is undoubtedly on the individual within the urban mass. The concern, in the last analysis, is to select the most appropriate strategy by which the maximum number of people may be persuaded to consider the claims of Christ on their lives."

The paper also mentioned the number of studies which have examined and debated a "preferential option for the poor" within deprived urban areas as an intrinsic part of the Church's mission. "This approach often puts the emphasis on a prophetic ministry of judgement, warning and hope, which addresses macro-economic and political issues for the sake of micro-communities." The paper suggested that "from the perspective of an interest in the evangelization of the city, there are two major gaps that need to be filled: first, a proper theological reflection on the nature and significance of the *modern* city; secondly, a discussion of the proper relationship between evangelization and prophetic mission." The paper finished by stating that "our task is to wrestle with the question as to whether the significance of Jesus Christ can be conveyed to corporate bodies, powers and structures, and if so, exactly how. It hinted at the fact that the message and practice of the first disciples of Jesus was not only directed towards the conversion of individuals and the creation of small communities, called churches, but that something more public was going on."

Initial Research

The group commissioned three independent papers to begin to take the process of reflection forward: one was designed to look at the history of the impact of the Gospel in the past on the formation of the city of Birmingham; a second one had the task of analyzing the "City Pride" document—a study, produced by the city council, of the social, economic and participatory realities of the city, with a view to setting in motion programs of regeneration, particularly of disadvantaged areas; a third was given the job of setting out guidelines for "a project that would deliberately involve a sustained effort by a significant number of Christians to listen to our fellow-citizens."

The papers produced background information on the city and, in the case of the listening project, a series of questions that, it was hoped, would provide "fresh, first-hand data, not so much on the quantitative aspects of life (which are covered in most other 'public' enquiries) as on the qualitative aspects and concerns of living, and of the potential for living, in this city." In this way it was hoped that, by discovering the mood of the public, a beginning would be made in understanding the significance of the Gospel as public truth. Some of the questions that were suggested at that time, and that would seem to have a wide resonance elsewhere, were: What helps or hinders people making friends in Birmingham? What do people hope to make of their lives, and in what ways does this city encourage or block them in fulfilling that purpose? What do people most want to encourage their children to discover in this life and does the city facilitate that? What can be done to make this city a better place to live in and which activities are most likely to harm a better quality of life? There are, of course, other relevant questions that could have been asked. The intention of the listening process would have been to gain a cross-section of opinions about people's assessment of life in the city and their aspirations and fears about the future.

Reading the "City Pride" document a decade and a half later makes fascinating and dispiriting reading. In terms of economic trends, little seems to have changed. High unemployment amongst certain groups in the population continues. Long-term unemployment, where there is little opportunity for the development of new skills, increases. New jobs in the city are being taken by those who live outside; whilst employment locations are moved to suburban and rural areas. The percentage of jobs being part-time or temporary goes up.

J. Andrew Kirk

The document claims that economically the U.K. is looking back on a century of relative decline, and has not found the mix of policies and strategies to halt the decline. After years of some progress in reducing poverty and disadvantage, inequality and squalor once more have begun to increase. The labor market is distributing national income in increasingly uneven ways. Once established, social breakdown, violence and anti-social subcultures are difficult to reverse. The picture that is painted is bleak. The analysis shows that in a globalized economy, economic survival is dependent on gaining competitive advantage in the market place. However, history shows that such an economic strategy has had the effect of increasing social disadvantage and creating divided communities.

A Process of Reflection

The group initiated a process of reflection on these background papers. Among the many contributions the following points were highlighted. Firstly, we need to try to move beyond the division between the evangelization of individuals and the city. The city is comprised of individuals and individuals are affected by the corporate reality of their urban environment. There is nothing properly called a "city" that is not people engaged in activities together. Secondly, the task of charting the powers and priorities which are in tension with or flagrant contradiction to the purposes of God is a gap which needs filling in understanding the task of evangelization. Thirdly, we need to establish relevant criteria for judging whether, or to what extent, the city is being evangelized. What, for example, would be the *spiritual* benchmarks for creating "human flourishing"? It may be possible to create an excellent external environment, but without achieving this flourishing.

So, can we work on envisaging a process which actually changes societies through the message of the Gospel? The group thought that there might be a clue in the thought of Augustine, who, before speaking about the City of God, began his great treatise with a thorough demolition of false idolatries. This suggests that before the Gospel can be proclaimed as public truth, Christians need to grapple with the powers, both hidden and overt, that maintain the social sphere captive to false ideologies and distorted reasoning. It was pointed out that institutions may have arisen out of the best of motives, and yet, because they end up serving themselves rather than the causes for which they were created, they become oppressive. Also, teenage young people in Aston, interviewed by a member of the group, talked about an attitude of hostility towards anyone who had aspirations for a better life than that enjoyed by their parents. This perspective could be interpreted as a cultural block (and, therefore, a "power") to change that sprang from and induced a pervasive atmosphere of futility and fatalism.

However, the group also sounded a note of caution. The church has to be able to demonstrate that it has proclaimed the Gospel first to itself by consciously seeking to live on the basis of its key components: grace, forgiveness, justice, integrity, humility, service, suffering, compassion and holiness of life. Its first message to the world, therefore, should be we are a group of imperfect people, who have gone astray from God's good purposes for living. Nevertheless, we know that we have been forgiven and accepted by God on the basis of his own sacrifice of himself by which he has dealt with the problem of evil once for all. We are striving, through God's strength, to lead lives worthy of God's intentions. All those who are aware of their own failures, do not seek to justify themselves and genuinely want to live a new life are welcome to participate in this community of failed and vulnerable human beings. The church has to discern the powers in its own midst which distort its life and resolutely seek to unmask and eradicate them.

Tentative Outcomes

So, how far did this particular group go in exploring the significance of proclaiming the Gospel as public truth in the city? These are some of the tentative conclusions to which it came. Firstly, the church has to act as both a counter-culture to some dominant, prevailing thought-processes and activities and be involved in the debate about the macro-issues of power and economics.[19] Secondly, there is a need for a new Augustine to interpret and speak to the break-down of the inherited civilization of the West. Thirdly, evangelization cannot be divorced from macro-issues that require Christians to develop powers of discernment, so that the good news of the kingdom of God can be related effectively to concrete realities. This suggests taking the risk of speaking the truth of God's word into the public arena in a forthright way (for example, about the objective nature of right and wrong or the corruption that occurs, when money becomes

---

19. It is intriguing to note that, already in 1996, the group was suggesting a review of alternative banking systems and the reasons for and ways in which money was being invested.

the master we serve). A prophetic ministry is concerned with enabling people to see the truth by cutting through lies and illusions. Logically, it precedes evangelization, because the good news that proclaims the reality of transformed human life follows the bad news that we are unable to save ourselves from the mess we have created.

In the event, the whole conversation over some three years achieved no major breakthrough in the actual practice of proclaiming the Gospel as public truth . . . to Birmingham. It did, however, break new ground in tackling the issue in the first place. It also began to uncover some of the major themes that have to be considered, if the evangelization of a whole city is contemplated. Unfortunately, the listening process never got off the ground, owing to a lack of resources and motivation. In the end the group did come up with the idea of a "Kirchentag-style" event to be held in 1999 under the title "Towards the Millennium: a Dialogue with the City." The German Kirchentag is a major happening that focuses in part on a serious reflection around a major topic of the church's mission and in part on a celebration of God's continuing providential and salvific presence in the world. In the case of Birmingham, it was suggested that the dialogue would encompass such areas of the city's life as patterns and goals for life-long learning, economic objectives, the built environment as a means of creating greater community cohesion, healthy lifestyles and the conversion of cultures of despair and meaninglessness.

It was intended that the gathering would be a high profile event, supported by all the Churches in Birmingham. It would be distinctively Christian, both as a symbol of the Churches common life in Christ and as an expression of the public significance of the Gospel of the kingdom of God. It would engage with those not previously attracted to the Christian faith by setting forth a renewed vision of life in the city that touched people in their daily existence. In theological terms it would combine *dialogue* with different sectors of the city, *prophecy* that combined the exposure of evil with a message of hope, forgiveness and the promise of new life through God's action, and *evangelism* in the form of a multi-media retelling of the story of Jesus as good news for every aspect of the city and for individuals within it.

CONCLUSION

Newbigin's writings largely stopped in the mid-1990s. Consideration of a possible pilot project, testing out the significance of the Gospel as public truth in Birmingham, came to an end around the same time. Whereas the significance of the Gospel for public life has not changed, the "plausibility structures" that drive forward change in society seem, in important aspects, to have hardened against Christian belief and moral values. So, Christians in the West have found in recent years that their freedom of belief and action is being gradually curtailed. Laws are coming into existence, which prohibit people of faith criticizing the beliefs and lifestyles of others. In particular, Christians are being dismissed from their jobs or having public funds withdrawn from their enterprises or charitable organizations, because they disagree with the state's formal recognition of same sex relationships. Paradoxically, in the name of tolerance and anti-discrimination practices, Christian views are being suppressed and Christians are being discriminated against.

Newbigin, were he still with us, might possibly interpret this trend as another step in the direction of the state arrogating to itself a kind of divine status, being the final arbiter of what can and cannot be believed or openly expressed. Where there is a palpable moral vacuum at the heart of Western societies, the state steps in to decide moral virtue and moral vice. Could it be that, in the terrifying imagery of George Orwell, dismissed as absurdly alarmist when he wrote about it,[20] the "thought-police" are on the march? Traditional Christian convictions could now be labeled as "thought crimes," for which it is perfectly possible to be prosecuted. This is a dangerous tendency, in at least some Western societies, to which Christians need to respond vigorously before it is too late. In one of his very last publications, Newbigin hinted at what might be coming in societies that deliberately promoted the separation of the secular public realm from the sacred private sphere of individual belief. He noted that such a strategy was fallacious. It is the result of sloppy thinking, based on a partial and partisan reading of history.[21]

> We must surely now recognise that it is an illusion to suppose that the State can be totally neutral in respect of fundamental beliefs. All deliberate action pre-supposes some belief about what is the case, about the meaning and direction of human life. The ideologically neutral state is a myth, and a very dangerous one. Insofar as Christians are in positions of political responsibility, they are bound to use the power entrusted to them in accordance with the Christian understanding of God's purpose

20. In Orwell, *Nineteen Eighty-Four*, passim.
21. See Kirk, *Future of Faith, Reason and Science*, passim.

for human life. This means that there will be resistance from those who take other views. For the reason just stated, namely for the reason that in Christ God has given us a space of freedom for dissent and disobedience, but also for witness to the kingly rule of God, a government shaped by Christian belief will ensure the preservation of this space. It will recognise that there is unending need for the spiritual warfare which is required if the truth of the Gospel is to prevail in the public realm. But it will not pretend to neutrality. It will use the power entrusted to it in accordance with its understanding of God's will as revealed in the Gospel.[22]

Here, then, is a brief synopsis of Newbigin's reasons for emphasizing the public nature of the Gospel. The story of Jesus has significance for every aspect of life. Human beings cannot be treated as persons apart from their immersion in the cultural, social, political and economic circumstances that affect their lives. These realities, if they are to conform to the purposes for which God has created them, and if they are to serve the genuine needs of the whole community, must be placed under the rule of Christ. However, there is no natural desire in the human heart to submit to this rule. On the contrary, human beings, apart from the grace of Christ, are inclined to follow their own desires, fashioning their own lives and creating institutions in ways that fail to understand what makes for true human flourishing in a world created by God to reflect his nature. On their own human beings do not know the way to fullness of life in every sphere. The Gospel provides the answers to the most basic of life's conundrums by showing how life under the rule of Christ works out, in individual lives, personal relationships and the public life of the human community. It does so, because its message is true, i.e. it reflects and responds to the fundamental moral laws of the universe and the devastation that is caused when these are broken.

If this is the nature of the Gospel, then the context in which it is communicated has to include the market place and the "Areopagus," the civic centers of community life. Because it claims to tell the ultimate truth about the origin, meaning and end of life and propose how humans should live, it cannot be treated as if it were one amongst many other opinions about the nature of reality. Truth-claims bring with them inevitable consequences: if they are valid, they should be believed and acted on; if they are not valid, then this can only be known by reference to other truth-claims that are undeniable.

22. Newbigin, "Modern Society."

Newbigin is right to draw two conclusions from this argument about the public truth of the Gospel. Firstly, it is impossible for the collective organs of the human community (the state) to remain neutral towards belief systems and core values. Decisions have to be made that imply the truth about one or another underlying set of convictions. If a consensus concerning the truth and orienting power of the Christian faith has been broken in Western societies, another truth claim will have to emerge to take its place. The current candidate appears to be a version of secular humanism that looks to the principle of human rights to undergird its moral vision. However, its intellectual base is incoherent, since secular humanism has no reason, in terms of its own ideology, to sustain a defense of human rights. It actually has to assume the correctness of the Biblical teaching on the nature of human beings to be able to make its case.

Secondly, given the plurality of beliefs and values current in Western societies, Christians are obliged to engage in dialogue and debate with all alternative views. The case for the public truth of the Gospel has to be made out and then advanced through persuasion and argument. We now live in an age that insistently questions all truth-claims. People are looking, not for dogmatic statements, but for convincing reasons, based on cogent evidence, that claims to truth are to be trusted. Christians, therefore, need to learn to live again (as did the early Church) as representatives of a minority faith, able to uphold their beliefs in the market place of ideas, explaining why the Gospel is true. The true value of a genuinely secular society is that it maintains a space for conflicting views to be held, consciences respected and a dialogue respectful of variant claims to be pursued. In so far as this space has been restricted in recent years by capricious laws, purporting to defend equalities, but in reality subverting them, Christians will need to defend basic liberties. They may even have to test the law in court by non-compliance. Paradoxically, current secularist ideas are undermining the kind of secular society that supports the free exchange and open expression of views, however unpalatable they may be.[23] Could it be that Christians will be the last to defend the truly secular?

So, if the good news of Jesus and the kingdom (Acts 28:31) is true, it is true in the public realm. And, if it is not being proclaimed as true in the market place, it is not the good news about which the apostles spoke and

23. Thus, for example, a case could be made out even for allowing ultra-extremists to deny that the holocaust under the Nazi regime ever took place. In open debate their views can be ridiculed by showing them to be the historical fantasies that they are. Passing laws criminalising such a belief adds to its attraction for some kinds of people open to the delusion of conspiracy theories.

wrote. This is the fundamental point that Newbigin was wishing to convey with his pithy aphorism about the Gospel as public truth. Christians that follow him need to learn how to articulate afresh and appropriately this core conviction for their particular generation in circumstances that are constantly changing. This will be a core part of the Church's mission.

BIBLIOGRAPHY

Chaplin, Jonathan. *Talking God: The Legitimacy of Religious Public Reasoning*. London: Theos, 2008.

Kirk, J. Andrew. *The Future of Reason, Science and Faith: Following Modernity and Post-Modernity*. Aldershot: Ashgate, 2007.

———. *Loosing the Chains : Religion as Opium and Liberation*. London: Hodder & Stoughton, 1992.

———. *Mission under Scrutiny : Confronting Current Challenges*. London: Darton Longman & Todd, 2006.

Newbigin, Lesslie. "Can a Modern Society Be Christian?" In *Christian Witness in Society: A Tribute to M.M. Thomas*, edited by K. C. Abraham, 95–108. Bangalore: Board of Theological Education/Senate of Serampore College, 1998.

———. *Honest Religion for Secular Man*. London: SCM, 1966.

———. *Truth to Tell: The Gospel as Public Truth*. London: SPCK, 1991.

Orwell, George. *Nineteen Eighty-Four*. London: Secker & Warburg, 1949.

Satyavrata, Ivan M. "Religious Pluralism." In *Dictionary of Mission Theology: Evangelical Foundations*, edited by John Corrie. Nottingham: Inter-Varsity, 2007.

The Congregation as Hermeneutic of the Gospel

Murray Rae

AN ENDURING CHALLENGE

L ESSLIE NEWBIGIN STANDS IN a line of prophetic figures who remind us
that participation in God's purposes for the world involves a transformation both of the individual and of our life together as the people of God.
Being a Christian is not a minor alteration of our lifestyle, a hobby that oc-
cupies but one portion of our lives. Rather, Christian discipleship involves
a renewal of our minds and a radical transformation of our way of being.
The church, that community of people drawn by the Spirit into the body of
Christ, ought therefore to have a distinct identity, an identity determined
by its faith in Christ and by the new life inaugurated and established in
and through the resurrection of Jesus from the dead. My purpose in this
chapter is to consider this challenge as presented to us in Newbigin's work.

Returning to the UK in 1974, after many years of ministry in South
India, Newbigin saw with fresh eyes the extent to which the church in the
West had become assimilated to a culture that was no longer Christian.
While the culture of Modernity that now held sway had brought many
benefits, the underlying beliefs and convictions of that culture were seen
by Newbigin to be antithetical to the Gospel. He spent the remainder
of his life articulating the need for a new mission to that culture, and a
distinctive witness to the creative and redemptive purposes of God. That
distinctive witness consists, above all, in a transparent faithfulness to the
God of Jesus Christ and a refusal to worship the many other gods that
invite our allegiance.

Newbigin reminds us further that the good news of the Gospel entails a reshaping of the whole of life—our economic order, our justice system, our politics, our education system, and so on. We must be clear that the mission is God's mission rather than our own. Nonetheless, the human community formed as Christ's body is called to participate in this transforming work under the headship of Christ. Articulating that calling, Newbigin writes, ". . . the most important contribution which the Church can make to a new social order is to be itself a new social order."[1] Here, I believe, is the most profound challenge that Newbigin leaves with the Church of the twenty-first century. He calls the church, by which he means, first of all, the local congregation, to be a "hermeneutic of the gospel,"[2] to be in its own life an enacted interpretation of and witness to the good news that in Christ God is making all things new.

VISIBLE COMMUNITY

Although Newbigin advocated that theme with renewed urgency on his return to Britain, his insistence that the form of the church's own life should bear witness to the gospel appears early in his writings, notably, in *The Household of God*, published in 1953. Newbigin's lifelong concern for the unity of the church is shown here to be intimately connected with the credibility of the church's witness. In the missionary situation especially, he writes, the disunity of the church is "an intolerable scandal."[3] It is scandalous because the disunity of the church constitutes a betrayal of the gospel of reconciliation through which those previously at enmity with one another are made one in the body of Christ (cf. Eph 2:11–22). Concomitant with his claim that the form of the church's life should be transparent to the gospel, Newbigin writes, ". . . I believe that the divinely willed form of the Church's unity is at least this, a *visible* company in every place of all who confess Jesus as Lord, abiding together in the Apostle's teaching and fellowship, the breaking of bread and the prayers. Its foci are the word, the sacraments, and the apostolic ministry. Its form is the *visible* fellowship, not of those whom we choose out to be our friends, but of those whom God has actually given to us as our neighbours. It is therefore simply humanity in every place re-created in Christ."[4]

1. Newbigin, *Truth to Tell*, 85.
2. See especially, chapter 18 of Newbigin, *Gospel in a Pluralist Society*.
3. Newbigin, *Household of God*, 18.
4. Ibid., 21 (my emphases).

The stress upon the visibility of the church recurs throughout *The Household of God*, and for several reasons, first because God's redemptive purposes for the world involve creation itself. We are not concerned here only with a spiritual reality but with the formation of a body that has a definite place in space and time. The salvation accomplished in Christ involves the reformation of the creature, the reconstitution in Christ of the creaturely existence that God has established for us and that God has deemed to be good. Because the Savior has come, therefore, and because the work of salvation has begun we should expect to see signs of the reconstituted humanity apparent in our cities, our towns, and in our local neighborhoods. "It is in accordance with the whole biblical standpoint," Newbigin writes, "that the sphere of salvation should be a visible fellowship marked by visible signs wherein God uses material means to convey His saving power, and wherein, therefore, there is an earnest and foretaste of the restoration of creation to its true harmony in and for God's glory, and of man to his true relation to the created world."[5]

The second reason for Newbigin's stress upon the visibility of the church is simply the mission imperative. God appoints a people, not for their own sake, but to be "His royal priesthood" and "the bearer of His light to the nations." Newbigin continues, "It is surely a fact of inexhaustible significance that what our Lord left behind Him was not a book, nor a creed, not a system of thought, nor a rule of life, but a visible community . . . a community called together by the deliberate choice of our Lord Himself, and recreated in Him, to make explicit who He is and what He has done."[6] To put it as Newbigin himself does not, but in a way consistent with his intent, the visibility of the community is the means of God's self-presentation. That there is on earth, gathered in particular identifiable places, a visible community of people constituted as Christ's body and enlivened by the Spirit, means that God makes himself available. God is not absent but enacts his promise to dwell with his people. To be sure, "this congregation is truly known only to faith"[7] but there should be apparent in the church's visible presence in particular communities a sufficiently distinct form of life to elicit from those outside the church an enquiry about who its Lord is. The life lived by the community of God's people should be sufficiently transparent to the gospel that those outside will demand an accounting for the hope that is in them (1 Pet 3:15).

5. Ibid., 65.

6. Ibid., 27. The point is repeated in *Gospel in a Pluralist Society*, 227.

7. Newbigin, *Household of God*, 26.

A third reason for Newbigin's stress on the visibility of the church is that the gathering of real men, women and children into a community whose character is determined by the reconciling and redemptive love of God is simply the content of the gospel. As Paul puts it in his letter to the Ephesians, ". . .now in Christ Jesus you who were once far off have been brought near by the blood of Christ. For he is our peace; in his flesh he has made both groups [Jew and Gentile] into one and has broken down the dividing wall, that is, the hostility between us. . ." (Eph 2:13–14). Whether Jew or Gentile as referred to here, male or female, slave or free, black or white, Israeli or Palestinian, Bosnian or Serb, and so on, the enmity typically characterizing such polarities is overcome in the community of the church, or else it is not the church. The content of the gospel is the redemptive and reconciling love of God. Where that redemptive and reconciling love is at work, the new covenant in Christ's blood is being enacted and the community of his body is being formed.

Of particular concern to Newbigin in *The Household of God* is the scandal of denominational division. We will not give extensive consideration to that matter in this paper, but it is worth noting, albeit only in passing here, the continuing challenge of Newbigin's claim that a federation of churches is not a sufficient expression of the unity of the body of Christ. We must continue to strive, he argues, for visible institutional unity.

A NEW ORDER

We have noted Newbigin's call to the church to be in its own life a new social order. The foundation and presupposition of this new order is the reordering of creation that has already taken place in and through the redemptive and reconciling life, death and resurrection of Jesus. Although the sinful ways of humanity still shape our life together, the resurrection of Jesus confirms that sin and death have no future. The future of creation is shown to rest with the God whose word is life. The resurrection, it is often and correctly said, is an eschatological event. It is an event of the coming kingdom by which God's final victory over sin and death breaks into the midst of history and begins to re-shape our present life. Newbigin supposes, following the witness of Scripture, that this re-shaping should be apparent, especially, but not exclusively, in the congregation of people who, through baptism, participate in the death and resurrection of Christ and are made one in his body.

The claims of Christian proclamation are momentous claims. They speak of the reordering of the cosmos, the overcoming of death, the redemptive presence of God in our midst, and the reestablishment of creation in its proper relation to God. Precisely because of their cosmic scope and because of their foundation in the improbable narrative of the man Jesus crucified and risen, they will not be credible claims unless the reordering of things to which these claims testify is somewhere visible. It cannot become visible in a series of claims, or in a written deposit. These are *mere* words. It becomes visible only in and through the formation of a differently ordered community. That is why Christ called men and women to follow him and why he established them as the new community of his body.[8] Following on from his call to the church to be itself a new social order, Newbigin writes, "More fundamental than any of the things which the church can say or do is the reality of a new society which allows itself to be shaped by the Christian faith."[9] Newbigin here upholds the principle evident in Jesus' response to the question posed by John the Baptist's emissaries: "'Are you the one who is to come or are we to wait for another?' Jesus answered them, 'Go and tell John what you hear and see: the lame walk, the lepers are cleansed, the deaf hear, the dead are raised, and the poor have good news brought to them.'" (Matt 11:33–5). Jesus points to the reordering of things that is going on around him. The wounds of creation are being healed, its travail overcome, and the light of hope dawns upon those who suffer. These are signs that the Messiah has come, that God has set about the work of bringing creation to its promised fulfillment. We should expect to see in the community that is Christ's body, similar signs of the new creation that God is bringing about.

THE CHURCH AFTER CHRISTENDOM

We face, however, the vexing question of what that new order should look like. The form that the body has taken through the history of Christendom has not always been recognizable as the form of Christ, the crucified servant and victor over death. For all the benefits that have been wrought through the church's alliance with state power and its privileged position in society, there have been compromises made along the way that obscure the gospel and have seen the church be complicit in the faults and failings

8. Newbigin comments, "The thread which binds the whole Bible story together is emphatically not the history of an idea but the history of a people." Ibid., 62.

9. Newbigin, *Truth to Tell*, 85.

of the old order. Newbigin's analysis of this reality is pertinent: "I have said that in the New Testament the Church is depicted as a body of people chosen by God and trained and empowered for a missionary task. It is a task force which exists not simply for the sake of its members, which would be absurd, but for the sake of the doing of God's will in the world. The visible structures of church life which we have inherited from the *corpus Christianum* of Medieval Europe do not correspond very obviously to that description."[10] More trenchantly still: "the Church [in Christendom] had become the religious department of European society rather than the task force selected and appointed for a world mission."[11]

Because the form the church took in Christendom is less transparent now to the gospel, it is looked upon by many in the Western world as a crumbling relic of the past rather than as the pledge and foretaste of a new creation. We have been slow to relinquish the habits of Christendom that, very often, were inimical to the gospel, not least because, as Bruce Hamill has put it, "it was assumed [in Christendom] that the state's use and threat of force had become the means of God's rule."[12] But, Hamill continues, "the resurrection of Jesus puts the cross at the centre of history as the definition of the power of God (1 Cor 1:17–18). . . [I]n the cross of Christ the power of God meets the dominion of the principalities and powers and is victorious (Col 2:15)."[13] We might say, therefore, that in Christendom the church was often visible in the wrong way. Its visibility took the form of political power and privilege, accumulated wealth, and the availability of its ministers sometimes to bless the sinful institutions and endeavors of a fallen world.[14] The church is called, however, not to bless, but to bear witness to the interruption of these endeavors by the life, death and resurrection of Jesus Christ.[15] Its witness must take the form of a different social order, an order determined by the death and resurrection of Christ.

10. Newbigin, *Honest Religion*, 105.

11. Ibid., 103.

12. Hamill, "Christendom Still in Our Hearts?"

13. Ibid.

14. The blessing of the Enola Gay and its crew before it flew on its mission to drop an atomic bomb on Hiroshima is but one notorious example. Father George Zabelka, a Catholic chaplain with the U.S. Air Force who gave this blessing, later came to believe that he had made a grave error. In a speech on the anniversary of the bombings he said, "War is now, always has been, and always will be bad, bad news. I was there. I saw real war. Those who have seen real war will bear me out. I assure you, it is not of Christ. It is not Christ's way." Zabelka, "Blessing the Bombs".

15. This point too is drawn from Bruce Hamill, "Christendom Still in Our Hearts?"

Hamill again writes: "Once we have learnt to appreciate the importance of the church's social otherness, we can then . . . explore what the church is called to be. For not just any kind of social otherness will do, certainly not a *reactionary* counter-culture. Missional otherness, of the kind that participates in the missional interruption of history we call Jesus Christ, will thus be both christological and cruciform. It will have its own positive form and content enabled by the Spirit."[16]

THE LOCAL CONGREGATION

What will this form and content be and where shall we find it? We turn our attention more fully now to the theme of this paper, namely, Newbigin's insistence that the primary locus of Christian witness and mission is the local congregation. It is in the local congregation that the credibility of the gospel becomes apparent, for that is the place where a real community of men and women, of young and old, of stranger and friend, are gathered into the reconciled fellowship of the body of Christ, hear the declaration that their sins are forgiven, and feast together at the table of the Lord.

Thirteen years after the publication of *The Household of God*, Newbigin published *Honest Religion for Secular Man*. Again in this work, we find Newbigin maintaining his stress upon the visibility of the church and the centrality of the local congregation. He laments the paucity of attention given to the latter in the tradition of missiological reflection. "Most talk about the Church as a missionary community" he writes, "has left untouched the centre of the Church's life. It is only within very recent years that the light of a missionary doctrine of the Church has been turned steadily upon the local congregation."[17] Newbigin would have welcomed, no doubt, the considerable momentum that has built up recently as local congregations grapple with what it means to be a "missional church." He would be anxious as always, however, to remind the "missional church" that while the form of the church's life must continue to adapt and evolve in order to meet the challenges of changing circumstances, and while it must "leave behind, if necessary, much of the baggage accumulated during a long encampment, to follow without procrastination wherever the Spirit leads,"[18] the Christian church must remain faithful to the gospel.[19]

16. Ibid.

17. Newbigin, *Honest Religion*, 105.

18. Ibid., 122.

19. On this note, I commend especially *The Gospel Driven Church* by Ian

> [T]he local Christian congregation, where the word of the gospel is preached, where in the sacrament of the Eucharist we are united with Christ in his dying for the sin of the world and in his risen life for the sake of the world, is the place where we are enabled to develop a shared life in which sin can be both recognized and forgiven. If this congregation understands its true character as a holy priesthood for the sake of the world, and if its members are equipped for the exercise of that priesthood in their secular employment, then there is a point of growth for a new social order. . . there is a sense in which the local congregation is the place where the truth of the gospel is tested and experienced in the most basic way.[20]

To believe and to live by the gospel requires first, that there is a people among whom the word of the gospel is proclaimed, and who are sustained and nourished by their sharing in the fellowship of Christ in baptism and at the Lord's table. Whether these things take place in a cathedral, in a café, or, as Newbigin himself commonly practiced in India, under a tree out in the open, the life of the church depends on their faithful execution by ministers of word and sacrament.[21] Summarizing Newbigin's stance on this matter, Geoffrey Wainwright writes, "At the heart of the church's life stands the assembled congregation, where the communication of the Gospel takes place through word and sacrament, and the response of praise and prayer is made to the triune God."[22] Preaching and the sacraments are the most readily available mode of corporate attentiveness to the gospel. There are other modes, of course. Newbigin was an advocate of the small group gathered around Scripture for study and prayer. That too is important, but preaching and the sacraments are more public and have a wider reach than the study and fellowship of the small group.

Stackhouse.

20. Newbigin, *Truth to Tell*, 86–7. See also *Gospel in a Pluralist Society*, 227.

21. I am not concerned here to enter into the debate about ordination, but rather to emphasize the importance of the ministry with which we are here concerned. It is essential to the life of the church that there be among its members people who are gifted and equipped to serve the body of Christ through faithful proclamation of the gospel and right administration of the sacraments.

22. Wainwright, *Lesslie Newbigin*, 270.

Preaching

Some commentators on the missionary situation in which the church in the West now finds itself have called for an abandonment of preaching. The contemporary generation, it is argued, is resistant to an authority that presents itself in brocaded robes, speaks from on high in a pulpit and delivers its message as a monologue. Perhaps it is true that these accompaniments to the preaching of the word should be consigned to history. There is no essential need for robes and pulpits, nor for a form of preaching that leaves no space for discussion and response. But there is need still for the congregation of God's people to hear the word proclaimed and to be attentive to God's address. Without attentiveness to the Word of God that calls forth, invites belief, forms a people of God, and sends them in mission, there is no church.[23]

The church does not live by a word of its own making but by the Word given to it by God. It is the preacher's task, therefore, to lead the congregation in giving attention to the Word. Preachers undertake that task by virtue of the fact that they spend time during the week in study and in prayer, giving attention themselves to what God is saying to the church. It is not the preacher's task, by contrast, to set Scripture to one side and then to speak for herself. The sermon is not the place for the preacher's home-spun wisdom or homely good advice. "As a servant of the Word, the preacher's job is not to propagate personal ideas but to expound the open Bible."[24]

It is one of the most astonishing acts of grace that God should enlist in his service the stumbling and inadequate words that we human beings typically muster in order to speak of God. But God does that, again and again. Putting one's trust in God to do that once more is the only justification the preacher can possibly have for undertaking the task of declaring to the gathered congregation the good news of the gospel. The preacher who has not said with Jeremiah, "Ah Lord, truly I do not know how to speak" (Jer 1:6), has no business being a preacher. But whoever confesses their inadequacy in preaching will likely hear in response something akin to the words spoken to Jeremiah: "'Do not be afraid [said the Lord]. . . for I am with you to deliver you'. . . Then the Lord put out his hand and

23. Newbigin notes the importance of preaching in Jesus' own ministry. See *Household of God*, 32.

24. The point appears in Geoffrey Wainwright's summary of Newbigin's lecture "Preaching Christ Today" delivered at Overdale College, Birmingham in 1979. See Wainwright, *Lesslie Newbigin*, 285.

touched [Jeremiah's] mouth; and the Lord said to [him], 'Now I have put my words in your mouth . . .'" (Jer 1:8–9). Everything said in preaching depends upon that act of grace, submission to which is precisely what the ministry of the Word is about.

Sacraments

Alongside the preaching of the gospel, the celebration of the sacraments is foundational to the life of the Christian congregation. Although not every service of worship includes a baptism or culminates in the celebration of the eucharist we ought to recognize that every occasion of corporate worship is in fact a living out of one's baptism. The sacrament of baptism bestows upon those baptized membership of a new community, a community that is distinguished, above all, by its worship of the triune God. In the sacrament of baptism a new person is brought into being, a person whose identity is determined by his or her belonging to Christ and to the people whom Christ has gathered into the communion of his body. Whenever people come from their homes and from their work, from their sickbed or from the marketplace, they are being bound by the Spirit into a new corporate reality, that of the Body of Christ. They are participating, furthermore, in the ongoing work of their formation as disciples of Jesus Christ.

Discipleship, we note, is not principally about the life of the individual. It is about the formation of a new people who have been gathered to share in Christ's work of service to the world. It is participation in a community that through its life and witness shows forth the redemptive purposes of God in the world and the coming kingdom of God. The practices are typically relational rather than individual—forgiveness, reconciliation, love of neighbor, *koinonia*. One has to be gathered into community in order for these practices to be worked out. Linking this life in community with baptism, Colin Gunton writes, "Baptism . . . gives social embodiment and expression to that different place in which justification sets the sinner, the place where the Word is heard and the Supper celebrated. To live under the discipline of the Word and the Table, *is* to be one whose way of being is altered. . ."[25]

When, on occasion, the sacrament of baptism is celebrated explicitly in worship and new members are joined to the Body of Christ, the congregation is called upon to reaffirm their own commitment to that body,

25. Gunton, *Christian Faith*, 146.

to share in the nurture and support of the newly baptized, and thus to contribute to the work of making disciples as they were commissioned to do when, at their own baptism, they were set free from sin and raised to new life in Christ.

Baptism is complemented in the life of the local congregation by the celebration of the Lord's Supper. Although the sacrament of the eucharist is other things besides, it is also an evangelical ordinance, a means of setting forth the gospel, of telling the good news. "This cup of blessing that we bless, is it not a sharing in the blood of Christ? This bread that we break, is it not a sharing in the body of Christ?" (1 Cor 10:16). With these words the minister speaks gospel and as the bread and the cup are taken and passed in service from one hand to another the gathered people of God live out the gospel by being actually reconciled with neighbors, and perhaps strangers, who would not otherwise be their companions.

The Lord's Supper is a development of course of the Jewish celebration of the Passover, commemorating and announcing once more the saving work of God. In the Passover liturgy particular emphasis is placed on the pedagogical function of the liturgy. In the instructions given in Exodus 12 for the celebration of the Passover, for instance, we read, "When your children ask you, 'What do you mean by this observance?' you shall say, 'It is the passover sacrifice to the Lord, for he passed over the houses of the Israelites in Egypt. . .'" (Ex 12:26–27). And again in Exodus 13:8: "You shall tell your children on that day, 'It is because of what the Lord did for me when I came out of Egypt.'" "This response," says Brevard Childs, "is not simply a report, but above all a confession to the ongoing participation of Israel in the decisive act of redemption from Egypt."[26] The Passover Haggadah takes up the challenge of proclaiming this redemption to succeeding generations. The children gathered at the table take a central role in the liturgy. It is they who ask after the meaning of the various elements of the celebration, and the liturgy itself is directed towards the purpose of assuring all who are gathered that the story here recounted is their story. A passage "of central importance" in the Haggadah reads:

> In every generation let each man look on himself as if he came forth out of Egypt.
>
> As it is said: 'And thou shalt tell thy son in that day, saying: It is because of that which the Lord did for me when I came forth out of Egypt.

26. Childs, *Exodus*, 200.

It was not only our fathers that the Holy One, blessed be he,
redeemed, but us as well did he redeem along with them.'[27]

I cite this passage as an exemplary instance of how liturgy contributes to the formation of a people. The Exodus and redemption here recounted "are not to be taken as happenings in long bygone days, but as a personal experience."[28] "It was not only our [parents] that the Holy One. . . redeemed, but us as well did he redeem along with them," the Passover liturgy proclaims. The celebration of the Passover is thus to be understood as an exercise of *paideia*, a process by which persons are formed. In continuity with this conception of things, the celebration of the eucharist is likewise a process by which a people's identity is established and a new society takes shape.

Returning to Exodus 13, the Israelites are further advised that the observance of the Passover ordinance and the festival of unleavened bread is to be undertaken "so that the teaching of the Lord may be on your lips" (Ex 13:9). Faithful utterance of the teaching of the Lord is grounded thus in a particular set of practices, and in membership of a particular community. Here too, there are salutary lessons for a church concerned with mission. Mission is grounded in a particular set of practices—the practice of worship, the practice of faithful transmission of that which has been received, the practice of participation in a community brought into being by the redemptive and liberating work of God. Participation in these practices week by week, in answer to God's call upon us, is the necessary antecedent condition of our being able to tell truthfully in mission the story that Scripture tells.

CONCLUSION

For the most part, we don't yet have much idea of how to be the Church beyond Christendom. We are still experimenting with the challenge of being a church ready to move on, travelling light with only the gospel at hand, and assurance of the Spirit's presence. We are reluctant, however, to leave behind the baggage of the past, land and buildings, investment funds, the paraphernalia of long established rituals and traditions, particular forms of ecclesial organization. . . These are things that made the church visible in Christendom but we must ask ourselves whether they are

27. Glatzer, *Passover Haggadah*, 59.
28. Ibid., footnote commentary, 59.

still transparent to the gospel. Newbigin found in the church of South India that these things were not essential. Essential instead was the existence of a community, a congregation of people, whose life together was ordered by its hearing of the Word and by its taking to heart the pattern of death and new life set forth in the sacraments of baptism and the Lord's supper. These are the foundation and content of the new social order to which the church is called.

After the Christian congregation has gathered to hear the preaching of the gospel and has participated together in the sacramental enactment of that gospel it is sent forth with a benediction, at once a commissioning and a blessing. Following a pattern seen in Scripture, encounter with God in worship involves also a commission. "Whom shall I send, and who will go for us?" the Lord asks (Isa 6:8). Encounter with God brings rest for the weary and heavy laden, a restoration of shalom between God and those who worship, but it also makes them restless for a "shalom" in this world not yet realized in its fullness. Thus in worship we are confronted with the question, who then will go to do the work of making peace, of telling good news, of searching out the weary and heavy laden? In the benediction we are commissioned for that work and assured of God's blessing. The blessing is assured because the work of mission is in fact a participation in what God is already bringing about.

The act of corporate worship thus comes to an end, but the liturgy as such does not. For "liturgy" in its original sense means "the work of the people." The gospel heard and enacted in worship now becomes the pattern of Christian life. The local congregation is commissioned to go forth with the gospel written on their hearts, to proclaim and to enact it and to participate thereby in God's mission to the world.

BIBLIOGRAPHY

Childs, Brevard. *Exodus: A Commentary*. London: SCM, 1974.

Glatzer, Nahum, editor. *The Passover Haggadah*. New York: Schocken, 1953.

Gunton, Colin. *The Christian Faith: An Introduction to Christian Doctrine*. Oxford: Blackwell, 2002.

Hamill, D. B. "Christendom still in our hearts?" Online: http://dbhamill.wordpress.com/2011/04/06/christendom-still-in-our-hearts.

Newbigin, Lesslie. *The Gospel in a Pluralist Society*. Grand Rapids: Eerdmans, 1989.

———. *Honest Religion for Secular Man*. London: SCM, 1966.

———. *The Household of God*. London: SCM, 1957.

———. *Truth to Tell: the Gospel as Public Truth*. Grand Rapids: Eerdmans, 1991.

Stackhouse, Ian. *The Gospel Driven Church*. Carlisle: Paternoster, 2004.

Murray Rae

Wainwright, Geoffrey. *Lesslie Newbigin: A Theological Life*. Oxford: Oxford University Press, 2000.

Zabelka, George. "Blessing the Bombs." Online: http://www.lewrockwell.com/orig6/zabelka1.html.

Confessions of a Journalist

A Case Study in Public Religion

Jenny Taylor

INTRODUCTION

LAPIDO MEDIA, THE MEDIA consultancy I set up with a friend in 2007, owes its birth in part to Lesslie Newbigin. Not that he had any fondness for the media. But his passionate belief in public truth resonated so deeply with me, a journalist and a new believer at the time I first encountered his work, that I determined to get to know him. In fact the encounter with his work reoriented the rest of my life. It generated the energy to sustain a long and continuous argument with the church that had, I felt, failed me by relinquishing its missionary responsibilities for the secular mainstream world in which journalists had to operate.

Lesslie's urgent call to a mission to Western culture—elucidated so compellingly in his short book, *The Other Side of 1984*[1]—recovers the rationale for a beleaguered profession. What had been so striking to me was his analysis of the privatization of thought: "We have been tempted either to withdraw into an intellectual ghetto, seeking to preserve a kind of piety in church and home while leaving the public world (including the world of scholarship) to be governed by another ideology. Or we have been tempted to regard the 'modern scientific world-view' as though it were simply a transcript of reality which we must—willy-nilly—accept as true."[2]

---

1. Newbigin, *Other Side of 1984*.
2. Ibid., 32.

Jenny Taylor

This echoed my own inability, both as I laboured in unbelief in the newsroom and then on coming to faith, to express the deepest intimations of my heart in my work. Who could I go to? Not some vicar—I thought vaguely—in case I might get sucked into a vortex of "religion" and a mental capitulation from which I might never escape. It was as if the things of the spirit had all been vacuumed up into a sealed-off place I could not and would not access, and there was no shred of it left on the newsdesk.

That Newbigin understood our epistemological predicament was evident even to a theological illiterate like me. His was a faith that was searching for souls like mine. It was wise, compassionate, and *out there.* That he had gone deep enough into all that was wrong with secular thinking in Britain to rescue those of us who were floundering down there was deeply felt. Faith was not a crutch but a searchlight by which to see things never known or understood before. It was not a retreat from inquiry and knowledge but the very means to wisdom, and insight. Immensely practical, his was a kind of faith that was not irrational as I had presumed, but revealed profound truths that reason could elucidate and utilize. It was not in fact a relinquishing of individual will, but offered a road out of inertia into fullness of personhood and community.

All this I had resisted, until from deep wretchedness on a tabloid newsdesk, I came to a new intellectually credible faith after reading Newbigin and found a reason to live. In the process my eyes were opened not just to the wonders of a far deeper connectedness with others and the world, but to the roots of the world's misery and a new way of reporting it. I will never forget the former Brahmin (high-caste) colleague I later worked with who told me that before his conversion, he had not known there was poverty in India. Christ gives us eyes to see what's there, and a heart to feel what we see.

The word "Lapido" means to "speak out" in the Acholi dialect of Northern Uganda. Journalists are largely off the missionary radar of the church and operate according to a rubric whose ethical deficit has been starkly exposed in the News Corp phone hacking "firestorm." Journalists exist to be avoided by the church, which is our prey, so our spiritual salvation is a hit or largely miss affair. Prostitutes, tramps, gypsies, even politicians get prayed for—but journalists are what you might call "a lost people group" in the strange argot of missions. Yet unless the media get the point of faith, get Christ in fact, how can they filter what really matters into their reportage? How do they know when to "blag," and when not to?[3]

3. To "blag" is the expression made famous by the NewsCorp scandal but which

Not that one would want them writing more about *religion*; but to write about world affairs with religious intelligence is surely something else. Lapido wants the spiritual ruled *in*, because it is not possible to do justice to the way the world is without it.[4] Not just that, but as I came to see (and describe later in this chapter), it is not possible to activate the switches that stop wars and prevent famine without recourse to non-secular language and categories.

Lesslie Newbigin's great guru was Michael Polanyi, whose work *Personal Knowledge* fired Lesslie's final campaign.[5] That Newbigin became my friend and changed the course of my life completely indicates the truth in Lesslie's own assertion that you can only know anyone or anything deeply by loving them. I regarded myself as his disciple. I edited his last papers, organized his reading as he became increasingly blind, stimulated the book *A Proper Confidence*[6] as we sat chatting in the office that doubled as a bedroom in his final Abbeyfield home in London's Herne Hill, and was the last civilian to hold his hand as he lay dying. The book we wrote together— *Faith and Power: Christianity and Islam in Secular Britain*—was published posthumously in 1998. Theoretical knowledge can never do justice to the fullness of truth. I kept vigil by his hospital bedside the night he died, and was able to explain to him that as he had been the beginning of my true life, I wanted to be there at the very end of his. His writing had transformed my mind, and strengthened my weak will after a difficult early life. Who he was seemed to have leeched into what and how he wrote, and its authority and compassion were incontrovertible. Once you've read it, you are changed. The power in Newbigin's words lies in the fusion of experience and expression under Christ; not the dry-as-dust ruminations of a career theoretician who never encountered pain, grief, poverty, hopelessness, but resonant with the very heart of Christ explored in the heat and dust of an alien country, India. His writing is saturated with the gospel heeded in the grand silences of that great country, in which he lived alongside the

every journalist practices to some extent, and justifiably so, if it means nailing a crook by pretending to be someone you're not, in order to get otherwise undisclosed information from them. This has been taken to ludicrous lengths in recent years to solicit juicy details of celebrities for no good reason other than to sell the paper.

4. Sarah Sands, Deputy Editor of the London *Evening Standard* wrote something very similar the week after the 2011 riots in the UK: "The party leaders sound like Baptist preachers in their dismay over the values of our society but none has actually mentioned faith. Yet in the riot-stricken communities faith has an enormous role" (16 August 2011).

5. Polanyi, *Personal Knowledge* (1958).

6. Newbigin, *Proper Confidence* (1995).

very poor, and through whose eyes he saw the world. His contemplation and prayer for them over the years created a vast hospitable space that also made a space for me at a dark hour. Too much of our modern project concerns a kind of knowing that—as Richard Rohr points out in *Simplicity*—is a "left brain" rationalist kind of knowing, and the negative results are increasingly clear.[7]

CONVERSATION AND ORIENTATION

I have tried in what follows to reflect the dialectic between Newbigin's writing and my own praxis, as it emerged out of the deep personal engagement that I was privileged to have with the man. Three particular events stand out as waymarks along this road, and form the substance of what follows, interspersed with reflections on them from Newbigin's writings. The first of these demonstrates graphically the privatization of faith which Newbigin frequently spoke about, and illustrates the rejection by a culturally "ghettoized" mission society of the use of mainstream media to "mediate" its good news. The second event highlights what happens to reportage when journalists—in this case the *Times* newspaper columnist Bernard Levin—become secularized and cut off from the church. And the third concerns the baleful effect of media blindness on the poor whose stories emerge out of religious worldviews that journalists can no longer even apprehend, let alone comprehend: in this case the devastation of children by a "religious" war in Uganda.

EPISODE 1: PLANE CRASH IN KATHMANDU

The Boeing 727 that slammed into the mountain east of Kathmandu in thick fog on the morning of 28 September 1992 with the loss of all 167 on board, had not been chartered by Interserve. But nonetheless, the Kennington-based missionary society, more used to occupying the small ads of *Evangelicals Now* than the front page of the red-top newspapers, found itself in the middle of an international media frenzy.

The switchboard was jammed with calls from journalists trying to find out who we were. Many of the passengers had evidently been returning aid workers and missionaries. I took several calls from journalists who must have conferred with each other, insinuating, by their line of

7. Rohr, *Simplicity*, passim.

questioning that we were a travel company who had chartered a dodgy plane to send religious eccentrics to a remote part of the world on some weird and doubtless covert enterprise. I was reeling, not just from the tone of the calls, but from what I'd seen out of the corner of my eye through the glass wall of my office on the mezzanine floor . . . three photographers with enormous flashguns already in the building, sitting tensely like quiescent sharks in a row in reception.

Suddenly the Development Director burst into my office. "We've got the press here. Say nothing."

"About what?"

"The Wilkinses. They were on that plane."

"We can't do that. They're here."

It seemed an odd reaction from a missionary to fellow humans simply doing their job; a part of all our lives every day of the week.

As Interserve's editor, who was occasionally allowed to do press releases, I had to think fast.

"But the press are already in the building. We can't say nothing."

The director glared at me, repeated his "say nothing" line and left.

We did not have a "crisis management" strategy or anything so grand. The only thing for it was to find out what was happening; embargo the story and call a press conference. I had no authority to do it. But this was a huge story. Was I to leave the building? Sit there with bungs in my ears? The photographers downstairs were all from the tabloids. A human interest story; the kind that comes along once in a decade had pitched us into a new world, without any warning or preparation.

I briefed Dorothy on the switchboard before phoning the Press Association to announce a press conference in two hours at the office. That bought me time to try and find out exactly what had happened, and who was in the plane.

To my dismay, the Personnel Director who had all the information I would need on the Wilkinses had left the building as soon as she heard about the media interest. The General Director was on leave. There was only one other director left who would cooperate—the Finance Director Simon Sheldon, who had the great presence of mind to locate the family's prayer card. All missionaries were required to have one as an aide memoire for their supporters. It contained a photo of the whole family, a prayer request—and a Bible text.

I managed to locate some prayer letters with information about what the family was intending to do back in Nepal for their second term of service. And I wracked my own memories of meeting them, which providentially were vivid, being impressed by their grace and gentleness; their professional skills (Andy was a hydropower engineer); their willingness to render themselves homeless and uncomfortable for the sake of the poorest nation on earth—and to do it despite their three children being small and vulnerable to illness, heat, altitude, pollution. Here was an unprecedented opportunity to talk about their lives and the meaning in their death. Here were modern disciples of Christ, and a media pack that wanted to know.

The press conference was packed out. We told the story; answering questions as fully as we could, aware that a wrong word or headline could jeopardize the future of the whole of the United Mission to Nepal. UMN was under agreement with the Nepal Government not to "proselytize." The rule of thumb for all missionaries posted there was to answer questions about their motivation only if asked; to let their work and their lives speak for themselves. Acutely sensitive to the common charge of "cultural imperialism," Interservers put themselves under the indigenous church leadership or under the Nepalis who ran the hydropower projects on which Andy Wilkins was working.

As a journalist trained by *Yorkshire Post* Newspapers, I was just following instinct. But by now I'd absorbed a lot of Newbigin's writing. Indeed, when I was first given a small synopsis of his work in a pamphlet called *Thinking Mission* I'd underlined whole paragraphs and tried to commit them to memory. It was water to a parched soul. I was also seconded, at my own request, to the Gospel as Public Truth Consultation just a few months away, and a golden opportunity had fallen into my hands.

And to our astonishment, we did it. Naturally enough, every single newspaper in the land ran the story of the crash on their front pages. Several however, including the *Daily Mirror*, the *Daily Mail* and the *Times*, led with the Wilkins' story, with pictures, and quotes about their motivation. "Sacrificing everything to help the poor in Nepal . . . they were real Christians," the *Mail* reported. And most amazing of all, the *Mirror* even published their prayer card in full on page 2. I cannot believe that the tabloids have ever before or since published the words of the gospel as part of a front-page lead. "I will lift up my eyes to the hills—where does my help come from? My help comes from the Lord, the Maker of heaven and earth" (Ps 121:1–2).

Of course, for the *Mirror* the story was the ultimate bad news: God had been rumbled. The pathos of prayer unanswered and faith obliterated on a Himalayan mountainside *is* the ultimate hard news story. Yet, it seemed to me as a journalist-turned-believer that we had had the last word. If you played bad news right, you could still get your side of the story told well.

Yet within what Newbigin calls the "fiduciary framework" of dogmatic neutrality that newspapers inhabit and reinforce, missions had—not surprisingly—given up trying to get any kind of a hearing. In "our culture" and for those who mediate it, faith is just a matter of personal opinion, not the basic fact on which the world is built. Secularization is reinforced by the churches' weariness, and as Newbigin saw it, the "adjustments they have made to the requirements of modern thought."[8] When the opportunity arose, for good reasons as well as bad, mission managers literally left the building.

Few if any journalists ever get close enough to the grassroots where profound change allied to spiritual transformation happens. This is partly because you only see what you already believe to be the case. And unless you *are* a hack with a faith, you will pursue only those stories and contacts that you, your peers and your readers regard as credible. If you've already ruled out Christians as sources because you or your news editor deem them to be "biased," or weird, you will probably never meet the kind of winsome, creative world-changers I stumbled upon as a new believer; and you will certainly never get right down to the bottom of things where the very poor have nothing and no one to help them except the brave and the maverick for whom altruism *is* a worldview.

The experience of the Wilkins' death made a profound impression. But perhaps not so profound as a blinkered article by the eminent *Times* columnist Bernard Levin, which also contributed to the founding of Lapido Media.

It was this episode that enabled me to appreciate fully the cultural problem that Newbigin had articulated: that the knowledge that comes from reason alone is too easily put off the scent of the terrible and wonderful things that emerge from the deepest human motivation where faith and belief operate. We do indeed live—and die—by faith, not by sight, and Bernard Levin, the most reasonable and reasoned of columnists, was blind.

8. Newbigin, *Other Side*, 32.

EPISODE 2:
CHRISTIAN PERSECUTION AND LEVIN'S "CARELESSNESS"

The twentieth century was the bloodiest in history. No doubt Genghis Khan's assaults on the tribal populations between China and Russia were gruesome enough, but no Tartar warlord was ever able to get as techno-logical about killing as Hitler, Stalin, and Mao were. And Christians were targets of all three. Anecdote has it that there were more deaths for the Christian faith in the twentieth century than all the previous nineteen centuries put together. This is hard to prove, but highly likely. I became aware of the extent of Christian martyrdoms in Islamic lands only when I began editing Interserve's international magazine *GO*, and every day read the evidence sent in by suffering churches: a tide of murders, massacres, imprisonments for blasphemy, gang rapes, abductions, torture, quasi-judicial killings and judicial execution of Christians everywhere from Iran, to Pakistan to Egypt. I had never before heard of such killings, or their motivation. The appalling toll of death reached a crescendo with the murders of pastors in Iran in 1994 just for the sin of being born Muslim and chang-ing their mind in adulthood about what they wanted to think—which is a crime called "apostasy"; concluding with the solitary confinement over two years, and imprisonment for seven years before that, of the Protestant pastor Mehdi Dibaj. The defence he gave at his trial, where he faced the death penalty for conversion, read like one of the letters of St Paul:

> He is our Savior and He is the (spiritual) Son of God. To know Him means to know eternal life. I, a useless sinner, have believed in this beloved person and all His words and miracles recorded in the Gospel, and I have committed my life into His hands. Life for me is an opportunity to serve Him, and death is a better opportunity to be with Christ. Therefore I am not only satisfied to be in prison for the honor of His Holy Name, but am ready to give my life for the sake of Jesus, my Lord, and enter His king-dom sooner, the place where the elect of God enter everlasting life.[9]

The Amnesty Campaign to release him, in which I was peripherally involved, succeeded—but he was found, just five months after his release, in an alley in Tehran, with a bullet in his back.

Levin had criticized Christians for complaining about such things. For a long while, his famous *Times* column had been required reading by

9. Dibaj, "Written Defense," lines 25–27.

a generation's élites. It was the acme of journalistic comment. When he wrote, governments quailed. He excoriated the Soviet Union over many years, and helped contribute to a climate in which the Berlin Wall could come down.

So when Levin asked (I paraphrase): "Why are Christians bleating about persecution? No one has been persecuted for their faith since Roman times, except the Jews," his ignorance and conceit finally threw the switches. Patrick Sookhdeo of Barnabas Fund and I, without consulting one another, simultaneously contacted Levin's office. We both sent a mass of evidence, Patrick on Iran, I on Pakistan. Levin's secretary—a Christian—phoned me back. The great man never dealt personally with sources for his column, she said, but he was impressed and shocked by the documents we had sent him. She told me he had been much moved by the detailed accounts of the Church of Pakistan, and impressed by the careful way they had been compiled and presented. Clergy in the Church of Pakistan on a visit to Britain had asked me to help them publicize the abuse of the blasphemy laws, under which people were being imprisoned and condemned to death (to blaspheme the Prophet is a capital offence) on the say-so of "one bearded Muslim,"[10] often seeking to settle a business score.

Levin went on to do a whole series of pieces, beginning with a shocker about crucifixion of Christians in Sudan called "Islam's Fearful Bloodletting" on 23 March 1993. On 15 February 1994, under the title "Martyred for his faith," he even reproduced verbatim the Dibaj testimony, without comment—so stark was it not just as a reflection on the state of freedom in Iran, but on a whole generation's ignorance of such horrors, and presumably of the entire British ruling class who took Levin as a standard bearer.

Levin immersed himself in the subject of Islamic persecution, and the inequality of faiths elsewhere in the world, and I believe marked the beginning of the end of the multifaith "all-religions-are-the-same" fallacy that governed British education policy and much else up to the beginning of the new millennium.

If the Wilkins' deaths indicated how the mission agencies strangely colluded in the privatization of their own faith, Levin's article—which was by his own estimation "careless"—demonstrated the prejudice and ignorance such privatization caused. Levin was sympathetic to Christianity and always wrote appropriate pieces at her great festivals or mentioned the incumbent Archbishop with somewhat exaggerated courtesy. He was

---

10. A beard was all that was required for a single Muslim testimony to be believed over against a non-Muslim testimony, and so far as I can tell is true still.

often humorous and undefensive about his own Jewishness. But his view
of Christianity—though more aware and respectful than many of today's
commentators—was parochial. Any sense that faith was transformative
and efficacious beyond the speechifying of bishops at Westminster, and
therefore a target for cruelty for foreign regimes, was surprisingly lost on
him. He had a common sense view of Christianity in common with his
class, but it did not encompass reality.[11]

Newbigin identified this rightly as an epistemological problem. He
wrote: '. . . what matters about religious beliefs is not the factual truth of
what they affirm but the sincerity with which they are held . . . a matter of
personal inward experience rather than an account of what is objectively
the case.'[12] Religion was no longer a matter of public knowledge but of
personal faith, said Newbigin, and Christians (according to Levin and
those like him), had no more right than anyone else to push their faith
claims on others. Since religion actually made no difference (in this view),
it could not be the case that believers might actually be being persecuted
as if it did.

EPISODE 3:
BREAKING THE SILENCE ABOUT NORTHERN UGANDA

The small Eagle Air Cessna touched down at Kitgum airport one blus-
tery morning in February 2003 on an inadequate strip of dust, patrolled
by chickens, and flanked by a long-drop loo with its door missing. I was
greeted with a broad toothy grin by a skinny man in a purple shirt and
dog-collar, the Church Mission Society's Partner bishop in this most
remote of all its Uganda dioceses, the Rt Revd Benjamin Ojwang. The
mission regularly sent small donations to the Anglican clergy in the two
northern Ugandan dioceses, but they had had no missionary there since
the mid-1980s Amin era. The organization that had brought education
and the Gospel to Northern Uganda in response to a request by the head
man of the Acholi tribe 100 years earlier, now deemed it too dangerous
as a mission post. A madman named Major General Joseph Kony had

11. The irony of finding myself writing this while the NewsCorp scandal unfolds
like waves crashing on the beach, should not be lost on the reader. Rupert Murdoch
professes to be a Christian. The former News of the World features editor Paul Mc-
Mullan describes Murdoch as "puritanical." If that is the case—and I believe it is—it
is a faith that has been totally privatized. Bernard Levin wrote for Murdoch's flagship
British newspaper.

12. Newbigin, *Gospel in a Pluralist Society*, 25f.

been waging war in the name of God against any whom he suspected of colluding with President Museveni. This was most of his own people in the northern belt of the country, along the border with Sudan, and more especially their children. Children were particularly vulnerable to the predations of the Lord's Resistance Army because they could be caught easily and indoctrinated. Without the moral capacity or physical strength to resist him, they could be turned into ruthless killing machines, without compunction or fear. 25,000 such children had been abducted over seventeen years, and only half had ever returned. What I could not believe was how little we in Britain knew of this horror, despite being the largest donor to Uganda. Britain was not just the source of Western-style education and literacy, but the home of its founding martyrs.[13]

The whole of the north was in lock-down. No business was being done. The atmosphere itself seemed frozen with terror, as if every nerve were strained and on maximum alert. Everyone had experience of the most savage atrocities. And the children who survived came back with wounds and stories too terrible to contemplate; missing eyes, ears, lips, sanity. How had this been allowed to go on so long? Seventeen years, and no westerners at work up there, only spasmodic calls in international forums for an end to it all, no "discourse"; what you might call the silence of the lambs.

I came home after just three days of mortal fear to launch the Break the Silence Campaign, which targeted the media—from Lindsey Hilsum on Channel 4 news, to Kampala's *New Vision* in which Museveni complained bitterly about the Church Mission Society's interference. We flew the Bishop of Kitgum, a former shepherd, over to Britain to meet the government minister responsible, and to take a petition with Ugandan children to 10 Downing Street. We got him onto Radio 4's *Today* programme, interviewed by James Naughtie. That helped mobilize the development world—including Human Rights Watch and Oxfam—and got the UN's Under-Secretary for Humanitarian Affairs Jan Egeland up to Kitgum ("This is worse than Iraq"). We somehow generated political will enough to kick Kony out of Uganda, and the huge 1,500,000 strong displacement camps began to be disbanded.

I experienced first-hand what can be achieved by judicious partnership with the media, hooking up the international agencies and above all, mobilizing ordinary people through international church networks. Six hundred churches in Britain were galvanized not just to pray and give to

13. See Taylor, "Taking Spirituality Seriously."

Northern Uganda, but also to send people out to learn and report back. The campaign was mentioned in speeches in parliament, and Bob Geldof filmed one of his six Africa programs from Kitgum. He was pictured weeping on his mobile phone to his wife. That's how it got to you. It created at last a mandate that politicians could use. They could begin to justify spending time on understanding the issues.

Yet again, it showed how little can be achieved by reason alone, without the passions mobilized by faith. It reinforced Newbigin's view that unless the West is re-converted, it will continue to evangelize its own illusions and face futility in its home and foreign policies.

There had been very little written about Northern Uganda. The secular world had written off this war as the madness of a voodoo priest, or the tribalism of the country's rulers. Neither analysis provided the motivation for action. The secular mindset is not adequate to solve the world's problems, because its default ideology is material, and the world's poor are spiritual: they have so little else, they have to face reality in the raw. The poor and war-locked will not respond to secular solutions, even when they're offered, because they do not reach the spot. Says Newbigin: "The pre-condition for effective action in any field is a true perception of how things are." He adds presciently: "Our culture has been confident, during the past two centuries, that it could change the world. Perhaps we may now have to insist that the point is to understand it."[14]

The unending "war" in Northern Uganda demonstrated for me the results, this time on a truly awful scale, of the media's blindness to the tenacious resilience of belief systems and their effects. Evil flourishes when the media fail to acknowledge the existence and importance of worldviews other than their own.

Joseph Kony's power was reinforced by fear and superstition within a revenge culture that had no authoritative legal redress. This is perfectly "understandable" only if you have not written off the situation in advance, through attitudes that are tantamount to racism. The power, shame and lack of forgiveness Uganda's armies fed upon had to be addressed at their spiritual/psychic roots, not simply dismissed. The altars where Kony literally "sacrificed" children for the magic it conferred had to be cleansed, because they were the hot, radiant core of what caused the terror and anomie in the population. Inhumanity and evil were allowed to go unpunished. In primal societies spirits rule, and take hold on personalities hospitable to them. Spirit possession is not always schizophrenia. Church leaders have

14. Newbigin, *Other Side*, 18.

to pray in the name of a Spirit stronger than any other if the people are to find the courage to return to their villages—and indeed, this was so. Ways also had to be found to guarantee not just safety for returnees, but *forgiveness* for their atrocities: a forgiveness this remarkable people were only too keen to administer because they had the religiously-derived cultural categories that could support it. And above all the Ugandans who were suffering had to sense they mattered to the outside world. Their sense of their own humanity had become so attenuated they could not activate their own inner resources, until CMS provided a kind of mirror to it. Only then could the work of rebuilding homes, businesses and lives begin. As one Acholi activist said to me afterwards, after seeing some of the TV footage: "When I saw Bishop Ojwang of Kitgum actually in front of Downing Street . . . this to me felt like humanity has the same language now."

That word "language" is instructive. Our campaign generated a common *discourse*, despite huge disparities in culture and geography, through the bridging work of the international Anglican church and the compassion mobilized by the Holy Spirit. It taught the lesson that the world stays poor, angry and catastrophic because we let it stay that way. And that's a failure of empathy, which is a failure of love. CMS *saw* the issues in Northern Uganda because of its religious literacy—and that is a literacy of the human heart, whatever its trappings. The Incarnation means that the Gospel is *comprehensively* good news .

SUMMING UP

Lesslie Newbigin inspired me to understand that the Good News is the lodestar by which to decide what *is* news. News is about change and decision, often bad, but implying good. The news potential of the Gospel is therefore there in every scenario. "The church is for the place Christologically . . . The Church is a movement launched into the world in the same sense in which Jesus is sent into the world by the Father," as he put it.[15]

For Newbigin, the question was always sharply raised against the moral skepticism of which journalists are sometimes guilty. Rationalism gives rise to skepticism, but worse is the moral "neutrality" that is often confused with objectivity. Objectivity is another word for fairness where reportage is concerned. Reportage concerns the even-handed presentation of facts that, if reported "fairly" will convey "the truth" of the matter. Both sides of any issue are to be faithfully recorded, and the reader will

15. Newbigin, "On Being the Church," 32.

decide the merits of each. All facts are relativized by *the* fact of history, since the death and Resurrection of Christ imparted life and freedom to all; and it is human flourishing and freedom that form the ground—however implicitly and however unacknowledged—on which all reportage is done. Newbigin says: "The question is, 'Do you believe or do you not?' Here is a fact, and of course it is not a religious fact. It does not belong to that little slot in *Time* magazine, between drama and sport, where religion is kept. It belongs to the opening section on world affairs. The Kingdom of God is at hand."[16]

This is the truth that compels us to speak up. Says Newbigin: "What is unique about the Christian gospel is that those who are called to be its witnesses are committed to the public affirmation that it is true—true for all peoples at all times—and are at the same time forbidden to use coercion to enforce it."[17]

For Newbigin, the whole human race is subject to this grace. The whole human race is the *oikumene,* the potential recipients of grace, not just the church or "our culture" or those bits of society that are like us, or that have a preference for that kind of thing. For him the church is potentially humanity in every place recreated in Christ. This is both inclusive and particular. But it allows for the transformation of the particular into something more fully and recognizably itself. The whole human race is truly multicultural and the treasures in those cultures are truly the objects of God's affirming action in Christ.

LAUNCHING LAPIDO

Lapido Media's slogan is "Religious literacy in *world* affairs." Its name was chosen in order to provoke questions that might testify to what happens when the media expunges religion from the political equation. My friends and a very few supporters took up Newbigin's challenge to see the Gospel as *the fact* that makes or breaks the news in the real world of other "facts"—both political and social. He dared me to "risk everything" in a radical encounter with that "real world."[18] If the Gospel is true, when we speak it into the questions and dilemmas that face us in the public domain we can expect difficulties—but also surprises.

16. Ibid., 33.

17. Newbigin, *Faith and Power,* 148.

18. Newbigin, *The Other Side of 1984,* 31.

Lapido Media was launched in December 2007 at the Frontline Club, a watering hole for foreign correspondents in Paddington, in the presence of some of the most senior journalists in the country who all admitted on the day that their biggest postbags always concerned any reference they had made to religion. Melanie Phillips of the *Daily Mail* and Aaqil Ahmed, later to become Head of Religion and Ethics at the BBC, came. The columnist Dominic Lawson agreed to interview Bishop Michael Nazir-Ali on the subject: "Neutrality or Truth? Reporting Islam post–7/7" which was intended to challenge journalists on their equivocation about religion after the London Tube bombings. Lawson wrote his "op-ed" in the *Independent* the next day under the headline: "Could a robust Christian response be the answer to Muslim extremism in Britain?" One tiny charity inspired by an old, blind missionary sparked the debate of the week. We secured extensive coverage on the BBC news website, three stories in the *Times*, inquiries from much of the other press including *The Sun*, as well as a live half-hour studio discussion with the presenter of CNN's worldwide *Correspondent* slot.

There is still a huge mountain to climb but a number of well-funded or connected new networks and partnerships are forming, taking the high ground of the culture and using the expression "religious literacy in world affairs"! Following the publication of *The Other side of 1984* in 1983, the paradigm shift in western culture to which Newbigin devoted his "retirement" is becoming more and more apparent as the reality about the "public square" in which Christians are called to bear witness. Lapido represents a refusal to be corralled within one ghetto or another. It is a kind of mission using the media to reach "our culture," not for preaching, but for reorienting the false perspectives that made the Rushdie *fatwa*—and later 9/11—such bolts from the blue to the secularized intelligentsia. In doing so, it has been one small harbinger of change.

BIBLIOGRAPHY

Dibaj, Mehdi. "The Written Defense of the Rev. Mehdi Dibaj Delivered to the Sari Court of Justice—Sari, Iran December 3, 1993." Online: http://www.farsinet.com/persecuted/dibaj.html.

Newbigin, Lesslie. *The Gospel in a Pluralist Society*. London: SPCK, 1989.

———. "On Being the Church for the World." In *The Parish Church?: Explorations in the Relationship of the Church and the World*, edited by Giles Ecclestone, 25–42. Oxford: Mowbray, 1988.

———. *The Other Side of 1984: Questions for the Churches*. Geneva: World Council of Churches, 1983.

Jenny Taylor

————. *Proper Confidence: Faith, Doubt and Certainty in Christian Discipleship.* London: SPCK, 1995.

Newbigin, Lesslie, et al. *Faith and Power: Christianity and Islam in "Secular" Britain.* London: SPCK, 1998.

Polanyi, Michael. *Personal Knowledge: Towards a Post-Critical Philosophy.* Chicago: University of Chicago Press, 1958.

Rohr, Richard. *Simplicity: The Freedom of Letting Go.* Revised ed. New York: Crossroad, 2003.

Taylor, Jenny. "Taking Spirituality Seriously: Northern Uganda and Britain's 'Break the Silence' Campaign" in *The Round Table—The Commonwealth Journal of International Affairs* 94, no. 382 (2005) 559–74.

SECTION THREE

Theology in Global Context

Theological Education in Historical and Global Perspective

Wilbert R. Shenk

INTRODUCTION

A{N UNEXAMINED ASSUMPTION OF} the modern mission movement was that theological education was essential to the well-being of the churches being established across the world. The missionaries in the vanguard of this initiative in the 19th century took with them the only model of theological education they knew, confident that this was the proper mode of training pastors, evangelists, catechists, and other church workers. When the concept of the *indigenous* church was introduced in the mid-19th century, no one anticipated the implications this necessarily would have for theological education. Indeed, the question of the appropriateness of the western model of theological education for churches in other continents and cultures would not be raised until well into the 20th century.

The argument put forward here is that *modern* western theological education, exported throughout the world as a part of the modern mission movement, has proved to be a serious impediment to training church leaders in other cultures whose task it was to develop contextually appropriate churches. Everything about this theological educational program was geared toward inculcating western ideals and values. Observers like W.A. Visser 't Hooft and Lesslie Newbigin, with the benefit of extensive cross-cultural experience, saw clearly the profound syncretism and re-paganization that was at work in Western Christianity throughout this period.[1] Surely, this model was not to be viewed uncritically. Jürgen Moltmann spoke directly to this point in an address in 1971. He warned of the "danger that academic theology may become so contextualized that it becomes fossilized theology, and all the more dangerous because we are not aware of it."[2] The academy was not a reliable ally of the church. It was increasingly clear that the decline of the church in the West, evident already in the 19th century, had accelerated in the 20th. In retrospect, western theological education, blinded to its own cultural captivity, was singularly ill-suited to participate in the development of indigenous churches in Asia, Africa, and Latin America.

Lesslie Newbigin was among the early critics of this unexamined assumption. From the time of his arrival in India in 1936 he began raising questions about various dimensions of the classical missions model, including theological education.[3] The International Missionary Council Assembly at Tambaram, near Madras, India in December 1938, stressed the importance of theological education for the churches of the non-western world, but the clouds of the coming war overshadowed everything. By the 1950s the crisis in theological education was being widely discussed. In response to this crisis, theological educators in Asia and Africa led the way in developing contextualization theory in the 1960s and '70s. This opened the way for a new model. The task of developing contextually appropriate theology and theological education remains a work-in-progress.

A WINDING JOURNEY

From the beginning of the modern mission movement, a standard line in instructions handed to outgoing missionaries was that the goal of missionary work was to establish the church. In the 1850s a consensus began emerging among mission leaders that the original formulation needed to be clarified. It was becoming clear that what must be emphasized is that

---

1. See Newbigin, *Foolishness to the Greeks:* "The result is not, as we once imagined, a secular society. It is a pagan society, and its paganism, having been born out of the rejection of Christianity, is far more resistant to the gospel than the pre-Christian paganism with which cross-cultural missions have been familiar. Here, surely, is the most challenging missionary frontier of our time" (20). This critique was adumbrated already in *The Other Side* and repeated in subsequent writings. Cf. Visser 't Hooft, "Evangelism in the Neo-Pagan Situation" and "Evangelism among Europe's Neo-Pagans."

2. Cited by Coe, *Recollections,* 272.

3. Newbigin, *Unfinished Agenda,* 39–40.

the primary goal of the Christian mission is the development of *indigenous* churches.[4]

The Indigenous Church

This change in terminology was far more than mere semantics. Two generations of experience had revealed a fundamental flaw in missionary methodology. Careful observers saw with growing clarity that mission-founded churches lacked staying power. These churches remained dependent on their foreign sponsors and were aptly described as "potted plants." This variety of church was incapable of taking root in local soil.

According to the new concept, the viability of any church was linked to indigeneity, i.e., a church had to be rooted in its cultural soil. This "rootedness" would foster a dynamic sense of self-responsibility, that is, it would be *self-supporting, self-governing,* and *self-propagating.* It was precisely these features that were largely absent from mission-founded churches. While most missionaries began to pay lip-service to the indigenous church ideal, they effectively resisted any fundamental change in missionary methods and practices. The western missionary seemed intent on tending "potted plants" rather than cultivating indigenous agency.[5]

Education was integral to missionary work from the beginning. In addition to setting up primary schools for basic education, local people were trained to be evangelists, catechists, and Bible women. Such training emphasized Bible knowledge and practical methods of doing the work. By the 1820s higher level theological schools began to be established. All formal education was based on the western model.[6]

By the turn of the 20th century relentless new forces critical of the modern mission enterprise were afoot. Essentially, this opposition took two forms: 1) rising criticism by indigenous people of Euro-American patterns of domination, and 2) self-critique of missionary ideology and practice. Inescapably, western missions became entangled in the growing geopolitical tensions. The founding of the Indian Congress Party in 1885

4. Several mission leaders had a hand in conceptualizing the indigenous church. Henry Venn, secretary of the Church Missionary Society, produced a comprehensive statement in 1863. Cf. Shenk, *Henry Venn,* 44–46.

5. Cf. C. P. Williams, *Ideal of the Self-Governing Church,* which traces the gradual abandonment of Venn's strategy by CMS.

6. The Enlightenment exerted pervasive influence. Cf. Bosch, *Transforming Mission,* chapter 9; Stanley, *Christian Missions and the Enlightenment;* and Toulmin, *Cosmopolis.*

caught the incoming tide of nationalist sentiment. This marked the beginning of organized independence movements in many of the colonies controlled by western nations.

China: Wake-up Call

Formally, China was not colonized by a western power, but following upheavals in the 1860s several western nations banded together to force China to accept a series of treaties that permitted them to establish enclaves on Chinese soil for the purpose of trade. These treaties included guarantees that Christian missionaries could continue working in China. The Chinese people resented these treaties deeply. As a consequence, periodic demonstrations erupted against the western presence in China. Finally, in 1900 the Boxer Uprising gave vent to these frustrations. Some 5,000 people, including several dozen missionaries, were killed and considerable property was destroyed. Alarm spread across the world. The colonial powers realized this might well be a portent of what was coming in their colonies.

The dominant voice in missionary self-criticism between 1912 and his death in 1947 was that of Roland Allen. In fact, he was neither the first nor the only one calling for reform of mission methods and policies. Allen was a young Anglican missionary living in Peking at the time of the uprising. The horrors of the Boxer rebellion were deeply etched in Allen's consciousness. He was especially troubled that Chinese Christians had been singled out by the Boxers and charged with embracing a "foreign" religion. In 1912 he published his seminal work, *Missionary Methods: St. Paul's or Ours?*[7] For the rest of his life Allen was a fierce critic of mission policies and practices that he believed insured that the church being planted by the missionary was irremediably foreign. He proposed an alternative, arguing that the Apostle Paul had followed a different model that was permanently valid. The churches the Apostle Paul established were indigenous from the outset. The modern missionary was in thrall to a model that created dependency, an approach antithetical to the formation and flourishing of indigenous churches.

Yet well before Roland Allen appeared on the scene, other perceptive observers were making essentially the same critique. During the last third of the 19th century, John L. Nevius, Presbyterian missionary to China, developed a strategy based on his experience both in church planting and

7. Cf. Allen, *Roland Allen* for overview and bibliography.

training Chinese evangelists for developing indigenous churches.[8] His missionary colleagues in China proved the dictum that a prophet is honored everywhere except in his own place for they never accepted Nevius' ideas.

Edinburgh 1910 and "Exotic" Churches

In the popular imagination the World Missionary Conference that met in Edinburgh in 1910 is recalled as the pinnacle of a foolhardy western Christian triumphalism. A closer reading of the proceedings shows that this is an inadequate evaluation.[9] Commission III's report on Christian education includes a chapter, "The Relating of Christian Faith to Indigenous Thought and Feeling." The section dealing with India opens with a series of pithy observations and self-criticism of the western agents of mission:

> When we come to India we come to the region where the peril of an exotic church is greatest . . . In the first place, the gulf which separates races in their deepest life is probably at its widest as between English-speaking people and Indians . . . English-speaking people are in India the conquering race, the ruling class . . . This has affected inevitably the relations of missionaries to those whom they were teaching . . . No doubt the religious prepossessions of our missionaries have not generally inclined them to expect to find anything but evils in an idolatrous world . . . We are an insular race. Wherever we go, religion suggests to us the habits of our own home . . . And the educational ideals of the missionaries have naturally been those of their own generation and race . . . If we have these considerations in mind, it will not surprise us to find that there has been a tendency in India to generate an exotic religion.[10]

Emphasis on the "exotic" nature of western religiosity and mission-sponsored institutions highlighted the inability to adapt to non-Christendom environments. The report goes on to acknowledge that "the evil of an exotic non-national Christianity exists and is largely connected with non-national English methods and ideas in education."[11] This criticism has special implications for training for Christian ministry: "We venture

8. Cf. Nevius, *Planting and Development.*
9. Cf. Stanley, *World Missionary Conference.*
10. WMC, 1910, *Commission III*, 256–57.
11. Ibid., 259.

to say that the training of the native clergy has commonly been, even to a ludicrous extent, western in type. For instance, in the Anglican communion, candidates for the ministry have, we believe, been submitted to the same examination as candidates in England, and have been required to instruct themselves in, and conform their minds to, the XXXIX Articles—a formulary full of points of western controversy upon which they might surely be excused from entering."[12]

Criticism of Western missionary ideology and methodology was offered in a plenary address to the Edinburgh 1910 assembly. In a stirring message the Indian churchman, V.S. Azariah, pleaded "give us friends." He paid tribute to the remarkable collegiality he had experienced working with western YMCA staff in India but criticized the implicit racism and consequent absence of positive working relations between Indians and missionaries in many of the churches.[13]

The British dominated Commission III in terms of membership and largely controlled the study process. Their formulation of the aims of mission education framed the final report. According to this view the goal of mission education was three-fold: *evangelistic, edificatory* and *leavening.*[14] Looking back on the work of this commission, it failed to engage the basic issues and had no long-term effect on educational missions.

Western Tone-Deafness

Edinburgh 1910 faltered at the point of the West's inability to hear the voices representing other continents and cultures. The western worldview at the turn of the century was deeply shaped by Social Darwinism. "Scientific racism" was an unquestioned assumption that framed discussions of culture and cultural development.[15] Robert E. Speer, one of the most influential American mission leaders of that generation, in a reflection on the Conference emphasized how similar the New and Old Churches were in their theological perspectives. Indeed, Speer lamented that the promised enrichment of Christian theology through the contributions of Asian and

12. WMC, 1910, *Commission III*, 263. In the late 1860s Henry Venn pointed out that the 34th article of the *Anglican Prayer Book* provided for adaptation to a local culture. See, Shenk, *Henry Venn*, 34.

13. Azariah, "Problem of Co-Operation." Cf. Harper, *In the Shadow of the Mahatma*, 62–66; 147–49.

14. Stanley, *World Missionary Conference*, 176.

15. Curtain, "'Scientific' Racism."

African theologians had not yet been realized.[16] No wonder V.S. Azariah sounded a note that mixed equal parts of exasperation and desperation. Several other Asians who participated in the Conference made the same earnest plea for genuine understanding and acceptance on the part of the Western church. And yet no direct response was forthcoming.

One person who keenly understood the issues was J. H. Oldham, the astute and effective organizing secretary for Edinburgh 1910. Oldham was founding editor of the *International Review of Missions* (IRM), launched in 1912, and general secretary of the International Missionary Council (IMC), founded in 1921. Using his multiple leadership roles Oldham kept the "indigenous church"—and the range of issues this entailed—before the missionary world over the next several decades.[17] He commissioned Asians and Africans to contribute articles to the IRM on culture, national-ism, and racism. A survey of the proceedings of IMC conferences shows that one theme sure to be addressed from one angle or another was the indigenous church. Although the need for effective theological education was widely acknowledged, action on this front moved at glacial speed.

Shanghai, 1922

The National Christian Conference, meeting in Shanghai, China, May 2–11, 1922, twelve years on, was essentially a re-run of the issues debated at Edinburgh 1910. Tensions between missionaries and Chinese were palpable. In a plenary address to the Conference, T. C. Chao highlighted strengths and weaknesses of the church in China. As to weaknesses, he argued "the Church is weak because she is still foreign and divided . . . She is foreign both in thought and form."[18] This *foreignness* is not inherent in the Christian faith; rather it is the result of the form western missionaries brought to China.

Speaking as general secretary of the International Mission-ary Council, J. H. Oldham put his concern before the Conference in a straightforward manner. He was aware that while most missionaries paid lip-service to the indigenous church ideal, they declined to allow Chi-nese shoulder full responsibility. He warned that "the National Christian Council . . . if it is to succeed it must be *national*, that is to say *Chinese*

16. Stanley, *World Missionary Conference*, 130–31.

17. See Oldham, *World and the Gospel*; and *Christianity and the Race Problem*; also IMC, *Christian Mission in the Light of Race Conflict*.

18. Rawlinson, *Chinese Church*, 208.

in its genius, outlook and expression" (emphasis added).[19] Oldham was disturbed by what he observed of missionary intransigence and evasive actions in China. He then read a minute summarizing an extended IMC discussion several months earlier:

> It has been brought home to the Council in an extended discussion that, notwithstanding all the efforts that have been made to carry out the aim of foreign missions, namely the establishment of an indigenous church, the Christian movement in a large part of the mission field, and in particular in India and China, labours under a serious disadvantage because of the foreign character which it bears in the eyes of the people—a disadvantage which can be overcome only in the degree that the main leadership and direction of the Christian movement passes into native hands.[20]

The Conference report included a section on training men and women for various ministries. An over-riding issue in relation to ministerial training was compensation for pastors and other church workers, an issue that plagued mission-founded churches across the world.

J. H. Oldham listened closely to the criticisms and appeals that kept coming from leaders of the African and Asia churches. The old order had to give way to the new. One of the official volumes of the 1928 Jerusalem Meeting of the IMC, was devoted to *The Relation between the Younger and the Older Churches*.[21] Oldham recognized this as a pervasive and crucial issue but missionaries seemed incapable of mounting a constructive response on their own. The integrity of the missionary movement was at stake. At Jerusalem the race problem was studied in terms of two well-known cases: the United States and South Africa.

TAMBARAM 1938

One of the most important functions of IMC leadership was to set the agenda, as it were, for the missionary movement. During the two decades following Edinburgh 1910, J.H. Oldham had taken the lead in focusing on three priorities: indigenous agency, racism, and secularization. In the 1930s attention shifted to the church and training leadership for the churches in Africa and Asia.

19. Rawlinson, *Chinese Church*, 665.
20. Ibid., 667.
21. IMC, 1928.

Intuitions and Intimations

A few missionaries who began their missionary service in India in the 1930s—and were attuned to the rapidly changing world—were troubled that the colonial pattern was still largely intact and the majority of missionaries felt no urgency about coming to terms with the emerging new situation. Shortly after arriving in India in 1936, Lesslie Newbigin recorded in his diary: "Everywhere the same gulf between Indian and missionary, the conviction that Indians are not fit for responsibility . . . More and more I feel the test of our sincerity must be: Are we putting the training of Indians in responsibility above the efficient running of the machine?"[22] Newbigin was not alone. Charles Ranson, who began his service in India in 1929, was similarly disturbed by the attitude projected by British colonials toward India and Indian people. William Paton, who succeeded J.H. Oldham as IMC general secretary, had held several various posts in India between 1916 and 1926 and was well aware of the issues.

Newbigin's critique, developed during the early years of his service in India working with poor rural villages, struck several notes: 1) Ecclesial reality is most accurately discerned at the local level. 2) The clearest picture of this reality is to be found in the rural villages. 3) The life of the church must be developed from the ground up so as to ensure that it is fully supported by the local body of believers. 4) The local Christian community has all the essential resources necessary to develop a vital Christian discipleship and witness. 5) It is essential that the vernacular be privileged over other languages, in the training of pastors, evangelists, and catechists. Newbigin reported that he discovered Roland Allen "when I was beginning missionary service in India."[23] Thereafter, he was unable to escape Allen's influence.[24]

The meeting of the International Missionary Council at Tambaram, on the outskirts of Madras, India marks the beginning of study, debate, and initiatives to address theological education in relationship to the development of the indigenous church.[25] By the time of this meeting in December

22. Newbigin, *Unfinished Agenda,* 40; Ranson, *Missionary Pilgrimage,* 46, 69, 75–76.

23. "Foreword" to Allen, *Roland Allen,* xii. This modifies Wainwright's statement that Newbigin "read the 'seminal' works of Roland Allen . . . during the early years of his episcopate in Madurai." *Lesslie Newbigin,* 21. Wainwright helpfully documents the importance of Allen's influence on Newbigin.

24. Cf. Newbigin, "Work of the Holy Spirit."

25. From the beginning of the modern mission movement education was a

1938, the Europeans had waged the Great War of 1914–1918, nationalist movements in the European-controlled colonies were gaining greater traction, and the Bolsheviks had wrested control of Russia from the Czar. Other ideologies, including National Socialism and Fascism, were bent on gaining geopolitical dominance and the ominous threat of another war was gathering force. Mahatma Gandhi, leader of the Indian crusade for independence from Great Britain, had become an international symbol of the quest of indigenous peoples round the world for political independence and self-government.

Contextualization Anticipated

In preparation for the Madras Assembly, the Dutch scholar, Hendrik Kraemer, was commissioned to write a study volume that was distributed in advance to all conference registrants. Kraemer titled the book, *The Christian Message in a Non-Christian World*.[26] His academic training in Islamics, History of Religions, and Linguistics, and subsequent service with the Dutch Bible Society in Indonesia, 1922–1935, had given him a strategic vantage point from which to observe and evaluate the modern mission enterprise. During this time Kraemer carried out a series of field surveys of the churches in various parts of the country, starting with the Moluccas and northern Sulawesi in 1926.[27] He paid close attention to the way these churches related to their local cultures. In one church after another he observed that the Christian faith was not engaging the culture effectively.

A generation before the term "contextualization" was coined, Kraemer was analyzing the missionary approach to culture and pointing out the barriers that consistently blocked effective communication. He called for a new kind of encounter with culture. Kraemer hailed those few missionaries who instinctively showed respect for context and developed appropriate evangelization. Based on his extensive field studies of mission-founded churches in Indonesia, he observed that many missionaries operated self-confidently within their western worldview. He had concluded his 1933 report on the Sundanese Church in West Java, with an astringent

---

concern of missions and missionaries. The argument here is that a shift takes place in 1938. While only a beginning a new conceptualization was requisite to real progress.

26. Kraemer, *Christian Message*.

27. Kraemer's reports were published in the 1930s in Dutch. A selection of these reports was translated into English and published as *From Missionfield to Independent Church*.

critique of the state-controlled Protestant Church—erstwhile sponsor of the Sundanese Church—which he characterized as being "indifferent to the propagation of the Gospel among the Sundanese."[28] As a consequence, the Indonesians understood that they were being offered the *religion* of their colonial masters. This attitude had a demonstrable withering effect on missions and evangelism. In an effort to break the cycle of western domination within the church, in 1934 Kraemer helped to establish an advanced level theological school in Jakarta, the first of its kind in the Dutch East Indies.

When Kraemer came to write *The Christian Message* in 1938, he could draw on his extensive academic training, now greatly augmented by his years of engagement with churches that had been founded through *western* missionary initiative. The thrust of his book was that if the church is to be faithful to its fundamental purpose in a changing environment, it must maintain complete fidelity to the Word, on the one hand, and develop profound understanding and respect for its cultural context, on the other.

Theological Education: A Priority

The "Findings and Recommendations" of the IMC Tambaram Assembly included a section, "The Indigenous Ministry of the Church, both Ordained and Lay."[29] A key observation was that there was widespread dissatisfaction with the system for training ministers. But exactly what kind of training would meet the needs of the churches was far from clear. On the one hand, many argued that the low level of training for church leaders meant that they were not respected in congregation or community. On the other hand, it was widely reported that the churches did not have the economic base for supporting a professionally trained ministry.[30]

The way forward would be to develop three types of theological training: Bible schools for unordained church workers, theological schools that trained pastors, and theological colleges, affiliated with a university, which

28. Kraemer, *From Missionfield to Independent Church*, 146.

29. IMC, *World Mission*, 77–86.

30. The continuing debates about the proper kind of education revealed the strong pull toward academic respectability, i.e., western-style education that inevitably required that pastors be salaried in the western pattern; but this was at odds with attempts to develop patterns appropriate to the culture and economy of the people. Far too often the academic western model won out because it was regarded as more prestigious.

offered advanced training. Concerning curriculum in the theological school, it was recommended that "the vernacular should be the medium of instruction . . . It is especially necessary that students should constantly read and study the Bible in the vernacular."[31]

The report concludes: "*It is our conviction that the present condition of theological education is one of the greatest weaknesses in the whole Christian enterprise, and that no great improvement can be expected until churches and mission boards pay far greater attention to this work*" (emphasis added).[32] It was acknowledged that the report had "been prepared on the basis of very inadequate information. We think that the time has come for a much more thorough investigation and survey of this field." Accordingly, the section ends with the following proposal: "We therefore instruct the Committee of the International Missionary Council to take action in this matter, in consultation with the churches, and that a commission be appointed as soon as possible, to arrange for the preparation of detailed studies of the situation, where these have not already been made, to visit the main centres of theological education, and to work out a policy and programme for the training of the ministry in the younger churches."[33]

Looking back on Tambaram forty years later, Lesslie Newbigin noted "Tambaram drew attention to the shocking neglect of ministerial training in the 'younger churches' . . . It called for a much higher priority for theological education."[34] In the event, the IMC was unable to initiate follow-up to these recommendations. The rapidly approaching world war required that IMC focus its energies on preparing for that dreaded probability. It was left to member churches to act on this recommendation as best they could.

The Changing Role of the Missionary

By the early 1940s the British Colonial Government had signaled its readiness to grant India political independence in 1947. In this political climate the Indian churches and missions sensed that this would also affect them. Although many people resisted confronting the question, the role of the missionary in the India of the future had to be faced. The parallels between

31. IMC, *World Mission*, 81.

32. Ibid., 85.

33. Ibid., 86. Based on the survey in IMC Madras Series, *Life of the Church*, vol. IV, chapter 4.

34. Newbigin, "Theological Education," 105–15.

India in the 1940s and China in the 1920s are striking. In both instances the majority of missionaries were unable to listen sympathetically to the aspirations of the churches and church leaders. For the missionary the main question seemed to be: How can the missionary's position be preserved in this new situation?

Lesslie Newbigin addressed this sensitive question in an article commissioned by the IRM. His answer stirred controversy.[35] Using the prevailing image of the missionary to frame his analysis, he traced the way the missionary's role had evolved over time from evangelist and pastor to that of administrator; he showed that the ecclesiastical and institutional structures the missions set up insured that the administrator was at the top of the pyramid. In the popular mind power was associated with the administrator. The argument that the missionary had handed over responsibility to the Indian pastor was nothing more than a smoke-screen. In reality, the missionary administrator through the power of the purse continued to control the church and institutions.

To change this pattern, the first step was for the missionary to relinquish all administrative positions, making way for Indians to be assigned these responsibilities. But this required a deeper change. The missionary had to experience a reorientation. To clarify what he meant, Newbigin sketched a "spirituality" of service for the missionary of the future—a spirituality marked by humility, devoid of racial arrogance, self-effacing, ready to serve rather than rule, and willing to take the place of a junior member in the Indian Christian fellowship. Not content only to speak about this new model of missionary servant, Newbigin and two of his Church of Scotland missionary colleagues put themselves under the authority of the Indian church. This entailed surrendering their rights as missionaries. Their action threw the Church of Scotland Mission office in Edinburgh into some confusion, occasioning considerable correspondence.[36]

In view of the dynamic political situation—the world war notwithstanding—it was evident to thoughtful observers that evaluation and planning for the future of ministerial training could not be postponed.

---

35. Newbigin, "Ordained Foreign Missionary." Cf., on future of missionary in India, Newbigin to A.S. Kydd, 6/13/1943, National Library of Scotland (NLS): Acc7548/A23.

36. A Special Committee was established to confer with the General Administration Committee, the Inter-Church Relations Committee and the Foreign Mission Committee, with a view to the matter being brought before the General Assembly for decision. Minute 7279, 3/21/1944, NLS: Dep298/Box 191. Special thanks to Dr. Mark Laing for supplying this citation.

Wilbert R. Shenk

The National Christian Council of India, Burma and Ceylon took the lead, developing and implementing a nation-wide survey in 1943–1944. A director of research was appointed, research tools were devised and surveys carried out. The first survey was conducted in India. Charles W. Ranson wrote the final report, *The Christian Minister in India: His Vocation and Training*. This report was widely read and well received. It included "A Plan for Theological Education in India."[37] Yet this admirable project and the fine published report did not produce the much-needed conceptual breakthrough. At best, it represented an incremental approach whereas a reconceptualization was called for.

THE CHALLENGE OF THEOLOGICAL EDUCATION

In 1948 Charles W. Ranson became general secretary of the International Missionary Council. Having directed the survey of ministerial training in India and writing the report, noted above, Ranson brought with him a clear sense of the urgency of addressing this issue globally.[38] He was aware that Tambaram had made this a priority and he was convinced that it was the right one. He observed that many mission agencies and churches had "passed pious resolutions on the subject" but no one seemed capable of addressing this fundamental issue. Ranson was determined that positive action would be taken.

The IMC Research Secretariat was assigned to initiate a survey and study process. During the years 1950–1954 it conducted a survey of training for Christian ministry in Africa. The results were made available in four separate reports between 1950 and 1955.[39] Bengt Sundkler, a member of the IMC Research Secretariat, initiated a further survey of pastors and theological students in Africa in 1954. This was eventually published as *The Christian Ministry in Africa*, the most thorough of all the studies

37. Ranson, *Christian Minister*, 192–236.

38. Ranson, *Pilgrimage*, 147. Newbigin acknowledged Ranson's indispensable role: "Mainly through the tireless and imaginative persistence of one man—Charles Ranson—the Ghana Conference of 1958 was able to launch an ecumenical venture designed to do what Tambaram asked". Newbigin, "Theological Education," 3.

39. Part 1, by Stephen C. Neill, "Theological Education in British East and West Africa," (1950); Part 2, by M. Searle Bates, Christian G. Baeta, Frank Michaeli and Bengt G. M. Sundkler, "Theological Education in 'Latin' Africa and Liberia," (1954); Part 3, by Norman Goodall and Eric W. Nielsen, "Theological Education in Southern Africa," (1954); and, Part 4, by Fridtjov Birkeli, Frank Michaeli, and Charles W. Ranson, "Theological Education in Madagascar," (1955).

234

conducted during this phase.[40] Studies of theological training in other countries or regions were also made in the Caribbean, the Pacific Islands and parts of Asia.

The findings from these various surveys and consultations became the basis for a major project that would be carried out under auspices of the IMC, namely, the Theological Education Fund. This project was formally launched at the Ghana Assembly at the end of 1957.

Theological Education Fund Established

At the Ghana Assembly of the IMC, Charles Ranson resigned as general secretary to become founding director of the new Theological Education Fund. The IMC had secured funding for a five-year mandate.[41] TEF's main goals were to strengthen indigenous theological education through the upgrading of facilities and libraries, the preparation of new textbooks in vernacular languages, and recruiting and training men and women to serve as teachers in these theological schools.[42] Throughout this founding phase there was intense debate as to what it meant to work for "excellence" in theological education. Did it mean to bring theological colleges and seminaries in Asia, Africa, and Latin America into line with European and North American expectations? Or, should not "excellence" rather be measured in terms appropriate to the culture for which a school was training ministers of the gospel? Based on his twenty years of missionary work and episcopal oversight of a rural diocese in South India, Lesslie Newbigin argued strongly for the latter option.[43] This was also what Tambaram 1938 called for. But there were influential leaders, often lacking cross-cultural experience, who refused to accept this view.

In 1963 TEF's mandate was extended to 1970 with James F. Hopewell as director. During the second phase the TEF was to concentrate on promoting the concept of the seminary as a Christian community, raising the quality of both faculty and students, and revising the curriculum. Although this work was important to the future of theological schools around the world, the essential model of theological education remained unchanged.

40. Sundkler, *Christian Ministry in Africa.*

41. Ranson, *Missionary Pilgrimage,* chapter 16, gives a personal account of the founding of the TEF.

42. Cf. Ward, "Theological Education Fund."

43. Newbigin, *Unfinished Agenda,* 150–51.

This was a time of muddled thinking. While it was agreed that the TEF mandate to promote excellence in theological education was important to the future of theological schools around the world, the entrenched western model of theological education remained the default position. It was becoming clear to some leaders that this fundamental question could not be swept under the carpet. Upgrading facilities, libraries, and faculty credentials were all positive steps; but, ultimately, the model of theological education had to be appropriate to the cultural context of the churches being served. In the event, an important conceptual development lay ahead that would shift the terms of debate.[44] It is necessary to trace this development more fully.

Toward a Conceptual Breakthrough

Addressing Asian theological education leaders meeting in Bangkok in 1956, Dean Liston Pope, Yale Divinity School, praised these schools for their good work but "went on to say that he saw nothing new in [their] patterns of theological education, that in fact it was simply *a good imitation of the pattern found in the West* (emphasis added)."[45] This seminal observation registered with at least one person in Pope's audience. This was C. H. Hwang, principal of Tainan Theological College.

In 1962 the TEF's Advisory Committee, assisting in the drafting of the Second Mandate, assigned Hwang the task of writing a position paper titled, "A Rethinking of Theological Training for the Ministry in the Younger Churches Today."[46] Hwang brought an unusual set of experiences to his task: born the son and grandson of Presbyterian pastors in Taiwan when it was a colony of Japan, educated at a Japanese university, pursued theological education in Great Britain, married a British woman, spent the war years tutoring the British military to speak Japanese, returned to Taiwan in 1947 and became principal of Tainan Theological College in 1948. With the arrival of Generalissimo Chiang Kai-shek and his government from Mainland China in 1949, Taiwan came under what Taiwanese regarded as another occupying power. The Presbyterian Church of Taiwan soon emerged as a leading critic of the Kuomintang government, especially for its retrograde policies toward the indigenous Taiwanese. As a

44. Laing, "Recovering Missional Ecclesiology," provides a valuable overview and summary of the background and implementation of the first phase of TEF.

45. Hwang, "Rethinking," 8.

46. Coe, "In Search of Renewal, 235.

theological educator and Presbyterian Church leader, Hwang found himself constantly embroiled in a range of issues.

During those years Hwang had grown increasingly uneasy about the *foreign* curriculum that theological colleges in Taiwan followed. The training offered Taiwanese students might be appropriate for ministry in Great Britain or North America but not Taiwan. The students were not receiving the formation and tools needed to understand their culture in the light of the gospel.

In his essay Hwang agonized over the "imported" patterns of ministry and training that characterized all mission-founded churches. He questioned, for example, whether the "set-apart" ministry is "a theological necessity?" How effectively was the set-apart ministry relating to the ministry of the Body of Christ? The examples of indigenous churches such as Mukyokai in Japan and the Little Flock in China forced Hwang to question the prevailing patterns. These indigenous churches were self-supporting and rejected the concept of a clerical class and yet demonstrated a vitality that was the envy of mission-founded churches. The ferment in Hwang's mind forced him to search for a new way to conceptualize the task of theological education. He continually pointed to the burden Asian and African churches carried because of the "irrelevant theological outlook" of the "inherited pattern" from the West.

In 1965 C. H. Hwang, known hereafter as Shoki Coe,[47] moved from Taiwan to Great Britain where he joined the TEF staff as area director for East Asia. In 1971 he was appointed TEF director, during its third and final mandate.[48] Looking back on his participation in the process leading to the establishment of TEF and defining its first two mandates, Coe recalled that he received both "encouragement and a challenge."[49] Tainan Theological College, of which Coe had been principal, was a direct beneficiary of TEF grants that enabled upgrading and expansion of program. But with this came a sense of unease and a nagging question: Was this initiative developing and strengthening "indigenous theological education?"[50] Indeed,

47. Taiwanese-born C. H. Hwang went to university in Tokyo in the mid-1930s when Taiwan was occupied by Japan. There he was Shoki Coe, the Japanese transliteration of C. H. Hwang. See Wheeler, "Legacy of Shoki Coe."

48. Several accounts have Coe becoming TEF director upon his arrival in Great Britain in 1965, the year he joined the TEF staff. C. W. Ranson was director, 1958–1962, followed by James F. Hopewell during the second mandate, 1963–1970. Coe was director for the third, and final, mandate, 1971–1977.

49. Coe, "In Search," 234.

50. Ibid., 235.

is it possible to build up indigenous theological education by pursuing the Western model and standards? Coe admitted, "Up till that time we had not questioned the suitability of the Western model; indeed, we had done our utmost to advance towards it."[51]

African and Asian leaders in theological education were well aware that the churches they were committed to serving now found themselves in an unprecedented situation. Rapid political decolonization impressed on these churches the urgent need "to achieve an authentic self-hood" and this could only be realized as these churches underwent a change of identity, from being the "object of missions" to the "subject in mission." TEF continually encouraged theological schools to work for educational excellence: "The excellence to be sought should be defined in terms of that kind of theological training which leads to a real encounter between the student and the Gospel in terms of his own forms of thought and culture, and to a living dialogue between the church and its environment."[52] Yet TEF reporting through the 1960s had been preoccupied with upgrading program, not critically examining the fundamental question of what kind of theological training was appropriate to achieve the most basic goals. The western model remained securely in place. Apparently Liston Pope's challenge was long since forgotten.

The decade of the 1960s brought disruption on multiple fronts: geopolitical, cultural, religious, and inter-generational. The TEF's First Mandate, which accepted the western model as a given, had called for "Advance." The Second Mandate, adopted as the culture wars of the 1960s were starting, was focused on "Rethinking." The Third Mandate was expected to concentrate on "Reform." In 1966 Shoki Coe addressed the inaugural meeting of the North East Asia Association of Theological Schools on "Text and Context in Theological Education."[53] This was the first clue that a conceptual breakthrough was starting to emerge.

Contextuality and Contexualization

In 1971 four, of five, TEF program directors were from Asia, Africa, and Latin America: Shoki Coe (Taiwan), Ivy Chou (Malaysia), Aharon Sapsezian (Brazil), Desmond Tutu (South Africa), and James A. Berquist

51. Coe, "In Search," 235.
52. TEF, *Ministry in Context*, 12. Cf. Mbiti, "Theological Impotence."
53. Coe, "Text and Context in Theological Education."

(USA). A programmatic statement of the Third Mandate was set forth in *Ministry in Context* (1972).

The premise undergirding the Third Mandate asserted: "We have come to the end of an era."[54] This was recognized as a liminal moment in which there is "travail" as to what theological education ought to be but more profound is the "travail" by which "Christ is formed in us" (Gal. 4:19). A liminal moment signals new opportunity and this calls for re-thinking the very nature of theological education. The New Testament calls for a three-dimensional process. As "Christ is formed in me," my *living, thinking,* and *working* become expressions of Christ's ministry. This perspective entails a change in focus. The accent ought to be primarily on *how* and *where* this kind of formation can take place. If this is the focus, "we are driven to the question of contextuality and contextualization."[55] The theological task must always be carried out in the midst of life "on the way." It will be *theologia in loco.* No one should romanticize this process. Becoming aware of and sensitive to "what is *real, there,* is painful, and it is even more painful to be courageous and take the risk of being involved in it as the Incarnate Word did for the liberation of [humankind]."[56] Every-thing—all living, thinking and action—must be oriented to the *Missio Dei.*

This crucial conceptual development did not occur in a vacuum. Conversation and debate were taking place in many quarters. One of the important post-Vatican II developments was what emerged in the late 1960s as liberation theology. Varieties of liberation theologies were spawned from different continents, each with their particular socio-historical context, and groups (e.g., Black, feminist). Asian, African, and Latin American theologians joined the debate. An early contribution to this new genre was Kosuke Koyama's *Waterbuffalo Theology,* growing out of his work as a missionary theologian in Thailand and subsequent service as director of the Southeast Asia Association of Theological Schools.[57]

Shoki Coe emphasized the importance of both *contextuality* and *contextualization.* The theologian or missiologist gladly uses all the tools available to understand a particular context, including sociology, his-tory, anthropology, and linguistics. But all of this must be oriented to the *Missio Dei.* This requires a two-step process. First we must understand

54. TEF, *Ministry in Context,* 15–16.

55. Ibid.

56. Ibid.

57. Koyama, "From Water Buffaloes to Asian Theology," hinted at what was to come. See collection of early writings associated with this development is Anderson and Stransky, *Mission Trends No. 3.*

a particular situation. Contextuality refers to the "critical assessment of what makes the context really significant in the light of the *Missio Dei*." The second step is to undertake appropriate contextualization. "Authentic contextuality leads to contextualization."[58] To speak about "contextual theology" or "contextualized theology" is to misunderstand. Contextualization is always a process, an action. The theological basis for contextuality and contextualization is the Incarnation.[59]

Coe did not set this new conceptualization over against the older concepts of *indigenous* and *indigenization*.[60] Rather, he called for a new and more radical engagement. This new movement was led by people from Asia, Africa, and Latin America. Focusing on contextuality and contextualization signaled that the outsider no longer held a privileged position. Indeed, those indigenous to a particular context were in a privileged position for they understood, related to, and embodied the context in a way no outsider could ever do. This meant that the outsider—regardless of qualifications or title—should always come as a servant sharing whatever gifts the Master Servant had entrusted to the outsider on behalf of the world.

WHITHER THEOLOGICAL EDUCATION?

This essay has explored the struggle over the course of more than two centuries to develop appropriate theological training for the churches that were established as a result of the modern mission movement. The theme of western dominance has run through the entire story. Even when no western staff remained to run a theological school in Asia, Africa or Latin America, the curriculum and pattern of operation inherited from the west continued to determine the way theological education was conceived and carried out. The theoretical breakthrough reported above offered clues for moving beyond this long-running pattern of domination.

Much has also changed in the past four decades since that conceptual change occurred. Globalization has relentlessly been at work in the economic, cultural, communications, and religious systems that tie the world together in new and powerful ways. The polarity between local and global has intensified. Often it seems that the local is co-opted and exploited by

58. Coe, "In Search," 241.

59. Ibid., 242.

60. Ibid., 242–43.

the global system. The issues are, if anything, more confused and difficult to sort out.

The Christian movement itself has experienced a remarkable demographic change over the past two centuries. A growing majority of Christian adherents are now found in Asia, Latin America, Africa, and the Pacific, continents and regions where there was little or no Christian presence before 1800. The earnest efforts made during the last half of the 20th century to improve theological training were laudatory. But Dietrich Werner is surely correct in speaking about the "unfinished agenda" of theological education.[61] It will ever be so.

BIBLIOGRAPHY

Allen, Roland. *Missionary Methods: St. Paul's or Ours?* London: Robert Scott, 1912.

Allen, Hubert J. B. *Roland Allen: Pioneer, Priest, Prophet.* Grand Rapids: Eerdmans, 1995.

Azariah, V. S. "The Problem of Co-operation Between Foreign and Native Workers." In *The History and Records of the Conference* (World Missionary Conference, 1910), 306–15. London: Oliphant, Anderson & Ferrier, 1910.

Bosch, David J. *Transforming Mission: Paradigm Shifts in Theology of Mission.* Maryknoll, NY: Orbis, 1991.

Coe, Shoki. "In Search of Renewal in Theological Education." *Theological Education* 9 (1973) 233–43.

———. *Recollections and Reflections.* 2nd ed. Edited and introduced by Boris Anderson. N.p.: Formosan Christians for Self-Determination, 1993.

———. "Text and Context in Theological Education." In *Theological Education and Ministry from the N.E. Asia Theological Consultation.* Seoul, Korea, Nov. 28–Dec. 2, 1966. Tainan, Taiwan: Presbyterian Bookroom, 1966.

Curtain, Philip D. "'Scientific' racism and the British theory of empire." *Journal of the Historical Society of Nigeria* 2 (1960) 40–51.

Goodall, Norman, et al., editors. *A Decisive Hour for the Christian World Mission.* London: SCM, 1960.

Harper, Susan Billington. *In the Shadow of the Mahatma: V.S. Azariah and the Travails of Christianity in British India.* Grand Rapids: Eerdmans, 2000.

Hwang, C.H. "A Rethinking of Theological Training for the Ministry in the Younger Churches Today." In *South East Asia Journal of Theology* 4 (1962) 7–34.

International Missionary Council. *The Christian Mission in the Light of Race Conflict.* New York and London: IMC, 1928.

———. *The Life of the Church.* Madras Series IV. New York and London: IMC, 1939.

———. *The Relation between the Younger and the Older Churches.* New York and London: IMC, 1928.

———. *The World Mission of the Church.* New York and London: IMC, 1939.

---

61. Werner, "Theological Education."

Koyama, Kosuke. "From Water Buffaloes to Asian Theology." In *International Review of Missions* 53 (1964) 457–58.

———. *Waterbuffalo Theology.* Maryknoll, NY: Orbis, 1974.

Kraemer, Hendrik. *The Christian Message in a Non-Christian World.* New ed. Bangalore: Centre for Contemporary Christianity, 2009.

———. *From Missionfield to Independent Church.* London: SCM, 1958.

Laing, Mark. "Recovering Missional Ecclesiology in Theological Education." In *International Review of Mission* 98 (2009) 11–24.

Mbiti, John S. "Theological Impotence and the Universality of the Church." In *Mission Trends No. 3: Third World Theologies*, edited by Gerald H. Anderson and Thomas F. Stransky, 6–18. Grand Rapids: Eerdmans, 1976.

Nevius, John L. *The Planting and Development of Missionary Churches.* 4th ed. Philadelphia: Presbyterian & Reformed, 1958.

Newbigin, Lesslie. *Foolishness to the Greeks: The Gospel and Western Culture.* Grand Rapids: Eerdmans, 1986.

———. "Mission in an Ecumenical Perspective." Geneva: WCC Ecumenical Centre Library, 1962.

———. "The Ordained Foreign Missionary in the Indian Church." *International Review of Missions* 34 (1945) 86–94.

———. *The Other Side of 1984: Questions for the Churches.* Geneva: WCC Publications, 1983.

———. "Theological Education in a World Perspective." In *Missions and Theological Education in World Perspective*, edited by Harvie M. Conn and Samuel F. Rowan, 3–18. Farmington, MI: Associates of Urbanus, 1984.

———. *Unfinished Agenda: An Autobiography.* Rev. ed. Edinburgh: St. Andrews, 1993.

———. "The Work of the Holy Spirit in the Life of the Asian Churches." In *A Decisive Hour for the Christian World Mission*, edited by Norman Goodall, et al., 18–33. London: SCM, 1960.

Oldham, J. H. *Christianity and the Race Problem.* New York: George Doran, 1924.

———. *The World and the Gospel.* London: United Council for Missionary Education, 1916.

Ranson, Charles W. *The Christian Minister in India.* London: Lutterworth, 1946.

———. *A Missionary Pilgrimage.* Grand Rapids: Eerdmans, 1988.

Rawlinson, Frank, et al., editors. *The Chinese Church as revealed in The National Christian Conference.* Shanghai: Oriental, 1922.

Shenk, Wilbert R. *Henry Venn—Missionary Statesman.* Maryknoll, NY: Orbis, 1983.

Stanley, Brian. *World Missionary Conference, Edinburgh 1910.* Grand Rapids: Eerdmans, 2010.

———. editor. *Christian Missions and the Enlightenment.* Grand Rapids: Eerdmans, 2000.

Sundkler, Bengt. *The Christian Ministry in Africa.* London: SCM, 1961.

Theological Education Fund (TEF) Staff. *Ministry in Context: The Third Mandate Programme of the Theological Education Fund (1970–77).* Bromley, Kent: The Theological Education Fund, 1972.

Toulmin, Stephen. *Cosmopolis: The Hidden Agenda of Modernity.* New York: Free Press, 1990.

Visser 't Hooft, W. A. "Evangelism among Europe's Neo-Pagans." *IRM* 65 (1976) 349–60.

————. "Evangelism in the Neo-Pagan Situation." *International Review of Mission* 63 (1974) 81–86.

Wainwright, Geoffrey. *Lesslie Newbigin: A Theological Life.* New York: Oxford University Press, 2000.

Ward, A. Marcus. "The Theological Education Fund of the International Missionary Council." *International Review of Missions* 49 (1960) 137–47.

Werner, Dietrich. "Theological Education in the Changing Context of World Christianity—an Unfinished Agenda." In *International Bulletin of Missionary Research* 35 (2011) 92–100.

Wheeler, Ray. "The Legacy of Shoki Coe." In *International Bulletin of Missionary Research* 26 (2002) 77–80.

Williams, C. Peter. *The Ideal of the Self-Governing Church: A Study in Victorian Missionary Strategy.* Leiden: Brill, 1990.

World Missionary Conference, 1910. *Report of Commission III: Education in relation to The Christianisation of National Life.* Edinburgh and London: Oliphant, Anderson & Ferrier, 1910.

World Missionary Conference, 1910. *The History and Records of the Conference,* vol.9. Edinburgh/London: Oliphant, Anderson & Ferrier, 1910.

The Finality of Christ and a Missionary Encounter with Religious Pluralism

Newbigin's Missiological Approach

Michael W. Goheen

INTRODUCTION

IT MIGHT APPEAR AT first blush unlikely that in a book that explores Lesslie Newbigin's global theological legacy for today an investigation of his reflection on world religions would be promising. Charles Ryerson is not the only one to complain that Newbigin did not demonstrate enough enthusiasm for research into other religions when he said that an empathetic study of religions remained an "unfinished agenda" in his legacy.[1] It is true that compared to other major themes that appear in his vast literary corpus the study of world religions does not seem to command a high priority. And yet to draw the conclusion that what he did write on world religions—which is by no means paltry[2]—should be bypassed for other issues would be a mistake.

---

1. Ryerson, "Review of *Unfinished Agenda*," 460.

2. By my count he authored approximately 15–20 journal articles and book chapters as well as a couple of small books specifically on the topic although there is repetition and overlap among a number of them. A PhD dissertation has also been written on the topic: Thomas, *The Centrality of Christ and Inter-Religious Dialogue in the Theology of Lesslie Newbigin*. Other books that have dealt with this issue in some detail are Hunsberger, *Bearing the Witness of the Spirit*, 194–234; Wainwright, *Lesslie Newbigin: A Theological Life*, 204–236; Wood, *Faiths and Faithfulness*, 115–68.

In today's climate where religious pluralism is perhaps one of the greatest challenges to the gospel, one cannot overlook Newbigin's vast experience as a missionary amidst the pluralism of India and his "long, instructive contact with Hindu friends and scholars."[3] He carried out his missionary role in the shadow of some of the most powerful Hindu temples in India for three decades. He was involved in primary evangelism in Kanchipuram, one of the seven most sacred Hindu cities, spent time there in studying Hindu sacred writings with Hindu monks, and engaged in nation-building in co-operation with Hindus and Muslims as bishop in the cities of Madurai and Madras. His engagement with the issue of world religions was no less intensive as he returned to Britain. His pastorate in Winson Green in the midst of a predominantly Asian neighborhood, his involvement in the Sacred Advisory Council on Religious Education in the public schools, his membership on a committee in the United Reformed Church on 'Mission and Other Faiths', his treatment of Islam as a growing global power, and his participation in the fiftieth anniversary celebration of Tambaram in 1988 which vaulted him into ongoing discussions with powerful pluralist voices all led Newbigin to devote himself to further reflection on the proper response to religious pluralism growing in Western cities.[4] Alister McGrath rightly observes that Newbigin's "substantial first-hand experience" makes him "one of the most perceptive analysts of the consequences of pluralism for Christian churches."[5]

Yet anyone looking for a scholarly tome on world religions from Newbigin will be disappointed. Wilbert Shenk describes him as a seminal thinker who identified the key issues of the day and sharply articulated them. "Time and again Newbigin led the way in introducing an issue that would become a dominant theme in the ensuing years."[6] One of the examples that Shenk notes in both of his brief tributes written on the occasion of Newbigin's death is that of world religions: ". . . he has forthrightly grasped the nettle of Christian witness in relation to other religions. He has faced the subtleties and complexities of the question without surrendering his commitment to Jesus Christ as lord and savior of all people."[7] Indeed, the places where Newbigin does address the topic of world religions

---

3. Hunsberger, *Bearing the Witness of the Spirit*, 210.

4. Newbigin, *Unfinished Agenda*, 243–246.

5. McGrath, "Challenge of Pluralism," 361.

6. Shenk, "Lesslie Newbigin's Contribution," 3.

7. Shenk, "Tribute to Bishop Newbigin," 4; cf. also Shenk, "Lesslie Newbigin's Contribution," 3.

remain helpful in articulating themes that have enduring importance to the present. His treatment of the topic developed as his context changed in different stages of his life. Nevertheless there are at least nine themes that remained relatively constant over four decades that given more space would warrant careful attention: his astute analysis of Western culture as it sets the terms for the discussion of religious pluralism; his definition of religion that highlights its radical and comprehensive character including in its scope 'secular' worldviews; his missiological approach to world religions that foregrounds a missionary encounter; his non-negotiable commitment to the finality of the Christ event in the context of universal history as the true standpoint for approaching other religions; his struggle with and insight into the problem of continuity and discontinuity; his insightful critique of ideological religious pluralism especially in its Western academic form; his reflection on the theological foundations of interfaith dialogue especially dialogue placed in the context of 'everyday' life; his reflection on the growing global power of Islam and its presence in the public square as a comprehensive vision of life; and his discussion of the destiny of those who haven't heard the gospel.

Newbigin's discussion of these topics is indebted to Hendrik Kraemer. Kraemer's voice dominated Christian discussions of world religions for over two decades in the middle part of the 20th century. Almost every theme in Newbigin's position mentioned above bears the imprint of Kraemer. Newbigin believed himself in the late 1980s to be "fighting the same battle that Hendrik Kraemer fought at Tambaram fifty years earlier."[8] As he reread the debates surrounding Kraemer's work, and especially the critiques of A. G. Hogg, the most penetrating critic of Kraemer's position, Newbigin comments that "I find myself more and more compelled to stand with Kraemer."[9] While there are differences between the two men, at the heart of the issue Newbigin has carried forward the rich and often misunderstood work of Kraemer into a new context.[10] It is my conviction

8. Newbigin, *Unfinished Agenda*, 243.

9. Newbigin "Sermon Preached at the Thanksgiving Service," 328. In 1994 when I first met Lesslie Newbigin, he ushered me into his small apartment in London. The first thing he did was to take down a picture of Hendrik Kraemer prominently displayed on a cabinet. It was one of only two personal pictures he said he had kept when he moved into a smaller place. He asked me if I knew who he was. When I responded that I did, he proceeded to talk at length about how much Kraemer had influenced him, including his own approach to world religions.

10. Contra James Cox who believes that "it would be wrong in this context to dismiss Newbigin as a latter-day exponent of Kraemer's position," a viewpoint with which George Hunsberger appears to be in sympathy (Cox, "Faith and Faiths," 254;

that there is much in this Kraemer-Newbigin legacy that is exceedingly valuable and needs to be mined to address pressing issues today.[11]

I cannot address the whole of this topic comprehensively or any of the various themes articulated above in any detail in an essay of this size. I will focus my essay on Newbigin's understanding of a missionary encounter which he believed to be the correct fundamental stance the church was to take toward other religions. This belief flowed from starting with the finality of Christ as the fullest revelation of God's purpose for universal history. I will note some common faulty approaches that Newbigin believed eclipsed a missionary encounter and end with a brief section on the implications of such an encounter for a missionary approach to adherents of other religions.

WHO CAN BE SAVED? STARTING WITH THE WRONG QUESTION

Starting points for a discussion are, of course, highly significant. They function like a surveyor's fixed benchmark that serves as a trustworthy reference point to faithfully orient further surveys. Newbigin is concerned that the starting point for most discussions of world religions has distorted the discussion from the start. Usually three different positions of the relationship of the Christian faith to non-Christian religions provide a framework for discussion. While there is no agreement on how to characterize these positions, generally the exclusivist position holds an exclusive place for Christ and the Christian faith usually requiring a response of faith to the gospel for salvation; the inclusivist position maintains the universal validity of the gospel yet believes it possible for those who have not responded to the gospel to be saved, also believing that other religions may be channels of Christ's salvation; the pluralist position holds that all religions offer alternative yet equally true paths to personal salvation. This categorization, Newbigin believes, "has been fatally flawed by the fact that it has been conducted around the question, 'Who can be saved?'"[12] Can the good non-Christian be saved? Where will she go when she dies? What happens to the non-Christian after death? Newbigin believes that these

---

Hunsberger, *Bearing the Witness of the Spirit*, 327, note 10).

11. Cf. Perry, "Significance of Hendrik Kraemer," 37–59.

12. Newbigin, *Gospel in a Pluralist Society*, 176–77.

are all variations of the same wrong question and, of course, "the quest for truth always requires that we ask the right questions."[13]

These questions are the wrong questions for three reasons. First, these questions misunderstand the final judgment of God. God alone is judge and we are only witnesses. Jesus' many warnings and parables make clear that the last day will be a day of surprises, of reversals, and of astonishment. The warnings of eternal judgment given in Scripture are given not to judge outsiders but to produce a godly fear and fend off presumption among God's people. Second, the question about the eternal destiny of the soul assumes an individualistic anthropology that abstracts individuals from the ongoing history of the world. It is reductionistic to speak of a person apart from the full embodiment of his or her life in the context of the history of creation. The final reason is that it focuses on the individual's need of salvation rather than God and his glory. When the question of the individual's destiny shapes the issue, the whole cosmic drama of salvation seems to culminate in the words "For me; for me . . ."[14]

Newbigin certainly demonstrates that to make the salvation of the individual the starting point is to skew the whole issue from the beginning. Yet we can ask if by rightly reacting against a distortion he has not overstated his case neglecting something important. The question of individual salvation is not the *only* or *central* question; but surely it is *a* legitimate secondary question.[15]

STARTING IN THE RIGHT PLACE—JESUS, THE CENTER OF WORLD HISTORY

If the salvation of individuals is the wrong place to start the question, the question of course, is where is the right place? It is Jesus who stands at the center of universal history revealing God's purpose for the creation. It is "virtually impossible to read anything ever written by Lesslie Newbigin without gaining a sense of his feel for history, his awareness of being part of a story, indeed of being caught up in *the* story of the unfolding drama of the purposes of God."[16] The claim made for Scripture is that it is universal history: "The Bible tells a story that is *the* story, the story of which

---

13. Ibid., 176–77.

14. Ibid., 179.

15. Ibid., 176–77. Cf. Matthew Thomas, "Centrality of Christ," 318.

16. Wood, *Faiths and Faithfulness*, 147.

our human life is a part."[17] It is possible for us to know the meaning of universal history because in Jesus God has decisively and finally revealed and accomplished the end. In an early discussion of the world religions, he articulates the gospel as "secular announcement." The gospel is an announcement of an event in which God has acted decisively and finally for the restoration of the creation. It is not "a religious message which brings to completion and perfection the religious teaching of the ages" but "an announcement which concerns the end of the world."[18] The gospel is news about the goal of universal history, the corporate and cosmic completion of God's purpose for the creation whereby in Christ all things and all of human life are restored to the unity for which they were created. This is not a message about God for individual people detachable from their place in the world nor a message about salvation if that is understood to merely be what happens to the individual soul after death. Rather it is about the ultimate destiny of this whole creation. It is not a message that is concerned with only one aspect of human life (something called "religious") but with the whole human situation—all people and the whole of their life.

Newbigin's ways of speaking of the exclusivity of Christ contrasts with other ways. It is in this way, as the center and revelation of universal history, which Newbigin speaks of the finality of Christ. The gospel "concerns the consummation of all things. Its character as 'final' lies in this fact."[19] Paul Knitter piles up terms that have been used to describe the truth claims made for the Christian faith: "unique, exclusive, superior, definitive, normative, absolute."[20] Each function within a different universe of thought and thus will express the truth of the gospel variously. Moreover each has different implications for relating the gospel to other religions. Newbigin consistently expresses the universal truth of the gospel in terms of historical finality, an event in which God has acted to reveal and accomplish the goal of cosmic history. In the biblical view "all of history is in some sense a unity, with the incarnation of the eternal Word of God as the centre which gives it meaning. It is only within the framework which this view provides, that we can understand the decisiveness of the Christ-event for all times and all peoples."[21]

17. Newbigin, *Open Secret*, 82.
18. Newbigin, *Finality of Christ*, 48.
19. Ibid., 49.
20. Knitter, *No Other Name*, 18.
21. Newbigin, "Christ and the World of Religions," 28.

The first question, then, is whether or not the historical testimony to this event and its meaning is true. If one believes it to be true it must be the starting point for thinking about everything else including the religious life of humankind. If one does not believe it, it will be on the basis of another more ultimate faith commitment that must serve as the clue to understanding the world and the meaning of history including other religions.

This way of expressing the Christian faith gives rise to a quite different way of understanding religion than is popularly conceived. Often in Western culture the word "religion" is used in a limited way to describe practices and beliefs regarding the transcendent, or more specifically regarding the relationship of God to the immortal soul. Thus it is a department of life concerned with such things as worship, prayer, reading sacred scriptures, an ethical system, beliefs about God and the afterlife, and so forth. Newbigin is impatient with this narrow understanding of religion. Religion defined in this way arises from commitment to a story different than that of the Bible. Religion is much more basic and comprehensive, and it is a peculiarity of Western culture to isolate the domain of religion from the rest of life.

> Neither in practice nor in thought is religion separate from the rest of life. In practice all the life of society is permeated by beliefs which western Europeans would call religious, and in thought what we call religion is a whole worldview, a way of understanding the whole of human experience. The sharp line which modern Western culture has drawn between religious affairs and secular affairs is itself one of the most significant peculiarities of our culture and would be incomprehensible to the vast majority of people who have not been brought into contact with this culture.[22]

Religion is a "set of beliefs, experiences, and practices that seek to grasp and express the ultimate nature of things, that which gives shape and meaning to life, that which claims final loyalty."[23] Thus religion includes not only what are traditionally referred to as the world religions

---

22. Newbigin, *Gospel in a Pluralist Society*, 172.

23. Newbigin, *Foolishness to the Greeks*, 3. George Hunsberger speaks of Newbigin's understanding of religion in a "totalistic sense" and a "limited sense." He believes Newbigin is not clear and that he exhibits an oscillation from one position to the other. Sometimes religion is an element, aspect, dimension, or sphere of human life. At other times it is comprehensive and all-pervading, ultimate and decisive beliefs that provide stances for living all of life. Cf. *Bearing the Witness of the Spirit*, 201–3.

but also the ideologies and comprehensive worldviews that shape Western culture like the modern scientific worldview in both its Marxist and its liberal-democratic-capitalist expressions.[24] The phenomena we tradition-ally call "religions" are comprehensive worldviews which are marginalized because they don't share the faith commitment in science of the reigning worldview: "The things now called 'religions' have very little in common with each other except that they dissent from the reigning 'public doc-trine'—the doctrine which denies the reality of anything that cannot be handled with the tools of modern science."[25]

If the gospel offers a comprehensive way of understanding and liv-ing in the world and all the world religions do as well this will mean that inevitably religions will meet in terms of a missionary encounter between ultimate faith-commitments. One does not adjust the claims of the gospel to fit other visions of life including a pluralist vision. Rather there will be a clash of ultimate and comprehensive visions of life. From the side of the Christian faith the gospel will challenge and call into question the funda-mental assumptions of all other ultimate faith-commitments. Ian Barns describes this missionary encounter well when he says that Newbigin's "purpose is not to make a 'space' for Christianity *within* a wide pluralism, but to recover the alternative universalist *counter* claims of Christianity based on the particular grammar of the life, death and resurrection of Jesus."[26] All three adjectives used by Barns to describe the claims of Chris-tianity are important: *alternative* because the gospel presents another way of understanding the world; *universalist* because the truth of the gospel is valid for all people and claims the whole of human life; and *counter* because the gospel challenges all other ways of understanding the world calling for repentance and conversion.

TWO APPROACHES THAT PRE-EMPT
A MISSIONARY ENCOUNTER

If one starts with the finality of Christ this means the proper approach to other religions is in terms of a missionary encounter between ultimate commitments. This excludes at least two common ways of interpret-ing world religions that ultimately eliminate a missionary encounter by covertly assuming the truth of its own ultimate faith-commitments and

24. Newbigin, *Open Secret*, 161–62.

25. Newbigin, "Question to Ask," 11.

26. Barns, "Christianity in a Pluralist Society," 29.

masking them in the widely-held plausibility structure of our culture. The first is the supposed claim to be able to stand outside of any religion in order to interpret all religions in a neutral and impartial manner. This is the way of comparative religion. Newbigin offers a definition of this discipline by one of its pioneers Friedrich Max Müller as "a science of religion based on an impartial and truly scientific comparison of all, or at all events, of the most important religions of mankind."[27] Müller calls upon the scientific community to "take possession of this new territory in the name of science."[28] This commitment to science is not neutral or impartial but as religiously committed in faith as one who believes the gospel. Indeed it manifests missionary zeal for its religious cause: "This is the confident language of the pioneer missionary who has not yet found it necessary to consider the truth-claims of the tribal myths and religions of the natives."[29] It is precisely the unchallenged dominance of the commitment to scientific neutrality in Western culture that enables Müller to conceal this as an ultimate faith-commitment. It is not envisaged by such scholars that maybe this faith commitment to scientific neutrality will be questioned by the alternative faith commitments of one of the religions studied. A missionary encounter is simply eliminated at the outset by assuming the truth of one ultimate commitment and camouflaging it in the language of scientific neutrality.

A similar problem emerges with the pluralist approach to world religions. This position also sets aside a missionary encounter by simply assuming its own ultimate faith-commitment and concealing that faith in the widely-held ideology of pluralism of the broader culture. In fact, Newbigin insists, "pluralism is itself one position among other possible ones. It also makes truth-claims that have to be set against rival truth-claims which have to be denied. It cannot pretend to innocence among its arrogant rivals."[30] The only reason it is able to pretend humility in the midst of supposed arrogant and dogmatic truth claims is that pluralism is the "contemporary orthodoxy" and "reigning assumption" today.[31] Its widespread acceptance allows the dogmatic and arrogant claims of the pluralist to go unrecognized. Newbigin is concerned to unmask this illusion so that

27. Müller, *Introduction to the Science of Religion*, 26.
28. Ibid., 26–27.
29. Newbigin, *Open Secret*, 161.
30. Newbigin, *Religion in the Marketplace*, 137.
31. Newbigin, *Gospel in Pluralist Society*, 156.

there can be a genuine missionary encounter between the gospel and all other fundamental loyalties including pluralist faith.

A closer look at the story of the blind men and the elephants is one way Newbigin accomplishes this unmasking. This story is often used to illustrate the humility of pluralism over against the dogmatic arrogance of the various religions. Each blind man takes hold of a different part of the elephant and all disagree on what the elephant is. One takes hold of the trunk and believes it to be like a snake; another touches the ear believes it to be like a fan; still another grasps the tusk and thinks it to be a spear; and so on. It ends: "And so these blind men argued loud and long. Each of them was partly right but all of them were wrong." And so, says the pluralist, each religion has part of the truth and their dogmatic and ex-clusive claims show they are blind to the fact that they only have a partial perspective on the bigger truth. But as Newbigin astutely observes the real point of the story is constantly overlooked. The story is told from the point of view of the king and his courtiers, who are not blind but can see that the blind men are unable to grasp the full reality of the elephant and are only able to get hold of part of the truth. The story is constantly told in order to neutralize the affirmation of the great religions, to suggest that they learn humility and recognize that none of them can have more than one aspect of the truth. But the real point of the story is exactly the opposite. If the king were also blind there would be no story. The story is told by the king, and is the immensely arrogant claim of one who sees the full truth which all world religions are only groping after.[32] From what standpoint can they make such a claim?

A distinction made by John Hick offers an example of a pluralist at-tempt to pre-empt a missionary encounter. John Hick distinguishes be-tween two kinds of dialogue—confessional and truth-seeking dialogue. Confessional dialogue is carried out in the context of the varying ultimate faith commitments of the adherents. For Hick, this kind of dialogue will end either "in conversion or in a hardening of differences."[33] Instead Hick calls for a shift to truth-seeking dialogue in which adherents of the faiths engage in Socratic dialogue for a mutually enriched understanding of the Transcendent Being. Newbigin argues that such a contrast is false: "There is no dichotomy between 'confession' and 'truth-seeking.' A confession of faith is the starting point of their truth seeking."[34] Hick does not seem to

---

32. Newbigin, *Gospel in a Pluralist Society*, 9–10; *Open Secret*, 162.
33. Hick, "Christian Theology," 7.
34. Newbigin, *Open Secret*, 168.

recognize this and accordingly substitutes his faith commitment for the truth and so pre-empts any kind of encounter: "On the basis that Hick proposes, there is in fact no encounter between faiths. It is eliminated at the outset by the dogma that only one set of presuppositions can provide the conditions for truth seeking."[35] Hick seems to be unaware that his view is only one of many ways in which people grasp their experience, one vision of life based on faith amongst others. This position allows for neither a missionary encounter nor dialogue: "There is only the monologue of the one who is awake addressed to those who are presumed to be asleep, or who have not yet wholly roused themselves from their 'dogmatic slumbers.'"[36] Hick has not eliminated the confessional stance at all; rather he has assumed and imposed his own and thereby eliminated a missionary encounter. It is true of Hick, no less than any other position, that "no standpoint is available to anyone except the point where they stand; that there is no platform from which one can claim to have an 'objective' view that supersedes all the 'subjective' faith-commitments of the world's faiths; that everyone must take their stand on the floor of the arena, on the same level with every other, and there engage in the real encounter of ultimate commitment with those who have also staked their lives on their vision of the truth."[37]

LIVING AS A MISSIONARY COMMUNITY IN A RELIGIOUSLY PLURALISTIC SOCIETY

If the fundamental stance toward other religious communities is that of a missionary encounter a pressing question is: what is involved in a missionary approach to adherents of other religions in a religiously plural society?

First and foremost, the church must tell the story that has been entrusted to it. One may come to certain kinds of truth through observation and experiment, and to other kinds of truth through rigorous dialogue. However, if ultimate truth is bound up in a historical event the only way one can possibly know it is if they hear it from someone else. In a pluralist setting dialogue has often been introduced as a more humble substitute for evangelism. Newbigin counters that dialogue can never be an alternative to evangelism: historical truth comes neither by modernist dialogue in which dialogue brings its partners nearer to the truth nor by postmodern

35. Ibid., 167.
36. Ibid.
37. Ibid., 168.

dialogue in which adherents share the riches of their religious tradition for mutual enrichment. "The problem here is that the message of Christianity is essentially a story, a report of things which have happened. . . . A fact of history does not arise out of dialogue; it has to be unilaterally reported by those who, as witnesses, can truly report what happened."[38] While arrogant and aggressive proselytizing has been only too real, this does not abolish the task to tell the story, to seek to convince others of the truth, and to aim at conversion and discipleship. This is not necessarily an act of dogmatic arrogance but simply discharging the task that we have been chosen for. "For those who have been called to be part of this community and commissioned to be bearers of this witness, it is simply unthinkable that one should keep silent about it, and unthinkable that one should be willing to allow this witness to be listed as merely an expression in story form of one of the varieties of human religious experience. It must be shared as the clue both to the whole human story and therefore to every person's story."[39]

Newbigin often adds—and this is the second point—that it is also necessary if the words of the gospel are to be believed that the church must "be the place where the reign of God is present and therefore where the battle with the powers of darkness is joined."[40] Words must be joined to deeds, and both must flow from a community where the new power of the kingdom is evident. "The life of the Church, its words, its deeds, its corporate life and—above all—its worship may in the providence of God provide the occasions for the inner witness of the Holy Spirit in the heart of an unbeliever. Christians must pray for that. But the answering of the prayer is in the hands of God alone."[41]

A third point, one that Newbigin never fails to mention, is that it is tremendously important for the church to "acknowledge, and welcome, and thank God for, and cherish, and admire, and reverence all the signs of the grace of God which we see so movingly among people of other faiths . . ."[42] The way Newbigin piles up verbs to make his point is indicative of the importance he attaches to this aspect of a missionary approach. His starting point is Christ: the same Jesus who appeared in history is also the Word of God active in all creation. There will be some evidence of

38. *Religious Pluralism*, 232–233.
39. Newbigin, "Christian Faith and World Religions," 334.
40. Newbigin, "Religious Pluralism," 239.
41. Ibid., 242.
42. Newbigin, "Confessing Christ in a Multi-Religion Society," 129.

Michael W. Goheen

His work throughout the creation including in the adherents of other religions. At the same time Newbigin does not shrink back from observing that "it is often the higher religions, and those in them who are ethically farthest advanced, that offer the most bitter resistance to the preaching of the gospel."[43] Since sinful humanity will "take the good gifts of God and make them into an instrument to cut ourselves off from God" it is important to stress that the gospel "confronts the claim of every religion with a radical negation."[44] Often Newbigin leaves these two poles of God's work and sin's corruption in a paradox but at other times draws them together: "In the light of the highest of human standards of truth and righteousness, Jesus appears as a *subverter*, as he did to the spiritual heirs of Moses, and as he does for the noblest and the most sensitive among the adherents of other faiths and ideologies. It is only after the total overturning of the traditional world of values that he is seen as the *fulfiller*, not the destroyer, of what went before."[45]

Fourth, the church is called to live at peace with other faith communities participating with them in the task of building a just and sustainable order. A missionary encounter does not mean a repellent and polemical confrontation that simply asserts an incommensurable Christian truth over against other religious accounts of the world or seeks to coercively displace them. Rather, the church should pursue cordial co-operation on many social, political, and ethical issues that is based on mutual respect. We share a common cultural task and participate in a civic order that draws together many faith communities. Our task is to "join hands with those of other faiths and ideologies to achieve specific goals, even though

43. Newbigin, *Faith for this One World?*, 73.

44. Newbigin, *Open Secret*, 176–77. Newbigin speaks of "fundamental continuity" and "radical discontinuity" between the gospel and other religions (*Christian Witness in a Plural Society*, 15). Although he does speak of radical discontinuity and negation, he is much quicker to stress God's gracious work among adherents of other religions. When Newbigin envisages a missionary encounter with the religious faith-commitments of modern Western culture he is quick to challenge the distortions and much slower to cherish the insights. With a missionary encounter with other world religions it is the opposite. Are these examples of the "fat man on the seesaw" principle? When there is a fat man sitting on one side of the seesaw it is necessary to jump very hard on the other side. In our climate is it necessary to stress the distortions in Western culture but the insights in world religions?

45. Newbigin, *Christian Witness in a Plural Society*, 15 (my emphasis). His use of the words "subvert" and "fulfill" are deliberate following Kraemer. Kraemer offers an exceedingly helpful notion of "subversive fulfillment" ("Continuity and Discontinuity," 2–4). Newbigin calls attention to this phrase approvingly in his article on W. A. Visser 't Hooft ("Legacy," 80–81; cf. Visser 't Hooft, "Accommodation," 13).

we know that the ultimate goal is Christ and his coming in glory and not what our collaborators imagine."[46] Newbigin suggests a "committed pluralism" in which various faith communities, including the church, take responsibility to know the truth and to enter vigorously into the struggle for truth in the public domain.[47] In this way the church avoids a ghetto mentality as well as the imperialism of Christendom.

It is precisely Newbigin's epistemology that enables him to both make exclusive claims for the gospel while affirming an ongoing search for the implications of the gospel for all of life that would include other faith communities. Christopher Duraisingh cannot easily reconcile Newbigin's post-empiricist epistemology and the story character of the gospel, on the one hand, and the final and exclusive claims made for the gospel on the other. He writes, "One may also sense a certain tension between the perspectival and the story character of the gospel and the absolute claims that are made for the gospel."[48] Yet it is precisely in the "story character of the gospel" that we find the absolute character of the gospel. The story of Jesus' life, death, and resurrection reveal and accomplish the end of history, and since this end encompasses all things, the claim has absolute and universal significance. This is the clue or light in which the church, as a hermeneutical community, explores and attempts to understand the world. All hermeneutical communities work in the light of some faith commitment, and so establish a tradition of rationality that attempts to grasp and understand the world. As the "Christian hermeneutical community" attempts to understand the world in the light of Christ, dialogue with other faith communities can lead to deepening insight. Ian Barns correctly observes that Newbigin's "tradition-based epistemology provides a basis for a non-coercive claim to truth because it opens the way for a dialogical engagement with culture."[49] The Christian church "does not claim to *possess* absolute truth: it claims to know where to point for guidance (both in thought and in action) for the common search for truth."[50] Barns comments that Newbigin's approach "enables him to engage more effectively in dialogue with alternative belief systems—a dialogue in which the language and more specific knowledges of other religions, cultures and

---

46. Newbigin, *Gospel in a Pluralist Society*, 181.

47. Newbigin, *Truth to Tell*, 56.

48. Duraisingh, "Foreword," viii.

49. Barns, "Christianity in a Pluralist Society," 36–37.

50. Newbigin, *Gospel in a Pluralist Society*, 163.

Michael W. Goheen

modern science can be critically interpreted in terms of the 'plausibility structure' and ecclesial practice of Biblical faith."[51]

The final dimension of a missionary approach to adherents of other religions is dialogue. Newbigin's concern is that dialogue is often placed in the context of religion narrowly defined. There is an "unspoken assumption" that religion understood as beliefs about God and the afterlife is "the primary medium of human contact with the divine."[52] Rather the proper "context for true dialogue" is the shared commitment to the business of this world.[53] The proper context for dialogue is our shared cultural, social, and political tasks. It enables adherents of different faith communities to explore the possibility of common action where they share common goals and objectives. It may also contribute to a civic society by opening up insight into the religious experience of others thus creating mutual understanding and so building friendship. Ultimately, it is a dialogue about the meaning and goal of the human story in the midst of our shared life together. In this way the purpose of dialogue is an obedient witness to Jesus Christ.

BIBLIOGRAPHY

Barns, Ian. "Christianity in a Pluralist Society: A Dialogue with Lesslie Newbigin." *St Mark's Review*, 158 (Winter 1994) 27–37.

Cox, James L., "Faith and Faiths: The Significance of A G Hogg's Missionary Thought for a Theology of Dialogue." *Scottish Journal of Theology*. 32 3 (1979) 241–56.

Duraisingh, Christopher. "Foreword." In Lesslie Newbigin, *The Gospel in a Pluralist Society*, vii–ix. Grand Rapids: Eerdmans, 1989.

Hick, John. "Christian Theology and Inter-Religious Dialogue." *World Faiths: Journal of the World Congress of Faiths* 103 (August 1977) 2–19, 30.

George R. Hunsberger, *Bearing the Witness of the Spirit: Lesslie Newbigin's Theology of Cultural Plurality*. Grand Rapids: Eerdmans, 1998.

Knitter, Paul. *No Other Name: A Critical Survey of Christian Attitudes Toward the World Religions*. Maryknoll, NY: Orbis, 1985.

Kraemer, Hendrik. "Continuity and Discontinuity." In *The Authority of the Faith. The Madras Series, Volume 1*, 1–21. New York: International Missionary Council, 1939.

McGrath, Alister, "The Challenge of Pluralism for the Contemporary Christian Church." *Journal of the Evangelical Theological Society* 35/3 (September 1992) 361–73

Müller, Friedrich Max. *Introduction to the Science of Religion*. London: Longmans Green, 1882.

Newbigin, Lesslie. "Christ and the World of Religions." *Churchman* 97/1 (1983) 16–30.

51. Barns, "Christianity in a Pluralist Society," 33

52. Newbigin, *Gospel in a Pluralist Society*, 172.

53. Ibid., 181.

———. "The Christian Faith and the World Religions." In *Keeping the Faith: Essays to Mark the Centenary of Lux Mundi*, edited by Geoffrey Wainwright, 310–340. London: SPCK, 1988.

———. *Christian Witness in a Plural Society*. London: British Council of Churches, 1977.

———. Confessing Christ in a Multi-Religion Society," *Scottish Bulletin of Evangelical Theology* 12 (Autumn 1994) 125–136.

———. *A Faith for this One World?* London: SCM, 1961.

———. *The Finality of Christ*. London: SCM, 1969.

———. *Foolishness to the Greeks: The Gospel and Western Culture*. Grand Rapids: Eerdmans, 1986.

———. *The Gospel in a Pluralist Society*. Grand Rapids: Eerdmans, 1989.

———. "The Legacy of W. A. Visser 't Hooft." *International Bulletin of Missionary Research* 16 (April 1992) 78–81

———. *The Open Secret: An Introduction to the Theology of Mission*. Revised edition; Grand Rapids: Eerdmans, 1995.

———. "A Question to Ask; A Story to Tell." *Reform* (November, 1990) 11.

———. "Religion in the Marketplace." In *Christian Uniqueness Reconsidered*, edited by Gavin D'Costa, 135–148. Maryknoll: Orbis, 1990.

———. *Religious Pluralism: A Missiological Approach*, *Studia Missionalia* 42 (1993) 227–244.

———. "A Sermon Preached at the Thanksgiving Service for the Fiftieth Anniversary of the Tambaram Conference of the International Missionary Council." *International Review of Mission* 77 307 (1988) 325–331.

———. *Truth To Tell: The Gospel as Public Truth*. Grand Rapids: Eerdmans, 1991.

———. *An Unfinished Agenda: An Updated Autobiography*. Edinburgh: Saint Andrew Press, 1993.

Perry, T.S. "The Significance of Hendrik Kraemer for Evangelical Theology of Religions." *Didaskalia* (Spring 1998) 37–59.

Ryerson, Charles. "Review of *Unfinished Agenda*, by Lesslie Newbigin." *Theology Today* 43/3 (October 1986) 459–60.

Shenk, Wilbert R. "Lesslie Newbigin's Contribution to the Theology of Mission," *The Bible in TransMission: A Tribute to Lesslie Newbigin (1909–1998)* (1998) 3–6.

———. "A Tribute to Bishop Newbigin," *The Gospel and Our Culture* (North America) Special Edition (April 1998) 4.

Thomas, V. Matthew. "The Centrality of Christ and Inter-Religious Dialogue in the Theology of Lesslie Newbigin." PhD diss., Wycliffe College, University of Toronto, 1996.

Visser 't Hooft, W.A. "Accommodation, True or False." *South East Asia Journal of Theology* 8 3 (January 1967) 5–18.

Wainwright, Geoffrey. *Lesslie Newbigin: A Theological Life*. Oxford: Oxford University Press, 2000.

Wood, Nicholas J. *Faiths and Faithfulness: Pluralism, Dialogue and Mission in the Work of Kenneth Cragg and Lesslie Newbigin*. Milton Keynes, UK: Paternoster, 2009.

"Who Is Jesus Christ?"

The Necessary Missionary Form of the Confession of the Trinity

John G. Flett

INTRODUCTION

ROWAN WILLIAMS OBSERVES THAT "our tendency is to think of 'mission' and 'spirituality' as pointing in different directions—the communicating of faith and the cultivation of faith."[1] While correct, the issue is surely much greater than "a tendency." One need not delve far into liturgical, theological, or ethical systems to discover this petrified binary and the concomitant priority given the cultivation of the now essentially non-missionary faith. This establishes what is meant by "internal" and "external" to the church and quite naturally feeds into the questions of order and the shape of "pastoral" ministry. Yet, as William's argument progresses, it is clear that this entrenched dichotomy contravenes many of the affirmations of fundamental theology. This is a curious observation and suggestive of the difficult contest that underlies the few theological attempts to ground mission in the trinity. That is, insofar as mission is understood as a community crossing of boundaries which is itself changed as a result of that movement, then this seemingly combats an understanding of growth in Christian maturity located in stability and visible continuity.

Such is the setting of Lesslie Newbigin's trinitarian grounding of mission. While his position is most fully developed in an introductory

---

1. Williams, "Doing the Works of God," 221.

mission text, his concern is not so much with an apology for missionary activity in a period of decline. His work is meditation on the one church as the historical confession of the Trinity. As the community of the Trinity, no space exists between the communication and the cultivation of the faith. The visible continuity of the Christian community is itself basic to missionary movement, and this movement shapes the church in obedience to the Spirit. In summary form: the gospel is the message of the reign of God the *Father*, the creator, sustainer and redeemer of all things, and the church exists in its proclamation, that is, the economy of history is the necessary realm of the church's acting. The *Son* is the presence of the kingdom, and as his body, the church bears in its own life the presence of the kingdom. The *Spirit* is the firstfruit of the kingdom, its prevenience, and the church forms in obedience to the missionary witness of the Spirit.

METHODOLOGY

Before turning to the substance of Newbigin's position, two methodological observations are in order. First, Newbigin's constructive theology is "occasional" rather than "systematic." He begins neither with prior treatments propagated by the theological lights of the church nor with traditional "problems," such as the relationship between the immanent and economic trinity. It is difficult to identify his position in terms of theological provenance and systematic outline.[2] Instead, the immediate backdrop and framing goal of his work is in service to the mission and unity of the church.

This means (1) that he appreciates the extent to which the discussion of normative theology is culturally embedded, and, as such, is deafened to the questions and claims posed by the non-western church.[3] His critical appreciation of the theological tradition can appear, at once, liberal with regards to the cultural possibilities available to the church, its confession and order, and conservative with regards to the centrality of Jesus Christ for the whole of human history and its consequences for the church's existence. He resists, in other words, received trajectories of interpretation, and needs to be read with this difference in mind.

2. A circumstance facilitated by his seeming phobia of citation.

3. Newbigin, for example, observes that "a great deal of the substance of the Western Christian tradition—its liturgy, theology and church order—was formed during the long period in which Western Christendom was an almost enclosed ghetto precluded from missionary advance" (Newbigin, *Open Secret*, 4).

(2) Newbigin understands theological formulations to be products of a particular historical and context. No theological utterance possesses a hallowed status that sets it apart from the economy of worldly discourse. By way of example, "the Nicene formula has been so devoutly hallowed that it is effectively put out of circulation. It has been treated like the talent that was buried for safekeeping rather than risked in the commerce of discussion."[4] This does not render every statement relative. Rather, theological formulations are to serve the missionary witness of the church, which for Newbigin means their proper location is in the contest of the public.

(3) This "location" of all theological discussion permits Newbigin to relativize the challenges history and culture present to the church. For example, in reaction to certain problems, including that of "religious pluralism," Konrad Raiser proposed a "Trinitarian" solution in opposition to a "Christological-universalism" that he understood as normative during the inception of the World Council of Churches (WCC).[5] One element of Newbigin's response consisted of the simple observation that by describing religious pluralism as a development of the past twenty-five years, Raiser has illustrated the euro-centric roots of his view.[6] By extension: throughout its history, not only has the church maintained its Christological commitments, but the doctrine of the Trinity developed in the context of religious pluralism in answer to the Christological challenges this context posed.[7] Newbigin's critical sense of the conditional nature of theological statements occurs within a long view of missionary engagement, one that understands that relativity within a continuity.

As a second methodological observation, Newbigin did not focus attention on any particular doctrine. Thus, while he published a great deal, the dataset for an investigation into his trinitarian framing of mission is largely limited to the 1963 *Trinitarian Doctrine for Today's Mission* and the 1978 *The Open Secret.*[8] While he bears some responsibility for

---

4. Ibid., 27.

5. Raiser, *Ecumenism in Transition.*

6. Newbigin, "Ecumenical Amnesia," 5.

7. "[T]he doctrine of the Trinity is the theological articulation of what it means to say that Jesus is the unique Word of God incarnate in world history." Newbigin, "Ecumenical Amnesia," 2.

8. Given the deep relationship between Newbigin and the "missional church" movement which helped give the term a wider audience, the extent to which he *avoids* the language of *missio Dei* is somewhat surprising. Newbigin's limited employment of the term typically occurs as a simple indicator of a theological position developed

the trinitarian statement at the 1952 International Missionary Council Willingen conference,[9] it is out of some dissatisfaction with the "witness" section for the 1961 New Delhi WCC conference that Newbigin came to recognize "a Trinitarian, rather than a purely christological understanding of the missionary task [as] more and more necessary."[10] To this end, and in recognition that the missiology in his *One Body, One Gospel, One World* reflected a too "church centric" position, Newbigin developed his *Trinitarian Doctrine for Today's Mission*. This first attempt at a trinitarian formulation, however, met with a cold reception: Willem Visser 't Hooft "disapproved of its theology, and my colleagues in the Division were not sufficiently persuaded to support me."[11] The problem, as it developed through the 1960s, was that reference to God's missionary being located God's acting first in secular history, beside which the church was a "postscript."[12] Newbigin states of this development that "on a theological level I had to recognize the big element of truth in what was being said, but I was acutely aware at the same time of what was being ignored or denied."[13] Newbigin's own 1963 contribution failed to inform the developments through the 1960s and, to quote, it was not until "nearly twenty years later that I had the opportunity to develop its argument in a full-length book, *The Open Secret*."[14]

---

during the 1960s. (Newbigin, "Recent Thinking on Christian Beliefs," 260–64.) This happens because of the negative relationship he understands that the phrase *missio Dei* has to the church. "This phrase was sometimes used in such a way as to marginalize the role of the church. If God is indeed the true missionary, it was said, our business is not to promote the mission of the church, but to get out into the world, find out 'what God is doing in the world', and join forces with him. And 'what God is doing' was generally thought to be in the secular rather than in the religious sectors of human life. The effect, of course, was to look for what seemed to be the rising powers and to identify Christian missionary responsibility with support for a range of political and cultural developments, sometimes bizarre indeed." (Newbigin, *Open Secret*, 18.)

9. For a discussion of the trinitarian developments of this conference, see Flett, *Witness of God*, 123–62.

10. Newbigin, *Unfinished Agenda*, 192. This comment was made in the context of thinking about the gifts of God given to people of other faiths and of no faith; that is, the language of the Trinity here references a space between the church and the action of God.

11. Ibid., 198–99. Such distrust formed against the background of the charge common against the WCC even during its early formation of being too "christo-centric." H. Richard Niebuhr, for example, advocated a "theocentric" position as a way of addressing a type of narrow Christological focus that resulted in problematic mission methods (Niebuhr, "Doctrine of the Trinity and the Unity of the Church," 371–84).

12. WCC Department, *Church for Others*, 70.

13. Newbigin, *Unfinished Agenda*, 175.

14. Ibid., 199.

John G. Flett

Although it developed with this historical distance, the key questions of the relationship between the acting of God in history and in the church, of a theological grounding for mission and its relationship to the church, and the question of unity as basic to the missionary task, shape Newbigin's contribution.

WHO IS JESUS CHRIST?

Newbigin enters his treatment of the Trinity through a reflection on authority. Nineteenth century missionary activity assumed, to a significant degree, a relationship between the Christian gospel and the superiority of western culture, thereby locating the authority of evangelism in cultural benefits. Today, the question, posed both within the lands formerly known as Christendom and in those lands which consider Christianity a foreign religion, is "what right do you have to preach to us?"[15] For Newbigin, this is the very question posed to Jesus through his ministry (Mark 11:28), and later to his disciples whose answer was simply "in the name of Jesus" (Acts 4:7–10). Jesus is himself the ultimate authority, the basic commitment of Christian mission.[16] This does not establish a general justification because "the authority of Jesus cannot be validated by reference to some other authority that is already accepted."[17]

Much hangs on this affirmation and it is certainly open to misinterpretation. Generally stated, the variety of charges associated with the language of "christomonism" or "revelational positivism," or even the more generic "fideism" seem, at base, to reflect a concern for the agency of the church with respect to the lived witness of the gospel. The fear is that the church retreats from the world, either by so emphasizing the agency of Christ, or by enclosing the church in a theological predicate non-accessible by the world. Against this position, reference to "theocentrism" or "trinitarianism" serves a transitioning purpose, that is, it seeks a wider purview for God's acting as the Father of creation, and as the Spirit that enlightens every culture. This position both acknowledges the merit of the breadth of human history and culture and establishes a ground and impetus for the church's commerce in, with, and for, the world.[18] Such deployment

15. Newbigin, *Open Secret*, 12.

16. Ibid., 14.

17. Ibid., 15.

18. The problem for Newbigin with this variety of position is that it often grounds the authority for the proclamation of the gospel in a type of universal that is true

of trinitarian language, however, establishes a seeming contest between Christology and the doctrine of the Trinity.[19] While Newbigin's account of the authority basic to the Gospel might seem open to the charge of withdrawal, it actually constitutes the basis of the church's active engagement with its neighbors. It does this precisely as a confession of the Trinity, and one that refuses any disruption between the Father, Son and Spirit.

Newbigin notes that the authority of the "name of Jesus" prompts the counter question: "Who is Jesus?"[20] With this entrance point, Newbigin's account of the Trinity is christologically determined. It is "non-negotiable the affirmation that in Jesus the Word was made flesh; there can be no

---

beyond the gospel itself. He, for example, takes issue with accounts of mission validated "by appealing to some other commitment—that is, by claiming that it ministers to human unity, to development, or to liberation . . . .The question of authority is not to be answered by trying to demonstrate the usefulness of missions for some purpose that can be accepted apart from the ultimate commitment upon which the missionary enterprise rests." (Ibid., 14.)

19. By way of example, in his review of *Ecumenism in Transition*, Newbigin cautions that "a Trinitarian perspective can be only an enlargement and development of a Christo-centric one and not an alternative set over against it, for the doctrine of the Trinity is the theological articulation of what it means to say that Jesus is the unique Word of God incarnate in world history" (Newbigin, "Ecumenical Amnesia," 2). Raiser responds with the affirmation that "the Trinitarian perspective cannot be placed as an 'alternative' over against the Christological confession but must be understood as its proper biblical frame of interpretation" (Raiser, "Is Ecumenical Apologetics Sufficient?" 50). His countercharge is that "we seem to disagree about what it means to take the Trinitarian faith seriously and specifically to appreciate the constitutive role of the Holy Spirit in understanding the Christ event." Given Newbigin's actual pneumatological expectations, this is an astonishing claim. Newbigin responds simply that "The Holy Spirit, the Spirit of the Father and of the Son, is known by the confession that Jesus alone is Lord" (Newbigin, "Reply to Konrad Raiser," 52). While this may appear somewhat abstract, for Newbigin it touches ground in Raiser's neglect of the doctrine of atonement and, by extension, his neglect of missionary engagement. While Raiser presents a more sophisticated version, Perry Schmidt-Leukel aptly exploits this variety of position in his startlingly disengaged response to Newbigin's work (see, Schmidt-Leukel, "Mission and Trinitarian Theology," 57–64). Colin Greene's response was surely correct: "I cannot see how Lesslie Newbigin, if he were here with us today, could do anything other than disavow the premises upon which the paper is based." (Greene, "Trinitarian Tradition," 65.)

20. One should note here the intimate nature of this question. While Newbigin argues that the church as a community must give an answer to this question, and thus it is a question of cultural and historical import, the question is itself a question posed in the context of a face-to-face encounter between individuals or small groups. Newbigin is also aware that it is not a question that can be answered "without using a language—and therefore a structure of thought—that is shaped by the pre-Christian experience of the one who asks the question." Moreover, the answer must be given in the language of the one who asked the question (Newbigin, *Open Secret*, 20).

relativizing of this, the central and decisive event of universal history."[21] Yet, it is precisely this affirmation that propels the church into the world. With Jesus Christ the center of history, "the only proper response to the question 'By what authority?' is the announcement of the gospel itself."[22] This missionary engagement secures the gospel against charges of fideism because this is how, to quote Colin Greene, "we test the claim that the gospel reveals the clue to the meaning of universal history."[23] With this, the act of "announcement" receives a precise form: the announcement must itself correspond to the claim. Against conceptions of the missionary task which ground it in a mandate, thus rendering it a burden, Newbigin grounds the task in an external compulsion evident as an "explosion of joy"[24] and depicts it as one of "creating believing communities."[25] It is in this communal form, with the "congregation as the hermeneutic of the gospel," that the announcement of the gospel is to be made.

It is here that the doctrine of the Trinity comes to the fore. Beginning with the historical development of the doctrine, Newbigin notes how the question of Jesus came into conflict with assumptions concerning the un-approachability of pure being, the accidental nature of human history, and the range of potential intermediary entities which bridge the gap between the two. At base, the struggle was over how God could be involved in hu-man history.[26] The doctrine of the Trinity developed as an answer to these fundamental assumptions concerning the nature and structure of human existence, and, as such, offered a new way of understanding and dealing with existence. To speak in the authority of the name of the Father, the Son and the Spirit is to offer "a model for understanding human life—a model that cannot be verified by reference to the axioms of our culture but that is offered on the authority of revelation and with the claim that it does provide the possibility of a practical wisdom to grasp and deal with human life as it really is."[27]

By the term "model" Newbigin does not regard the Trinity as simply a pattern available for instantiation across historical and cultural bound-aries. Rather, the community, as the form of the announcement of the

21. Newbigin, "Reply to Konrad Raiser," 51.

22. Newbigin, *Open Secret*, 18.

23. Greene, "Trinitarian Tradition," 69.

24. Newbigin, *Gospel in a Pluralist Society*, 116.

25. Ibid., 121.

26. Newbigin, *Open Secret*, 25.

27. Ibid., 28.

gospel, is located in history and culture but at some distance due to the nature of its authority. It is so because this form corresponds to the acting of the Trinity.

PROCLAIMING THE KINGDOM OF THE FATHER

Though Jesus Christ is the determining fact of all his thinking,[28] Newbigin has no trouble relating the acting of the Father to that of the Son. As Jesus is the beloved Son of the Father, "it is impossible to think of him or to speak of him truly apart from the Father."[29] Such an affirmation stems simply from the beginning of Mark's gospel: "The time is fulfilled, and the kingdom of God has come near; repent, and believe in the good news" (1:14–15). Jesus' message is of God's kingdom. As such, he "submits himself wholly to the Father's ordering of events."[30] This is the basis of the church's expansive vision; expansive not in reductive geographic terms, but as the church stands under God own ordering of history so history becomes the necessary realm of the church's acting.

"The Bible *is* universal history."[31] Its narrative begins with the breadth of the creation of the whole cosmos and the tribes of humanity. At each stage, however, its cosmic perspective undergoes a progressive narrowing. With each narrowing it becomes clear that God is choosing people to bear a blessing for the sake of all people. It finally narrows to the singular and unrepeatable event of Jesus Christ's birth, life, death, and resurrection. He "bears the whole purpose of cosmic salvation in his own person."[32] This is the center of history and gives meaning to the whole of human history. From this point on, the story broadens out with the proleptical inclusion of all the nations at Pentecost and ends with a vision of the whole redeemed cosmos living with God. With this universal vision, the biblical message gives a clue to the "meaning of the human story as a whole."[33]

---

28. Here reference must, of course, be made to Newbigin's "a vision of the cross" and its effect over his entire subsequent ministry (see Newbigin, *Unfinished Agenda*, 11–12).

29. Newbigin, *Trinitarian Doctrine*, 39.

30. Ibid., 39.

31. For a primary treatment, see here "The Bible as Universal History," in Newbigin, *Gospel in a Pluralist Society*, 89–102. See also, Hunsberger, *Bearing the Witness of the Spirit*, 113–55.

32. Newbigin, *Open Secret*, 34.

33. Newbigin, *Gospel in a Pluralist Society*, 91.

John G. Flett

Clearly and without equivocation, Newbigin places Jesus Christ at the center of the whole human story. With this cornerstone in place, the reign of God is neither a movement nor a cause. It is, tautologically, "the reign of God, the fact that God whom Jesus knows as Father is the sovereign ruler of all peoples and all things."[34] He is creator, sustainer, and redeemer, and holds all in his hands. What changes with Jesus is that the kingdom is no longer remote, but is present, "the one great reality that confronts men and women now with the need for decision."[35] It is present in such a way, however, that it is best described by parables: "a 'mystery,' at once both hidden and revealed,"[36] with the cross the ultimate parable. The reign of God is not something that can be won through human mobilization or power; it is "a reality that remains hidden unless it is revealed by the action of God."[37]

In the narrowing of the Bible's history to the man Jesus, Newbigin lays great stress on God's "electing" of people to serve his purposes for the blessing of all.[38] The revealed and hidden nature of God's reign as seen in the cross finds correspondence in the resurrection. This proclamation of victory was not made visible to all, but to those who were chosen by God to be witnesses. As witnesses of the *resurrection*, Newbigin notes that they themselves were "firstfruits" of God's promised harvest (1 Cor. 15:23). Jesus does not begin a religious "program for private deliverance."[39] His sending of the disciples is not to propagate a doctrine or program. "He sends them out as witnesses to men of the fact that the decisive event of all history has arrived and is impending,"[40] to the "the hidden reality by which the public history of humankind is to be understood."[41] They do

34. Newbigin, *Open Secret*, 34.

35. Ibid.

36. Ibid., 35.

37. Ibid.

38. In term of the contemporary question of the borders of God's self-revelation, Newbigin notes that "It is not true, though it is often said, that the risen Jesus manifested himself only to believers. Saul of Tarsus was not a believer" (Newbigin, *Open Secret*, 36). For a primary material on election, see here "The Logic of Election," in Newbigin, *Gospel in a Pluralist Society*, 80–88. See also, Hunsberger, *Bearing the Witness of the Spirit*, 45–112.

39. Newbigin, *Open Secret*, 37.

40. Newbigin, *Trinitarian Doctrine*, 40.

41. Newbigin, *Open Secret*, 37.

this as they themselves submit to the Father's ordering, renouncing any claim to "a masterful control of history."[42]

Two observations follow. First, as universal history, as the reign of God, no division exists between a sacred and a secular history. The events of secular history do not form merely a "background for the story of the Church, or merely scenery for the drama of salvation."[43] The Bible refuses such a distinction. "The coming of the Messiah precipitates the crisis of human history."[44] Newbigin here incorporates the "indisputable" insight dominant in 1960s missiology that God is at work in the world.[45] Such an insight includes a de-privileging of "religion" as the proper realm of God's acting.[46] Negatively stated, without a doctrine of secular history the theology of mission breaks down, reducing often to mere proselytism. The missionary draws people out of the secular world into his or her own, and, as such, the missionary seeks "adherents for his cause and opinions."[47] Positively stated, the vulnerable engagement in history as formative of mission method renders the openness to the development of structures and confessions a theological necessity.[48]

Second, this openness, in that it corresponds to the center of history, has a determined form. The Father alone reveals the meaning of history to whom he chooses. His chosen witnesses are to follow the Lamb and in so doing bear witness to the true meaning of history. They are to offer a "concrete alternative" to all people and nations.[49] This is the way of the cross, and it is "projected across the picture of world history. It is not to be a smooth story of successful struggle leading directly to victory. Rather it

---

42. Newbigin, *Gospel in a Pluralist Society*, 118. See also, "The Church is not the instrument of God's governance of the world, but the witness of his governance both by speaking and by suffering" (Newbigin, *Trinitarian Doctrine*, 45).

43. Newbigin, *Trinitarian Doctrine*, 26.

44. Ibid., 27.

45. Newbigin, *Open Secret*, 37. He continues that "[w]hat can and must be disputed is that the apparently successful movements and forces are the work of God." The problem is not that God works in history, but that we expect to discern his working in a way different from the type of victory gained on the cross.

46. "We have often made it appear as though we believed God to be interested only in the religious questions.... it appeared that we tried to assert the uniqueness of Christ by denying the splendour of God's work in creation and the spirit of men" (Newbigin, *Trinitarian Doctrine*, 27).

47. Ibid., 22.

48. Ibid.

49. Ibid., 27.

is a story of tribulation and faithful witness, of death and resurrection."[50] Mission is the action of victory hidden within which "seems to be its opposite—suffering and tribulation for his people."[51] Mission takes the form of the cross.

SHARING IN THE LIFE OF THE SON AS THE PRESENCE OF THE KINGDOM

"The Father rules all things and works through whatever way he chooses. He is not confined to the Church. He can and does use what and whom he will to serve him."[52] For Newbigin, this strong statement intrudes no breach between the universal acting of the Father and the particularity of the Son. The Father's "working has a visible centre and point of reference. Jesus Christ, the God-Man, eternal and yet part of history, is the Omega; it is in his coming in the flesh, as a man of a certain place and time, that the ultimate issues are posed for men."[53] As the particularity of the Son is the presence of the universality of the Father, so the church makes its particular Christological claims in the movement toward a universalism which does not destroy difference but which demands this difference as part of the fullness of Christ's lordship. What this means for the relation of the authority of Jesus in relation to every cultural location becomes clear with reference to Newbigin's pneumatology. The mutuality of the Father and the Son, however, indicates the necessary missionary form of the church understood as the presence of the kingdom.

Jesus sent his disciples to proclaim the kingdom, but the substance of this message is that, in Jesus, the kingdom is a present reality. Jesus "embodied in his own person the presence of the kingdom."[54] While he expends some space on the exegetical grounds for this position, this succinct statement proves exhaustive for Newbigin. Furthermore, it launches him into the question of if and how one might speak of "the church as being a body commissioned to continue the ministry of Jesus after his death."[55] After a brief treatment of baptism, the sharing of the body and the blood, and eschatology, he concludes that the "presence of the kingdom" now

50. Newbigin, *Open Secret*, 38.

51. Ibid., 39.

52. Newbigin, *Trinitarian Doctrine*, 52–53.

53. Ibid.

54. Newbigin, *Open Secret*, 41.

55. Ibid., 44.

exists, "in a secondary, derivative, but nonetheless real sense," in the life of the church as a continuous historical institution.[56] Given the extensive theological baggage associated with this language, such a statement requires unpacking.

First, Newbigin does not depict the church as a continuation of the incarnation. Its continuity with Jesus is grounded in its participation in his baptism.[57] Drawing on the John 20:19–23, Newbigin links Jesus' sending of his disciples (v.21), the scars of his passion as the authentic marks of the mission of his body (v.20), and the gift of the Spirit to his baptism (v.22). Here, the Spirit anointed Jesus for his mission and, as such, the cross marks the "fulfillment of his baptism."[58] This fulfillment opens the way for the disciples to share "in the complete baptism that is baptism in water and the Spirit for the bearing of the sin of the world. The disciples are now taken up into that saving mission for which Jesus was anointed and sent in the power of the Spirit."[59] To be baptized, as the entrance into the Christian community, "is to be incorporated into the dying of Jesus so as to become a participant in his risen life, and so to share his ongoing mission to the world. It is to be baptized into his mission."[60] As participants in his baptism by virtue of the reception of the Sprit, his disciples share in the authority of his name and this includes the authority to forgive sins (v.23). Jesus did not commission the disciples to propagate a timeless truth, but to bring forgiveness "in the only way that it can be done so long as we are in the flesh—by the word and act and gesture of another human being."[61] And all of this is set within Jesus' first words of greeting: "peace be with you" (v.19). This, for Newbigin, is the presence of the kingdom: "peace, shalom, the all-embracing blessing of the God of Israel." The church is to bear in its own life the peace of God.

Second, Newbigin, with the language of "presence," indicates the essentially communal nature of the church's confession, its limited, particular, contingent and crucifix form. Newbigin's own missionary experience in India, especially as he reflects on how conversion occasions a "radical break" with the local context, indicates the need for the church to become

56. Ibid., 53.

57. This account of baptism underlies equally Newbigin's account of the Spirit, see: ibid, 57–58.

58. Ibid., 48.

59. Ibid.

60. Newbigin, *Gospel in a Pluralist Society*, 117.

61. Newbigin, *Open Secret*, 48.

in truth a new community, a need and corresponding form which is not perceptible within "Christian" cultures like the West.[62] The life of the community is itself the mission precisely because of the comprehensive nature of salvation, but this means "the church will be delivered from the tendency to turn in upon itself and will always be turned outward to the world."[63] Newbigin remains wary of settled church structures due both to their tendency to project western political categories on non-western churches and to their innate neglect of the active missionary act. "[P]articipation in Christ means participation in His mission to the world, and that therefore true pastoral care, true training in the Christian life, and true use of the means of grace will precisely be in and for the discharge of this missionary task."[64] This does not intrude on visible continuity. Mission, understood precisely as "the creation of believing communities," includes this revision of received church structures as basic to the task of proclaiming the authority of Jesus Christ.

Third, understanding the church as the "presence of the kingdom" does not lead Newbigin into a discussion of an ideal or invisible church, a church prefigured before the creation of the world. The church is "the presence of the kingdom *in the form of death and resurrection*."[65] The eucharistic celebration is central to the life of the church because here the gathered community partakes in Jesus' death and resurrection which itself takes the form of being sent into the world to witness to the power of God's acting.[66] This is no triumphal procession. "It is important to remember how relentlessly the New Testament emphasizes the reality of sin in the

62. See Newbigin, *Household of God*, 14–18.

63. Ibid., 146.

64. Ibid. It is for this reason that Newbigin is critical of the Protestant tradition's "theological defect" with regards to thinking of the church as a continuing historical institution (he even espouses an understanding of the historical episcope as a proper form of the church's unity). By this community focus, however, Newbigin is not simply advocating a catholic position. One of the chief theological problems within the theology of mission is the dichotomy of mission from church. This dichotomy tends to identify "mission" with a critical stance toward the institutions of the church and "church" with an attitude that identifies mission as a theological redundancy. For Newbigin, this approach is fallacious because it depicts the problem in terms of a competition whereby one theological truth is asserted at the expense of another. By contrast, the missionary nature of the church is properly located within its being the presence of the kingdom. With this, a church without mission constitutes a "radical contradiction" of its being, and a mission "which is not at the same time truly a Church is not a true expression of the divine apostolate." (Ibid., 148.)

65. Newbigin, *Open Secret*, 52.

66. Ibid., 54.

Church."[67] It is the visible church, in its very sinful and divided nature, which is the power of God in weakness and his wisdom in foolishness. As the church lives in history in the dying and rising of Jesus, so it is the place where the kingdom of God is present. This again directs it to its missionary form. The presence of the kingdom is baptism into Jesus' own baptism and thus into his mission and its crucifix form.

BEARING THE WITNESS OF THE SPIRIT AND THE PREVENIENCE OF THE KINGDOM

If describing the church as bearing the "presence of the kingdom" represents certain problems, it does so, for Newbigin, due to an inadequate understanding of the Spirit. The Spirit is himself the foretaste or prevenience of the kingdom. While Newbigin advocates a strong account of visible, historical continuity, reference to the Spirit serves not to ratify existing church order. The New Testament evidence indicates, instead, a missionary pattern of the church, one which remains normative for Newbigin because "the picture given us in the Acts is one that is constantly being reproduced in the missionary experience of the Church."[68] Thus, while "the real presence of God's own life lived in their common life will be the evidence, the witness to all the nations, that the full reality of God's victorious reign is on the way," this results, not from "a command, but a promise. The presence of the Spirit will make them witnesses."[69] The Spirit, as the foretaste of the kingdom, demands the corresponding missionary form of the church.

Mission is and remains an action of God. The church is initiated into mission by the sovereign act of the Spirit, and this mission remains that of the Spirit.[70] The church's "own" mission is its "obedient participation in the action of the Sprit by which the confession of Jesus as Lord becomes the authentic confession of every new people, each in its own tongue."[71] Newbigin is critical of depictions of mission activity based in bureaucracy with the goal of the salvation of individual souls, or in church growth or in the humanization of society.[72] Yet, he is equally critical of mission ac-

67. Ibid., 52.

68. Ibid., 64.

69. Ibid., 58.

70. Ibid.

71. Ibid., 20.

72. Newbigin, *Gospel in a Pluralist Society*, 121.

John G. Flett

counts in which the church self-propagates the "power that inheres in its life."[73] This takes practical form as the exportation of ecclesiologies formed in a European political milieu as necessary to the gospel message. Such things, for Newbigin, are unnecessary accretions to the name Jesus Christ and thus hinder the church's witness by putting the church above the action of the Spirit.[74]

Not confined to the walls of the church, the Spirit, precisely as promise, goes ahead of it. Newbigin, again, while establishing a wide purview for the Spirit's acting imposes no contest between the Spirit and Christ. The Spirit as foretaste determines the nature of the church's response: as the Spirit "is himself the missionary,"[75] so the church witnesses to the kingdom as it conforms to the missionary witness of the Spirit. Newbigin uses the account of Peter and Cornelius in Acts 10 to illustrate the point. With Cornelius' conversion "it is not as though the church opened its gates to admit a new person into its company, and then closed them again, remaining unchanged except for the addition of a name to its role of members. Mission is not just church extension."[76] Conversion is a process that runs in two directions. The Spirit "both convicts the world (John 16:8–11) and leads the church toward the fullness of the truth that it has not yet grasped (John 16:12–15)."[77] This observation comes with a warning. Peter, with reference to the law, had solid theological reasons for his hesitancy to follow the Spirit's lead. This ground, however, could not prevail against the visible action of God. Nor are such challenges confined to the first 100 years of the church's existence. The church must so follow the Spirit's lead if it is to be faithful, for "the mission is not ours but God's."[78] As it follows the Spirit, the missionary church crosses human boundaries and articulates the gospel in terms of this new situation.

Missionary movement characterizes the visible continuity of the church. The twofold dynamic of convicting the world and leading the church into the fullness of Christ is one and the same action of the Spirit. "The mission of the Church to all the nations, to all human communities in all their diversity and in all their particularity, is itself the mighty work of God, the sign of the inbreaking of the kingdom. The Church is not so

73. Newbigin, *Open Secret*, 56.
74. See his unpublished paper, "Missions in an Ecumenical Perspective."
75. Newbigin, *Trinitarian Doctrine*, 71.
76. Newbigin, *Open Secret*, 59.
77. Ibid.
78. Ibid., 64.

274

much the agent of the mission as the locus of the mission."[79] It is as the church follows the Spirit beyond its natural boundaries, into those things that divide the world, and lives as the one body of Christ that it witnesses to the power of kingdom. Nor is this quite radical need for the church to order its life around its mission simply a functional structuring according to the variability of context. Such ordering results from the Spirit's control of the mission. "His fresh works will repeatedly surprise the church, compelling it to stop talking and to listen . . . The church's witness is secondary and derivative."[80] Missionary vulnerability is the church's proper weakness. It has no claim to the mastery of history. Its only claim is the foolishness of the cross. But this is the power of the Spirit: to take this weakness "mirrored in the life of the community, and make it the witness that turns the world upside down and refutes its most fundamental notions."[81]

CONCLUSION

"There is no participation in Christ without participation in His mission in the world."[82] This statement from Newbigin's pen is, for him, no mere rhetorical embellishment. To live in the authority of the name of Jesus Christ is to live in an authority that demands its public announcement and the associated questioning and contest. In that the question "who is Jesus?" follows claims to act in his name, this directs the church to name the Father, Son, and the Spirit as a full description of who Jesus Christ is. Living in this authority gives the church a particular communal form. God the Father as creator holds the whole of history in his hands and calls a particular people to bear his blessing in history for the whole of humanity. God the Son as the presence of God's kingdom left not a book but a community which, by the power of the Spirit, participates in his baptism, and thus in his own cruciform mission. God the Spirit is the prevenience of the kingdom, is the missionary Spirit that convicts the world and leads the church into the fullness of the confession of Jesus Christ. In this Newbigin eschews the all-too-normative distinction between mission and spirituality. Mission is simply "an acted out doxology. That is its deepest secret. Its purpose is that God may be glorified."[83]

79. Newbigin, *Gospel in a Pluralist Society*, 118–19.
80. Newbigin, *Open Secret*, 61.
81. Ibid., 62.
82. Goodall, *Missions under the Cross*, 190.
83. Newbigin, *Gospel in a Pluralist Society*, 127.

John G. Flett

BIBLIOGRAPHY

Flett, John G. *The Witness of God: the Trinity, Missio Dei, Karl Barth and the Nature of Christian Community*. Grand Rapids: Eerdmans, 2010.

Goodall, Norman, editor. *Missions under the Cross*. London: Edinburgh House, 1953.

Greene, Colin J. D. "Trinitarian Tradition and the Cultural Collapse of Late Modernity." In *A Scandalous Prophet: The Way of Mission After Newbigin*, edited by Thomas F. Foust et al., 65–72. Grand Rapids: Eerdmans, 2001.

Hunsberger, George R. *Bearing the Witness of the Spirit: Lesslie Newbigin's Theology of Cultural Plurality*. Grand Rapids: Eerdmans, 1998.

Newbigin, Lesslie. "Ecumenical Amnesia." *International Bulletin of Missionary Research* 18, no. 1 (1994) 2–5.

———. *The Gospel in a Pluralist Society*. Geneva: WCC Publications, 1989.

———. *The Household of God: Lectures on the Nature of the Church*. London: SCM, 1953.

———. "Missions in an Ecumenical Perspective." Unpublished paper, 1962. Online: http://www.newbigin.net/assets/pdf/62mep.pdf.

———. *The Open Secret: An Introduction to the Theology of Mission*. 2nd ed. Grand Rapids: Eerdmans, 1995.

———. "Recent Thinking on Christian Beliefs: VIII. Mission and Missions." *The Expository Times* 88, no. 9 (1977) 260–64.

———. "Reply to Konrad Raiser." *International Bulletin of Missionary Research* 18, no. 2 (1994) 51–52.

———. *Trinitarian Doctrine for Today's Mission*. Carlisle, UK: Paternoster, 1998.

———. *Unfinished Agenda: An Autobiography*. Geneva: WCC Publications, 1985.

Niebuhr, H. Richard. "The Doctrine of the Trinity and the Unity of the Church." *Theology Today* 3, no. 3 (1946) 371–84.

Raiser, Konrad. *Ecumenism in Transition: A Paradigm Shift in the Ecumenical Movement?* Geneva: WCC Publications, 1991.

———. "Is Ecumenical Apologetics Sufficient? A Response to Newbigin's 'Ecumenical Amnesia.'" *International Bulletin of Missionary Research* 18, no. 2 (1994) 50–51.

Schmidt-Leukel, Perry. "Mission and Trinitarian Theology." In *A Scandalous Prophet: The Way of Mission After Newbigin*, edited by Thomas F. Foust, George R. Hunsberger, J. Andrew Kirk and Werner Ustorf, 57–64. Grand Rapids: Eerdmans, 2001.

WCC Department on Studies in Evangelism. *The Church for Others, and the Church for the World: A Quest for Structures for Missionary Congregations*. Geneva: WCC Publications, 1967.

Williams, Rowan. "Doing the Works of God." In *A Ray of Darkness: Sermons and Reflections*, 221–32. Cambridge, MA: Cowley, 1995.

Contemporary Ecumenical Challenges from the Legacy of Lesslie Newbigin

Geoffrey Wainwright

IN THEIR INTRODUCTION TO the *Dictionary of the Ecumenical Movement*, the editors—of whom I was one—speculated that "if church history continues to be written, future historians will almost certainly regard the ecumenical movement as one of the most remarkable features of the twentieth century. To a degree never witnessed before, Christianity became a worldwide religion, spread over the whole inhabited earth. And an unprecedentedly large number and range of Christian communities, hitherto separated by doctrinal and institutional factors, set about a serious process of consultation, cooperation, communion and even union among themselves, inspired by the prayer of the Lord that his followers 'be one,' 'so that the world may believe' (John 17:21)." However, there was "much work still to do; several traditionally controversial issues remain unsettled among the churches; new questions arise for the Christian faith as a global culture develops with its own characteristics in economics, geopolitics, the religious field, science and technology, information and communication; the kingdoms of this world have not yet become the kingdom of God and of his Christ (Rev. 11:15)."[1]

Lesslie Newbigin was a towering figure in twentieth-century ecumenism, active and influential in his own time, and who had moreover a prophetic gift of anticipating the future which not only proved itself while he was yet alive but also stretched beyond in ways relevant to succeeding generations. It seems appropriate and feasible, therefore, to look not only for the challenges left by the ecumenical achievements to which he contributed but also those sketched by his own further-reaching vision.

1. Lossky et al., *Dictionary* (1991), xi; (2002), xv.

The modern ecumenical movement is classically seen as comprising three streams which—at least at certain times and places—flowed together: faith and order; mission and evangelism; life and work. Lesslie Newbigin contributed powerfully in all three areas; and while current interests and structures may no longer fit so neatly into that threefold pattern, its three parts cover concerns that must permanently occupy any serious ecumenism, and so we may conveniently follow that triad in seeking to detect the impact and provocation of Newbigin's ideas and example for the present century.

FAITH AND ORDER

My own initial acquaintance with Newbigin came by hear-say. I knew of him as one of the first bishops in the episcopally and synodically constituted Church of South India which had recently brought into ecclesial union the fruits of evangelistic labors largely on the part of missionaries from British churches: Anglicans, Presbyterians, Methodists and Congregationalists. And my first direct contact with the Church of South India occurred shortly after I began my theological studies at the University of Cambridge in 1960. I attended a celebration of the Lord's Supper that was led by a furloughing presbyter from the CSI (as the newly united church became almost universally known). The liturgy, freshly shaped by that body, was a weave of elements from the constitutive traditions, drawing in also litanies from the Syrian Orthodox long present in India, and even the lovely "Adesto" invocation from Mozarabic Spain: "Be present, be present, O Jesus, thou good High Priest, as thou wast in the midst of thy disciples, and make thyself known to us in the breaking of the bread."[2] The hope of ecumenists on "the home front"—including already some of us seeking ordination—was that the "sending" churches might soon come to a similar "organic union" in Britain that would significantly embody structural and liturgical features from the recognizable riches of classic Christianity. Alas, that was not to be; nor indeed did too much result from the looser "covenantal relationship" that both Lesslie Newbigin and I worked on some fifteen or twenty years later—he having returned to Britain from three or four decades missionary service in India and I from a much shorter stint in West Africa.

2. It turns out that the concluding allusion to Emmaus (Luke 24:31, 35) was Newbigin's liturgical suggestion; see Wainwright, *Lesslie Newbigin*, 274.

It was perhaps predominantly from a "faith and order" perspective that the vision of church unity was classically formulated at the New Delhi Assembly of the World Council of Churches in 1961, its chief drafter having been none other than Lesslie Newbigin in the context of the Faith and Order Commission. The unity for which "we believe we must pray and work" was described thus:

> We believe that the unity which is both God's will and his gift to his Church is being made visible as all in each place who are baptized into Jesus Christ and confess him as Lord and Saviour are brought by the Holy Spirit into one fully committed fellowship, holding the one apostolic faith, preaching the one Gospel, breaking the one bread, joining in common prayer, and having a corporate life reaching out in witness and service to all and who at the same time are united with the whole Christian fellowship in all places and all ages in such wise that ministry and members are accepted by all, and that all can act and speak together as occasion requires for the tasks to which God calls his people.[3]

The phrase most readily picked up from that description was, in fact, "all in each place." Early in the twenty-first century we still confront—and perhaps more acutely than ever—the question(s) of the nature and structures of the "local churches" that can or should be seen to be "truly united" (visibility being a necessary dimension of true unity according to a Christian faith that is incarnational and sacramental), and the networks by which such local units are (to be) integrated in the Church universal. Whether at local, intermediate, or universal level, Newbigin firmly held that the full, visible unity of the Church would properly be "organic" in all its aspects, not merely "federal."

As to ecclesial unity at the local level, I myself can imagine a local church consisting of several mutually open smaller communities, shaped perhaps by various historical and cultural backgrounds, among which there would exist ample opportunity for spiritual fellowship, sacramental communion and joint action, all held together by a reconciled confession of faith and by ministerial and governmental structures of a collegial, synodical and communal kind.[4]

As to the integration of the local units at the universal level, I can do no better than to cite what Lesslie Newbigin saw already in 1948 as perhaps

3. *New Delhi Report*, 116–17; see Newbigin's article, "Unity of 'all in each place'" in Lossky et al., *Dictionary* (1991), 1043–46; (2002), 1175–78.

4. See my remarks on "the topography of unity" in Wainwright, *Embracing Purpose*, 157–59.

no more than a speck on his prophetic horizon: "However far-reaching may be the transformation required both of the Protestant Churches and the Roman and Eastern before union can be a matter even of discussion, there ought to be nothing to prevent our looking now towards the restoration to the whole Church of a visible unity with a central organ of unity such as Rome was for so many vital centuries of the Church's history."[5] Not even Newbigin prophesied the event of the Second Vatican Council (1962–65), but a couple of years before Lesslie's own passing, Pope John Paul II could, in 1995, issue an encyclical under the title *Ut Unum Sint*, in which he invited the leaders of other churches and their theologians to "a patient and fraternal dialogue" as to how the Roman see, without forfeiting its historic claims, might exercise a "universal ministry of unity" in new ways in a new situation. That dialogue remains to be pursued. The eschatological thrust of Newbigin's ecclesiology—to be noted later—characteristically led him to be open to what God's future work might entail for the realization of the divine purposes. It was openness to the future that led the framers of the CSI constitution to declare its provisional character.

One further development needs to be mentioned before we shift the emphasis of this chapter from "faith and order" to other dimensions of ecumenism. In his ecclesiological treatise *The Household of God*, Newbigin argued that a Protestant emphasis on "the people of God" or "the congregation of the faithful" and a Catholic emphasis on "the body of Christ" or "the sacramental institution" needed a Trinitarian completion through what he tentatively called a Pentecostal emphasis on "the community of the Holy Spirit."[6] What both the Protestant and the Catholic side have tended to forget in their historic controversies, wrote Newbigin, is a third term: the Holy Spirit, for "the Church lives neither by her faithfulness to her message nor by her abiding in one fellowship with the apostles"—though both these strands must be tightly clung to—but "by the living power of the Spirit of God," by which alone we can abide in Christ's communion and bear witness to his grace. Here was Newbigin paying prophetic attention to a Pentecostal movement that was barely half-a-century old, and whose style he later confessed he had hitherto "regarded with the distaste of a well-educated university graduate." A new understanding and experience of the Holy Spirit, to which Pentecostals might introduce them, might help Protestants and Catholics to break their own deadlock, while the fissiparous Pentecostals for their part had something to learn from

5. Newbigin, *Reunion*, 189.
6. Newbigin, *Household*, 94–122.

"the growth of real charity between the great confessions" that provided "evident tokens of the Spirit's working in the experience of the ecumenical movement." In the early twenty-first century, it may be that Protestants, Catholics, and by now "traditional Pentecostals," all alike face the challenges and opportunities posed by the rise of "spiritual communities" of very varied kinds in the various parts of the world.

Not only Newbigin's ecclesiology but also his missiology was henceforth firmly marked by the Trinitarian pattern. Already from the 1950s we find him interpreting the Church's mission in terms of collaboration in the *missio Dei*, the Father's sending of the Son and the Spirit into the world for its redemption and renewal, and finally its participation in the life of the Triune God. That pattern is briefly set out in Newbigin's booklet of 1963 entitled *The Relevance of Trinitarian Doctrine for Today's Mission*, and it governs the entire book *The Open Secret*. As late as 1993, in the context of a dogmatics conference in Edinburgh, Newbigin could seek to counter the enfeebled grasp of Trinitarianism on the part of much modern Christianity with a lecture on "The Trinity as Public Truth":

> The development of the doctrine of the Trinity was not the result of any kind of theological speculation within the tradition of classical thought. It was the result of a new fact (in the original sense of the word *factum*, something done). God had done those things that are the content of the good news that the Church is commissioned to tell, the Gospel. This fact required a rethinking of the word "God." One could, of course, decline to believe the "facts" alleged in the Gospel. This is always a possibility. But if one believes that they are true, then this has to be a new starting point for thought . . . For nearly a thousand years—the years that shaped the barbarian tribes of the western extension of Asia into a cultural entity that we call "Europe"—it was this way of thinking that shaped public discourse. The liturgy, the preaching, the drama, and the art of Christendom all took this apostolic record as the framework within which public discourse took place.[7]

Having thus noted Newbigin's location of the Trinity at the heart of the Christian faith and message, it may now be safe to shift our main attention to "mission and evangelism."

7. Published in Vanhoozer, ed., *Trinity in a Pluralistic Age*, 1–8.

Geoffrey Wainwright

MISSION AND EVANGELISM

By the time of the New Delhi Assembly of the World Council of Churches in 1961, Newbigin had already served for a good two decades as missionary and evangelist in India; and through the integration of the International Missionary Council with the WCC at the start of that Assembly, he himself was soon transmuted from general secretary of the IMC into director of the new Division of World Mission and Evangelism in the WCC. It was in this context that I first met Lesslie in person, while I was studying at the Ecumenical Institute of Bossey, near Geneva.

I will not dwell on Newbigin's flirtation with "the secular meaning of the gospel" and his desire to provide "honest religion for secular man" during his brief Genevan period (he returned to India for another near-decade in 1965). Rather I will draw upon some of his thought in connection with the needed "(re-)conversion of the West"—a phrase more recently borrowed by Lesslie from the Indonesian soldier and theologian T. B. Simatoupong—that had begun to occupy Newbigin in substance well before his return to Britain in 1974. In his teaching (at the Selly Oak Colleges in Birmingham), in his own practice (he served for most of the 1980s as pastor of a local congregation of the United Reformed Church in the socially, ethnically and religiously complex inner suburb of Birmingham officially known as Mary Hill but popularly described as Merry Hell), in his itinerant lectureships (on both sides of the North Atlantic), and in his prolific publications, Lesslie's missionary theory could almost be condensed into a single preposition: especially in a "pluralist society" the local church was to be a church "for" its particular place: "a Christian congregation . . . is God's embassy in a specific place."[8]

Like John Calvin, Newbigin knew well, of course, that the Gospel must not only be preached but also heard:

> The Gospel must be heard as relevant. It must speak of things which are real in the life of the hearer. It must therefore begin by accepting his issues, using his models, and speaking his language. But relevance alone is not enough. The Gospel must at the same time challenge the whole world view of the hearer. It must cause him to question things that he has never questioned. It must bring him to the place where he hears spoken to his whole world of understanding and experience that word of

8. Newbigin, *Gospel in a Pluralist Society*, 229.

282

grace and judgment which marks the end of one world and the beginning of another, a death and a new birth.[9]

Throughout the 1980s Newbigin devoted his best spiritual and intellectual energies to that kind of "contextualization" of the Gospel in relation to "the powerful paganism of our Western world." That challenge has lost nothing in importance since then.

But who, in practice, is to speak and perform that Gospel? In *The Gospel in a Pluralist Society*, in fact, Newbigin devoted a chapter to expounding "the congregation as hermeneutic of the gospel."[10] This community "has at its heart the remembering and rehearsing of Jesus' words and deeds, and the sacraments given by him through which it is enabled to engraft new members into its life and to renew this life again and again through sharing in his risen life through the body broken and the lifeblood poured out." For the Church to "be fully open to the needs of the world and yet have its eyes fixed always on God," a congregation would be marked by six features that made it both the interpreter and the interpretation of the Gospel: it would be a community of praise, truth, concern, service, mutual responsibility, and hope. At worship, the Christian congregation is "a place where people find their true freedom, their true dignity, and their true equality in reverence to One who is worthy of all the praise we can offer . . . A Christian congregation is thus a body of people with gratitude to spare, a gratitude that can spill over into care for the neighbor." As a community of truth, the congregation, by virtue of its "constant remembering and rehearsing of the true story," counters other regnant "plausibility structures" with "the Christian understanding of human nature and destiny." A Christian congregation "does not live for itself but is deeply involved in the concerns of its neighborhood"; its members "are willing to be for the wider community." The congregation is where Christian men and women with their various gifts are prepared for, and sustained in, the exercise of their royal priesthood on God's behalf in the world. In contrast with the individualism of its surroundings, the congregation will be a community of faithfulness and mutual responsibility as at least "the foretaste" of "a new social order." And finally, amid the "virtual disappearance of hope" in contemporary Western culture, with its literature "full of nihilism and despair," the recovery of hope will only come through movements that begin with the local congregation in which the reality of the new creation

9. Newbigin, "Mission in the 1980s"; cf. Wainwright, *Lesslie Newbigin*, 196. For Calvin, see the *Institutes* I.9.2, and IV.1.9–10.

10. *Gospel in a Pluralist Society*, 222–33.

is present, known, and experienced, and from which men and women will go into every sector of public life to claim it for Christ." For the true nature of the Church—within the eschatological purposes of God—is to be the "sign, instrument, and foretaste of God's redeeming grace for the whole life of society."

In setting out thus what Lesslie might have called—according to the title of a WCC program of the 1960s—"the missionary structure of the congregation," we have at points to wet our feet in the third stream of ecumenism, namely "life and work." That is not surprising, given the degree to which Newbigin shared the interest and engagement in civic and social concerns that is characteristic of theologians in the Reformed tradition.

LIFE AND WORK

Newbigin's first book, written on board the *City of Cairo* during his first voyage to India in 1936, was entitled *Christian Freedom in the Modern World*. For a genuinely Christian understanding and practice of freedom, he argued, both sides of the seeming paradox of Law and Gospel have to be maintained: "The morality of obedience to duty by itself leads to bondage, and yet simply to eliminate obedience to duty from the good life is impossible." God from his side—from the side of the objective moral order—has provided the solution which man from his side could not, being himself the problem. Announcing the redemptive action of God in Jesus Christ, the Gospel "proclaims a quite new fact as the basis of a quite new motive. The new fact is forgiveness, and the new motive is gratitude." [11]

There is, therefore, a "Christian life" to be lived both by each believer and by the faithful community, but the "works" that may thereby be accomplished will remain modest both at the individual and at the social level. Perhaps dating from his studies in economics at the University of Cambridge, amid "the great depression" of the 1930s, Newbigin was gravely suspicious of the "modern" optimism that man's "essential goodness" needs only to be "educated." Confronted, then, with the outbreak of a second world war on the terrain of "Christian Europe," Newbigin in 1941 framed his "Bangalore Lectures" on "The Kingdom of God and the Idea of Progress" which continued to shape his own views throughout the rest of his life. The barriers of sin, failure, corruption, and death mean that "there is no straight line of development from here to the Kingdom." Yet Christians are not to wait passively for the full realization of God's Kingdom at

11. Newbigin, *Christian Freedom*, 82.

the final resurrection. Christian action in this world is to be regarded, with Albert Schweitzer, as "a prayer for the coming of the Kingdom": "Christian action, done as in the sight of God, for His sake, acknowledging that He alone is final judge, and that the Kingdom must be His gift, . . . is a kind of prayer offered to God that He may hasten His Kingdom. It is a prayer that He can and will answer, because it is one where praying itself makes us and the world more fit to receive the answer."[12] Having observed that by far the greater part of the problems facing humanity in the technical, economic, and demographic conditions of modern life are problems calling for political solutions, Newbigin asserts already in the Bangalore Lectures the impossibility of Christians avoiding politics. Given an authentically Christian view of history and eschatology, Christians will in practice exert their influence "rather against the tendency to exercise the imagination in making blueprints of a new and perfect world order, and in favor of efforts of a humbler kind to deal concretely with existing evils and put them right."[13]

To the end, Newbigin would stress the essential importance of God's action in history and its expected goal in the final Kingdom as the context for Christian life and work. In place of the "fiduciary framework" inherited from the Enlightenment, Christian discipleship—Newbigin wrote, looking around George Orwell's iconic year of "1984"—will rather be "concerned equally in the private and in the public spheres to make visible that understanding and ordering of life which takes as its 'fiduciary framework' the revelation of himself which God has given in Jesus. It will provide occasions for the creation of visible signs of the invisible kingship of God."[14] Even before 1990 and the collapse of Marxism (which Newbigin had rejected for its ideological utopianism) and of the Soviet Empire (which he had condemned for its practical totalitarianism), Newbigin had voiced fierce moral criticism of "unrestrained capitalism" and the effects of its global spread. The ideology and practice of the "free market" was driven by the covetousness which the Apostle Paul called idolatry (Colossians 3:5). In *The Other Side of 1984*, Newbigin wrote:

> An international economic order which works steadily and inexorably to divide the world into a rich sector which expects

---

12. The Bangalore Lectures remained unpublished in Newbigin's lifetime. They can be found with other similarly "new" materials in the volume that I edited and introduced and published under his name with the title *Signs amid the Rubble*; here 48–52.

13. So in the fourth Bangalore Lecture; see *Signs*, 53–55.

14. Newbigin, *Other Side of 1984*, 37.

to become richer with each year that passes, and a poor sector which sinks ever deeper into poverty, is in flagrant contradiction to the will of God as revealed in Christ. There can be legitimate differences of opinion for the ordering of the economic life of the nations, but when the cause of Christianity is identified with the resolute defence of the existing capitalist structure, if necessary by the use of nuclear weapons, then the question about the limits of permissible diversity, the question of apostasy, has to be raised.[15]

With that we are coming close to our final ecumenical topic: the Gospel in a global culture. But first we may take a look at what Newbigin proposed on a smaller national scale by way of "a Christian vision for society" in chapters written for a book that was posthumously published in 1998—with Lamin Sanneh and Jenny Taylor as co-authors—under the title *Faith and Power: Christianity and Islam in "Secular" Britain.* Newbigin's basic assumption, stated in the preface, is that "the Christian Gospel, with all its uniqueness and specificity, has validity for all people, and that failure to recognize the crucial significance of religious beliefs is causing and will continue to cause confusion, misunderstanding, and alienation at all levels of national life."[16] Already in his contribution to a 1988 report on "Faith in the City of Birmingham," he had recommended Christians to welcome wholeheartedly "the evidences of God's grace in the lives of people of other faiths and people of no religious faith"; it is "not our business to ferret out the sins of our non-Christian neighbors," for Christ alone is judge, and "our business, as fellow-sinners, is to recognize and rejoice in the light that enlightens every person of whatever faith or no-faith." Consequently, Christians should "seek out and develop those areas of our civic life in which people of all faiths can cooperate for the common good"; in particular, friendly contacts with Muslims, Hindus, and Sikhs could initiate collaborative enterprises to restore hope in the deprived areas of the City. And local congregations should be places "where people of all faiths can find a welcome," for "the good news of which we are the bearers is for all," and "it would be an intolerable sort of racism to suggest that the Gospel is only for people of a certain ethnic origin." Christians have much to learn from their willing Muslim and Sikh interlocutors, even while testifying to the good news that, in Jesus Christ, "the sovereign Lord of all creation has

15. Newbigin, *Other Side of 1984*, 43.

16. Newbigin et al., *Faith and Power*, x; cf. Wainwright, *Lesslie Newbigin*, 235–36; 432, note 71.

acted in infinite love to deliver all humankind from the power of sin and death and to open for us the gate of life."[17]

Now how might all that look when transposed to the global level at the start of the new century?

THE GOSPEL IN A GLOBAL CULTURE

In our opening paragraph we noted the perception of the editors of the *Dictionary of the Ecumenical Movement* that at the start of the twenty-first century, "new questions arise for the Christian faith as a global culture develops with its own characteristics in economics, geopolitics, the religious field, science and technology, information and communication." In late 1996, Newbigin addressed for the last time a world conference on mission and evangelism; it was held under WCC auspices in Salvador de Bahia, Brazil, under the title "Called to One Hope: The Gospel in Diverse Cultures." In a brief two-part speech that was not originally part of the program, Lesslie made a short, simple and strong statement of the final position that he had come to on the themes of "Gospel" and "culture" and their interrelation.[18] The Gospel, he said, is not "Christianity" (for that is "what generations of us have made of the Gospel, and we know that we have made a mess of it"); nor is the Gospel "religious experience" (which is "a very ambivalent affair"); rather, the Gospel is "a factual statement," namely, "that God, who is the author, the sustainer, the goal of all that exists, of all being and all meaning and all truth, has become present in our human history as the man Jesus, whom we can know and love and serve; and that by his incarnation, his ministry, his death and resurrection he has finally broken the powers that oppress us and has created a space and a time in which we who are unholy can nevertheless live in fellowship with God who is holy." The implication is that final authority lies with Jesus, as declared in Matthew 28:18. All of us need to know who is ultimately in charge and our specific responsibility as Christians and as Church is to bear witness to the Lord. The Gospel has to be carried in understandable and relevant words and deeds into whatever culture. Not taken in by "postmodernism," Lesslie declared the most pervasive current culture to be the "modernity" that is based on science and technology and channeled

---

17. Newbigin was generally reckoned to be the principal writer of the sixth chapter of the report, the "theological chapter" entitled "Christian Perspectives on the City," which occupied 111–29 of the final report; cf. Wainwright, *Lesslie Newbigin*, 378–82.

18. See Newbigin, *Signs*, 111–21.

through the ideology of the free market; and he saw the chief rival to the Christian faith for the challenging of that culture to be Islam.

Newbigin viewed "the globalization of the whole human family" as "probably irreversible in the near future," and "we must expect increasingly to see ourselves as one global city." With his gift for going to the heart of a matter, Lesslie forecast that "in the century that lies ahead of us, these are the three major factors which will compete for the allegiance of the human family: the Gospel, the free market, and Islam." Like none of the other world faiths, Islam makes a claim of universal truth and allegiance. In seeking control of the political order, Islam punishes dissent (and Newbigin confessed shame at the silence of the British media about the sufferings of Christians in some Muslim countries); by contrast, the Christian Gospel affirms that God's sovereignty was manifested not by power or might but in the humiliation of the Cross and that the victory of that seeming defeat was made known not as a great public demonstration, which would mean the end of human history, but as a secret to a very small community chosen to be witnesses, so that the Kingdom of God could come through freely given love and obedience. How can Christians challenge the idolatry of the market? Only God can create a genuinely free and just society. The Gospel provides space and freedom for dissent, and only faith can sustain a truly free society and lead to salvation. If God has done what the Gospel story tells us, the only response can be praise and thanksgiving, and mission is the work of sharing that joyful response with others.

In its comprehensive character, that may be a sufficient ecumenical challenge for the twenty-first century. To tackle it properly will take all of "faith and order," "mission and evangelism," "life and work"—by whatever instrumental forms the Triune God's ecumenically uniting Church may appropriately evolve. From his reading of God's history with the world Newbigin knew that there was no easy, straightforward way to the final Kingdom.

BIBLIOGRAPHY

Lossky, Nicholas, et al., editors. *Dictionary of the Ecumenical Movement*. Geneva: WCC Publications; Grand Rapids: Eerdmans, 1991; 2nd ed., 2002.
Newbigin, Lesslie. *Christian Freedom in the Modern World*. London: SCM, 1937.
———. *The Gospel in a Pluralist Society*. Grand Rapids: Eerdmans; Geneva: WCC Publications, 1999.
———. *The Household of God*. London: SCM, 1953; New York: Friendship, 1954.

————. "Mission in the 1980s." In *Occasional* [later renamed *International*] *Bulletin of Missionary Research* 4 (1980) 154–55.

————. *The Open Secret: Sketches for a Missionary Theology*. London: SPCK; Grand Rapids: Eerdmans, 1978. Rev ed. *The Open Secret: An Introduction to the Theology of Mission*. Grand Rapids: Eerdmans, 1995.

————. *The Relevance of Trinitarian Faith for Today's Mission*. London: Edinburgh House Press, 1963 (= *Trinitarian Faith and Today's Mission*. Richmond, VA: John Knox, 1964.)

————. *The Reunion of the Church*. London: SCM, 1948.

————. *Signs amid the Rubble: The Purposes of God in Human History*, edited and introduced by Geoffrey Wainwright. Grand Rapids: Eerdmans, 2003.

Newbigin, Lesslie, et al. *Faith and Power: Christianity and Islam in "Secular" Britain*. London: SPCK, 1998.

Vanhoozer, Kevin J., editor. *The Trinity in a Pluralistic Age: Essays on Culture and Religion*. Grand Rapids and Cambridge, England: Eerdmans, 1997.

Visser 't Hooft, W. A., ed. *The New Delhi Report: The Third Assembly of the World Council of Churches 1961*. London: SCM; New York: Association, 1962.

Wainwright, Geoffrey. *Embracing Purpose: Essays on God, the World and the Church*. Peterborough, UK: Epworth, 2007.

————. *Lesslie Newbigin: A Theological Life*. New York: Oxford University Press, 2000.

Going Public with Lesslie Newbigin

*Public Theology and Social Engagement
in an Islamic Context*

Ng Kam Weng

GOSPEL AS PUBLIC TRUTH

LESSLIE NEWBIGIN TIRELESSLY CHALLENGED western Christians to recover the historic role the church played in shaping public life in western society. His insistence that the gospel is public truth is also vital for Christians in an Islamic context like Malaysia and Indonesia who exist as minority groups under pressure to yield the public arena to Islamic *shariah* law. Malaysia and Indonesia provide valuable case studies of nations that adopted Federal Constitutions that were essentially secular when they gained independence from their colonial masters. However, over the last two decades Islamic activists have successfully pressured their parliaments to amend their constitutions so that Islamic values become dominant in legislation of new laws.

Likewise, the public sphere and civil society in these countries are increasingly contested by aggressive Islamic activists and government officials who are willing to use the instruments of the state to stifle democratic dissent. Minority groups, including Christians, are faced with the specter of being reduced to second class citizens. Indeed, one major doctrine of Classical Islam (the *dhimma* system) teaches that Muslims may tolerate Christians on condition they accept a subordinate status in the majority Muslim community—symbolized by payment of a protection tax (*jizya*)—and restrict the practice of their faith to within the household or within the church premises.

Muslims justify the marginalization of the Christian community by claiming that Jesus Christ came only to preach love and personal piety. In contrast, Muhammad was both a prophet and a statesman who bequeathed a comprehensive system of law (*shariah*) for the ordering of both private life and society at large.

This rationalization is wrong on both counts. First, it ignores the Old Testament as part of the Christian canon of Scripture which provides a "social cosmos" as a paradigm for the ordering of public life. Second, it exaggerates the contribution of Muhammad as a legislator. A closer examination of the Quran shows that it contains mostly moral injunctions which Islamic jurists later augmented with examples taken from the *Hadiths* (traditions relating the words and deeds of the Prophet that provided authoritative guidelines for conduct). The first written compendium of law, the *Muwatta'* was produced by the Medinan scholar Malik ibn-Attas (d. 796). Even then, for centuries Islamic laws have functioned more as cultural guidelines for arbitration rather than laying down the equivalent of a modern legal system with written judgments based on explicit legal principles and binding precedents.[1]

Newbigin did not directly critique the historical foundations of Islamic jurisprudence which contemporary Muslim activists rely on to justify their demand for a comprehensive application of *shariah* law to civil society. However, he expressed succinctly both the commonality and the crucial difference in the way Christianity and Islam approach public doctrine and the ordering of society:

> The issue of public doctrine cannot be evaded. It is an evasion to say that we are taught to criticise all dogma for that is merely to state a dogma which has to be criticised. Muslims and Christians share a common belief that life is not to be understood or managed without reference to God. Christians must welcome the challenge which Muslims bring to our belief-system and begin to recognize how much dogma is built into our accepted public doctrine.... Christianity and Islam have differing beliefs about

1. Coulson concludes after a survey of early Islamic laws that, "Under the Umayyads, then the basic material of the local customary law had been modified by the elaboration of the Quranic rules, overlaid by elements of administrative regulations and infiltrated by elements of foreign legal systems. The process of growth had been haphazard, the fusion of these heterogeneous materials been largely fortuitous and depending ultimately upon the discretion of the individual judge." See Coulson, *History of Islamic Law*, 34.

how God rules in human affairs. The heart of the difference is in the fact of the cross. The Prophet rode into Mecca to conquer; Jesus rode into Jerusalem to die. The crux lies there. And that means that Christians cannot use coercion in the struggle between two different ultimate faiths. But struggle there must be. The field is the whole of our public doctrine.[2]

That is to say, while Christianity and Islam agree on the theistic foundation for public morals, they disagree on how public morals should be exemplified and regulated, especially in a plural society. In particular, contemporary Christianity gives priority to embodying moral ideals rather than impose moral rules and regulations backed by punitive measures. The basis for this Christian approach rests on the understanding that the church's exemplary moral life best represents how the gospel redeems culture.

THE CHURCH AS A CATALYST FOR SOCIAL RENEWAL

It is arguable that culture is more fundamental than politics, in that cultural values underpin social institutions that include the state, schools, and the marketplace. Democratic processes are shaped by fundamental cultural values. As such, Newbigin's reflection on faith and culture is relevant for Christians who wish to explore how best to engage wider society.

Newbigin's writings on the gospel and the redemption of culture naturally reflected the controversies between scholars regarding the issues of mission, culture, and contextualization from the 1960s to 1990s. It should be noted that these running battles focused on external aspects of church life rather than on the relationship between the church and wider society.

Reflection on public theology begins with the church as a "sign, instrument, and foretaste of God's purpose for all human culture." It is in the midst of culture that is both glorious and fallen that the church must "so live, act, and speak within each culture that its words and deeds and its life communicate in a way which can be understood the judgment of God upon that culture and his promise for it."[3]

Indeed, the church as the first fruits of redemption provides resources for the renewal and flourishing of culture. "An essential part of the history of salvation is the history of the bringing into obedience to Christ of the rich multiplicity of ethical, cultural, spiritual treasures which

2. Newbigin, *Muslims, Christians and Public Doctrine*, 1–2.
3. Newbigin, *Open Secret*, 163.

God has lavished upon mankind . . . All these gifts will be truly received and understood when the Holy Spirit takes them and declares their true meaning and use to the Church."[4]

The social impact of the church comes primarily through a community that acts as a catalyst for cultural and social renewal. As Newbigin famously puts it, "The congregation as the hermeneutic of the Gospel"[5]—the church is inevitably a social embodiment of its message. In remembering and re-enacting the life of Jesus' word and sacrament the community both incorporates new members into the church and transforms them. These members then impact wider society by their exemplary life and deeds: "The congregation has to be a place where its members are trained, supported, and nourished in the exercise of their parts of the priestly ministry in the world. The preaching and teaching of the local church has to be such that it enables members to think out the problems that face them in their secular work in the light of their Christian faith."[6]

But Newbigin was insistent that the impact Christians seek comes not through imposition by a dominant majority as was the case in the early days of Christendom. It is begins with grass-roots communities, whose members are empowered and released to unmask ideological illusions by the truth of the gospel, who transform social life through the redeeming grace of God.

> If the gospel is to challenge the public life of our society, if Christians are to occupy the "high ground" which they vacated in the noon-time of "modernity," it will not be by forming a Christian political party, or by aggressive propaganda campaigns. Once again it has to be said that there can be no going back to the "Constantinian" era. It will only be by movements that begin with the local congregation in which the reality of the new creation is present, known, and experienced, and from which men and women will go into every sector of public life to claim it for Christ, to unmask the illusions which have remained hidden and to expose all areas of public life to the illumination of the gospel. But this will happen as and when local congregations

4. Newbigin, "Basis, Purpose and Manner of Inter-Faith Dialogue," 262–63.

5. The Bible functions as the final authority within a community that is committed to faith and obedience. The hermeneutical circle operating within the community means that "tradition and Scripture are in a constant developing reciprocal relationship." Therefore, "it is not the Bible itself but the church confessing the mystery of faith that is spoken of as a pillar and bulwark of the truth (1 Tim 3:15–16)." See Newbigin, *Foolishness to the Greeks*, 58.

6. Newbigin, *Gospel in a Pluralist Society*, 230.

renounce an introverted concern for their own life, and recognize that they exist for the sake of those who are not members, as sign, instrument, and foretaste of God's redeeming grace for the whole life of society.[7]

Newbigin seemed haunted by the excesses of Christendom. He appreciated too well the reality of contemporary plural society than to privilege the church with unique spiritual and sociological insights on how to run modern society. Naturally he refrained from spelling out concrete details on how Christian faith can impact society and shape public life. He eschewed the formation of Christian political parties but instead placed his hope on movements grounded in the local congregation since the church as God's new society is the first fruits of God's redemption for the whole of social life.

Newbigin rightly pinpointed that social change starts with grass-root communities, but he did not go far enough. Granted, social change comes from people who are first renewed within grass-root communities; but how are these renewed people to go about renewing society? They will surely need competence on how to address facts at the ground level, that is, the dynamics of social institutions. This requires concrete analysis of the process of social transformation, how social institutions could be configured to bring about justice and peace and if necessary, how to restore broken democratic institutions. Admittedly, it would be unrealistic for Malaysian and Indonesian Christians to expect detailed guidelines from western Christians as they work out for themselves strategies for social political engagement and offer alternative schemes for rightly ordering of society.

QUEST FOR SOCIAL-POLITICAL LEGITIMACY

Public discourse in the west still rests on unacknowledged underlying Christian values and social institutions continue to draw from the social capital inherited from Christianity. As such, the right of the church to participate in social society is still acceptable, although it is increasingly contested by western secularists. Newbigin therefore challenged the church to present the gospel as public truth to defend its right to participate in social ordering of society.

7. Newbigin, *Gospel in a Pluralist Society*, 232–33.

To be fair, Newbigin recognized that "culture is not an ethically neutral entity, and cultural change cannot be a matter of ethical indifference."[8] He identified cultural dynamics with what the Bible calls the "powers": the powers of state, religion, law, and custom which were created by and for Christ are to provide an ordered framework for life. These powers rebelled against Christ, but Christ through his death disarmed them and "their claim to absolute authority has been disallowed."[9] The powers now "must serve the purpose of Christ and they are open to challenge by those who are in Christ to whom has been entrusted the secret of God's purposes."[10] Hence the church can successfully contest against these powers and shape public life.

The challenge from these powers against the church is not so overwhelming that Newbigin felt compelled to defend the church's continuing involvement in western society. In contrast, Christianity in post-colonial societies like Malaysia and Indonesia is often conveniently stigmatized by the authorities as an undesirable legacy of colonialism. The continuing presence of the church is regarded as a hindrance to the project of nation building. Many government officials seeking to erase the public presence of Christianity conveniently suggest that Christians should accept the implementation of *shariah* law for public order since Christians have no equivalent public laws.

Christians have two options in responding to the realities of plural society under Islamic hegemony. First, they can appeal to the words of Caesar, that is, use the language of the Quran since there are sections of the Quran that enjoin justice and divine righteousness. But this approach to find common ground is perceived by Muslims as evidence that Christians have finally accepted the fuller (and therefore superior) revelation of the Quran that came later than the Bible.

Second, Christians may simply acknowledge that despite some commonalities, in the end Christianity and Islam represent incommensurate paradigms for social and religious life. This being the case, the task of Christians engaging in dialogue with other religious authorities is to present the truth of the gospel on its own terms (both through proclamation and in the life of the Christian community). Such a presentation should aim at making evident the fact that Christians genuinely seek to build a community of peace and righteousness, and work towards a just social

8. Newbigin, *Open Secret*, 161.

9. Ibid., 159.

10. Ibid., 160.

order. This strategy of presenting the Christian faith on its own terms shares affinities with Newbigin's sentiments as he argued that there can be no context independent criterion of truth as demanded by the European Enlightenment rationality. That is, Christians do not need to submit to some universal or public ethical standards to present their case since there is none.

BUT HOW DO WE SPEAK IN THE PUBLIC SQUARE?

But some nagging questions arise: How can truth be public and not be universal? How can we talk to those outside the Christian community if there are no "context independent criteria" of truth? And, if there are no universal truths so that one must by necessity speak in terms spelled out by different traditions, how can dialogue be possible? Do we not just end up preaching at one another? These problems seem insurmountable even when dialogue is pursued in a spirit of goodwill. How much more difficult it is when different communities and religious traditions are caught in the midst of ongoing social conflict. Put epistemologically, how do we resolve competing claims to truth represented by the various religious traditions?

One helpful approach to resolving the impasse is offered by Charles Taylor who builds on the insights of Alasdair MacIntyre. Taylor agrees that we cannot appeal to "neutral" criteria to adjudicate between competing traditions. Nor should we compare rival positions against independent facts. Rather, we should lay out how the new conclusion must be accepted on premises which both sides accept. Taylor explains MacIntyre's position: "What may convince us that a given transition from X to Y is a gain is not only or even so much how X and Y deal with the facts, but how they deal with one another . . . In adopting Y, we make better sense not just of the world, but of our history of trying to explain the world, part of which has been played out in terms of X."[11] Taylor modestly suggests that the claim is not that Y is absolutely true, but that whatever is "ultimately true," Y is better than X. It is, one might say, less false . . . whatever else turns out to be true, you can improve your epistemic position by moving from X to Y; this is a gain.[12]

We can translate Taylor's abstract epistemology into the following social processes. It has to be acknowledged that religious conflicts in history have driven people to the ideology of secularism that seeks to exclude

11. Taylor, *Philosophical Arguments*, 43.

12. Ibid., 54.

religion from the public arena. It is undeniable that religion has exacerbated social conflict, but religion per se is neither intrinsically conservative nor revolutionary. However, religion is only part of a complex of social factors which includes race and economics which can be used for exploitation and conflict. The task for any religion seeking to shape public life is to demonstrate that it can provide adequate (if not the best) moral resources for building common life in civil society. Two immediate challenges come to mind.

First, religions must offer ethical resources vital for building consensus and harmony in society. The studies of Robert Bellah and his team of researchers highlight that the problem of contemporary society is not merely the precariousness of the bonds of citizenship but a more fundamental problem of people's inability to bond and have meaningful relationships.[13] Obviously such bonding needs to be stimulated by primal patterns of association exemplified by religion. That is to say, religion contributes to the nurture of robust moral individuals with social conscience. These individuals will in turn bring morality into the public square and the marketplace without harboring an illusion of religious aggrandizement characteristic of religious clerics who see themselves as harbingers of social progress. The apt phrase coined by Reinhold Niebuhr, "moral men in immoral society" succinctly captures the positive function of religion. Religion then promotes healthy national life by ensuring that it is underpinned by "communities of character."[14]

Democracy has emerged as the unchallenged political ideal in the modern world. But democracy requires disciplined citizens if it is to function properly. J. Philip Wogaman explains, "[a] democratic society is well served by a citizenry not fanatically attached to single issues or causes but capable of rounded judgment and a careful weighing of ambiguous alternatives. That maturity is grounded, first, in a secure sense of personal worth. And it is at this point that the personal faith of Christians is a distinct contribution to democratic disciplines."[15]

It is vital that each religion spells out how its beliefs specifically contribute to the building of a common society where human dignity is respected and where the only force accepted is the force of truth in a fair and equal dialogue.

---

13. Bellah, *Habits of the Heart*, 137.

14. Suggestive recommendations on how "community of character" constitutes effective social witness may be found in Hauerwas, *Community of Character*.

15. Wogaman, *Christian Perspectives on Politics*, 175.

Second, religion must support a public philosophy that allows for diversity in unity. Social conflicts arise when different communities fail to practice tolerance and mutual acceptance of recognized differences. All too often integration is on terms set by the dominant community because it is assumed that unity requires homogeneity. Should we not instead accept plurality within unity as a given reality in the contemporary world even if we want to place plurality within a wider framework of transcendent values? In this regard the Christian doctrine of the Trinity provides resources for social pluralism. To amplify this point Max Stackhouse offers some insightful words worthy of a full quotation:

> For those of us who believe that the Trinitarian God is the true God, pluralism is a normative theological belief as well as an ethical or social belief. The metaphysical-moral grounds for dealing with pluralism are at hand. Pluralism within a dynamic unity, understood in terms of persons in community and the community of persons . . . gives metaphysical-moral articulation to the proper foundations and limits of pluralism. Christians oppose monolithic definitions of ultimate reality, but their pluralistic beliefs are governed by a broader belief in unity. The triune God is integrated. Thus polytheism, the theological form of pluralism without unity, is condemned as strongly as is imperious singleness without differentiation. In using these terms, we see that both pluralism and unity can become blessings or curses, depending on whether our view of pluralism has an ultimate coherence, or whether our view of unity has a place for diversity.[16]

Obviously, each religion will adopt a distinctive approach in its goal to nurture moral individuals and democratic discipline. As such, the state should protect the right of each religious group to meet and promote its views and values on an equal basis to ensure a sense of mutual tolerance and respect amidst diversity. Put concretely, a secular order is necessary to manage the tension and potential violence that could arise from religious plurality.

The suggestion of the secular state may alarm some western Christians. But it should be noted that the relationship between religion and the secular order in Malaysia and Indonesia is different. In the west, religious communities have to argue for a legitimate right to enter the public arena where secularism is increasingly dominant. In Malaysia and Indonesia, it is secularism that has to defend the proposal to keep religion out of the

16. Stackhouse, *Public Theology and Political Economy*, 175–76.

public arena. The reality is that religion continues to define the way of life for the majority of the people. As such, secularism will be rejected if it is perceived to be hostile to their way of life. Hence it is necessary to lay aside the notion that the secular state is inherently inimical to religion.

RELIGION IN PLURALIST DEMOCRACY—SECULAR STATE AND RELIGIOUS LIBERTY

Newbigin himself experienced the tension between conflicting religious traditions in India (specifically Islam and Hinduism). It is not surprising that at that time he had positive regard for keeping civil society secular as a means of managing competing/conflicting religions. He observed that secularization "is accomplishing the kind of changes in patterns of human living for which Christian missionaries fought with such stubborn perseverance a century and a half ago—the abolition of untouchability, of the dowry system, of temple prostitution, the spread of education and medical service, and so on."[17] He argued that the secular order ("a system of thought and practice which lies, so to say, outside the direct responsibility of religion, but in which the will of God is to be done"), is a Christian idea."[18]

Secular institutions replace the "ontocratic," sacral institutions of traditional society that restrict human conduct, set people free, and make personal choice and responsibility possible. Newbigin concluded that secularization is a "summons to greater personal freedom, and the responsibility freedom entails."[19] The "de-sacralizing of great areas of human life is all part of the journey by which God leads the world to the ultimate issue of faith and unbelief in Jesus Christ."[20]

Such statements from Newbigin would surprise western readers who read only his later writings that were polemical against secularism in the west. However, Malaysian and Indonesian Christians would find the earlier Newbigin more relevant than the later Newbigin. The change of tone in Newbigin's writing on secularization should alert the reader to the fact that theological terms assume different connotations in different contexts. For example secularism and multi-culturalism that seek to undermine the prominent role of Christianity in public life would elicit negative connotations in the west. But Malaysian and Indonesian Christians would appeal

17. Newbigin, *Honest Religion for Secular Man*, 17.
18. Newbigin, *Faith for This One World*, 21.
19. Newbigin, *Honest Religion for Secular Man*, 68–69.
20. Newbigin, *Relevance of Trinitarian Doctrine*, 62.

to the secular polity in their struggle against Islamic activists who demand that only Islam be authoritative in shaping public policy.

Some clarification however is necessary to set aside a wrong perception among Muslims who consider the secular state as antipathetic towards religion. By a secular state is meant a state that adopts religious neutrality in a pluralistic society.[21] Notice that neutrality is a far cry from hostility towards religion. Indeed, a secular state should maintain benevolent neutrality that respects the integrity and equality of diverse religions of the nation.

Two consequences emerge if we demarcate a clear boundary between state and religious institutions. First, the state is judged as lacking competence in matters religious. The Latin term *saeculum* (from which the word "secular" comes) means pertaining to temporal matters. The call for a secular state is to remind state authorities in a democratic society that the electoral mandate given to them in elections only pertains to temporal matters in society. The state should respect the autonomy of religious institutions even though both institutions work together in promoting a moral society.

The act to remove religious institutions from state sovereignty should not be seen as an act to undermine religion. On the contrary, the act elevates the status of religion since its institutions become independent public institutions capable of censuring state authorities should the latter arrogate for themselves the final say over human affairs. If anything, state authorities are held morally accountable to a higher transcendent authority.

The fundamental nature of a state that respects the integrity of different social institutions of society is one that accepts its limits in the

21. The secular state is one in which government is limited to the *saeculum* or temporal realm; the state is independent of institutional religion or ecclesiastical control and, in turn, institutional religion is independent of state or political control. It is a state that is without jurisdiction over religious affairs, not because religious affairs are beneath the concerns of the state, but rather because religious concerns are viewed as being too high and too holy to be subject to the prevailing fallible will of civil authorities or to popular sovereignty. In application, the secular state is one which denies the use of political means to accomplish religious ends or the use of religious means for the accomplishment of political ends. Because its power is limited to temporal affairs, the relationship of the state to religion should be one of neutrality, toward both various faith communities and to irreligion, a state where citizens are neither advantaged nor disadvantaged because of their religion. It is a state where government is denied the right of domination over the institutions of religion and the institutions of religion are denied the right of domination over the state. See Wood, "Apologia for Religious Human Rights," 470.

regulation of religious life. That is to say, the state must limit the exercise of its power to secular matters and not assume a religious mantle. Is it not the case that a faith that is coerced is a false faith? More dangerously, a state that demands religious allegiance turns itself into an idol since it has demanded an ultimate loyalty that is due to God alone.

The state must see itself as only one institution among many institutions in wider society. The state must support and sometimes adjudicate conflicting interests when authorities from one sphere of human activity transgress into another, like when a local government denies parents their right to oversee the education of their children and insists that children's education must take place only in state-sponsored schools. In the end, government intervention must respect the legitimate rights of parents within the family institution. Jack Donnelly goes further to suggest that such a state will also provide "private security" for all citizens. In his words: "Nonetheless, a state that does no active harm itself is not enough. The state must also include protecting individuals against abuses by other individuals and private groups. The 'classic' right to personal security, for example, is about safety against physical assaults by private actors, not just attacks by agents of the state. The state, although needing to be tamed, is in the contemporary world the principal institution we rely on to tame social forces no less dangerous to the rights, interests, and dignity of individuals, families, and communities."[22]

The goal of strengthening secular democracy sets a positive agenda. Acceptance of plurality is a vital prerequisite for building overlapping consensus among citizens with different ideologies and religious beliefs. In this respect, plural democracy provides manageable platforms for the resolution of differences among citizens. That being the case, there should be a separation between religious and state institutions to ensure that national consensus emerges from grass-root interaction rather than being imposed from above.

Fundamental to secular democracy is the recognition of equal rights of persons regardless of their religious affiliation and their unrestricted participation in civil society. This is based on three democratic principles. First, the *libertarian* principle, or principle of toleration, which requires the state to simply recognize the inalienable right of citizens to profess, practice and propagate religion. It is therefore inappropriate for state institutions to interfere with this religious freedom.

22. Donnelly, *Universal Human Rights*, 35–37.

Second, the *equalitarian* principle requires impartiality of the state in not favoring a particular religion to the extent that it discriminates against other religions. This principle also demands that public offices should not be restricted exclusively to citizens professing a certain religious affiliation. While this principle accepts that there can be different degrees of establishment of religion, in general, it deems the establishment of religion as an obstacle towards the maturing of democracy.

Third, the *neutrality* principle says that the state should not favor citizens simply because they are religious. The state must maintain impartiality toward both the religious and the non-religious, and toward citizens of different religions. A plural democracy promotes a citizenry that is capable of transcending partisan politics.

The rationale for non-interference is the undeniable reality that there is no consensus on adoption of a single system of belief or comprehensive way of life in the modern world. If there is no agreement and given the basic acceptance of moral equality of all human beings, then the principle of tolerance should prevail and individual citizens should be allowed to determine for themselves what belief and religion they wish to embrace. Such religious freedom should include the following components: 1) liberty of conscience; 2) free exercise of religion; 3) religious equality; 4) separation of church and state; and 5) non-establishment of religion. These components cannot be separated from one another; they complement one another and together they weave an ethos of religious freedom and religious pluralism.

A secular state must respect the plural nature of modern society with its mingling of diverse cultures and religions. Any attempt to impose a uniform public morality can only result in injustice to minority groups. A secular state is limited in its power to enforce public morality, even though some common good would thereby be served. The violation of minority rights becomes likely if the state goes beyond moral influence and applies force to coerce citizens to conform to a homogeneous culture.

We must accept that diversity will go a long way to encourage genuine debate and exploration of new perspectives. This ensures people remain capable of adaptation and development. Rather than relativize the search for truth, the challenge of competing faiths promotes an understanding of the complexity of truth in personal beliefs and social life.

REALISTIC SOCIAL ENGAGEMENT

While Christians do not hide the fact that their social views are shaped by their religious heritage they are not exempted from the task of speaking in the language of public discourse for the sake of achieving a common social agenda with their neighbors. Their recommendation of public policies may be supported by public arguments that should go beyond simplistic quotation of scriptures and naïve moralism.

This calls for a hermeneutical retrieval of Christian political theory that was vigorously developed in church history. I have in mind the Christian understanding of "Statecraft" which is defined as the "art of careful reasoning, judging, and acting in the process of making, executing, and adjudicating public laws." Christian public theology must move from general theological principles and social ethics and analyze the mechanisms underlying social institutions and the dynamics of political action. The truth is, theologians sound like they are merely moralizing when they fail to provide sociological insights on how public institutions develop and how their public policies can shape citizens' perception and values. Their view of society is fragmentary and social processes are reduced to individual choices and their consequences. They fail to explain how public institutions work, how their policies fit together and how dominant political ideologies push society in a certain direction, whether towards greater economic inequality or towards social justice. In this regard, the goal of public theology is not to theorize about an ideal social order, but to identify options that will deal justly with specific situations. Theologians achieve unity of theory and praxis when they are able to offer viable strategies for social change.

Achieving this unity of theory and praxis in public theology requires expertise in theology, social-economic theory, history, and law. Public theology is challenging in its demand for holistic analysis and political action. But the Christian community has to rise to the challenge and pool together its intellectual resources to inform its social engagement. Otherwise it will by default remain divided and confused by the conflicting political dogmas and buffeted by social currents. It will be easily intimidated by hostile political groups, will passively accept a political agenda that is imposed on it, and remain ineffective with *ad hoc* and piecemeal participation in the public arena. The challenge to develop a Christian political perspective that is coherent and comprehensive is indeed urgent. Christian witness demands nothing less than the fulfillment of a contextualized Christian public theology that can assist citizens in the task of strengthening democratic institutions that uphold freedom and justice.

BIBLIOGRAPHY

Bellah, Robert, et al. *Habits of the Heart: Individualism and Commitment in American Life*. New York: Harper & Row, 1985.

Coulson, Noel J. *A History of Islamic Law*. Edinburgh: Edinburgh University Press, 1964.

Donnelly, John. *Universal Human Rights in Theory and Practice*. Ithaca, NY: Cornell University Press 2002.

Hauerwas, Stanley. *A Community of Character: Towards a Constructive Christian Social Ethic*. Notre Dame: University Notre Dame Press, 1981.

Newbigin, Lesslie. "The Basis, Purpose and Manner of Inter-Faith Dialogue." *Scottish Journal of Theology 30* (1977) 253–270.

———. *A Faith for This One World*. London: SCM 1958.

———. *Foolishness to the Greeks: The Gospel and Western Culture*. Grand Rapids: Eerdmans, 1986.

———. *The Gospel in a Pluralist Society*. Grand Rapids: Eerdmans, 1989.

———. *Honest Religion for Secular Man*. London: SCM 1964.

———. "Muslims, Christians and Public Doctrine." *The Gospel and Our Culture Newsletter* (UK) 6 (1990) 1–2. (Also online: http://www.newbigin.net/assets/pdf/90mcpd.pdf.)

———. *The Open Secret: Sketches for a Missionary Theology*. Grand Rapids: Eerdmans, 1978.

———. *The Relevance of Trinitarian Doctrine for Today's Mission*. Edinburgh: Edinburgh House, 1963.

Stackhouse, Max. *Public Theology and Political Economy*. Grand Rapids: Eerdmans, 1987.

Taylor, Charles. *Philosophical Arguments*. Cambridge: Harvard University Press, 1997.

Wogaman, J. Philip. *Christian Perspectives on Politics*. London: SCM, 1988.

Wood, James E. "Apologia for Religious Human Rights." In *Religious Human Rights in Global Perspective*, vol. 1 edited by John Witte and Joan D van der Vyver, 455–483. The Hague: Martinus Nijhoff, 1996.

Appendix

Newbigin Centenary Reflections

IN PREPARATION FOR THE two Day Conferences that were organized in December 2009 in Birmingham and Edinburgh, UK to mark the centenary of Lesslie Newbigin's birth, a number of leading scholars and thinkers from around the world were invited to contribute their own reflections and reminiscences about Newbigin and the enduring significance of his life and work.

RT REV'D BRIAN CARRELL
Anglican Bishop in retirement and ex-CMS General Secretary, New Zealand

Back in the 1980s, as Vicar of one of the largest NZ Anglican parishes, I was becoming more and more aware of the growing gap between the church tradition I was committed to represent and the secular society in which I was bound to live. How did one connect the gospel of grace to a culture of indifference? I struggled to discover what needed to be done differently in our received ministry patterns. Up to this time anything I had read about Christianity and secularism invariably dismayed. Pessimism about the future of the church, confusion about the nature of the gospel, and virtual salutes to the brave secular spirit of the age, were hallmarks of much of this despondent literature.

Fortuitously, friends from other denominations in our city were found to be facing much the same questions. Between us we came across first Lesslie Newbigin's *Foolishness to the Greeks,* then his follow-up *The Gospel in a Pluralist Society.* For two years we successively worked through these books in turn, chapter by chapter, paragraph by paragraph, constantly applying their content to the perplexities of our own situations. David

Kettle, then ecumenical Chaplain at the local University, was convener of these studies within our home.

Within this monthly study group "gospel and culture" took root and understanding began to emerge. A decade later I was in Birmingham on study leave, pursuing this same, but now much more enriched, vein of insight. A highlight was an invitation to visit Lesslie in his home with an opportunity to tease out some of the nuggets of wisdom his writing had introduced to the world down under. His personal courtesy and attentiveness on this occasion was impressive, his comments apt and helpful.

One persistent word to me, repeated again as we parted at his cottage door, was to remember always that critical to addressing global concerns and answering philosophical questions raised by issues of gospel and culture was the place of the life and worship of the local congregation. The significance of this did not fully register with me at the time, but over subsequent years, while exercising episcopal ministry in New Zealand, I came to see the pertinence of his advice.

This period of study leave in 1996 also enabled me to advance my writing of *Moving Between Times: A Christian View of Modernity and Postmodernity*, that expressed the liberating understanding I had come to discover concerning the Christian faith and contemporary Western society. What I was able to record there owed more to Lesslie Newbigin, his various writings and penetrating insights, than to any other single individual.

DR SIMON CHAN

Professor of Systematic Theology at Trinity Theological College, Singapore

There is no question that the works of Lesslie Newbigin have deeply impacted the church especially in Asia, and will continue to reverberate far and wide in the years to come. Newbigin is not only a pioneer mission theologian and churchman, but also in every true sense a prophet. Long before any scholar had hit upon the idea, Newbigin had already recognized the significance of the Pentecostal movement which he regarded as necessary for the development of a holistic church. The convergence movement that is gathering momentum in recent years among evangelicals and charismatics has been shaped decisively by his far-sighted vision.

In India, where he was bishop for many years, and in much of Asia, his legacy lives on among many evangelicals who found his bold and thoughtful commitment to the "scandal of particularity" an invaluable resource for their own proclamation and defense of the gospel in a religiously plural context.

His expansive vision also affected the ecumenical movement. Newbigin, together with men like D. T. Niles, contributed to the movement's attaining its high watermark in the mid-twentieth century. But unlike other ecumenists like M. M. Thomas who tried to "generalize" the truth and blur the distinction between the church and world, Newbigin insisted that the church catholic is determinate, with a distinctive identity shaped by a particular historical narrative. The church is big, but it is not borderless!

Perhaps his greatest legacy is to help Christians in the late twentieth century come to see the church as central to the mission of God where for too long they have been pursuing mission as a parachurch activity. Newbigin locates it at the very heart of the church. What is now called missional ecclesiology is largely the result of his ecclesiological insights.

Newbigin's legacy will live on because it exemplifies what C. S. Lewis (and before him, Richard Baxter) calls "mere Christianity"—a Christianity solidly grounded in the Tradition and yet open to the continuing work of the Holy Spirit.

DR GABRIEL FACKRE

Abbot Professor of Christian Theology Emeritus, Andover Newton Theological School, Massachusetts, USA

My first exposure to Lesslie Newbigin was a film shown to Pittsburgh parishioners in the 1950s of his work drafting a World Council of Churches' document. My memory is dim, but it must have been the powerful statement from the second Assembly on "Christ—the Hope of the World." The steelworkers were impressed and so was I. This reaction illustrated Newbigin's capacity to communicate to all sorts and conditions over the decades of his rich ministry.

My contacts with him continued in correspondence over half a century, and sharing the platform with him at a Mansfield College, Oxford conference in the 80s. What a giant in the many worlds of ecumenism, mission, overseas and at-home national Church leadership, pastor to a congregation, intellectual pioneering on agitated theological issues of the day from pluralism and postmodernism to Christian faith as public truth.

He was modest about his sorties into academic theology. Example: his relation to Karl Barth. I once asked him about it and he wrote on June 16, 1988: "Until I retired from India at the age of 65 I had only read Barth in outline (except for a dip into the volume on Creation) and was totally turned off by him. However, meeting Barth personally and coming to realize what a great human being he was, I decided that on retirement I would set myself two tasks : to read right through the Dogmatics (and incidentally also the Qu'ran). I found the Dogmatics absolutely absorbing, but I began with IV and worked backwards back through III and II until I came to I, which almost defeated me. Yes, I was enormously impressed by this experience. I don't think it radically changed my understanding of the Gospel, but it gave me an enormously renewed confidence in preaching it."

Barth will surely be long remembered. But so will Newbigin who was able to take the Grand Narrative that Barth probed so deeply and give it wings that took it to places and people far and wide. No doubt, as Barth looked forward to his conversation with Schleiermacher in the world to come, so he will relish the lively engagement with Lesslie Newbigin.

MICHAEL PAUL GALLAGHER SJ

Emeritus Professor of Fundamental Theology and previous dean of the
Theology Faculty, Gregorian University Rome

One little phrase of Lesslie Newbigin's gives me a springboard for these considerations in his honor. In an article entitled "Evangelism in the City" (1987) he speaks of "the assumptions that we breathe in from every part of our shared existence." Culture, which was one of his key concerns, can be understood as a zone of hidden assumptions rather than of explicit meanings and values. What he would rightly call the non-neutrality of the lived culture, and its power to trivialize life, lies in those hidden assumptions rather than in overt philosophies.

But where does that everyday culture have its greatest impact for good or ill? I want to suggest that to mediate God's Word today we need to reach people's freedom *through their imagination*. This ministry has both purifying and creative dimensions. A friend of mine has a provocative question he puts to young people: who is imagining your life for you? The implication is that we may be less in control of our self-images than we think, that dehumanising forces take over the imagination like an occupying power.

We talk much about a crisis of faith today. But perhaps it is often a crisis of imagination. Many so-called unbelievers have never had their imagination touched by the gospel. They have encountered only the externals of religion, and found them alienating, empty, not so much incredible as unreal. What they need is a surprise for their imagination. William Lynch (1908–1987) was an American Jesuit who wrote several books about the power of images in our culture, and whose ideas would probably have been congenial to Lesslie Newbigin. Lynch wrote that "all around us imagination is traumatized and addictive" but that it is also a source of our Christian healing. In his view Christian faith is a form of imagination, shaped by Christ as Lord of imagination, where we gradually learn to imagine reality with God.

However, to enter that adventure in contemporary culture, in the light of Newbigin's discernment, we may first need to resist the imprisoning imagination, and then communicate new images and embodiments of faith. Faith has to be courageously counter-cultural but not in a merely negative spirit. In the spirit of the parables of Jesus, it is religious imagination that can create receptivity for the Word, mediate the new vision of the Gospel, and ultimately can be transformative of our world. To quote Paul Ricoeur we experience "redemption through imagination" because in "imagining our possibilities we act as prophets of our own existence."

GEORGE R. HUNSBERGER
Professor of Missiology at Western Theological Seminary and author of Bearing the Witness of the Spirit: Lesslie Newbigin's Theology of Cultural Plurality (Eerdmans, 1998)

In the days following Bishop Newbigin's death, I found myself acknowledging him to have been a twentieth-century "Apostle of Faith and Witness." I am not in the habit of throwing the term "apostle" around lightly. But here was someone whose Spirit-given role among us drove me to it. I said at the time, "I never was around Bishop Newbigin when he was not working hard to cultivate for the church a sense of its authority to preach the gospel, and its authority to believe that it is true. In deep response to the crisis of missional nerve in the churches of the West, which had become ultimately a crisis of faith, he seemed to have been called to be pastor to us all" (*The Gospel and Our Culture* [North America], Special Edition, April 1998, p. 2).

Newbigin was—and remains—a pastor and mentor to the world church. In his later years, that became especially poignant for us in the churches of the West. "He gave us ways to believe, whether under the privatizing effects of modernity or the pluralist social arrangements of postmodernity. In our progress-and-success culture, he helped us see that death finally mocks all our greatest achievements and our only hope lies in the risen Christ, not in the permanence of our accomplishments" (*ibid.*).

If pastors everywhere today were to do nothing more than cultivate for the churches a sense of their authority to preach the gospel and to believe that it's true, I am tempted to say, it would be enough! But that makes it sound too simple and easy. The demonstration that this is not easy, but yet is simple in the sense of its singular focus, is among those facets of Newbigin's legacy that remain important and immense for us today.

It is a scant hundred years since Newbigin was born, and not quite a dozen years since his death. His influence in a wide array of historic traditions and contemporary movements is a testament to how closely Newbigin attended to the church's most pressing challenges and deepest longings for meaningful life and witness. His influence shows no signs of receding. In fact, it seems to grow all the more as he is discovered by community after community. Neo-Calvinists and Emergent leaders, Roman Catholic theologians and Mennonite peace activists, seminary educators and disciples in their daily workplaces—all find something in Newbigin that is wonderfully resonating with their own quests to be faithful.

Two features of Newbigin's work occur to me to be especially important contributions for the long haul. One is his sense—theologically and biblically—of the dynamic encounter of the gospel with any and every human culture. This is often overlooked by people who are otherwise drawn to his missional vision. Or if noted, these themes of gospel and culture are simply transposed into notions about adapting the message for a new audience. What still needs to be learned from Newbigin (and companion missiologists such as Andrew Walls, Lamin Sanneh, and Kwame Bediako) is all that is at stake in this dynamic encounter. His summary of missiological wisdom on the dynamic, found in the initial ten pages of *Foolishness to the Greeks*, is an amazing description: short, in a sense, on anthropological sophistication; long, however, on framework for cultural interpretation; and vivid with respect to the essential rootedness of the gospel in culture after culture. His arresting statement on page 4 continues to captivate people: "Neither at the beginning, nor at any subsequent time, is there or can there be a gospel that is not embodied in a culturally conditioned form of words. The idea that one can or could at any time separate out by some process of distillation a pure gospel unadulterated by any cultural accretions is an illusion." That vision, so rooted in the incarnation itself, opens up for people a sense of the "baptism of languages" and their respective cultures that Newbigin sees in Acts 2.

I am sensitive, of course, to debates and critiques within the Indian context that have engaged Newbigin regarding his own ways of playing this out in matters such as liturgy, conversion and baptism. But I suggest that something like his sense of the "triangular relationship" between gospel, culture, and church is the ground upon which there is reason to take even the challenges of his critics seriously.

A second major contribution, running like a thread through everything Newbigin did, lies in the area of ecclesiology. I have sometimes been asked, "Which of Newbigin's books do you think is the most important, or the one most likely to be around for another century or more?" My answer is consistently, *The Household of God*. With a touch of trinitarian completeness, and with a mid-twentieth century sense of current historical movements (particularly, the rise of Pentecostalism), he deftly addresses the loggerhead that had tended to keep ecclesiological breakthroughs at bay. He contends that the struggle between the Roman Catholic "Body of Christ" imagination and the Protestant "congregation of the faithful" imagination continues precisely because a third biblical imagination is missing: the church as the "community of the Spirit." With this pneumatological dimension in hand, and in this more fulsome trinitarian scope, he goes on to commend a sense of the church that is both eschatological and missionary. This set of core affirmations about the church guided Newbigin's hand from then on, attending to whichever of the church's challenges the moment required.

BRIAN MCLAREN
Popular U.S. author, speaker, pastor, and networker among Christian leaders, thinkers, and activists exploring emergent church

I am among the many people whose thinking and ministry have been profoundly enriched by the work of Lesslie Newbigin. Back in the 1990s, a friend recommended *Foolishness to the Greeks*, which I devoured in a matter of days and after which I read *The Gospel in a Pluralist Society* and then many more of his books. A few times as I read, I remember him mentioning the word "election" and I assumed he meant what most conservative Reformed people meant by the term. Yet it seemed he was getting at something different. It wasn't until I was reading *The Open Secret* that I realized how simple and radical a critique Newbigin was making of the traditional understanding of election shared both by Calvinists who embraced that traditional understanding and Arminians who rejected it.

Newbigin wasn't merely arguing about the scope of election: he was deconstructing the very concept and proposing in its place a profoundly different understanding: to be chosen by God is not a matter of exclusive privilege, where one is selected to the exclusion of others. Rather, to be chosen by God is to be chosen for service, to be chosen on behalf of others, to be blessed so one can bring blessing to them. That simple insight struck me as revolutionary when I first "got it," and I feel that I am still coming to terms with the implications of it.

Whenever I am confronted with a new idea that upsets some of my theological assumptions, I try to hold it in suspension for a year or two, neither accepting it nor rejecting it. During that time, I keep it in mind as I read the Scriptures, and I test it by the Scriptures. As I tested Newbigin's concept of election against the Scriptures, again and again I realized how true and right it was. It wasn't only my concept of election that was transformed, but my whole understanding of salvation and the gospel and the *Missio Dei*. In fact, it wasn't until I was writing *A New Kind of Christianity* that this singular insight had its full effect on my understanding of the biblical narrative(s).

The impact of Newbigin's re-conception continues to impact me. Just a few weeks ago, I noticed something I had never noticed before in Paul's Galatian epistle (3:8). Paul says that God preached the gospel in advance to Abraham . . . in the very passage Newbigin focused on so intently, Genesis 12:1-3. This is a gospel not of how to be saved from hell after death and outside of history, but rather how God is bringing blessing to the world in history. That one insight from Newbigin has been truly transformative in my life and ministry.

Of course, there have been other impacts as well. For example, Newbigin's reading of John's Gospel (*The Light Has Come*) is one of the freshest Bible commentaries I ever read, and his general approach to interfaith dialogue has been catalytic for many of us in that important endeavor. His concept of "proper confidence" has provided us with an alternative to the excessive and dangerous certainty of colonialism/rationalism/fundamentalism/absolutism on the one hand and the excessive and identity-eroding uncertainty of relativism on the other. But I would have to say that there have been few single insights that have had a more transforming impact on my theological life than Newbigin's critique of "election as exclusive privilege," which he called the greatest heresy in the history of monotheism. His rediscovery and re-articulation of the call of Abraham as being chosen instrumentally to bring blessing to others has filled my life and work with greater hope and joy than I could have had otherwise. I thank God for Lesslie Newbigin, and only wish I could have met him and thanked him personally.

IAN PACKER
Assistant Director, ETHOS: EA Centre for Christianity and Society, Australian Evangelical Alliance.

Lesslie Newbigin challenged us to recapture the meanings of the gospel's "publicness." His penetrating insight into the necessary missionary encounter between the gospel and the culture of modernity came not only from his wide reading in history, philosophy and social theory but from his captivating grasp of the biblical story and the gospel at its climax. For all the skill with which he deployed his reading, for me it was his capacity to tell the Story itself as public truth that continues to inspire, energize and equip my work in the church, academy and wider world. His effortless movement between the Story and the insights of others inside and beyond the church was itself a key witness to the gospel as public truth.

But Newbigin's concern for the Christian community as the hermeneutic of the gospel sums up well a vital issue we must grapple with in the midst of any enthusiastic talk about public truth and "social transformation." As we creatively adapt to the emergence of post-Christendom society, our resistance to the privatisation of the gospel must be primarily cultivated in Christian communities as genuine witnesses to a new way of life. The gospel must be public in both senses, as a claim about the world and as embodied reality among Christian people as they gather and as they are scattered in their everyday lives and social roles. Newbigin holds much promise for keeping together the best insights of both the Reformed Kuyperian declaration of "Christ as Lord over all of life" and the Anabaptist rootedness in an alternative, parallel, missional community. Newbigin is neither an advocate for a pre-Christendom primitivism nor a Christendom triumphalism but rather a rich resource for genuine post-Christendom theology and praxis.

VINOTH RAMACHANDRA
Sri Lankan Author and IFES Secretary for Dialogue & Social Engagement

It is no exaggeration to say that Lesslie Newbigin was a twentieth-century prophet for the universal Church. Like all true prophets his writings were addressed to specific local contexts, yet are profoundly relevant beyond those contexts. Straddling Western Europe and South Asia, and the misleadingly labeled "ecumenical" and "evangelical" wings of the Church, he built bridges of mutual listening and challenge.

Newbigin confronted the abject surrender of the Gospel by the Church to a secularist mind-set which manifests itself in a variety of ways: for instance, seeking a social justice uninformed by the message of the Cross, reducing missiology to techniques of cross-cultural church planting, separating proclamation and dialogue, or endorsing a pluralistic perspective on religious traditions that denies the servant-reign of the risen Christ over all cultures. Newbigin did more than challenge shoddy thinking and unchristian practice. He showed us an exciting alternative: mission "in Christ's way." This is mission that is Trinitarian in both foundation and conception, incarnational in practice—unmasking and confronting the false gods of the age with a bold humility, in sheer vulnerability and dependence on the Holy Spirit.

Newbigin's stress on the public character of Christian witness remains a refreshing antidote to the contemporary focus on multiplying church programs, privatizing the Gospel in "seeker-friendly" homogenous churches, and therapeutic forms of preaching. He demonstrated that evangelical passion and intellectual rigor need not be divorced, indeed that the former demands the latter. Mission is not primarily command or duty, but "the overflowing of joy," he wrote somewhere. Joy, love, justice and truth form an interconnected moral web, and living within that web and embodying it in the world is the calling of the Church. Such an integral vision is Newbigin's legacy. It is a vision that he tirelessly announced and faithfully obeyed.

DR ELAINE STORKEY
English broadcaster, author and President of Tear Fund

Lesslie Newbigin enabled British Christians to see their Christian intellectual history from a global perspective. His insights into the effects of the European Enlightenment and post-Enlightenment thinking were forged through his reflections and experiences in India. The urgency of theoretical engagement, the inter-relatedness of the Gospel and culture and the calling of Christians to an integrated Christian life and worldview were what he impressed upon us. These were not unique insights, and they dovetailed with much that had been bequeathed us from the Dutch Christian intellectual tradition, but they were delivered in a creative and accessible form. They were much needed and much valued, and inspired a whole new generation of thinkers.

As I got to know Newbigin personally, I encountered a man whose fine mind and prophetic challenge was accompanied with humility and gentle humor. He lived the deep integrity that he commended and it was impossible to be with him and not to realize how central the disciplines of prayer and Bible reading were to his life. Today, Newbigin still points us to how biblical teaching unlocks the truths about who we are; he also points us to the depths and reality of the love of God.

JANNIE SWART
Pastor of Second Presbyterian Church in Oil City, Pennsylvania, USA, and Consultant of Church Innovations Institute facilitating local churches in missional transformation.

The enduring significance of Lesslie Newbigin is well documented in terms of his contributions to the macro theological and philosophical conversations on the relationship of gospel and culture. However, many more stories will emerge in the future coming from pastors in local congregations who can testify to how Newbigin's vision for the posture of the church in a post-christendom era shaped their own leadership for leading congregations to a socially-embodied and missionally-oriented existence in neighborhoods and communities. I am one of those who turned to Newbigin for guidance ten years ago when I was given the transformational leadership task in a local congregation to lead that congregation into mission in a post-apartheid South Africa. This influence eventually became one of the main motivations for pursuing my PhD in a unique program at Luther Seminary in Saint Paul, Minnesota (USA), called "Congregational Mission and Leadership" (which originated out of an interest in the missional church conversation).

Newbigin's enduring significance for leadership in local congregations is fundamentally related to his trinitarian foundations for mission (e.g. in *The Open Secret: An Introduction to the Theology of Mission*). As he writes in *The Gospel in a Pluralist Society*, "The mission of the Church is to be understood, can only be rightly understood, in terms of the trinitarian model." Such a trinitarian foundation shapes the vision for a *participatory* understanding of the congregation's vocation as Christian people who are participating in how God is already present and active in their neighborhoods and broader communities (*missio Dei*). It also cultivates a *posture* of engagement through

315

which congregations no more think of themselves in relationship *to* others, but rather *with* others. It challenges the benevolence model of mission (always framing the missional question as *what* God wants us to do *for* others by bringing the Gospel *to* them), and promotes a relational understanding of mission (the people *who* God is calling us to be in relationship *with*). In such a participatory and relational understanding of mission, congregations discover that the church itself is also transformed when encountering the other through participating in God's presence and activity in the world. As Newbigin writes, "This means that their (the church's) mission will not only be a matter of preaching and teaching but also of learning."

DR KANG-SAN TAN

Executive Director for AsiaCMS, and former Head of Mission Studies at Redcliffe College (U.K.), and from Malaysia

Lesslie Newbigin called Western Christians to carry their faith into the public realm, but his call is a summons also to minority Christians in the non-Western world. For myself, growing up in a Chinese church tradition in Malaysia dominated by Islam, Newbigin's challenge to Western Christians was a formative influence for me. While the *content* of his Christian engagement with the public realm was particular to Western culture, I recognized that the underlying *principle* of engagement was paradigmatic also for Asian Christian engagement with World Religions.

Some have seen Newbigin's approach to Western enlightenment perspectives as robust and confrontational, while his approach to World Religions was more conversational. However, I do not think we can appreciate fully his approach to other religions by means of this comparison. His views cannot be easily categorized within the "exclusivist or inclusivist" paradigm. Asian Christians engaging with Asian Religions need to discover Newbigin's own approach of "bearing witness to the truth" in a spirit of humility, dialogue and cooperation. Confrontational models of engagement have not served the minority churches of Asia. Rather, the church is offered in Newbigin's work various postures that are at once dialogical and contextual and at the same time missional. Rather than retreating into private religiosity, the church could benefit from Newbigin in learning how to bear witness in multi-religious contexts, how to take risks, and how to discover glimpses of truth from other religious traditions.

Many studies of Newbigin have focused on his engagement with Western culture, and this has also been the focus of the Gospel and Our

Culture Networks in Britain and North America. However, as a new generation of Asian thinkers rediscover Newbigin, it would not surprise me if Newbigin's enduring legacy were eventually found in his theology of religions rather than Christian engagement with secular cultures.

With the globalization of Christianity in the non-Western world, and as the church seeks to find new ways to articulate the Christian Gospel in the midst of religions, we have in Newbigin a cosmopolitan apologist par excellence!

REVD DR CARVER T. YU
President and Professor in Dogmatic Theology at the China Graduate School of Theology

In the onslaught of secularization engendered by the Enlightenment project of culture, in which ideologies of rationalism, positivism, scientism and autonomy prevails, the Christian faith has been pushed into the realm of the private and has become almost totally marginalized. Bishop Newbigin took up the challenge of presenting a Christian critique of Western culture. He was one of the very few theologians who dared to employ insights of Polanyi and sociology of knowledge to unmask unexamined "faiths" underlying the Western scientistic culture. He rejected the privatization of Christian truth and insisted that the Church had to make the gospel a public truth. To him, the Christian faith has to be translated into public values. At the same time, he was not unaware of the possible menace of postmodernism when driven to its logical conclusion. And so, the gospel has on the one hand to be contextualized, be it a scientistic culture or postmodern culture, yet on the other hand, it has to be contextualized in such a way as to provide a transcendent perspective for the critique of culture. In doing so, he showed us what theology ought to be if theology is to be true to its task. In this sense, he is not only a prophet, he is also one of the most important theologians of our time.

As a Chinese theologian, I can perhaps more easily appreciate Bishop Newbigin's contribution in his critique of the Western culture. Not only have I been able to witness how devastating the process of Westernization has had on the Chinese cultural tradition, I can also see much more clearly than my Western colleagues the pitfalls of Western culture from the perspective of another tradition. Bishop Newbigin was someone who understood our Asian perspective and took it seriously. For this, I am deeply grateful to him.

Printed in Great Britain
by Amazon.co.uk, Ltd.,
Marston Gate.